Britain and Europe

Series Editor: Keith Robbins

Britain and Europe

In preparation, volumes covering the periods:

1100–1500	Anne Curry and Donald Matthew
1500–1780	Ralph Houlbrooke
1789–2000	Keith Robbins

Already published

Britain in the First Millennium   Edward James

Britain in the First Millennium

EDWARD JAMES
Professor of History, University of Reading

A member of the Hodder Headline Group
LONDON
Co-published in the United States of America by
Oxford University Press Inc., New York

First published in Great Britain in 2001 by
Arnold, a member of the Hodder Headline Group,
338 Euston Road, London NW1 3BH

http://www.arnoldpublishers.com

Co-published in the United States of America by
Oxford University Press Inc.,
198 Madison Avenue, New York, NY 10016

British Library Cataloguing in Publication Data
A catalogue entry for this book is available from the British Library

Library of Congress Cataloging-in-Publication Data
A catalog record for this book is available from the Library of Congress

ISBN 0 340 58688 5 (hb)
ISBN 0 340 58687 7 (pb)

1 2 3 4 5 6 7 8 9 10

Production Editor: Rada Radojicic
Production Controller: Iain McWilliams
Cover Design: Terry Griffiths

Typeset in 10/12pt Sabon by Phoenix Photosetting, Chatham, Kent
Printed and bound in Great Britain by MPG Books Ltd, Bodmin, Cornwall

Contents

List of maps

Acknowledgements

I should like to thank various people for their help with this project: Keith Robbins, the general editor, and Christopher Wheeler, of Edward Arnold, for their gentle pushing; students over the last thirty years, from Dublin, York and Reading, for trying to get me to think about the problems of early medieval British and Irish history, even when I thought I would never write a book that was not about Gaul; and above all some ex-students – Simon Burnell, Ken Dark, Julie Ann Smith, Victoria Thompson, David Thornton and Simon Trafford – and Farah Mendlesohn, all of whom looked over the text with expert eyes and made very helpful suggestions. If there are flaws and errors remaining, they are either the result of my own wilfulness or incompetence, or a product of the fact that no one person can any longer be familiar with all the problems and debates involved in over a thousand years of British history.

I shall never be able sufficiently to acknowledge all the debts, incurred over nearly thirty years, to Columba James, née Maguire, who died on May 20 2000. I met her in 1965, on an excavation of an Iron Age hill-fort in Herefordshire, just before she began studying archaeology at Oxford; we married in 1969, and she supported, encouraged and helped me throughout my studies in Oxford, my research in France, and my career in Dublin and York. Her kindness, warmth and good humour, her enthusiasm for all things medieval, and her great talents, particularly as artist, sculptor and musician, will be missed by so many people. In faint recognition of what I owe her, I should like to dedicate this book to her memory.

General editor's preface

Years, decades, centuries, millennia come and go but Britain's relationship with its European neighbours remains consistently complicated and, on occasion, acutely divisive. It forms the stuff of contemporary political arguments both in 'Britain' and 'Europe', debate which is sometimes strident and ill-informed.

The heat may perhaps be excused on the grounds that there are issues of personal, national and continental identity at stake about which people have strong feelings. The ignorance, however, is not excusable. Whatever views may be taken about contemporary issues and options, here is a relationship which can only properly be understood if it is examined in the *longue durée*. That is what this series aims to do.

It becomes evident, however, that in regard to both 'Britain' and 'Europe' we are not dealing with fixed entities standing over against each other through two millennia. What may be held to constitute 'Britain' and what 'Europe' changes through time. The present is no exception. In a context of political devolution how Britain and Britishness is defined becomes increasingly problematic as new patterns of relationship across 'the Isles' emerge. And what are perceived to be new patterns turn out on examination to be reassertions and redefinitions of old identities or structures. So is it also with 'Europe'. The issue of 'enlargement' of the current European Union brings up old problems in a new form. Where does 'Europe' begin and end? At long last, to take but one example, the Turkish Republic has been accepted as a candidate for membership but in earlier centuries, for some, Europe stopped where the Ottoman Empire began, an outlook which can still linger, with violent consequences, in the Balkans.

In effect, therefore, the series will probe and chart the shifting of boundaries – and boundaries in the mind as boundaries on a map. Where Britain 'belongs', in any era, depends upon a multiplicity of factors, themselves varying in importance from century to century: upon ethnicity, language, law, government, religion, trade, warfare, to name only some. Whether, in particular periods, the islanders were indeed 'isolated' depends in turn not only on what they themselves thought or wanted to believe but upon the patterns prevailing in 'Europe' and what might be thought to constitute the 'mainstream' of its development. The historians in this series are well aware that they are not dealing with a simple one to one relationship. They are not committed to a common didactic agenda or rigid formula. Different periods require different assessments of the appropriate balance to be struck in tackling the ingredients of insularity on the one hand and continental commonality on the other. Propinquity has itself necessarily brought the communities of Britain into closer contact, in peace and war, with some continental countries than with others and to have established (fluctuating) affinities and enmities, but the connection is not confined to immediate neighbours. Beneath the inter-state level, different sections of society have had different sorts of relationship across the continent. There is, therefore, in reality no single 'British' relationship with something called 'Europe' but rather multilateral relationships, sometimes in conflict and sometimes in co-operation, across Europe both at the state and non-state levels which have varied in content and intensity over time. And what has been happening in the 'wider world' has in turn affected and sometimes determined how both 'Britain' and the countries of 'Europe' have perceived and conducted themselves.

The study of a relationship (just like the living of one) is one of the most difficult but also the most rewarding of tasks. There is, however, no single title for this series which really does justice to what is being attempted. To speak of 'Britain and Europe' does indeed risk carrying the imputation that Britain is not 'part of' Europe. To speak of 'Europe in British Perspective' would mislead as to the extent of the concentration upon Britain which remains. To speak of 'Britain in Europe' or even of 'Europe in Britain' both have their difficulties and advantages. In short, in the event, there is something for everybody!

The difficulty, though perhaps also the urgency of the task, is compounded for historians by the circumstances of history teaching and learning in schools and universities in the United Kingdom where, very largely, 'British History' and 'European History' have been studied and written about by different people who have disclaimed significant knowledge of the other or have only studied a particular period of the one which has been different from the period in the other. The extent to which 'British history' is really a singular history and the extent to which it is a particular manifestation of 'European history' is rarely tackled head-on at any level. This series attempts to provide just that bridge over troubled waters which present European circumstances require. It is, however, for readers to decide for themselves what bridge into the future the past does indeed provide.

Keith Robbins
Vice-Chancellor
University of Wales, Lampeter

1
Introduction

This volume in the series 'Britain in Europe' innovates in a number of ways. It is the first time that Britain has been studied over the whole of the first millennium – or what we might call the 'long' first millennium, from the middle of the first century BC until near the end of the eleventh century AD. It is the first time that an attempt has been made to study *Britain* in this way: the whole of Britain, from Cornwall to the Shetlands, rather than (usually) England or (sometimes) Wales or Scotland. And it is the first time that Britain in this period has been presented in its full European context, rather than as a self-sufficient island occasionally invaded or visited as if by aliens from another world. In what ways *does* British history differ from European history? In what ways *is* Britain part of Europe?

I use the word 'attempt' in the previous paragraph advisedly. It may be that readers will find that I have failed. Don't I betray my English origins by the fact that there is indeed much more about England than about Scotland and Wales? Why don't I actually say very much about Cornwall at all, or the Shetlands? Why don't I say more about Europe? There are obviously the constraints of space: even though this is a long book, there is not room for everything. Some things have been put in simply because I realise that this might be someone's first introduction to British history in this period, and some basics therefore have to be here. Some things have been left out simply because I am not interested in them, or sufficiently well-versed in all the problems. But to a large extent the shape of this book, and what is in it and what is not in it, is dictated by the survival of evidence. There is very much more written evidence surviving from England (and Ireland, for that matter, although that is largely outside the scope of this book) than there is from Scotland or Wales. If I say little or nothing about the Shetlands, it is because no written evidence survives for this period; and because there is a limit to how much space I can devote to mentioning yet another excavation which demonstrates that people living in this particular village or farmstead lived much like people in most other villages or farmsteads. Some parts of Britain remain essentially in the prehistoric or protohistoric period throughout the first millennium: that is, they do not use writing, or if they do, it does not survive. The Isle of Man makes its appearance in Chapter 9 because of some spectacular Viking-period tombs; the Orkneys burst gloriously onto the scene in the same chapter, because of the survival of the Icelandic saga known as the *Orkneyinga Saga*. Some parts of Britain, however, remain throughout largely beyond our ken.

The book begins with the first contact with the Romans and the subsequent Roman Conquest, and ends with the aftermath of the Norman Conquest. (The eleventh century is treated briefly: for a fuller discussion, see the second volume in this series.) That the period should be framed by two invasions and conquests from across the Channel is an apt illustration of some of the ways in which Britain at this time – more than at any subsequent period in its history – was linked very intimately to the history of Europe as a whole. Partly because of this, this period is fundamental for the historical and cultural development of these islands. The incomplete nature of the Roman Conquest lies behind the separate development of Ireland and northern Scotland, and perhaps Wales. The events of the fifth and sixth centuries, the so-called Migration Period, led to the remaking of the linguistic map of these islands, with Irish colonisation bringing Gaelic to western Scotland, and the invasions of the Angles, Saxons and Jutes bringing English to what became England and southern Scotland, and at the same time confining the British (Welsh) language to the western part of Britain. The coming of Christianity to all these islands between the third and seventh centuries was a major unifying event of the period in cultural terms. The arrival of the Vikings ultimately brought about the unification of the English kingdom, and aided in the unification of the kingdom of Scotland, the two most significant political developments of the latter part of the period, while the Norman Conquest inextricably tied subsequent medieval English monarchs into the politics of France.

This book will examine the ways in which developments in Britain mirrored, or differed from, developments in the rest of Europe, and look at the ways in which contacts with the rest of Europe changed in kind and quantity throughout the period. It is France, the Low Countries, North Germany and Scandinavia with which we shall mostly be concerned, and also Ireland, which will be treated as part of Europe and not, as so often, as some kind of appendage to Britain. Wales and Scotland will form an integral part, together with England, of the whole story. If the period sees the emergence of England as the most powerful political unit in these islands, it also witnesses to the historical emergence of other cultures which were later to play an important role in British history: not just Wales and Scotland, but also northern England, or Cornwall, or other regions of what is now England. Regional diversity, created by historical accident as well as geographical factors, will be a continuing theme throughout.

The traditional way to picture regionalism in Britain is to think of a basic

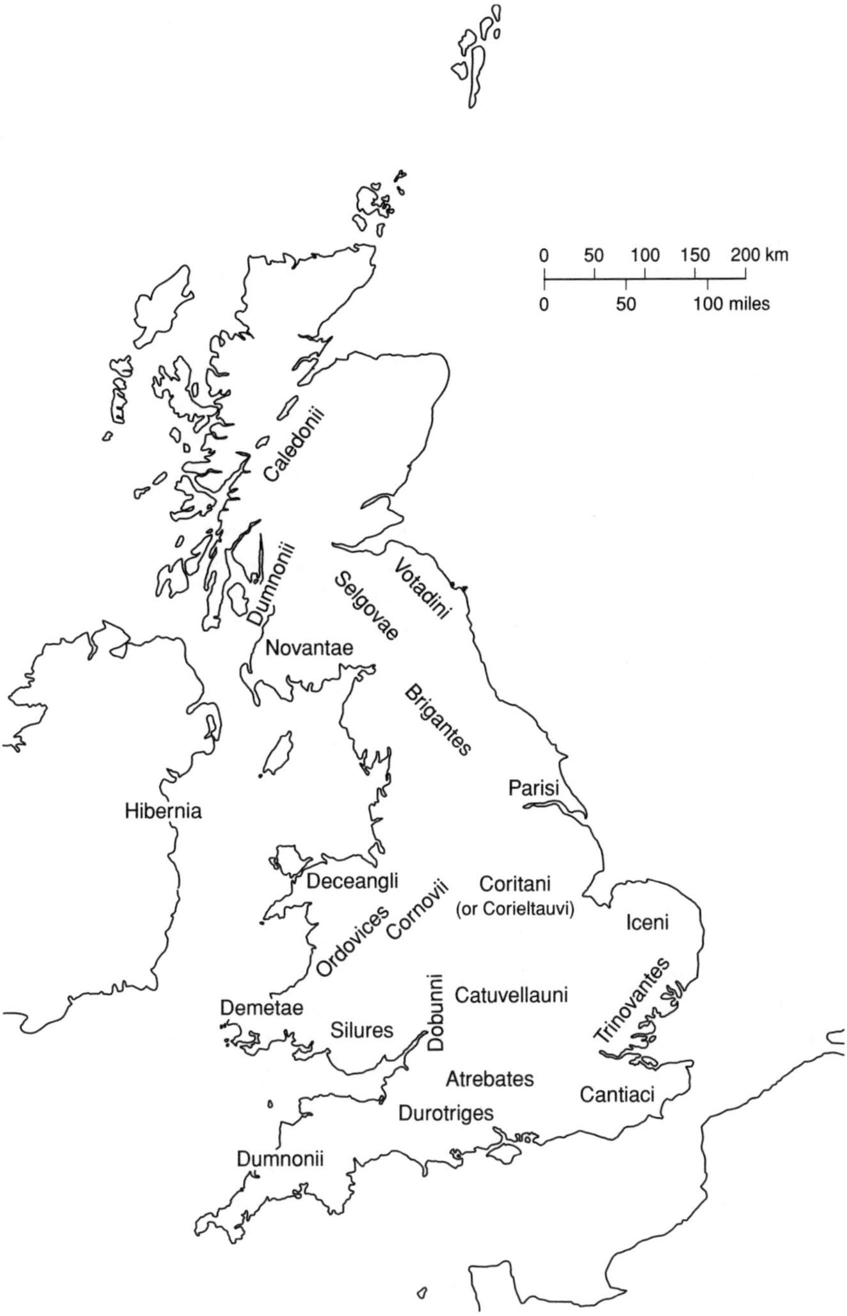

Map 1 The peoples of Britain at the beginning of the first millennium AD

geographical division into lowland and highland, with the dividing line going diagonally on the map, roughly from Devon up to the mouth of the Tees. To the north and west of this line is the 'militarised zone' in the Roman period, characterised by garrisons and scattered settlements; to the south and east is the 'civilian zone', characterised by Roman villas. In the sixth century, north and west of this line are the British kingdoms; to the south and east are the Anglo-Saxons. To the north and west is poor agricultural land and a reliance on pastoralism; to the south and east is rich arable country, and the real wealth of the island. If there is a certain very rough truth behind this division, it is also riddled with exceptions. While the *real* highland areas (the Scottish Highlands and Snowdonia) have high rainfall and offer very inhospitable agricultural conditions, parts of the 'highland zone' (Cornwall) have a very mild climate, while some parts of the lowlands (the Midlands and East Anglia) can have very harsh winters. There are good soils in parts of the highland zone, and poor soils in parts of the lowlands. The traditional idea that highland areas were largely pastoral and lowland areas largely arable is another simplification that does not meet the facts; whatever actual practice has been since prehistoric times, almost all Britain apart from the 'real highlands' offers opportunities for mixed farming.

Extrapolating from what Greco-Roman writers said, prehistorians used to assume that before the Romans arrived Britain was a land dominated by forest, and relatively little touched by the plough or the axe. Increasingly, scholars are thinking that the rural landscape may not have been so much different from today. It was intensively exploited, by a farming population that may not have been very much smaller than that engaged in farming in Britain in 1901.[1] Analysis of pollen from archaeological sites certainly shows that parts of the highland region may have been more wooded than they are today; but some parts of the lowlands, by the Roman period at least, were actually less wooded than they are now.[2] In other ways too the face of Britain was not quite what it is now. In particular, changes in sea-level and in land-level operated to make parts of the coast-line very different: the Wash was much more extensive; the area known as the Somerset Levels was largely under water; the coastline around the Ribble and the Dee, drastically altered by early-modern attempts to dredge the rivers (the Wirral peninsula is in large part a by-product of this engineering), was in the first millennium very different from now; a channel, now entirely silted up, existed between Thanet and the rest of Kent, providing Romano-Britons and their successors with some excellent ports for cross-Channel traffic.[3]

'Britain'

People coming to the history of Britain for the first time are often confused by the geographical and ethnic terminology. This confusion, indeed, is part of daily life. The English – and the Americans even more so – frequently annoy the Welsh and the Scots by using 'England' when they mean 'Britain'. Only slowly are English football fans learning to display their flag of St George rather than the Union Flag; in the World Cup year of 1998, commentators still occasionally talked about the *British* football hooligans in France. The period dealt with in this book is precisely the period in which the terminology becomes established, and it is important to note what the words mean, or, rather, the way in which I intend to use them in a vain attempt to avoid stepping on the more active parts of this minefield. Some phrases I shall simply ignore. I shall not use 'the British Isles', because people on the mainland of Britain often use it to mean 'all the islands to the north-west of the mainland of Europe', including Ireland, unaware that many in Ireland bitterly resent their island being described as 'British'. I shall try to avoid, however, what (during my eight years of teaching at the National University of Ireland) I was told was the politically correct alternative – 'these islands' – because outside Ireland that is an ambiguous phrase. The adjective 'insular' – meaning Britain and Ireland together, as opposed to 'continental' – is sometimes useful, however, and is frequently used by scholars of the period when the culture of the two islands was particularly close, in the seventh and eighth centuries.

When I write 'Britain', I shall mean the mainland of Britain, with the Isle of Man and all the islands except Ireland and those islands lying immediately off the Irish coast. I shall not talk about 'the north-east' and 'the north-west', without being more specific, because although the English often use those phrases to refer to the part of England north of the Tees and north of the Mersey respectively, the Scots do not. For the English 'the north-east' means Newcastle; for the Scots it means Aberdeen. 'Scotland' cannot really be used, at least in any political sense, before the ninth or tenth century. Until around AD 400, perhaps, there were no Scots in northern Britain, and even then 'the Scots' – *Scotti* is the Latin word for the inhabitants of Ireland – were a minority, living in the west of what is now Scotland, and in the Isles. 'North Britain' might be a useful alternative, but it has pejorative overtones for some who live north of the Border.

'England' and 'Wales' are another problem. One cannot use 'England' before the arrival of the English (the Angles and Saxons) in Britain in the fifth century AD, but for several centuries thereafter the territory controlled by the English does not correspond to modern England. Cornwall is not part of England until near the very end of the first millennium. It would be quite useful to think of England as the slowly expanding territory controlled by the English; in that case, should 'Wales' be used of the slowly shrinking territory controlled by the Welsh? Our word 'Welsh' comes from the English word meaning 'foreigner', and for several centuries after the fifth century the foreigners in question, all speaking a language which was recognisably Welsh, lived not only in Wales, Cornwall and Devon, and in Lancashire and Cumbria, in areas which had been part of Roman Britain, but also north of Hadrian's Wall, in the whole area of Scotland south of the

Scottish Highlands. A king of Strathclyde existed in the Glasgow area until the tenth century, and he and his people were possibly still Welsh-speaking. It would thus be highly confusing to use the word 'Wales' to refer to the whole area controlled by the Welsh; it is also difficult to avoid using the word 'Wales' for the 'peninsula' of western Britain north of the Bristol Channel which is the modern principality of Wales: there is no other obvious word for it. I shall not use the word 'Welsh' very much at all, in fact; for much of the book I shall use the word 'Briton' and 'British' to refer to the indigenous inhabitants of this island. I shall try to make my meaning clear at all times, and shall refer to the several maps in this book, and at times I shall have to resort to the clumsy phrase 'in what is now Wales [or England, or Scotland]'. If it seems confusing, take note of this explanation, which can be found in *1066 and All That*, by Sellar and Yeatman:

> The Scots (originally Irish, but by now Scotch) were at this time inhabiting Ireland, having driven the Irish (Picts) out of Scotland; while the Picts (originally Scots) were now Irish (living in brackets) and *vice versa*. It is essential to keep these distinctions clearly in mind (and *verce visa*).[4]

Bede (*c.* 670–735), an Anglo-Saxon monk and the most famous historian writing in Britain in the first millennium, began his *Ecclesiastical History* with a description of the island, much of which was stitched together from sentences and phrases taken from classical Roman writers like Pliny, Solinus and Orosius. Something of the exoticism with which the Romans viewed Britain comes through, but also something of Bede's own experience as someone who lived all his life by the Tyne and Wear, in the late seventh and early eighth centuries AD. (In another work Bede was the first writer in either Greek or Latin to offer a detailed discussion and explanation of tides, of which someone in Britain had much greater experience than someone living in the Mediterranean.)[5] Britain, once called Albion, Bede writes, is an island in the Ocean, off Germany, Gaul and Spain. It stretches 800 miles from south to north, and 200 miles from east to west, except where promontories extended land further. At one end of the island, closest to Gaul, is Rutubi Portus, 'which the English now corruptly call Reptacæstir [Richborough]', and which is just fifty miles from Boulogne; at the other end lie the Orkneys. Bede only makes one regional distinction in his enumeration of the island's richness in crops, trees and pasture: he writes that only in some districts can vines be grown. There are plenty of birds and fish (especially salmon and eels); seals and dolphins, and even whales, are frequently caught. There are numerous shellfish, including pearl-bearing mussels and whelks from which a fade-proof scarlet dye can be made. There are hot springs where people can bathe; rich veins of metal; jet, which, when burned, drives away serpents or, when rubbed, attracts things, as amber does. 'Because Britain lies almost under the North Pole', it has short nights in summer, so short that at times the sun hardly seems to set. Once, all the inhabitants of Britain were Britons, he wrote; then the Picts came to the North of Britain (from the Black Sea area via Ireland), and, more recently, some Irish moved eastwards to settle in part of Pictland and, last of all, came the English. There are four peoples in Britain today, says Bede, but five languages, because 'through the study of the scriptures, Latin is in general use among them all.'[6]

Bede seems to have been right that the Britons had once inhabited the whole of the island: at least it seems now that before the Romans all those on the island did speak the same general dialect of the Celtic group of languages, known as *p*-Celtic or Brittonic: the other main dialect, *q*-Celtic or Goidelic, was until the fourth or fifth century AD restricted to Ireland, and was only then, as Bede implies, brought by the Irish to the western parts of Pictland. (The terms *p*-Celtic and *q*-Celtic derive from a basic difference between the two variant Celtic languages: words beginning with 'p' in one began with a 'q' or 'k' sound in the other, as in *pen* or *ceann*, which are Welsh and Irish words for 'head'.) Bede was wrong about the exotic origin of the Picts, however: this probably derived from an Irish legend, which, by stating the Picts had once lived in Ireland, explained or claimed some close relationship between the Irish and the Picts. Indeed, there were still some people in Ireland in the early Middle Ages, living in Antrim, the closest part of Ireland to mainland Britain, whom the Irish knew as the *Cruthin*, a word derived from *Pritani*, or British, but in Irish meaning 'Picts'.[7] But a close relationship between Picts and Irish may relate to the later political situation in Scotland, where the two peoples were vying for dominance. Place-name evidence does suggest that the Picts in Scotland were *p*-Celts, like the rest of the Britons, thus speaking a language markedly different from that of the Irish. We must not be misled by the modern popular fascination with the Picts, which has been dubbed 'Pictomania', to imagine that the Picts were some mysterious indigenous pre-Celtic inhabitants of Britain: by the time they emerge into the historical record they are as 'British' as the rest of the Britons.

The idea that Britain had once been called Albion was taken by Bede from the Roman encyclopedist Pliny (d. AD 79), who had derived it ultimately from a very early traveller to the north from the Greek colony of Marseilles: Pytheas, who probably lived c. 325 BC. There may have been early confusion with the tribe of the Albiones, who lived in the north-west of Spain, but it does seem that there was a British word **albio*-, meaning 'the country'. (The asterisk indicates a word or word-element that does not survive in any text, but is hypothesised by linguists, extrapolating backwards from what we know about linguistic change.) Even if 'Albion' had dropped out of usage among Latin writers by Pliny's day, it survived in Irish and Scots Gaelic right up to the twelfth century: *Alba* was the normal name for Scotland north of the Forth. The word was taken up by some as a politically neutral term to symbolise the union of Picts, Irish and others in Scotland: Constantine II's men fought against the Vikings in 918 with the battle-cry *Albanaich!* In the fifteenth century, the word was revived in the title of the Duke of Albany – *Albania* in Latin.

It seems that the inhabitants of southern Britain, at least, called themselves **Pritani* or **Pretani*, possibly meaning 'tattooed people'. The tattoos of the British crop up again and again in Roman descriptions, as does the blue woad with which they painted their skin. Herodian in the third century AD says that they tattooed themselves with designs of animals, while as late as AD 400 Claudian refers in his poem *On the Consulship of Stilicho* to the tattooed cheeks of the goddess Britannia.[8] **Pritani* gave the Romans their *Britanni* or *Brittani* and gave the Welsh *Prydain*, meaning Britain (and, because of the change from initial *p* to initial *q*, also gave the Irish their *Cruthin*, *Cruithni*, meaning 'inhabitants of northern Britain', or Picts). *Britannus* was a form found in Latin, but the usual Roman word for a Briton was *Britto*, which in the plural became *Brittones*, *Britones* or *Brettones*. *Britannia* was the standard Latin word for the island after the Roman conquest, although *Brittania* eventually became almost as common. The Greek geographer Ptolemy distinguished between Μέγαλη Βρεταννία, and Μικρά Βρεταννία, where Great Britain was the larger island and Small Britain was Ireland; but when Romans wrote *Britanniae*, 'the Britains', they were not referring to these two main islands, but to the various provinces into which they had divided that part of mainland Britain which they controlled.[9] And in case anyone thinks that Ptolemy's usage justifies us in lumping Britain and Ireland together as 'the British Isles', we should note that Ptolemy's distinction was not preserved. Our 'Great Britain', *Magna Britannia*, derives from the desire not to confuse the main island with *Britannia*, the 'French' province colonised from Britain in the fifth century AD, which we now call Brittany. The French still need this distinction: *La Bretagne* and *La Grande-Bretagne*, Brittany and Britain, are separated from each other by what we on this side of the water call the *English* Channel.

The sources and their study

Historians of the first millennium AD – like historians of any period – must be prepared to study everything that survives from the past in order to help them understand what happened, how people lived, and how people thought. Historians of the first millennium, however, are rather more used than, say, nineteenth-century historians, to trying to draw whatever conclusions they can from the most meagre and bizarre sources. There has been very little effort devoted to sifting through Victorian rubbish pits, or excavating Victorian town-houses: we can know a great deal about Victorian habits of consumption or living conditions from the vast array of written documentation, and the considerable expense of archaeological excavation may just not be worth the effort. But in the first millennium AD the written sources are much more scarce, and often very difficult to interpret, and rubbish pits become valuable documents. Surviving evidence will include artefacts – objects made by humans, such as books, place-names, pottery and earthworks – but also other things from the past: pollen which will tell the historian something about the vegetation, river sediments that may give climatic information, or skeletons which may inform the historian about disease or mortality.

I perhaps ought to explain my rather tendentious usage of 'historian': it is one I have come to after doing a DPhil in Archaeology, and after occasionally teaching early medieval archaeology, even though I have always been employed in Departments of History. For me, History is the study of everything that has happened in the past: that is, before you, the reader, took your most recent breath. In many if not most cases historians will be dealing with written texts: governmental records, poems, historical works, novels, inscriptions. But they ought to be prepared to take into consideration anything that has survived from the past: hoards of gold coins, rubbish pits, languages, paintings, earthworks, skeletons, memories. Before the rise of modern universities, in the days of Hume and Gibbon in the eighteenth century for instance, this used to some extent to be the case. But in the twentieth century professional historians in universities have sat feebly by as segments of the past have been sliced off and taken away from them: stolen by Departments of English Literature, Sociology, Political Science, Economics, Religious Studies, Art History, and Archaeology. To view it as theft is, of course, in many ways false, in part because in a sense historians gave these areas up themselves. History was being defined by professional historians in the late nineteenth century in an increasingly narrow way, so that Real History became virtually restricted to matters such as political and constitutional history. The growth of other university disciplines served to fragment matters still further. In particular, the study of Britain in the first millennium became almost impossible to do within a single university department: Departments of History in Britain have left Ancient History to Departments of Classics, and taken medieval and modern for themselves. (Except for the University of Oxford, where there is no 'medieval', Modern History was, and still is, defined as beginning with the end of Ancient History, with the accession of Diocletian in AD 284.) Late Roman and early medieval studies tended to fall into the gap between the two: too late to interest the classicist, and too early for the medievalist. The approaches of the two types of department often differed, too. Departments of Classics are more likely to preserve a holistic approach to the past: they frequently contain historians, literary scholars, linguists, archaeologists, art historians, and sometimes individuals who fulfil two or more of those specialisms. Departments of History have not been so sensible. As a result much of the research which supports this book has been undertaken not in History, but in Classics, Archaeology, English and Celtic Studies, as well, of course, as outside the university system totally, in museums or in archaeological units, and by amateurs.

The division between Classics and History in particular has not been kind to the treatment of the early history of Britain. It is notable that the only single-authored study of the first millennium of which I know has been written by Klavs Randsborg, who not only comes from Denmark, whose history was only marginally affected by the Roman Empire, but is also an archaeologist, much less affected by the institutionalised division between 'Roman' and 'medieval'. From where he stands, the first millennium can appear as some kind of unity. Enough continuity can be seen even in Scotland, which was effectively outside the Roman Empire, for a history of the first millennium to be written for Scotland (by Alfred Smyth). But in Britain as a whole, and above all in England, the break caused by the fall of the Roman Empire has seemed to be a justification for a division of its study between Romanists and medievalists. This disciplinary Hadrian's Wall is seldom breached, even by those people who peer into the obscurities of the British 'Dark Ages', the fifth and sixth centuries. Disciplinary boundaries which make it difficult for an Anglo-Saxon historian to understand the concerns of a Romano-British archaeologist, and vice versa, make it relatively easy for both to think of the fifth century as a watertight barrier which separates one period of history from another. However, these boundaries are starting to break down. And they must. After all, we are dealing with one population, which emerges from prehistory not long before AD 1, and which, despite all the invasions and migrations of the first millennium, remained largely the same population, and one which deserves its own history.

All too often a false dichotomy is drawn between Archaeology and History. It is not difficult to present the written evidence as static, largely unchanged and unaugmented since the nineteenth century, and thus to portray archaeology, where new discoveries are made each week, as something which is much more exciting. It would be misleading, however, and would offer a distorted picture of the relationship between written and non-written materials. It is true that the written evidence available to the historian now is hardly greater in quantity than that which was available in the year 1900. It is very seldom that a significant find of written material comes to light. There is nothing to rival the mass of letters found in the excavations of the Roman fort at Vindolanda, between 1973 and the present (see below, p. 47). The odd new manuscript does show up, perhaps in a Continental library; in the 1980s a National Trust employee even found a page from one of the three Bibles produced at the orders of Bede's abbot Ceolfrith in the early eighth century, wrapping up a set of sixteenth-century estate-documents. Discoveries of new texts are not likely to be any more common in the future. However, enormous advances have been made in our *understanding* of written sources, which parallel the advances made in our archaeological knowledge.

In many ways the intellectual aims and processes involved in History (in its narrow sense of the study of documents) and Archaeology are very similar. A written text has to be treated to some extent like an archaeological site, even though the historian does not destroy her document, page by page, as she reads it, in the way that an excavator destroys the site in the process of excavating. As an end product, both text and site have to be published carefully and to high academic standards. In both cases there needs to be not only description, but interpretation: a hypothetical reconstruction of the original, taking into account the various processes by which the original has degraded or otherwise changed. It is obvious that on an archaeological site much that was once there has disappeared, victims of the laws of chemical and biological decay. But texts too 'decay'. Most historical texts from this period do not survive in the handwriting of the author: most have been copied by a scribe, often more than once, and it is the copy, or the copy of a copy, which survives. A mediocre scribe will make all kinds of mistakes, particularly if he (or, perhaps quite rarely, she) is copying down a document in Latin, which he or she knows imperfectly. An intelligent scribe may be even more dangerous, making 'corrections' or otherwise editing the text while copying it. A good printed edition of an historical work will take account of all the surviving manuscripts of a text, and, if there are several, may well produce a version which does not correspond to any of them, but which is an editor's opinion as to what the author actually wrote. Let us take the biography which Tacitus wrote of his father-in-law Agricola, one of the early governors of Roman Britain, around the year 100. The earliest manuscript is one produced in a monastery in Gaul in the mid-ninth century, which the modern editors have had to augment by two fifteenth-century copies of missing texts from an earlier century. Needless to say, the scribes operating in the ninth or fifteenth centuries did not understand all that they wrote, in particular the personal names. The modern editors made the decisions, for instance, that *inde Cangos* was actually a reference to the British people called the Deceangli, and that *castris Antonam* actually referred to the River Trent, and should have been *cis Trisantonam*.[10] But these are hypotheses rather than facts, just as many of the interpretations of the excavator are. It is the editor of written texts who, like the excavator, makes sense of the raw data, and presents it in a fashion which can be used, though with caution, by the historian.

Once the edition is there, one has to be able to understand it. One of the most valuable contributions to our historical knowledge of the early history of these islands has been Daniel Binchy's massive edition of early Irish legal texts, which are a precious window into the non-Germanic and non-Roman legal world. The fact that this window is totally opaque except to a small handful of experts in Old and Middle Irish shows that there is another specialist discipline which the historian ought to be able to deal with – linguistics. The advances made this century not just in the comprehension of Old Irish, but also in Old Welsh, Old English and Latin itself have been of inestimable value to historians. But a large part of the progress made by historical studies has been due to the firmer application of critical techniques.

These techniques are not exactly new. As David Dumville has pointed out, the techniques are basically those of the medieval Irish scholar who said that one should always ask four questions of any work, the questions of place, time, author and cause.[11] Where was it written? When? By whom? And why? But there is a fifth question which any historian will want to ask – how did the author acquire the information?

As an example of this questioning, and how it changes the way in which historians operate, let us take one of the best known historical texts from this period, the *Anglo-Saxon Chronicle*. It has long been understood that this record of British history, starting with the early Roman period and continuing, in one manuscript, as late as the reign of Henry II of England (1154), was first compiled in the kingdom of the West Saxons under King Alfred the Great, in the 890s. Where? It was written initially in Winchester, but subsequently kept up by scribes in different centres: clearly the authors were limited by their sources of information, which were likely to be better the more local they were. When? After the 890s, the record of historical events was sometimes kept up year by year: it is as near a contemporary record as one could hope for, subject to all the problems of contemporary records. By whom? By monastic scribes, who may thus be inspired to write particular things because of the nature of their calling. Why? To preserve a monastic tradition; to record God's actions as revealed in human history; to preserve the memory of the kings of former times, so that their own monastic records could be put into context; to celebrate their own monastery, their own locality, their own kingdom. Because of these purposes, of course, all kinds of things which would fascinate the historian today were simply left out: details of economic life, for instance.

When we look at the *Anglo-Saxon Chronicle*'s account of the period *before* the 890s, however, our questions might have a rather different purpose, and a different result. The text was written in Winchester, Alfred's capital, during Alfred's continuing struggle to defend Wessex from Viking attack. It was written by someone relatively close to Alfred, who had no knowledge that anyone would necessarily continue the *Chronicle* from his day into the 1150s: it was initially intended not as a contemporary chronicle, but as a record of past events. It was written to glorify Alfred and his dynasty, and to show how the West Saxons (and not the Anglo-Saxons as a whole) came to inherit the glory of the Roman Empire. What about the fifth question – how did the author acquire the information? The information for Roman times came from Roman sources, sometimes mediated by Bede's great *Ecclesiastical History of the English People* (finished AD 731); the information for the seventh and early eighth centuries came almost exclusively from Bede; presumably earlier annals, now lost, were the source for much of the later eighth and early ninth century information. But what about the information for the fifth and sixth centuries, which provides us with almost all we know about the earliest activities of the Anglo-Saxon kings in Britain? Up until the 1960s, and even beyond, historians used the precious evidence of the *Anglo-Saxon Chronicle* to reconstruct the progress of the Anglo-Saxon conquests of Roman Britain, and in particular the history of the earliest West Saxon kings.

How *did* the chronicler acquire that information? The information clearly comes from an Anglo-Saxon source, since the names of Saxon kings are given, but rarely the names of their British enemies. But the Anglo-Saxons had no written documents during the fifth and sixth centuries. Could it have come from the oral tradition? If it did, how is it that the events are dated by the AD system of dating which was first used for historical purposes by Bede, in the early eighth century? Some stories may well derive from oral tradition, such as the story of the arrival in Britain of the founders of the West Saxon dynasty with their five ships. But some of these traditions might be quite late, and invented to explain origins and derivations. The name of a Welsh king, Natanleod, was given to 'explain' the name of the battle of *Natanleaga* (which is Netley, a word actually meaning 'the wet wood'); Portsmouth was explained by the invention of a hero called Port; while the name of the war-leader Wihtgar actually derives from the Latin name for the Isle of Wight, which he supposedly ruled. A very reasonable conclusion would be that much of the detail, and certainly the order of events and the dates, was simply invented by the Chronicler in order to fill out an otherwise rather blank couple of centuries. But Barbara Yorke has suggested that a much more interesting reason lies behind the invention.[12] The founders of the West Saxon dynasty are shown by the Chronicler to be fighting the British in Hampshire and the Isle of Wight. Now, the West Saxons should not be there at all in the fifth and sixth centuries. The archaeological evidence suggests that the origins of the West Saxon kingdom was on the Middle and Upper Thames, a long way north of Hampshire (the first bishopric of the West Saxons was established at Dorchester-on-Thames), while Bede says that the Germanic people who settled in Hampshire and the Isle of Wight, as well as in Kent, were the Jutes, who were neither Angles nor Saxons. A number of cemeteries found in this region have a material culture which is almost identical to that of contemporary Kent, which supports Bede's statement. Indeed, Bede specifically writes about what came to be called Hampshire as 'that part of the kingdom of Wessex which is still today called the nation of the Jutes'.[13] Yorke suggests that the Anglo-Saxon Chronicler is writing in part for the contemporary descendants of the Jutes, who preserved a memory of their independence, in an effort to prove to them that they had no ancestral right to the land which they claimed. It is a piece of ninth-century propaganda on behalf of the West Saxons. Elsewhere she has said that the *Chronicle* was less 'fictional' than 'factional', apparently meaning that elements of fact lay behind the text.[14] But it is also 'factional' in that it was written with a very definite political purpose.

This exercise shows something important about historical texts. What they tell us may not be true; but the way they tell it to us, and the very fact that they are telling it, may be of great interest. We will get more out of a text if we approach it with our five questions in mind before we ever start to ask the sixth question: 'what does it tell us about the past?' It is not until we have understood precisely why Bede wrote his *Ecclesiastical History of the English People*, what his concerns were, and where he may have got his information from, that we can start using the *History*, tentatively, to write our own history of the English church and people in the seventh century. Bede's *Ecclesiastical History*, like almost every text, informs us first of all about the author, and about the author's perceptions of the world: we have to move cautiously if we want to use that text to establish our own independent perceptions of that world. And we must remember not to fall into the trap of thinking that what the historian must do is to establish what *happened*. History is no longer, if it ever was, the relation and explanation of *events*. Bede's *History* tells us *first* about his mind, and only secondarily about England itself. Nowadays many historians are just as interested in trying to understand Bede's mind as the politics of Bede's England.

All kinds of written texts survive from the first millennium to help us flesh out our view of the past. There is great history like the *Ecclesiastical History*, and great poetry like *Beowulf*: not so dissimilar as they first appear, since both are literary works which to some extent follow the conventions of their genre, and which demand the techniques of the literary scholar for their explication just as much as those of the traditional historian. There are legal texts: law-codes, land-deeds (which are called 'charters'), legal treatises and so on. There are treatises on theology and philosophy and other subjects, private (or not so private) letters, historical annals, the very occasional biography and the much more frequent hagiography (that is, the *Life* of a saint, which may tell one more about the ideals of Christian living than about an historical human being). There are inscriptions, ranging from epitaphs to the dedications of buildings or curses. There is a whole range of material, in short, which must be approached with an understanding of the way the author is following the conventions of the genre and with our five questions firmly in mind. Throughout this book the written sources will be quoted, in order to show the problems of actually using them to reconstruct the past.

Great advances were made in the twentieth century in the way in which historical sources are treated and exploited. But those advances are nothing compared to the advances made by archaeology. At the beginning of the century, archaeology was a spare-time activity for scholars or for amateurs; it was not an academic subject at universities. By century's end, archaeological research has become a highly specialised and professionalised academic and scientific area, which is better funded than historical research (largely because its techniques are very expensive, and becoming more so all the time) and involves a large number of people, not just in universities, but in museums, in archaeological units, in institutions like the Royal Commission for Historical Monuments, and in the three national bodies: English Heritage, Historic Scotland and Cadw: Welsh Historic Monuments.

(Indeed, so professionalised and expensive has archaeology become that many are now worried about how the amateur is increasingly excluded, or pushed into what professionals sometimes regard as the disreputable world of the metal-detecting clubs.) At the beginning of the century, something was known about Roman Britain from archaeological work, largely because large-scale fortifications, stone buildings and sculptures were relatively easy to locate and to identify, but very little was known about the early medieval period, apart from the metalwork and pottery found in graves, and the sculpture and churches which survived above ground. Over the last hundred years not only has the database expanded enormously, but it has increased in terms of its social range: we now believe that we have peasant homesteads as well as villas and churches, and field systems as well as fortresses.

Archaeological advances can be summarised under three heads: improvements in excavation technique, the use of scientific methods for the study of sites and artefacts, and, most recently, the development of self-consciously theoretical approaches, which have allowed archaeologists to investigate questions of social and political development which were once thought to be virtually beyond the scope of the subject. Excavators can now extract much more evidence from a site than was once possible: indeed, valuable material can even be extracted from the spoil heaps left by earlier excavators. Some of this material might be examined using scientific techniques unknown before: obvious examples would be the study of insect remains from Viking houses in York, which can inform us about the domestic environment, or the pollen remains from many sites, which can be used to reconstruct the balance between the natural and farmed landscapes of different periods. Techniques such as C-14 analysis allow a date to be obtained for organic material, though, in this historical period, we obtain a bracket of probability over a century or more rather than an absolute date; dendrochronology (based on the analysis of tree-rings), on the other hand, can obtain a precise AD date for the cutting down of a particular piece of timber.

Although archaeologists are interested in contexts, and in relationships within and between sites, they are dependent upon all kinds of specialists for the information about what they have found: not just specialists in scientific techniques, but also specialists in the various categories of artefact and object which they find. An excavation report these days is usually accompanied by a whole array of specialist reports, on the pottery, the animal bones, the coins, the stone and so on. Pottery and animal bones, in particular, can be recovered from a site in huge quantities: 55,000 sherds of pot and 75,000 fragments of non-human bone from Anglo-Scandinavian levels at 16–22 Coppergate, York, for instance.[15] Their proper study not only demands familiarity with the material itself, but with the computing and statistical techniques needed to make sense of the material. Here it is worth underlining the particular importance of coins – the only artefact which is also a written document to be regularly found in excavations. Coins can often be dated relatively precisely, but can be used for far more than just helping to date archaeological contexts. The legends written on them may provide valuable evidence of political propaganda, or be the sole evidence for the name of a particular monarch; their regional distribution may be a clue to political or economic territories.

Another very specialised kind of human artefact which has great historical value is language. Through a study of the first millennium forms of language (whether Latin or one of the Germanic or Celtic languages) we can learn about cultural variation and cultural borrowing. The study of, for instance, the words which came into the English language through the influence of the Scandinavian settlers of the ninth and tenth centuries gives us a fascinating insight into the process of the development of the English language as well as of the impact of the Vikings themselves. Each new language also brought a new set of names for settlements and for features of the natural landscape. Through a study of place-names we can learn about the impact of newcomers, and about settlement patterns. Place-names are not necessarily easy to date, particularly when their first appearance in the written records is often centuries after their creation, nor are the historical interpretations of place-names without dispute. Are the many place-names in eastern England – above all in Lincolnshire and Yorkshire – which end in the Danish *-by*, for instance, a sign of mass settlement by Scandinavians in the Viking period, or are they the record of the takeover by a few hundred Scandinavian warriors of Anglo-Saxon estates?

No-one should be surprised, given the relative paucity of sources and the difficulty of those sources which we do have, that writing the history of this period is fraught with difficulty. Usually it is simply not possible to write a straightforward history: all that can be done is to present alternative hypotheses. In what follows, there will inevitably be a discussion of the debates which have taken place – or are still taking place – on many different aspects of the story, many of which are still unresolved. To those who are new to this period, this may seem at times tedious, or at least frustrating; but it is precisely the debates which, to the initiate, make this period so fascinating. This period is the most formative period in British history: the time when the three nationalities who were to dominate the history of this island have their very different roots. But it is also true that there is no other period of British history (taking 'history' in its narrow sense of 'period for which we have written sources too', as opposed to 'prehistory') where there is still so much uncertainty, or where the appearance of one new piece of evidence or one new hypothesis can have such repercussions that a reassessment of a whole century is required. There is no other period of British history, in other words, which is quite so exciting.

2

Rome and the Britons

Britain in the first half of the first millennium AD was dominated by the Romans. Much of Britain was ruled by the Roman Emperor, and even those parts that remained outside the Empire – most of modern Scotland – were inevitably strongly influenced by this massive political machine. In this chapter we shall see how the Romans came to Britain, and look at the limits of their conquests in the north; in the following two chapters we will examine the impact that Rome had upon Britain. On the surface that impact appears ephemeral; of all the aspects of Rome which were introduced into Britain, only Christianity continued as a major cultural force, and over much of Britain that was a reintroduction rather than a direct continuation of Roman beginnings. Nevertheless, the fact that Rome held the greater part of the island for four centuries was of crucial importance for the subsequent development of civilisation in Britain. For long afterwards the memory of Rome's greatness was a powerful fact in the British consciousness, and one that could hardly be ignored. What an Old English poem referred to as the 'work of giants'[1] littered the British countryside – ruined towns, fortifications, roads, villas, memorial epitaphs and sculptures: all of which contributed to that sense of sadness and loss which permeates Old English poetry. Rome cast a long shadow even in the tenth century AD, as it did, in a very different way, in the first century BC.

In 59 BC Julius Caesar was one of the two consuls of Rome, and for his post-consular appointment wangled for himself control of a large territory, which included Cisalpine Gaul (northern Italy) and Transalpine Gaul (southern Gaul), the command of four legions and the right to appoint legates and to found colonies. He had exploited the turbulent political situation in the Republic of Rome in order to gain this extraordinary command, and was determined to use the opportunity to increase his personal prestige and power. It was rivalry among the political leaders in the Republic, and the particular constitution which allowed civilian politicians to have command of legions, that had encouraged the territorial growth of the Roman state: several of the acquisitions of Rome had been the direct result of the political ambitions of individual politicians. By around 100 BC Rome had long been in control of the whole of Italy; Greece had been conquered and Asia Minor annexed; victory in three Punic Wars had given Rome the former kingdom of Carthage in North Africa and, indirectly, much of Spain; and Rome was consolidating its hold along the rest of the western Mediterranean coastline.

Once all schoolchildren knew one thing about Caesar's Gaul – the opening words of Caesar's *Gallic Wars*: that it was divided into three parts. This is patently wrong. Caesar, at the beginning of his own commentaries on his Gallic War, was referring to the three parts of Gallia Comata (long-haired Gaul) – the part of Gaul as yet unconquered on his arrival in Gaul, made up of Belgica, Aquitania and Gallia proper. The southern coastal area of Gaul – Transalpine Gaul, or 'Gaul on the other side of the Alps' – was a fourth part, firmly incorporated into Rome's Empire and a strong base for further expansion, while Cisalpine Gaul – 'Gaul on this side of the Alps', in northern Italy – was a fifth, it too inhabited by one of the Celtic-speaking groups who had populated much of central and western Europe in the early Roman period. Caesar's conquest of Gallia Comata began almost immediately after his arrival, when he used the excuse of the movement of the Gallic tribe of the Helvetii westwards (apparently to escape pressure from the Germans beyond the Rhine) to attack both the Gauls and the Germans. By 56 BC, the various separate peoples or tribes of Gaul had all submitted, and the resistance of the Veneti of north-west Gaul had been crushed ferociously, their leaders executed and the population sold into slavery: a deliberate lesson for other peoples. Caesar turned his gaze to the Ocean, and beyond the Ocean, to Britain.

Caesar's own description of the Britons made much of their primitiveness: they were savages, who painted themselves blue with woad. It is worth thinking about the actual differences between the two peoples, Romans and Britons. In the nineteenth century, British historians would have thought in terms of a comparison between western Europe and, say, central Africa: civilisation on the one hand, and barbarism on the other. With a system of Victorian values which was itself partly based on Greco-Latin literature, this is hardly surprising. 'Barbarian' was a Latin word deriving from the Greek for 'foreigner', but in Caesar's day it was already acquiring the association with inferiority and absence of civilised values. It is true that Julius Caesar stood at the apex of a massive and highly centralised military and political organisation, geared towards the exploitation of its conquered provinces. Rome possessed an urban-based culture; a system of education which used writing and the Latin language to foster a sense of identity among the elite; a sophisticated legal system; a technology which allowed large-scale building in stone; and an infrastructure of roads, aqueducts and sewers which enabled the cities of the Mediterranean world to thrive and expand. But in some ways – such as in the area of agricultural production – Rome was hardly more advanced than the Gauls or Britons, and a postmodern and above all post-colonial scale of values might not rate the Roman achievement quite so highly as the Romans did themselves. The Gauls and Britons themselves had a developed literary and legal culture, even if it was preserved orally rather than in writing; nowadays we value their decorative arts if anything rather more highly than the often vapid Roman imitations of the Greek. In terms of their political ruthlessness, or of their frequent inhumanity to foreign peoples and their own slaves, the Romans were morally speaking no better than, or even worse than, barbarians. But, of course, people who use the term 'barbarian' are, like Pratchett's Mrs Whitlow, 'not, for some inexplicable reason, trying to suggest that the subjects have a rich oral tradition, a complex system of tribal rights, and a deep respect for the spirits of their ancestors. They are implying the kind of behaviour more generally associated, oddly enough, with people wearing a full suit of clothes, often with the same insignia.'[2] Many historians in the last two centuries, oddly enough, have rather admired the clothed and uniformed Romans, whose idea of warfare emphasised discipline and ruthlessness, rather than the individual heroism of the Celtic warriors. It is more difficult in a post-colonial world with a post-fascist consciousness.

Our written information about Britain in the Iron Age or early Roman period comes exclusively from Greek and Roman writers: from the records of the earliest Greek traveller Pytheas, from the Greek geographers Strabo and Ptolemy, from the Roman scientist Pliny, and from those who wrote about the conquest of Britain, like Julius Caesar himself, who described his two visits to Britain in 55 and 54 BC, or Tacitus, who related the career of his father-in-law Agricola, governor of Britain between 78 and 84 AD. None of this material should be taken at face value: the geographers never left the Mediterranean, and those who described Rome's contacts with the Britons may well have been swayed in one direction or another for political reasons. We have the picture of a largely wooded island from Strabo, who notes that the Britons are 'unskilled in horticulture or farming in general'.[3] Although Caesar says that 'the population is exceedingly large, the ground thickly studded with homesteads, closely resembling those of the Gauls, and the cattle very numerous', he also thinks that 'most of the tribes of the interior do not grow corn but live on milk and meat, and wear skins' and that women are shared by groups of ten or twelve, and especially by brothers, and by fathers and sons.[4] These are very typical statements by which 'civilised' peoples define themselves against the barbarian, partly in order to justify their interference in the name of 'progress'; very similar, and equally untrue, comments were made about the Irish by those Anglo-Normans who were trying to take them over in the twelfth century.

The Britons may have spoken the same, or related, dialects, but there were considerable regional and other variations between them. The Romans themselves thought that these variations might denote racial difference: Tacitus noted that the red hair and large size of the Caledonians showed that they were really Germans, that the swarthy inhabitants of South Wales with their dark curly hair were clearly from Spain, while those in the south-east were just like the Gauls.[5] There have been modern scholars who would accept these suggestions, at least to the extent of thinking of British prehistory as a series of invasions and settlements of people from different parts of Europe. Archaeologically one can see cultural differences, some of which may indeed relate to influence of some sort from the Continent. In the fifth century BC, for instance, a distinctively Continental culture appeared in East Yorkshire, characterised by chariot burials: the closest parallels on the Continent are to be found in the Marne valley in northern France. In Caesar's day the people of East Yorkshire were called the Parisi: it is normally assumed that there must be some kind of link with the Gallic tribe of that name from near the Marne who would eventually bequeath their name to Paris.

The question of the relationship between Briton and Gaul, and particularly those Gallic peoples whom Caesar categorised as 'Belgae', is still a very vexed one. Caesar said that the coasts of Britain had been settled by immigrants from the Belgae of northern Gaul 'who came to plunder and make war – nearly all of them retaining the names of the tribes from which they originated – and later settled down to till the soil'.[6] There seems little doubt about the close links between some of these peoples north and south of the Channel: the Atrebates of central southern Britain, for instance, have the same name as a people in northern Gaul (who gave their name to modern Arras), and after Commius, one of the Gallic Atrebates, had fled Gaul around 52 BC he is to be found minting coins among the British Atrebates.[7] As with the Parisi, the question of whether this connection resulted from a large-scale migration, or conquest by a warrior elite, still remains the object of considerable debate. Although Caesar presents the Belgic influence in southern Britain as being well-established, it is possible that their presence was relatively recent; indeed, Caesar's own conquest of Gaul, completed only two years before his first visit to Britain, may have occasioned a flight of Belgic refugees north of the Channel. It is around then that the strongest Gallo-Belgic influence can be detected, in the coins that are being minted in southern Britain. There may even be coincidence, or linguistic parallels, at work: as Salway points out, no-one suggests migration to explain the fact that there are Celtic peoples called Veneti in north-west Gaul and also in north-east Italy (giving their names respectively to the modern towns of Vannes and Venice).[8] Such parallelism in tribal names was not uncommon among the Celtic peoples. It has been argued that there were three tribes in Britain known to Romans as the Cornovii, for instance: in Shropshire, north-west Scotland and Cornwall. The *civitas Cornoviorum* is the territory around Wroxeter in Shropshire; but the name actually survives in the modern term 'Cornwall'.[9] Some of the links between Britain and Gaul mentioned by Caesar are intriguing, but on the face of it implausible: such as his remark that earlier that century Diviciacus, king of the Suessiones (a Gallic tribe from around Soissons, east of Paris), had 'controlled not only a large part of the Belgic territory [in Gaul], but Britain as well.'[10] Caesar's main excuse for invading Britain – if, in their expansionist zeal, the Romans needed an excuse – was that the Britons were liable to help their newly conquered Gallic cousins in an uprising. We can thus by no means put our trust in Caesar's reliability.

The Belgic nature of the south-east British peoples is the first appearance of the type of academic debate which is going to become all too familiar by the end of this book. How should the various interventions by foreign powers in Britain (Belgae, Romans, Anglo-Saxons, Vikings, Normans) be regarded? The last four are clearly military interventions, but to what extent were those military interventions accompanied by large-scale migration? Was cultural change the result of migration and settlement, or the impact of a fairly small military elite? For prehistorians the debate goes back much further than the time of the Belgae: 'invasion' or 'diffusion' have been rival ways of explaining the appearance in Britain of each new material culture with an apparent Continental origin. As far as the pre-Roman peoples of Britain are concerned, however, the consensus seems now to be that there was no large-scale invasion from the Continent. The Iron Age peoples of Britain partook of political and cultural developments that were happening right across northern Europe. Material culture of the type known to archaeologists as Hallstatt appeared in southern England around 500 BC; a century or two later, La Tène culture also appeared in the south. At some point during this period, and in a process which is quite unknown to us, the Celtic language also came to Britain, presumably from Gaul, and seems to have replaced the pre-Celtic languages: the personal names of the British recorded by Roman writers are exclusively Celtic in type. In Caesar's day the 'Belgic' peoples north and south of the Channel do appear to be in close cultural contact with each other: the Romans may have thought of the Channel as 'the Ocean', a significant psychological barrier, but for the peoples on either side it may well have been a route and a point of connection.

The pre-Roman Iron Age peoples of Britain are generally referred to as 'Celtic', which as we have already seen is a linguistic term. Thanks largely to the racial theories of the nineteenth century, which have had such a damaging impact upon the twentieth century, those writing about the period have often used it in a much broader sense, writing not just of the 'Celtic race', but of Celtic society, Celtic religion, Celtic art and so on; later (pp. 164–70) we shall see the misconceptions that have crept in thanks to the modern invention of the 'Celtic Church'. The archaeologist Simon James caused a great stir in 1999 when he argued that 'the Celts' are a modern construct, offending the self-styled Celts of today from Scotland down to Galicia. But his argument that projecting the modern nationalist (or racialist) idea of Celticness back into prehistory obscures the complexities of Iron Age society, and hides the high level of continuity between late Bronze Age societies and those of the Iron Age, is one that would be shared by many prehistorians, who have for a long time been worried about the concept of the Celts. A phrase like 'Celtic society' is often a convenient shorthand, and certainly more euphonious than, for instance, 'LPRIA society' (using Millett's abbreviation for Later Pre-Roman Iron Age Society).[11] But because of the racial content of 'Celtic' these phrases tend to become *explanatory* as well as descriptive. If LPRIA culture can be seen to have things in common with cultures on the Continent, this is possibly because the LPRIA aristocracy shared that culture, for reasons of their own, and not because there was a mass migration, let alone some kind of racial programming.

The numbers now estimated for the population of Britain at the end of the first century BC in fact preclude any idea of mass migration. It used to be thought that the population was barely more than a quarter of a million, living in scattered groups within a largely forested and uncultivated island, with plenty of opportunities for ambitious immigrants. Pollen analysis now suggests that certainly over the southern part of Britain the landscape had been largely cleared of forest, and may not have looked much different from today; in the highland regions too deforestation was already advanced.[12] The evidence of cultivation and settlement revealed by aerial photography has suggested to some that the population of Roman Britain at its height may have reached four or five million: a figure not reached again until the eighteenth century. Even if four million is too high, the population was still larger in the Roman period than the population of around two million which is argued for England in 1087 (at the time of the Domesday survey).[13] Even though the population may have begun to rise rapidly from around AD 1, the numbers of people in Britain before the arrival of the Romans may still have been measured in the millions.

Julius Caesar and after

Once Julius Caesar had conquered Gaul, the nature of the contacts between Gaul and Britain changed dramatically. The British were no longer equals and 'cousins' of their Continental neighbours, but potential supplicants of a much greater power, and the nature of their trade changed, as they gained access to an important manufacturing and trading area. There was over a century between Julius Caesar's conquest of Gaul, in the 50s BC, and the full-scale invasion of Britain led by his great-grandson Claudius in 43 AD: a century in which the Britons slowly adapted to the presence of Rome south of the Channel. Caesar's raids on Britain in 55 and 54 BC were minor interruptions in this slow evolution.

Caesar's own justification for his raids rings fairly hollow. He claimed that, in the wake of the revolt of the Veneti, any fresh Gallic revolt would be assisted by the British. He mentioned a number of close links between Britain and Gaul: he alleges, for instance, that the Belgic nobles of the Bellovaci (from the Beauvais area), who had urged resistance to Rome, had fled to Britain in 57 BC. But one must suspect that these were excuses: Caesar's main ambitions were for power in Rome. Victories on the frontier, against no matter whom, could only serve to increase his prestige and strengthen the loyalty of his troops.

If we can trust our main source – Caesar's own *Gallic Wars* – the first expeditionary force in 55 BC consisted of some hundred transports, carrying two legions and a cavalry force. It was not a surprise attack: Caesar had sent Commius, whom he had made king of the Gallic Atrebates and who was, Caesar wrote, greatly respected in Britain, to contact peoples in Britain to persuade them to come over to the Roman side. The Britons must have been well-prepared, and indeed, when Caesar got within sight of the coast, he saw British warriors posted on the cliffs. Caesar soon discovered that the white cliffs of Dover did not make an ideal landing place; and in fact he had some trouble in disembarking his troops in the face of British defence. When he did land, the troops were unable to pursue an attack, because the cavalry had not disembarked. 'This was the one thing that prevented Caesar from achieving his usual success,' wrote Caesar.[14] Storm damage to the ships, compounded by the fact that (as Caesar admitted) the Romans had not realised that the tides were particularly high at full moon, further hampered his advance; part of the Seventh Legion was annihilated while foraging for food. Caesar eventually persuaded the British to meet him in pitched battle and he put them to rout, as Roman troops normally did when meeting barbarians on the battlefield. Caesar went home, with hostages. He had achieved his political purpose: Book IV of his *Wars* ends with the Senate receiving his dispatches and decreeing a public thanksgiving of twenty days.

Caesar had not finished with Britain, however. While he was in Italy during the winter of 55/54, a much larger invasion force was being built, including ships better able to disembark troops on beaches, and in 54 BC, on his return, it sailed: some 800 transports, with five legions and 2000 cavalry. The Britons had found a new leader, Cassivellaunus; but he was no match for the Romans. He was defeated once in north Kent and once when Caesar took his troops across the Thames. Caesar accepted an alliance with the Trinovantes, whose king had been exiled to Gaul by Cassivellaunus, and other Britons followed their lead. Caesar departed, with hostages, promises of tribute, and an alliance. His expeditions had done little to quell the danger of Gallic rebellion: indeed, he probably withdrew from Britain when he heard rumour of the impending rebellion by Vercingetorix in Gaul, which threatened his conquests and his career. Nor had his expedition been profitable. As Cicero wrote to Trabatius (joking about the British use of war-chariots, unknown to Greco-Romans except in Homer's *Iliad*): 'I hear there's no gold or silver in Britain. If this is so, I advise you to get a war-chariot and hasten back to us as soon as possible.'[15] Caesar had not proved that Britain was a necessary addition to Rome's massive empire. But he had conquered the Ocean, which was a great psychological barrier for the Romans; he had, as Plutarch put it, 'sailed through the Atlantic'.[16]

For the next ninety years Rome consolidated its hold on Gaul, and turned the Gallic aristocracy into a Romanophile elite. The Roman Empire inevitably exerted a strong influence on its neighbour, a few miles away across the Channel. To qualify this: Rome exerted a strong influence on *south-east* Britain, perhaps distorting the differences which were already present between the south and the rest of Britain – differences which are distorted still further by the fact that we know more about the south-east, archaeologically and historically, than we know about the rest of the island. Some of our information comes from the Romans themselves, and some from archaeology. But we also have the information from coins, from their distribution and from the names of the rulers inscribed on them. Although coins were minted in Britain from the late second century BC, it is only in the last years of the first century BC that names are first used on them: names in the Latin alphabet, sometimes with the Latin REX ('king'). This may not just reflect the importation of a Roman custom, but possibly also the emergence of a more fluid and competitive political system which favoured the propaganda value of coinage. It does not necessarily mean a close political relationship with Rome, any more than does, say, the rich burial at Lexden near Colchester: this contained Roman luxury goods, including a Roman stool which may be a Roman symbol of authority.[17] The Romans may simply have given Iron Age chieftains a new way of displaying their power in order to impress their rivals. As far as we can see, the Romans did their best to exploit rivalry between peoples: this was a normal means of dealing with barbarians. They harboured and helped political exiles; they played one king off against another by alliances and gifts. If this created a destabilising effect, then that too might benefit Rome. Archaeological evidence suggests that increased trade with the Continent came with the Roman conquest of Gaul; that too may have had a destabilising effect, as some kingdoms were able to prosper at the expense of others. Several of the tribes mentioned by Caesar had disappeared by the first century AD; kings seem to have become more common and more powerful.

If we look at the political structure of Britain from the Roman point of view we inevitably begin with Kent, the main entry-point for anyone coming from the Continent. Kent, or Cantium, which seems to mean 'corner land' or 'land on the edge',[18] was, according to Caesar, the home of the most civilised (*humanissimi*) of the Britons, by which, of course, he meant the most ready to import and imitate Roman ways.[19] But it was not a strong kingdom: the territory in Caesar's day was divided between four kings (ruling either four separate kingdoms, or perhaps ruling jointly, as is known elsewhere in pre-Roman Europe). The true power lay north of the Thames, in the tribes who, at the time of Caesar's attack, had placed themselves temporarily under the leadership of Cassivellaunus. By the first century AD, two generations later, the Trinovantes and the Catuvellauni had come together under a single ruler, and were perhaps the most significant destabilising factor in the south of Britain, extending their power south into Kent and into the territory of other neighbours to the north and west. It is likely that the Iceni of East Anglia and the Corieltauvi (or Coritani) were among the peoples dominated by the Catuvellaunian federation: the fact that neither seem to have had a unified kingship may have made them more vulnerable.

The main opponents of Catuvellaunian power were the Atrebates, south of the Thames. We have already noted their connection with the Atrebates in Gaul: the associate of Caesar, Commius, from the Gallic Atrebates, joined Vercingetorix against the Romans in 52 BC, and then fled to the British Atrebates, apparently becoming their king, since his name appears on their coins. He was succeeded by his son Timcommius, and then by Verica, whose coin proclaimed him (in Latin) to be REX COM. F., 'king, son of Commius'. Beyond the Atrebates were the Durotriges of Dorset, the Dobunni of the West Midlands, and the Cornovii of what would become the Welsh marches: each of these peoples used numerous hill-forts, suggesting a fragmented political structure. There are numerous hill-forts too among the various peoples in what is now Wales, about whom little is known beyond their names: the Silures and Demetae in the south, and the Ordovices and Deceangli in the north. Apart from the Parisi in East Yorkshire, the rest of what is now northern England seems to have been occupied by a single people (or probably a more or less closely-knit federation) called the Brigantes. The Brigantes did not have hill-forts: a sign for some scholars,[20] oddly, of their *lower* level on the evolutionary scale – far lower than the Belgic peoples of the south-east, who, the same scholars think, were too *sophisticated* to need hill-forts. To the north of the Brigantes were those who were, in the eyes of the Romans, even more barbarous than their southern neighbours: civilisation diminished the further one travelled from Rome. In the Scottish Lowlands there were the Novantae, Belgovae and Votadini, with the Damnonii in the area between the Forth and Clyde; north of them were the various peoples whom the Romans normally lumped together as Caledonii. Until the attempted conquest of Scotland under Agricola, Romans had virtually no knowledge of these peoples, and Roman writers barely recorded more than their names.

Not all changes in pre-Roman British society need be attributed to the proximity of the Romans, of course. And it is clear that society was changing rapidly, particularly in the south and east. In the Thames Valley, patterns of land-use seem to be changing, in a more marked way than actually occurred at the time of the Roman conquest a hundred years later.[21] There is a change in the characteristics of the farms, but also a shift from open pasture to enclosed fields and hence, perhaps, to a different type of land ownership. The archaeology of the late Iron Age also suggests that there was a growing tendency for the emergence of important central places – if not towns, then institutions that were on their way to being towns. In areas where there had been large numbers of small hill-forts, much larger hill-forts were being created which, in the cases of Maiden Castle (Dorset) and the Wrekin (Worcestershire), were eventually replaced by Roman towns. In areas where by the beginning of the first millennium hill-forts had ceased to be used, new tribal centres emerged, which we now call *oppida*. These were on low ground, and were sometimes defended and sometimes not: a few, known as 'territorial oppida' extended over a huge area. Camulodunum (Colchester, Essex), the capital of the Trinovantes, is a classic example. It is not a town in our sense at all, in that the settlement is scattered over 32.5 km^2, but within that area, delimited by dykes, was a major religious site, with a defensive site next to it (a royal centre?); an important burial site; places where coins were minted; and a concentration of imported goods from the Roman world. These territorial oppida were not restricted to the lowland region: there is one at Stanwick (North Yorkshire) in the territory of the Brigantes.

There are a number of possible reasons for these changes, including a trend towards an increasingly hierarchical society, produced by the growth of a class who were able to increase their wealth and prestige by trade with Rome. There were other signs of a much more tangible link with the Continent, most notably in the emergence of coinage, as we have seen. Coins had been produced by Gallic tribes before the Roman conquest, and in type the British coins were similar; they are restricted to the south-east of Britain, which emphasises this continental context. The coins are gold and silver: not for use in small-scale transactions, but produced perhaps for reasons of making payments of tribute, or even largely for prestige purposes. A small number of sites with coin-making activity are known, and it is interesting that a number of these later became important Roman towns, suggesting that already they were political centres before Roman conquest: Canterbury, Colchester, St Albans, Silchester and Winchester. Although many of the coins had purely symbolic designs, depicting horses, boars or stylised human beings, some had Latin inscriptions. The White Horse carved into the chalk downs at Uffington (Berks), on the Ridgeway by the hill-fort of Uffington Castle, resembles the horses on the coins produced by both the Dobunni and the Atrebates: it has been suggested that the Horse might have been a sign of a territorial boundary.[22] Even if the White Horse is actually Bronze Age in date,[23] it could still have been used for that purpose, and it may even have been located at the only point where, judging from the distribution of coins, four territories converge: those of the Catuvellauni, Atrebates, Durotriges and Dobunni.[24] Coins may have been another sign of increasing politicisation and territorialisation, and we might be able to detect the particularly powerful from the amount of coins they produce and the breadth of the area over which they are spread. If so, Cunobelinus was of considerable importance, issuing coins in great numbers from both Camulodunum (Colchester) and Verulamium (St Albans).

Coins are probably not evidence of trade, but there is plenty of evidence for trade nevertheless. What survives archaeologically is certainly only a tiny element of the total material traded, but also a seriously misleading element. Look at what Strabo says about trade. He records that the exports of

Britain were grain and cattle, gold, silver, iron, hides, slaves and hunting dogs, and that they in turn imported ivory, amber and glass.[25] Of these exports, nothing would survive archaeologically on the Continent that could clearly be shown to be British in origin: indeed, precious little would survive at all, since all except for the metals in Strabo's list were perishable. There is some evidence of the slave trade, however: slave chains such as those found at the hill-fort of Bigbury (Kent). As in West Africa in the eighteenth century, the presence of a market for slaves across the water may have brought considerable exploitation and social disruption.[26]

Trade across the Channel had always been of some importance, but there is little doubt that it increased through the century after Julius Caesar. There are clear signs that established patterns of trade were transformed by Caesar's conquest of Gaul. According to him, the Veneti of north-west Gaul had the largest fleet of ships, with which they used to trade with Britain;[27] and indeed, archaeology suggests that the main area of Gallic contact before Caesar's day was with southern and western Britain, with goods arriving at places like Hengistbury (Dorset) and Mount Batten (Devon). But Caesar brutally crushed the Veneti, and destroyed their fleet; in the second half of the first century BC, most of the trade seems to have been between north-east Gaul and south-east Britain. The earliest amphorae, evidence of the trade in Roman wine, are found near Hengistbury; the late first-century amphorae are found largely in the south-east. This change in trade patterns must have benefited the Catuvellaunian-Trinovantian confederacy in the south-east, and helped in the extension of its power.

The history of Britain in the early part of the first century AD is normally written around the rise of Catuvellaunian power, which does seem to have been the major political development. Around the beginning of the first millennium we see (through coins) Tasciovanus among the Catuvellauni; Dubnovellaunus among the Cantiaci; and Timcommius among the Atrebates. The coins of Dubnovellaunus are found in Essex too, apparently in Catuvellaunian territory. Then the coins of both Dubnovellaunus and Timcommius stop, around AD 7, and two people called 'Dumnobellaunus' and 'Tim——' (the rest of the name is not clear) appear in Emperor Augustus's official record of his reign, as suppliant British kings who had come to his court. It seems highly likely that these two kings had been expelled by the Catuvellauni. Their coins cease at about the same time as Cunobelinus – Shakespeare's Cymbeline – begins to mint coins in Colchester, and shortly afterwards in St Albans. It is possible that Cunobelinus was a Trinovantian, putting an end to the Catuvellaunian domination of the federation, for the centre of his power remained at the Trinovantian centre of Colchester. He ruled for over thirty years, undoubtedly the most powerful British king in the last years of British independence, maintaining his independence from Rome yet profiting from imports of wine and other luxuries. One of his last acts was to expel his son Adminius, who fled to Gaul in around AD 40 and surrendered to the mad Emperor

Caligula; the Emperor treated this as a great victory and began preparations for an invasion.

This was not the first time that an invasion had been mooted since the time of Julius Caesar: Caesar's heir Octavian, better known as Augustus, the first Roman Emperor, had had plans to invade on at least two occasions, but they came to nothing. It is interesting that Strabo puts forward an economic argument to explain why the Romans did not press forward with invasion plans with rather more urgency. The Britons were no military danger, and they were very friendly:

> Some of the chieftains there, having gained the friendship of Caesar Augustus through embassies and paying court to him, have set up votive offering on the Capitolium and have almost made the whole island Roman property. In addition they submit so readily to heavy duties both on the exports from there to Gaul and on the imports from Gaul ... that there is no need to garrison the island. For at the very least one legion and some cavalry would be needed to exact tribute from them, and the expense of the army would equal the money brought in.[28]

As with Caesar's raids, it was politics rather than economics which decided the events.

During the Roman Republic, individuals who wished to make a political name for themselves, like Julius Caesar, would often undertake expeditions against the enemy: not only did they win prestige, but, just as important for a successful career at home, they won large amounts of booty and the loyalty of an enriched army. The pressures were different for the Emperors who were to succeed Augustus and to rule in the West for the next four centuries and more. They had to try to ensure that potentially profitable conquests did *not* take place, unless they themselves were in charge, in case victorious generals should turn their attention to usurping imperial power. Sensible Emperors did not even want to go outside the Empire themselves, partly because defeat would have been politically suicidal, but also because leaving Rome for lengthy periods of time might be equally dangerous. After the defeats that the Romans had suffered beyond the Rhine, under Augustus in AD 9, there were actually very few attempts to extend the Empire beyond the bounds which Augustus had created. But Emperor Claudius decided that he ought to try. The very particular circumstances of the time conspired to make this a sensible course of action for him.

Firstly, Cunobelinus had died, bringing political turmoil to Britain. His two sons Togodumnus and Caratacus divided power between them; Verica of the Atrebates was thrown out of his kingdom; and Claudius was faced with demands by an obviously hostile Catuvellaunian federation to return the various political exiles who had come into the Empire. Thanks to Caligula, a blueprint for invasion existed. Claudius's own position was uncertain: he had been given the Empire after Caligula's assassination not from merit, but because he was the only surviving member of Augustus's family. Claudius must have thought that invasion of Britain was a very obvious way to increase the army's respect for him, to pacify a troublesome neighbour, and with luck to refill the empty treasury that had been bequeathed to him by Caligula.

Claudius's invasion of Britain

Claudius had four legions to send to Britain in AD 43, drawn from the forces stationed on the Rhine: 20,000 fighting men, many of them probably Italian-born. These were many more troops than Caesar had sent, and they were also in a much stronger position than Caesar's troops had been ninety years earlier. The provinces of Gaul were now well-established, prosperous, and (at least in the upper echelons) enthusiastic supporters of the Empire. One wonders how many British nobles looked at the current wealth and power of the descendants of Caesar's Gallic nobles and speculated about whether Roman dominion would bring them the same security and opportunities.

The aims of Claudius's forces were probably clearer too: Caesar never seems to have had clear military or political aims in mind, beyond cowing those native British he met into submission, but Claudius must have intended to turn Britain, or at least the southern part of it, into a Roman province. The exact course of the invasion is not nearly so certain as that of Caesar's expeditions, because those historians who wrote about it did so much later, with no great enthusiasm for Claudius, and with little detail. Dozens of Roman fortifications – from marching camps created to shelter advancing troops overnight to large-scale garrisons – have been investigated by archaeologists, but it is not possible to do more than sketch in the broad lines of a campaign when such camps can rarely be precisely dated. It does seem that one part of the Roman forces landed at Richborough, where the Claudian camp is still visible. Aulus Plautius, the Roman commander, did meet resistance, but won several battles, defeating forces led by Caratacus and Togodumnus. After crossing the Thames, he killed Togodumnus. It was at that point that Claudius crossed to Britain, with a group of senators and, according to Dio Cassius (probably the most reliable source), a number of elephants. Later historians dismissed Claudius's own role, but Dio Cassius says that he personally defeated a British army and captured Colchester, and received the surrender of other peoples. The triumphal arch that was later raised in Rome proclaimed that he 'had received the surrender of eleven British kings, defeated without loss, and for the first time had brought barbarian peoples beyond the Ocean under Roman rule'.[29]

A province was set up, with Aulus Plautius as first governor, and with the capital at Colchester: Cunobelinus's palace and the temple enclosure were both obliterated by the establishment of a Roman fort. At first, much of

Britain remained hostile or neutral, but the security of the new province was to some extent assured by establishing friendly relations with the king of the Iceni, in the northern part of East Anglia and by making Cogidubnus, a trustworthy Briton (or possibly even a Gaul), a king in the Sussex area: 'an example of the long-established Roman custom of employing even kings to make others slaves', as Tacitus acidly comments.[30] It has been suggested by Barry Cunliffe that the grand villa at Fishbourne was his 'palace' , though Reece has called this 'total fantasy' and Braund has pointed out that Cogidubnus was probably dead by 75, and that the palace was dated by Cunliffe himself to 75–80.[31] Fishbourne was, however, one of a number of large first-century villas in the area controlled by Cogidubnus, exceptionally luxurious for Britain at this time, that showed that some people there were already doing very well out of the new regime. The Romans may even have appointed a client king in the territory once controlled by Cunobelinus, although no Roman historical text mentions such a person. But a grave was excavated at St Albans, dating from around AD 50, which was 'the most sumptuous burial ever to have taken place in this country'.[32] The huge funeral chamber, and the cremation pit with its quantity of charred objects and molten metal, stood in the midst of an enclosure 115 by 170 metres in size: vastly larger than the usual aristocratic burial enclosure of some ten metres by ten. Perhaps it belonged to a son of Cunobelinus, or a rival, installed as king by the Romans: in either case, it must modify the picture of the conquest derived from the written sources.

Even as the new province was being established, conquests were continuing. One hero of the British campaign, Vespasian (who rose from the ranks to become Emperor in AD 69), was active in the south-west, fighting numerous battles and subduing two formidable peoples, presumably the Durotriges and the Dobunni. The Fourteenth Legion were active in the Midlands; the Ninth seems to have pushed northwards. Ostorius Scapula crushed a revolt that broke out when he replaced Aulus Plautius as governor in 47, and turned against the Deceangli of what is now north Wales, only to be deflected by hostilities led by the Brigantes. No sooner had that been quelled than a leader of the British resistance emerged, among the Silures of southern Wales: Caratacus, the son of Cunobelinus. He was a major threat, and Ostorius responded by removing the legion from Colchester, safeguarding that area by setting it up as a *colonia*: a settlement of veterans, rewarded by an allotment of land. Ostorius defeated Caratacus's forces, probably on the Severn near Newtown, and captured Caratacus's family: Caratacus himself was handed over by Queen Cartimandua, ruler of the Brigantes, to whom he had fled for protection. Claudius paraded Caratacus in triumph in Rome, and won political points for himself by sparing his life.

New governors had fresh threats to deal with, from the Silures and the Brigantes. But the most serious rebellion came from the client kingdom of the Iceni. King Prasutagus had hoped to make the Emperor co-heir to his kingdom together with his two daughters, thus preserving the power of his family. But on his death Roman officials moved into his kingdom, evicting nobles from their lands, plundering the king's household and, in the end, flogging the king's widow and raping the two daughters. The widow, whom Victorians called Boadicea and whom it is customary now to call Boudicca or Boudica, led a revolt, which was immediately joined by other peoples, including the Trinovantes, whose territory (with its capital at Colchester) had been at the heart of the Roman province. It is possible that the new Roman *colonia* had been allotting land that the Trinovantes thought was theirs, and/or that they had been lent money, possibly to buy office or to pay taxes, and that these loans were being called in. Colchester was sacked; part of the Ninth legion wiped out; and Verulamium destroyed. 'Roman and provincial deaths at the places mentioned are estimated at seventy thousand', claimed Tacitus.

> The British did not take or sell prisoners, or practise other war-time exchanges. They could not wait to cut throats, hang, burn, and crucify – as though avenging, in advance, the retribution that was on its way.[33]

The retribution came, of course. The forces of the Roman governor Paulinus met those of Boudicca somewhere in the East Midlands; and Tacitus records that 80,000 British men and women were killed, with a loss of 400 Romans. Boudicca died shortly afterwards; Paulinus went on a rampage of destruction (signs of violence at a number of excavated sites have been ascribed to this period), until his discreet recall to Rome.

By 65, therefore, southern Britain was largely pacified, although the long process of rebuilding had to begin. Tacitus's description of Agricola's approach to this problem nearly twenty years later is worth quoting, both for its perception and its cynicism:

> The following winter was spent on schemes of social betterment. Agricola had to deal with people living in isolation and ignorance, and therefore prone to fight; and his object was to accustom them to a life of peace and quiet by the provision of amenities. He therefore gave private encouragement and official assistance to the building of temples, public squares and good houses. He praised the energetic and scolded the slack; and competition for honour proved as effective as compulsion. Furthermore, he educated the sons of the chiefs in the liberal arts, and expressed a preference for British ability as compared with the trained skills of the Gauls. The result was that instead of loathing the Latin language they became eager to speak it effectively. In the same way, our national dress came into favour and the toga was everywhere to be seen. And so the population was gradually led into the demoralising temptations of arcades, baths, and sumptuous banquets. The unsuspecting Britons spoke of such novelties as 'civilisation', when in fact they were only a feature of their enslavement.[34]

This process no doubt began earlier than Agricola, and continued through the eventual mopping up of any resistance. Cartimandua was expelled from her Brigantian kingdom by her ex-husband Venutius, and he in turn was expelled by the Roman general Cerialis, who established a legionary fortress for the Ninth at York. Legionary fortresses were also built at Caerleon and Chester, after Cerialis had subdued the Silures: a measure of how much of a potential threat the peoples of Wales were. Other towns were founded under Cerialis and his successor Frontinus, and the work of what Tacitus ironically called 'civilisation' proceeded.

Frontinus was succeeded by Agricola, the Roman governor about whom we know more than any other, thanks to the biography by his son-in-law Tacitus. Agricola was clearly a wonderful governor: decisive, just, efficient, a paragon of all the old Republican virtues in an age characterised by imperial vice and incompetence. It is just possible, of course, that Tacitus, his son-in-law, was not telling the unvarnished truth.

The Romans in the north

Under Agricola, who was governor between AD 78 and 84, the Romans first penetrated north of the line on which, in the next century, they were to build Hadrian's Wall. Agricola advanced from Chester, building forts as he went, and then invaded via the eastern route, up to the Tay, building forts along the Forth–Clyde line. He moved into Galloway, and was perhaps able to look at northern Ireland across the narrow channel that separates it from Britain.

> An Irish prince, expelled from his home by a rebellion, was welcomed by Agricola, who detained him, nominally as a friend, in the hope of being able to make use of him. I have often heard Agricola say that Ireland could be reduced and held by a single legion with a fair-sized force of auxiliaries; and that it would be easier to hold Britain if it were completely surrounded by Roman armies, so that liberty was banished from its sight.[35]

In 83 and 84 came the most significant campaigns. Agricola moved north of the Forth, using both troops and warships, and breaking up a Caledonian attack. The troops, according to Tacitus, were very optimistic:

> They declared that nothing could stop men like them, that they ought to drive deeper into Caledonia and fight battle after battle till they reached the farthest limits of Britain.[36]

The following year Agricola advanced again, to meet an army of some 30,000 Caledonians (says Tacitus), gathered from all among the Caledonians, at the unidentified site of Mount Graupius. Tacitus 'reports' the pre-battle speeches of the Caledonian spokesman Calgacus and of

Agricola himself. The former spoke, very convincingly, about the tyranny, arrogance and lust for power of the Romans, and how the choice was between victory on the one hand or taxation and slavery on the other; Agricola (rather less convincingly, to modern minds at least) spoke about toil, bravery and glory. Agricola nevertheless seems to have inspired his men: some 10,000 of the enemy were killed, for a loss of 360 Romans. Agricola progressed through the cowed provinces, while his admiral sailed around the north coast of Britain: symbolic gestures, both, to signify the conquest of the whole island of Britain. The Emperor Domitian rewarded Agricola with a triumph at Rome, recalling him as soon as he could, suspicious of his power.

'Britain was conquered and immediately abandoned', commented Tacitus.[37] We can see this most graphically not through the written sources (which, after Tacitus, very rarely mention any detail about campaigns against the Caledonians), but in the archaeology. The most massive monument to Agricola's campaigns was the fortress of Inchtuthil, on the southern edge of the Scottish Highlands. Agricola reused a site that had been a fortification in prehistoric times. It was intended for some 6000 troops: an entire legion plus auxiliary troops. It was built in stages, with sixty-four barracks, each 84 metres long, in nine groups of six, intended for the finished camp. Aerial photography has discovered a nearby labour camp, for the workers building the fort, and beyond that a quarry from which some 8500 cubic metres of stone had been taken. It was a massive undertaking, which was left unfinished; and it seems to have been systematically dismantled only three or four years after Agricola's recall. The most recent coins are those of Domitian, dating to around AD 86 or 87. Stone walls were taken down, gutters blocked, and a million iron nails hidden under the floor of a workshop, perhaps so that they might be recovered in a future operation, or simply to hide that valuable resource from the Caledonians.[38]

Some 200 other Roman forts have been discovered from the area to the north of the future Roman frontier, Hadrian's Wall, most of them by aerial photography. Only five were built of stone: one of these was Inchtuthil and four were from the period of recovery under Antoninus Pius. But those 200 forts were built during a series of relatively short periods during which the Romans tried to recover all or part of Agricola's gains. It was Trajan (88–117) who decided to withdraw entirely from what is now Scotland, and to build a line of forts from the Solway to the Tyne which were eventually consolidated by his successor Hadrian (117-38) as the stone and turf wall which bears his name. Hadrian's own successor Antoninus Pius (138-61) decided at the beginning of his reign, perhaps largely for reasons of prestige, to advance northwards again: he began the turf wall, the Antonine Wall, 40 Roman miles (60 km) long, across the narrow isthmus between the Forth and the Clyde, together with its associated forts. In the mid-150s there seems to have been an uprising which brought this occupation to an end, though perhaps only briefly. Marcus Aurelius (161-80) had to send an army north to control the frontier, while Dio Cassius says that under Commodus (180-92) the northern peoples came over the wall (presumably Hadrian's Wall) and defeated the Roman forces, killing their general. Commodus's governor restored order, but did not, apparently, regain control over the forts north of Hadrian's Wall.

The last Roman Emperor to be involved in attempts to move into Scotland was Septimius Severus (193–211). Dio Cassius tells us that by his time the two major powers in Scotland were two large confederacies: the Caledonians and the Maeatae (whose name survives in place-names such as Dumyat and Myot Hill, near Stirling).[39] It is unclear whether the Maeatae included such British peoples north of the Wall as the Damnonii or the Votadini. Septimius's governors had little success containing these peoples, and in 208 or 209 the Emperor himself decided to campaign north of the Wall. The Maeatae and Caledonians were not as rash as their ancestors, who had met Agricola in pitched battle; their guerrilla tactics were very successful, and the Romans lost thousands, if not tens of thousands, of men. Severus nevertheless reached the far north of the island, apparently, and forced the Caledonians to surrender. He withdrew to York; and when he died there in 211, his son Caracalla soon gave up his gains. Rome once more withdrew to Hadrian's Wall, which Severus had reconstructed. (Indeed, it was not actually until archaeological work began on the Wall in the nineteenth century that it was realised that the Wall was indeed substantially that of Hadrian rather than of Severus himself.)

Rome's conquest of Britain was accompanied by numerous feats of engineering: the building of forts like Inchtuthil or the building of military roads (such as Dere Street in Scotland), but Hadrian's Wall is surely the most considerable. It was 76 Roman miles (113 km) long, punctuated by small forts every one Roman mile and larger forts each seven miles or so. Hadrian's Wall was not actually a frontier itself, but a crucial part of the system of defences that operated both north and south of it. The Wall was in stone, towards the east some 3 metres wide and some 4 metres high; initially, it was to be defended from forts further south, but it was later decided to build forts actually astride or adjoining the Wall. Immediately to the south of the Wall was the vallum, built after the forts had been added. It was a ditch 6.2 metres wide and 3.1 metres deep (20 and 10 Roman feet respectively), flanked on each side by banks 6 metres high: the width of the whole construction was 37 metres, or 120 Roman feet. The vallum was clearly important: it continues for almost the entire length of the Wall, with just a few gaps in it to permit access to the main roads and to the forts, and it must have required almost as much labour as the building of the Wall itself, but its function is actually a matter for dispute. It prevented people coming to the Wall unobserved from the south; it restricted the number of entry points to the fortification area itself. Perhaps it was designed to regulate (and tax?) the movement of people and livestock between north and south, helping to prevent small-scale raiding and the cattle-rustling which was virtually a

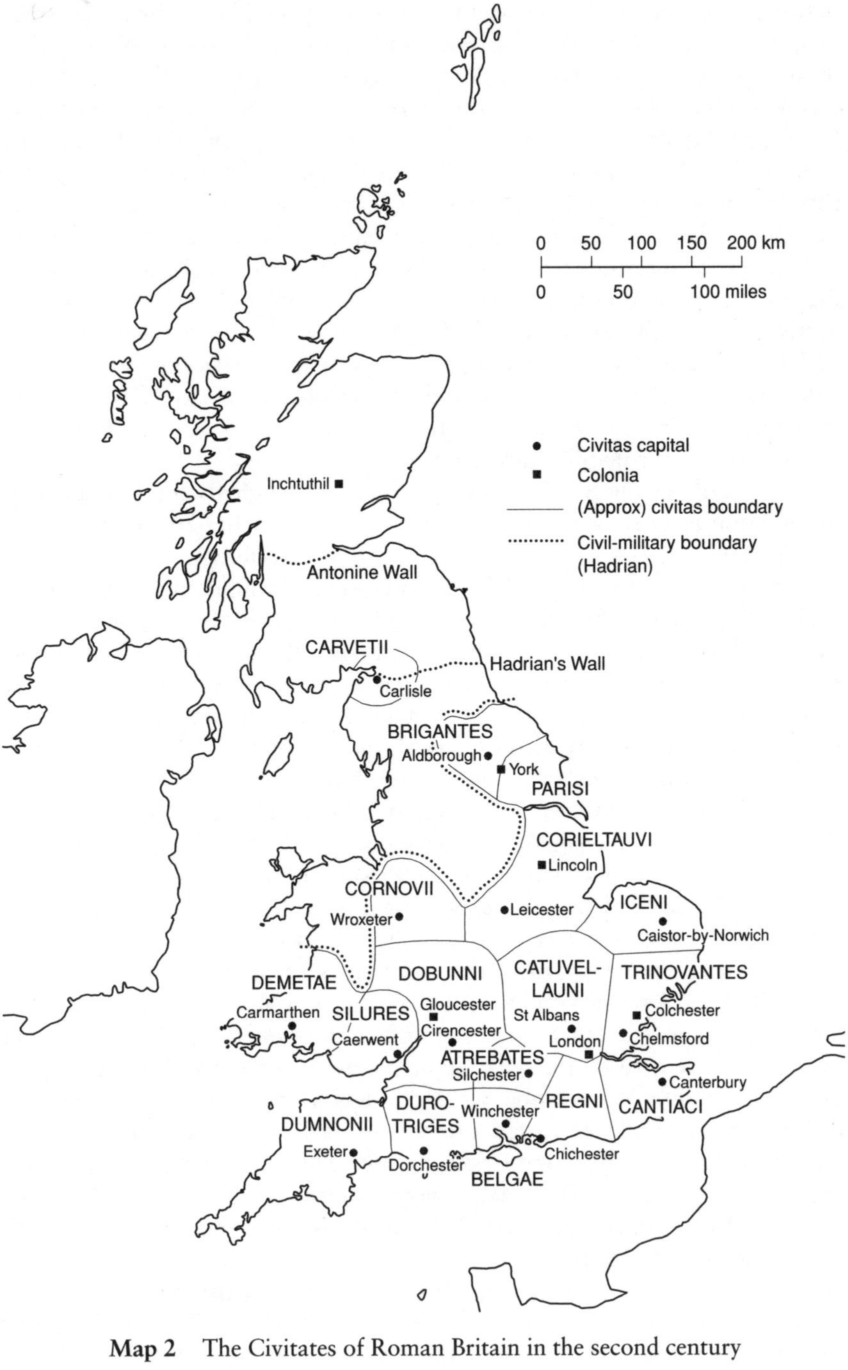

Map 2 The Civitates of Roman Britain in the second century

national sport among some Celtic peoples, or simply to protect Roman property. Indeed, both the Hadrianic and Antonine Walls have been called 'bureaucratic in concept, not military'.[40] They were to do with control. And the Wall was not just aimed at the 'barbarians' to the north: it also probably reflected distrust of the Brigantes – the Britons who lived in the territory to the south. There were a number of forts along the Pennines, well within the Roman province, indicating that the Pennines were to some extent a militarised zone; indeed, at the time of Antoninus Pius the Brigantes seem to have launched a serious rebellion. Arguably Hadrian's Wall, and its vallum, did not represent a natural frontier at all, but a line which deliberately separated peoples who had some affinity, and if ever in alliance would offer a real threat. But whatever its purpose, the defensive system was a clear demonstration of Roman power in the north; as well as, given the massive investment it entailed, a demonstration that Rome had no intention of trying to conquer the peoples further north.

The middle of the third century was marked by chaos throughout most of the Empire. There were invasions by Germanic barbarians from north of the Danube and east of the Rhine, and military troubles encouraged rebellion by numerous would-be Roman Emperors. Throughout this period the northern frontier of Britain seems to have been perfectly tranquil. Despite the fact that troops were probably taken from the frontier, or withdrawn from Britain, there were no disturbances in the north major enough to be mentioned in the sources. The defences did become run-down, however. An inscription from the fort of Birdoswald, on Hadrian's Wall, from between 296 and 306, states that the commander's house had fallen down and been covered with earth; the inscription records its rebuilding, and the repair of the headquarters building and the bath-house.[41] This was part of a general reorganisation of defences under Constantius Chlorus.

It was also under Constantius, in a panegyric addressed to him, that the word 'Pict' first appears, while the last appearance of the word 'Caledonian' is in a text from the early years of his son Constantine the Great. The Picts seem to be a confederation of Caledonians and Maeatae and of the various other northern tribes mentioned by the geographer Ptolemy; henceforth that is the only name given to the peoples north of the Forth. Ammianus Marcellinus, writing in Rome in the later fourth century, claims that the Picts consisted of two peoples, the Dicalydones and the Verturiones: the former word presumably relates to the Caledonii, while the latter is preserved in the later word *Fortriu*, the Pictish word for the southern part of their kingdom. Neither the Romans nor modern historians know very much at all about the early Picts, though the Romans did recognise them to be a real threat to the stability of the northern part of their province through much of the fourth century. The most serious Pictish attack came in 367, and the Roman response was probably the most intensive restoration of Hadrian's Wall and other frontier defences since the time of Septimius Severus. But it was the last attempt to keep the northern defences in place; there is little evidence for continued occupation of the forts after the 380s.

The presence of thousands of Roman troops on Hadrian's Wall for over two centuries, and, for a brief period, the occupation of Scotland right up to the Forth–Clyde line, must have had some impact upon the different groups of Britons who lived there. Wealth did certainly flow northwards at times. In 197, for instance, 'the Romans had to buy peace from the Maeatae for a considerable sum, recovering a few captives.'[42] There are several hoards of Roman coins from Scotland which may reflect such payments. The best evidence came from the hill-fort of Traprain Law, in East Lothian (some twenty miles east of Edinburgh). It is the only hill-fort which can be shown to be occupied throughout the Roman period, and has the largest assemblage of Roman artefacts in Scotland from a civilian site. It may have been the central site of the kingdom of the Votadini, and the artefacts may hint at some close diplomatic relationship with Rome, as well as trade, but it has also been suggested that the finds may have been offerings to a temple on that site. The most spectacular find, the Traprain Treasure, is likewise impossible to categorise with any certainty. It consisted of fragments of around fifty metal objects, such as jugs or dishes, most of them silver: these items had been broken up in antiquity. The objects date from around 400, and may represent loot, from the time that northerners were taking advantage of the collapse of the Roman frontier to raid within the province, or perhaps payment or subsidy from the Romans in return for action against the Picts to the north. All our sources refer to the Picts and the Scots as the real danger in the north, not the British peoples (like the Votadini) who lived beyond the Wall.

Other items of Roman manufacture – coins, metalwork, glass, pottery wine-jars – have been found all over Scotland, as far north as the Orkneys and Shetlands. Whether these arrived as items of trade or loot, or came with Romans or with returning Caledonians, is impossible to say. Most of the Roman goods arriving in the north were relatively high-quality items: a comparison of the artefacts found on ordinary British farmsteads immediately south of Hadrian's Wall with those found immediately to the north show that mundane artefacts did not cross the border.[43] After the third century there is very little.[44] It is not easy to detect archaeologically whether the presence of Rome actually made a great deal of difference to the peoples beyond the Roman frontiers. Perhaps the presence of the Romans encouraged the various Caledonian peoples to come together as one federation – or even one people – of Picts. Perhaps those British peoples sandwiched in between the Picts and the Romans, between the Forth–Clyde line and the Tyne–Solway frontier, continued to exist as separate peoples because the Romans fostered their existence as client, buffer, states. It has been noted, for instance, that the earliest known kings of some of these peoples in the fifth century seem to have Roman names. The kingdom of Strathclyde, for instance, heirs to the Damnonii, had kings called Cluim and Cinhil

(Clemens and Quintilius?) and the first king of Galloway (or Man) was Annwn (Antonius), while the kings of the Gododdin (Votadini) were Catellius Decianus, Tacitus, Aeternus, and 'Patern Pesrut', Paternus of the Red Cloak (the garment possibly some sign of Roman official status). Most of these names come in medieval genealogies, written to promote the interests of ninth- and tenth-century kings of Gwynedd, who wanted to promote themselves as kings of Britain: there might thus have been plenty of incentives to add Roman names to their ancestry, and we probably should not believe any of them were necessarily historical. But Cluim's grandson Coroticus was: he came into conflict with St Patrick (as we shall see on p. 82). His name was Celtic rather than Roman, but he was, on the other hand, a Christian – and thus, for St Patrick, it would seem, in that sense a fellow-Roman. The Britons north of the Wall may have resisted most of the blandishments of Romanisation, but they succumbed, eventually, to Christianity, that most successful of the Roman religions and that most insidious – if belated – aspect of Romanisation.

3

Britain in the Roman world

'Romanisation'

The process by which Britain became 'Romanised' has been one which has exercised archaeologists and historians of Roman Britain throughout the twentieth century. How did the process operate? *How* Romanised was Britain? And, of course, what do we *mean* by Romanisation? Are we dealing with something profound, that affected Romano-British society at every level, or is it in fact a process which only touched an elite and their dependents? How can we assess Romanisation; how can we *measure* it?

When one starts to think in terms of quantification, realisation soon sets in that what we are talking about is essentially unmeasurable. (And when we add to that the fact that there is almost no evidence which is measurable either, we have real problems.) We might compare it with the process of Americanisation that Britain, and the rest of Europe, has gone through during the twentieth century. The wearing of jeans, trainers, T-shirts and baseball caps has become nearly universal as leisure-wear; most major forms of mass entertainment, above all music and film, are produced in or inspired by the USA; many companies are wholly or partly subsidiaries of American companies; our foreign policy has for a long time been largely tied to that of America; our language has been Americanised so deeply that few people are aware of the extent of it. How many now realise that *reliable*, *influential*, *talented* and *lengthy* were all denounced as 'vile and barbarous' Americanisms in the early nineteenth century, or that *to belittle* was attacked hysterically by English commentators when Thomas Jefferson used it in 1787?[1] A reliable list of influential American effects on our culture would be lengthy, and difficult to belittle; and many of them would be significant and physically durable enough – Coca-Cola bottles, for instance – to register among the finds on any fourth-millennium excavation of our material culture. Yet, whatever our material culture might suggest, and although some may feel besieged by these cultural invasions (and others, such as lovers of jazz and American science fiction like myself, might welcome some of them), there is little doubt that despite these 'invasions' most of us feel safe in our identity as British (or English, Scottish, and so on). There are almost certainly rather more people whose identity feels threatened by the European Community than by the USA. So 'are we Americanised?' That is obviously the wrong question: the situation is more complex than that.

Clearly the analogy of Americanisation cannot be transferred wholesale into the second or third century. But it might remind us that even when we have a mass of evidence, it is difficult to use this concept of '-isation' precisely. In the case of Roman Britain it is even more problematical, because of the very one-sided nature of our evidence. All our written sources are in Latin, whether they are literary texts, inscriptions or graffiti, or even (as in the amazing finds from the fort at Vindolanda) private letters: the thoughts of those who are not thus 'Romanised' do not survive. What did the average man on the Ermine Street cart think about the Roman Empire and his place within it? We shall never know. Apart from our few written sources, we are confined to a study of the surviving material evidence. And, of course, our most visible archaeological remains are towns, villas, forts and other defences, decorated pottery, imperial coins, imports from the Mediterranean and so on: again, the evidence of 'Romanisation' predominates, and overwhelms the 'average' men or women, who lived and died in the countryside, probably working on the same piece of land that had been worked by their ancestors in pre-Roman times, with few material possessions, and those seldom obviously 'Roman' in type and often very difficult to date archaeologically. The presence of 'Roman' artefacts on a site tells us nothing about 'Romanisation' without a proper context. A find of Samian ware indicates Roman cultural imperialism about as effectively as a find of willow-pattern china on a Victorian site shows the cultural domination of nineteenth-century Britain by Manchu China. We need to refine our concepts, and our use of evidence; or else simply to ask different questions.

Whatever 'Romanisation' was, it did not mean the wholesale importation of Italian culture, or a concerted attempt to crush British ways. Many of those involved in the colonisation of Britain, to start with, were not Italians, but provincials. Some of the origins of the earliest Roman soldiers are known from inscriptions: Longinus, son of Sdapezematygus, from modern Sofia;[2] Rufus Sita, another Thracian; Valerius Genialis, a Frisian, from the Lower Rhine; Vitellius Tancvisu, from Lusitania (Portugal); and so on.[3] The Romans had never tried to (and had never had the power to) eliminate provincial cultures, and so the 'Romans' who initially came to Britain brought with them a whole range of cultures, backgrounds and concerns. But there was an attempt to bring at least the British aristocracy into what was becoming a universal Roman aristocratic mindset. This was achieved largely through that kind of gentle persuasion offered by Agricola to the British aristocracy, as reported by Tacitus in the words quoted on p. 31, whereby they were urged to build towns, to compete for honour, to acquire an education, to speak Latin, and to wear the toga.

> And so the population was gradually led into the demoralising temptations of arcades, baths, and sumptuous banquets. The unsuspecting Britons spoke of such novelties as 'civilisation', when in fact they were only a feature of their enslavement.[4]

The aristocracy hardly needed to be taught competition for honour; Greco-Roman writers at least portrayed the Celtic aristocracy as hungry for honour. But this was a new type of honour: in pre-Roman times honour and status had been acquired through military ability and through wealth. Competition through wealth obviously continued; but the imposition of Roman authority made one vital change to the nature of British society. Civilians were all disarmed; possession of a military weapon became a criminal offence. (We might wonder how effectively this was policed outside the 'villa zone'.) Henceforth, the only legal way to acquire a military reputation was by opting for a career in the Roman army; and since the normal length of service was twenty-five years, this was not something that every aristocrat wished to do. This separation of the military from the civilian was one of the most significant changes that the Roman Empire brought to the peoples it conquered. It is worth noting that although, technically, an imperial diadem was in every legionary's rucksack, and although there were North Africans, Spaniards and Gauls who, through military service, reached the position of general and then Emperor, no Briton ever achieved this; indeed, the British aristocracy do not seem to have had many imperial ambitions. That in itself, perhaps, is a measure of their 'lower' level of Romanisation – or of their sensible resistance to the dubious blandishments of an imperial career.

The administration

With the coming of the Romans, for the first and (so far) last time in British history Britons became subjects of an Empire of which they constituted only a tiny part. It was an Empire which stretched from Scotland to the cataracts of the Nile, and from the Saharan deserts to the banks of the Rhine and the Danube. Although at times, especially in the fourth century, the Emperor was resident in the north, at Trier, or even at York, the normal residence of the Emperor was firmly within the Mediterranean world: if not at Rome, then at Milan, or Split or, later, Constantinople and Ravenna. The wealth of the Empire was concentrated on the Mediterranean, and so were the activities of its political leaders. Although it has been estimated that in the second century about 12.5 per cent of the whole Roman army was stationed in Britain, the British probably constituted under 5 per cent of the total population of the Empire.

As we have seen, the imposition of Roman rule on Britain came by stages, not only as the invasion progressed but as the province expanded to take over the three main client kingdoms: those of Cogidubnus and of the Iceni and Brigantes. By the mid second century all Roman Britain was administered as one province, under a governor whose capital was London; there were three *coloniae*, settled by veterans (Colchester, Gloucester and Lincoln), and three legionary fortresses (Caerleon, Chester and York). There were about fifteen towns recognised as *civitas*-capitals: the centres of the basic governmental units of the Empire, the largely self-governing territories called *civitates* ('cities'). As in Gaul, the full names of these capitals mostly preserved the old name of the pre-Roman people; unlike Gaul, the modern names do not normally preserve the names of the peoples. Thus, Petuaria Parisiorum [Petuaria of the Parisii] is Brough-on-Humber, but Lutetia Parisiorum is Paris; Calleva Atrebatum [Calleva of the Atrebates] is Silchester, but Nemetocenna Atrebatum is Arras. There were legal distinctions between different 'grades' of city-status. For instance, in a *colonia* Roman law was used, while local provincial law could be used in the bulk of the *civitas*-capitals, which had the legal status of a *municipium*. The Romans made no effort to replace local systems of law anywhere in the Empire, with the result in Britain that pre-Roman 'Celtic' legal principles were able to survive into post-Roman times.

These towns with their attached territories were the basic building-blocks of the Roman Empire. With them, and their councils, rested the administration of justice and the collection of taxes and, if they fulfilled these tasks properly, they would operate without much interference from central government. If anything the pressure would be in the other direction: the local aristocracy would put pressure on people at the centre for the bestowal of patronage. The council (*curia*) appointed the magistrates and other officials, and was responsible for submitting the taxes to the centre. The council members (*decuriones*) themselves were supposedly elected by all the citizens, but in practice the councils soon became oligarchies representing the landed aristocracy of the *civitas*. In the early Empire the position of decurion was probably prized: it conferred status, and, possibly, the opportunity to extend private wealth at the expense of the public purse. By the last century of the Empire, however, things had changed: the largest section in the *Theodosian Code* of 438 records the efforts of successive emperors in the fourth and fifth centuries to stop those who qualified as decurions by their landed wealth from dodging their municipal responsibilities. It is usually assumed that it was the greater tax-burden combined with a faltering economy which made the responsibilities of tax-collection something to be avoided by the fourth century.

The citizen electorate for the city councils in the first and second century was a fairly small group. Citizens in Britain in the first and second century comprised those citizens who had migrated to Britain; veterans of the Roman army in Britain (still largely a citizen army in the first and second centuries), who were encouraged to settle in the province; the freed slaves of citizens, who could themselves become citizens; and those who had been granted citizenship by the Emperor or his higher officials. Many of the latter were, presumably, the aristocracy of the pre-Roman period and their descendants. If granted citizenship by the Emperor, it was normal to take the imperial names. Thus the client-king Cogidubnus took the full name of Tiberius Claudius Cogidubnus, while the British woman whose charm the poet Martial celebrates (despite being 'raised among the sky-blue [=woad-painted] Britons'), was probably descended from someone granted citizenship at an early date, since she was called Claudia Rufina.[5] Citizenship could also be achieved, on retirement, by those who joined the Roman army as auxiliaries. Sometimes their diplomas survive, detailing their demob privileges. There is one from Wroxeter, issued by the Emperor Hadrian in 135 in favour of those auxiliaries who had served for twenty-five years in a whole list of regiments (Asturians, Dalmatians, Thracians, Batavians and others). They were 'granted citizenship for themselves, their children and posterity, together with the right of legal marriage with the wives they had when citizenship was granted, or, if they were unmarried, those they have subsequently married, so long as there is only one.' The copy that survives, made of bronze, was issued for Mansuetus, from the Trier region of Gaul, from the second cohort of Dalmatians commanded by Julius Maximus (who was himself from the city of Rome):[6] it was found in a room off the great hall (basilica) to the west of Wroxeter's forum, which contained a number of locks and fittings from chests, and which presumably served as some kind of archive.[7] Similar diplomas are known from the Continent, issued to Britons serving in auxiliary regiments in other parts of the Empire, and we know about these British servicemen sometimes from epitaphs: the first known British sailor was Aemilius, whose tombstone in Cologne records that he served in the *classis Germanica*, the German fleet, and who came from *Dumnonia* (Devon).[8] Auxiliary soldiers not only acquired citizenship, of course: through service they also acquired Latin, and some sense of commitment to the Empire. The non-citizens who formed the bulk of the population of Roman Britain still in the second century were known as *peregrini*, literally 'strangers' or 'foreigners'; they were all made citizens, along with the *peregrini* of the rest of the Roman Empire, by a decree of Caracalla in 212.

Britain was a single province until the end of the second century, under a governor who was a high-ranking senator, and someone who had previously held one of the two consulships in the Empire. It was regarded as one of the more important positions a senator could occupy, partly because the governor automatically became commander of one of the largest provincial armies in the Empire. He held the rank of imperial legate, and was in office between three and five years. He supervised the administration of the *civitates*, although a separate official, the *procurator*, supervised the imperial revenue. It was perhaps because of the excessive power wielded by the governor that at the beginning of the third century the province was divided into two: the contemporary writer Herodian links this change with the civil war of 193-97, when the governor Clodius Albinus nearly defeated the eventual Emperor, Septimius Severus. The southern province, *Britannia Superior*, continued to be governed by a legate of consular rank; *Britannia Inferior* was ruled from York by a praetorian legate, of lesser rank. Henceforth neither governor would be able to command more than two legions.

Despite this reorganisation, the disturbances of the mid-third century allowed Britain, with its significant army, to secede from Rome on two occasions. In 260 Postumus set up a 'Gallic Empire', which maintained its independence from the central power in Rome, under himself and his successors Victorinus and Tetricus, until 273. There is nothing to suggest that any of these emperors crossed to Britain, but inscriptions show that they were able to count on British support. The second 'secession' came only ten years later, in the wake of the successful attempt of Diocletian to unite the Empire after two generations of invasions and civil war. Diocletian decided that the Empire needed to be ruled by two Emperors, and chose Maximian as his deputy. Maximian appointed a Gaul from the Low Countries, Carausius, to a military command in the Channel area. Carausius was an effective naval commander, but rumours arose that he was actually conniving with the Saxons and Franks who were making sea-borne raids on the Gallic and British coasts. Diocletian demanded his execution; Carausius proclaimed himself Emperor and seized Britain. Despite the wishful thinking of some British historians, Carausius and his successor Allectus do not appear actually to have been trying to secede and to set up an independent Britain, any more than Postumus had been trying to set up an independent Gaul. They were all in the tradition of Roman usurpers, whose ultimate ambition was invariably to seize the whole Empire. Carausius claimed that he was a legitimate Emperor, a colleague of Diocletian and Maximian: he issued a coin with the portraits of the three of them, and the inscription CARAVSIVS ET FRATRES SVI: 'Carausius and his brothers'. Britain remained independent of the rest of the Empire for ten years, from 286 until 296, when in two campaigns Diocletian's colleague Constantius Chlorus restored Roman authority. Hardly any Romans fell, says the poet who wrote the panegyric on Constantius – 'all those plains and hills were littered only with the prostrate corpses of our loathsome enemies': the poet maintains the fiction that the troops of Carausius and Allectus were all barbarian Franks, or traitorous Romans who imitated them 'in styles of dress and long blond hair'.[9] The latter comment is interesting. It shows that the Franks were distinctive in their appearance (and long hair is known to have been a sign of the status of a free Frank male). But it is also one of several late Roman texts which suggest that disaffected Romans sometimes did adopt barbarian identity. The event the panegyrist describes is also recorded on the Arras Medallion: the mounted Emperor stands over the personification of London, kneeling in front of a Roman warship, with the inscription

'Restorer of the Eternal Light'.[10] An even more interesting memorial of this episode was the discovery of massive timber foundations in the western part of the city of London: the analysis of the tree rings shows that the timbers were felled in 294. The building itself was not complete. Was it the palace started by Allectus, and left unfinished after his death in 296?[11]

A further reorganisation of the province followed soon afterwards, as part of the great programme of reform of the Empire's institutions that was carried out by Diocletian and his colleagues (after 293 he had three colleagues: one other senior emperor, the Augustus, and two juniors, the Caesars). All over the Empire there was a reorganisation of provinces, with a general trend towards subdivision (probably to reduce the power of individual governors). The most senior governor in Britain, of consular rank, remained based in London, but the southern province was divided into two, with *Maxima Caesariensis* created in the south-east, and *Britannia Prima* in the south-west, with its capital probably at Cirencester. The northern province was also divided into two, with *Britannia Secunda* probably having its capital at York and *Flavia Caesariensis* at Lincoln. It seems that there was even a further subdivision in the late 360s, with the addition of a province called *Valentia*. It is quite unknown where this province lay, though the consensus is that it was in the north – if it was not a renaming of an old province rather than a new creation.

Although by the fourth century there were four (or five) provinces instead of the original one, the military efficiency was enhanced by amalgamating all together as a *diocesis* for military purposes, and the civilian governors were largely stripped of their military responsibilities. A military commander was appointed, a *dux* (duke), whose authority ran across the whole of Roman Britain. Another military rank is also known, that of *comes* (count): by the later fourth century, for instance, there was a Count of the Saxon Shore, the commander of the coastal defence system set up in the south-east to defend Britain from Saxon raiders.

The obvious point which emerges from all this is that Britain was fully a part of the Roman Empire throughout its more than three and a half centuries of Roman rule. The main governors were of consular rank, which meant that they were (as far as we can tell) invariably appointments from outside the province. Most of them never seem to have been to Britain before their appointment.[12] That does not necessarily mean that they were not qualified: during the 50s, when there was campaigning in Wales, three men were appointed who had all served in mountain campaigns elsewhere in the Empire, and there are definitely five governors, and perhaps more, who had served on the Rhine frontier before being moved to Britain, and who thus had experience of a frontier province. For the first eighty years nearly all the governors were Italians, with the exception of two who probably came from Gaul, and a third – Agricola himself – who came from the southern Gallic *civitas* of Forum Iulii (Fréjus).[13] After that, however, an Italian was a rarity: in the next eighty years there was only one. Governors came from Spain, Gaul, North Africa, and there were at least two from the Eastern Mediterranean, whose first language was presumably Greek. Much less can be said about the third and fourth centuries, after the division into two provinces: because of the lack of inscriptions from southern Britain there are great gaps in the list. The northern governors are better known, because of the wealth of inscriptions on Hadrian's Wall. But it is clear that Britain was usually ruled as a colony, by outsiders – even during its periods of 'independence' under Postumus and Carausius.

The army

The army must have been a major agent of Romanisation. As we have already seen, the army brought in provincials from elsewhere in the Empire, and settled them as veterans in Britain; it also attracted British recruits, who thereby gained citizenship and a much greater understanding of the Roman way of life. Supplying the army with provisions must also have had a profound economic impact: shifting the wealth from one part of the country to another (collecting taxes in the wealthier south, and moving cash and provisions to the north, where most of the troops were stationed), and accustoming the British to new economic processes and goals. Indeed, the distribution of wealth must have affected Britain as a whole: it is estimated that the 40,000 men in the army in the first century must have brought in about 6.5 million *denarii* per year: some 1890 kg of gold.[14]

Dio Cassius, writing about Germany, illustrated the way in which the presence of Roman troops might change native society – apart from ensuring greater political stability than northern barbarians had known before.

> The Romans were holding parts of the country and their soldiers were wintering there and settlements were being founded. The barbarians were adapting themselves to Roman ways, were becoming accustomed to hold markets and were meeting in peaceful assemblages. They had not, however, forgotten their ancestral habits, their native manners, their old life of independence, of the power derived from arms. Hence, so long as they were unlearning these customs gradually and by the way, as one might say, under careful watching, they were not disturbed by the change in the manner of their life, and were becoming different without knowing it.[15]

Ironically, however, it is where the army was mainly stationed, in the Pennines up to Hadrian's Wall, that other signs of Romanisation are weakest: there were no large towns north of Aldborough, and no villas at all. Yet it was on the Wall, or at a fort on the line of fortifications which in Hadrian's reign became the Wall, that we have our best evidence for life on the Roman pattern.

This evidence comes from the fort at Chesterholm, although the finds are now generally known after the Roman name for the fort: Vindolanda. Over a thousand writing-tablets have now been found there, some 250 of which have yielded substantial texts, telling us an immense amount about Roman life on the frontier between AD *c.* 85 and *c.* 130. These tablets were cut from thin leaves of wood, about the size of a postcard, and written on directly in ink with a reed pen (rather than scratched onto a wax layer with a stylus, as seemed more common before the Vindolanda discoveries). The letters include military reports, accounts, and a large private correspondence, particularly that of the prefect of the Ninth Cohort of Batavians, Flavius Cerialis, and his wife Sulpicia Lepidina, from between 97 and 102 AD.

Vindolanda is a reminder that the administration of the Roman army involved a massive amount of paperwork – or, in this case, woodwork. Elsewhere in the Roman world, apart from Egypt, almost none of this kind of bureaucratic material survives. It has been estimated, for instance, that in the first three centuries of the Empire 225 million pay-records would have been produced for the army – of which precisely *three* survive.[16] Through the bureaucratic records at Vindolanda we can see something of the activities of the Roman army who were mostly, in this period, at peace. One of the military reports shows that skirmishes are happening, but also shows a very Roman contempt for the barbarian enemy: 'The Britons are unprotected by armour. There are very many cavalry. The cavalry do not use swords nor do the wretched Britons (*Brittunculi*) mount in order to throw javelins.'[17] The auxiliaries stationed at Vindolanda in peacetime were actively engaged in building: the reports mention builders, plasterers, men dealing with lead, clay, cement and wood. One letter mentions the urgent need for lime; another refers to the transport of stone. There is a shield-maker, called Lucius, and possibly makers of weapons; one letter refers to the despatch to Vindolanda of hubs, axles and spokes, which suggests that carts were assembled on site. Many of the letters relate to the supply of clothing and of provisions: two individuals are mentioned, Gavo and Atrectus *cervesarius* (the brewer), who may have been civilians involved in supplying the frontier army. Other professions mentioned were a bathman, a doctor, and two veterinary doctors, while other named individuals seem to be slaves, responsible for running the prefect's household: it seems that most of the slaves at Vindolanda were personal rather than state property.

Bowman's book on the Vindolanda tablets lists the foodstuffs mentioned in the texts,[18] which gives an idea of the diet of the officers at least: apart from the venison, pork and goat, which may have come from local sources, and the items which must have come from elsewhere in Britain (such as oysters), there are a number of imports – olives and wine from the Mediterranean, and pepper from Ceylon or even East Asia. Hunting of deer may well have provided an important addition to the diet: Flavius Cerialis writes to his friend Brocchus: 'if you love me, brother, I ask that you send me some hunting-nets'.[19] Brocchus's wife Severa writes in her turn to Cerialis's wife Sulpicia Lepidina, asking her to a birthday party, and mentioning a visit to Vindolanda. But the letters are not just from the elite of Roman or Gallic society. In fact, perhaps the most important lesson which the Vindolanda documents teach us is how widespread the use of written Latin was in frontier society; and if it was abundant in frontier society, then one might suppose that it was even more deep-rooted elsewhere. There are several hundred different hands which can be identified: even in those letters written in Vindolanda, rather than sent there from elsewhere, there are very few written by the same hand, suggesting that the writing was not done by scribes, but by the soldiers and slaves themselves. The dozen or so letters from soldiers requesting leave are not forms with a blank left for the name of the soldier: each is individually written, and several seem to come from the lower ranks.[20] Some are indeed written by secretaries, like the two letters from Severa to Lepidina, but Severa's party invitation has three lines written at the bottom in Severa's own hand: 'Farewell, sister, my dearest soul, as I hope to prosper, and hail.'[21] What one cannot tell, of course, is the extent to which this literacy, very largely restricted to military personnel in the surviving tablets – and many of those, as members of the conquering army, from outside Britain – actually percolated through into the native population. One might argue that if even the most petty administrative transactions were done by letter in the army, then this might be true too on larger country estates, or in towns; if one wishes to argue that the army is a special case, then we have to remember that veterans frequently settled in the provinces to farm or to live in the towns, and that they could easily have transferred their skills to civilian life. This clearly has a bearing on the whole vexed question of the level of Latinity in Roman Britain, which we shall look at in the final section of this chapter.

The role of the army in the cultural process undoubtedly changed in the later Roman Empire. This was part of a process of change, and of military organisation, which occurred throughout the later Roman Empire. Under Constantine there was a decision to divide the army into two groups: soldiers with the responsibility for frontier defence (*limitanei*) and troops in a more mobile field-army (*comitatenses*). There was also a considerable expansion – perhaps a doubling – of the number of soldiers in the Roman army. This in itself had direct effects: a considerable increase in the tax burden (which alienated tax-payers and made the municipal obligation to collect taxes an unwelcome burden on the municipal councillors), and a real difficulty in finding sufficient recruits. These two factors are related: soldiers conscripted into the army were tax-payers lost to the system, as well as farmers lost to the agricultural labour-force, and on both accounts landowners would be reluctant to part with them.

One response to this problem was to begin recruiting soldiers from non-tax-payers: that is, from the non-citizen barbarians both inside and outside the Empire. The barbarians inside the Empire were the prisoners-of-war, or their descendants, settled within the Empire as *laeti*, with the agreement to serve in the army in return for their land – or, one might say, for the right to live on their reservations. Barbarians from outside the Empire could be recruited as individuals, or as whole peoples, under their kings, after a formal treaty. (The treaty was a *foedus*; such barbarian soldiers were *foederati*, or federates.) Sometimes the exact terms under which barbarians are serving in Britain or elsewhere is unclear. For instance, it has been said that the Alamanni under King Fraomar were serving as federates in Britain in the 360s; what actually happened was that there was a unit of Alamanni, a Germanic people from south-west Germany, serving in Britain, who were given Fraomar, from a royal Alamannic family, as their commander in 367.[22] It was not unusual for aristocratic Germans to have high military command in the fourth-century Empire: indeed, it had a considerable advantage for an emperor, in that successful Roman generals might be tempted by ambition to try for imperial power themselves, while German generals seem to have accepted the fact that, as non-citizens, they could never themselves be Emperor. At one point in the fourth century two Germans, both Franks – a people living just across the Channel, at the mouths of the Rhine – held supreme military power in the Empire: Richomer was *magister militum* (commander-in-chief) of the Eastern Roman Army (388–93), while his nephew Arbogast was *magister militum* in the West (390–94).[23] After the fall of this Frankish family, and after the death of the Emperor Theodosius I in 395, a Vandal general called Stilicho effectively acted as regent in the West, until his own fall in 408.

There are occasional references to German barbarians in the army in Britain, but it is unclear how numerically significant they were. On the Continent, barbarians made up perhaps half the effective forces of the Roman army, and were particularly prominent in the *comitatus*, the field-army. In Britain, however, the field-army itself was not especially important, perhaps only some 5000 men out of a total of 35,000.[24] The frontier forces were divided into two, under the *dux Britanniarum*, who looked after the troops in the highlands to the north and west, and the *comes litoris Saxonici*, the Count of the Saxon Shore, who was in command of the troops defending the south-eastern shores of Britain from attack by Saxons, and these probably made up the bulk of the military strength of the island. The military problems of the fourth century and very beginning of the fifth century were such that Britain never loomed large in the minds of Roman emperors. There were several occasions when British troops were withdrawn to take action on the Continent, and what were left were probably well below their second-century strength. Archaeology suggests that there was reduced accommodation for troops available in the fourth century at two legionary fortresses, Caerleon and Chester, and reduction was just as marked at Wall forts like Housesteads and Wallsend. 'By the end of the fourth century *Legio II Augusta* which had once filled the fifty acres of Caerleon was now housed in eight-acre Richborough.'[25]

The reduction of Roman troops in Britain to a fraction of their second-century size obviously reduced the capacity of the army to act as a factor in

'Romanisation'. However, much more important was that the troops were largely *limitanei*, and, if patterns in the rest of the Empire were repeated in Britain, the greatest part of the *limitanei* would have been recruited in Britain itself. Did the garrisons still communicate with each other in Latin, as they did in the days of the Vindolanda tablets in the earlier second century? Or were these *limitanei* already using their indigenous language – which later Anglo-Saxon immigrants would call 'Welsh'?

Towns

The army was perhaps the most obvious Romanising force, but if not the army, then the town. As agents of Romanisation, towns are actually complementary to the army in several ways. To begin with, there is a very different regional distribution: very roughly speaking, the area of most significant urban development did not have a major military presence, through most of the period of the Empire, while the areas where large towns were thin on the ground (the area between York and Hadrian's Wall, the highland region of Wales) were the places where the military were present in some numbers. But the presence of the army could sometimes be crucial in the process of urbanisation. This was true not only of major fortresses such as York and Chester, where civilian settlements developed adjacent to the legionary fortress, but also of some of the smaller towns of Roman Britain. Although much attention has been given to the *civitas*-capitals, it is now clear that there were many smaller settlements which deserve the name 'town', and that many of these had been Roman forts.

As we have seen, the *civitas* was the basic administrative unit of the Empire, and its capital was thus a major social and cultural as well as administrative centre: a place where the local dignitaries could meet, where major religious ceremonies took place, where educational establishments were to be found. It was thus a centre of Romanisation. Indeed, Rome stamped its identity on the town just as firmly as on the fortress: each might well be built to the same pattern, regardless of where in the Empire they were to be found. Each town had its grid-system of streets, with a central forum and a major temple or two; each had its baths and fountains, supplied by a managed water-system; each had other public buildings, such as an amphitheatre and/or theatre; each, by the beginning of the fourth century, had its own ring of walls and fortified gateways to protect it.

As in northern Gaul, major *civitas*-capitals were very thin on the ground compared to Italy, North Africa or southern Gaul. This is not necessarily anything to do with a lower level of urbanisation outside the Mediterranean world: it was largely a result of the desire of the Romans in the parts of Gaul taken by Julius Caesar and in Britain to preserve the territory of the pre-Roman peoples as a basic political unit. The size of the *civitas*-territory was thus largely dependent on the size of the pre-Roman kingdom. In some parts of the Western Empire this led to startling continuity of territory: in western Gaul, for instance, the territory of the pre-Roman tribe of the Petrocorii became the *civitas* of Vesunna Petrocoriorum, which became the medieval diocese of Périgueux and the province of Périgord, and, at the French Revolution, the département of Dordogne. There is the possibility of similar continuity in Britain, but it is rare and uncertain: Higham suggests a possibility in the case of the territory of the Cornovii, which became the *civitas*-territory of Viriconium Cornoviorum (Wroxeter), and then, in post-Roman times, successively the territory of the Anglian people of the Wreocensaete, the diocese of Lichfield and, just before the Norman Conquest, the earldom of Edwin.[26] It is not at all clear how old the pre-Roman territories enshrined by the *civitas*-system actually were. But although there were changes (like the late creation of the territory of the Carvetii, with its *civitas*-capital at Carlisle), the structure set up in the first century had itself a continuity of at least several centuries.

It is important to discuss the origin of Roman towns in this administrative way, rather than thinking of them in economic terms. The main Roman towns were primarily seats of administration, justice and religion. Secondarily, they were significant social centres: places where the aristocracy of the territory might meet and, as members of the council, do political business, perform ceremonies as aediles ('part-time' priests), and also, one presumes, create and sustain the networks of patronage and alliance which was at the basis of local social and political structures. It was in the town that the aristocracy could display their wealth, in particular by paying for public buildings whose dedicatory inscriptions would publicise their founder's name. The stage-building of the theatre at Petuaria (Brough-on-Humber), for instance, was funded by M. Ulpius Ianuarius, aedile of the vicus of Petuaria. Inevitably, the town attracted commerce and industry: but one might wonder if it is right to argue that 'no matter how much official help a town might have received at its inception, all would come to nothing unless there was a sound economic reason for its continued existence'.[27] A Roman town was not necessarily like a nineteenth-century town, existing primarily as an economic enterprise.

To make generalisations in such a way, however, is to risk condemnation; indeed, any generalisations about Roman towns will risk condemnation from some quarter or other, because there is a good deal of unresolved debate about towns. Each of the major areas of debate in a sense relate to the question of Romanisation – of the degree to which the Romans affected British society, and how this actually happened. Firstly, there is the question of the role of the Roman army in the process of urbanisation. Secondly, and much more fundamental, is the question of whether Britain was truly urbanised, or whether Roman towns were a temporary imposition on the surface of Romano-British society. Thirdly, and related to the last, is the question of whether towns were parasitic on the rural economy, or whether they made a contribution towards the general economy. Are we hopelessly misled as to the nature of Roman towns because we make unconscious comparisons with the things called towns in our own world? Even our definition and mental image of 'town' almost certainly makes incorrect assumptions about the nature of the Roman town. Richard Reece, the most refreshingly controversial of Romano-British specialists, prefers to use the acronym 'TCTs': 'Things Called Towns'.

The role of the army in the origins of urbanisation was first developed by Graham Webster back in 1966.[28] Traces of early military settlements had been discovered at numerous places which became towns, and he suggested that towns often, or usually, developed from the civilian settlements which sprang up to supply and service the garrisons: when the army moved on, as Britain was pacified, the civilian establishments stayed and prospered. Cirencester would be an example. Although it is clearly in one sense a successor of Bagendon, the political centre of the Dobunni, the fact remains that Bagendon was 5 km away, and Cirencester developed on the site of the Roman fort and its civilian settlement. In some cases, whether fort or pre-Roman political centre was more important in urban origins is impossible to decide: and we must remember that the Romans often sited important forts at places which had been *oppida* or other pre-Roman centres. Thus, at Chichester a Roman military fort was established within the dykes forming the boundary of the *oppidum*, which was then levelled for the building of the forum. As a further argument for military origins, it has been noted that at some Roman towns in Britain the plan of the forum was more similar to that of a military headquarters building in a legionary fort than that of a normal civilian forum on the continent.[29]

It is probably important to make a distinction between the *civitas*-capitals and the smaller towns, about which we are much better informed than we used to be thanks to the last generation of archaeological investigation.[30] The *civitas*-capitals, whether they were close to a pre-Roman *oppidum* or not, all become the major centres for the territory. The Roman authorities may have encouraged their development as Roman towns, but the local élites were probably responsible for the actual building. The speed at which the public buildings of the towns were constructed varies. Some *fora* were started in the 70s, but some as late as the 90s or later; the Leicester forum may have started in the 80s or 90s, but was not completed until at least 120, while the Wroxeter forum was dedicated at the end of the 120s. The public baths came even later: those at Leicester, Wroxeter and Exeter probably not until the middle of the second century.[31] In some cases, the prior existence of a Roman fort, which was perhaps a very ephemeral establishment, may have been irrelevant; in other cases, the fort might have been there long enough to have encouraged the growth of a network of roads, which may well have encouraged the town's growth. At Cirencester, the fortress continued for nearly thirty years.

Nowadays it is recognised that there are numerous small towns in Roman Britain, which may not have merited the word 'town' in Roman eyes (that is, did not fulfill their criteria for an *urbs* or a *civitas*), but which were in some ways more urban, in our sense, than the *civitas*-capitals. They were 'natural' towns, that is, economic centres, acting as local market and production centres. These towns were unplanned, without the street-grid or standard pattern of the *civitas*-capitals, and, as far as we know, lacking any administrative or political role. Few of them seem to have been on Iron Age sites; many of them show traces of early Roman military settlement. Again, however, it may be the roads which were laid down to link these small forts which were crucial in the development of the small towns, not the fact of the army's presence. In some cases in the north of Roman Britain – where the army remained a sizeable presence through most of the Roman period – it is sometimes difficult to know whether we are dealing with a fort with an ancillary civilian population, or with a 'proper' town. Places like Carlisle and Corbridge are often regarded as 'garrison towns' or 'frontier towns' to recognise this problem. Small forts could give rise to much larger towns. The fort at Binchester, on a hilltop above Bishop Auckland (Durham), covered an area of four hectares, but the civilian settlement in the fourth century covered an area twice that, with a surviving depth of archaeological deposits of three metres.[32]

Our second area of controversy relates to the nature of urbanisation in Britain. Richard Reece has written: 'To what extent this foreign transplant ever took root and grew in Britain is highly problematic, because we are always dealing with stones and mortar, while the real town is rooted in the need and belief of its inhabitants.'[33] Most people agree that towns in Roman Britain were very small by modern standards, but also perhaps by the standards of some of the greatest towns of the Roman Mediterranean. Rome, at over a million, was very much an exception, but towns like Alexandria or Antioch certainly ran into the hundreds of thousands. Malcolm Todd reckons that a population of 10,000 would be regarded as large in Roman Britain, and that *medium* rank cities like Leicester, Winchester and Wroxeter had populations between 2000 and 4000.[34] Sheppard Frere notes that the towns of Elizabethan England were very similar in scale: only one provincial town was larger than 10,000, most were on the level of three to four thousand, and there were many active towns with a population of around 1500.[35] There were more towns in Elizabethan England than in Roman Britain: but, in both periods, towns were not just small in absolute terms, but in relation to the size of the population as a whole. Probably no more than 5 per cent of Romano-Britons lived in towns.

In both Elizabethan England and Roman Britain, London was the great exception. Londinium was not a *civitas*-capital, but it was the governor's residence, and was a major port and commercial centre. Its luxury was exceptional: buildings were decorated with a wealth of imported marbles and porphyry from southern Gaul, Italy, the Greek islands, Asia Minor and Egypt.[36] The large-scale excavations carried out in the last two decades by the Museum of London have found remains of the bridge across the Thames and of the urban development on the south side of the river, the massive timber quays, the warehouses behind the quays, and something of the administrative and residential areas of the main part of the city north of the river. As with other cities, however, there were clear and relatively early signs of retrenchment. Several buildings were falling out of use by the late second century; in the third century various buildings were dismantled and were found covered by a layer of dark earth. There was development in other areas of the city, however, and new buildings: 'but these buildings were much less concentrated than their early Roman counterparts and all of these features were set in a very different landscape from before'.[37]

Leaving aside London, however, were Romano-British towns a Roman idea that never really caught on, 'a tender Mediterranean plant in foreign soil'?[38] Some of them certainly do not suggest the crowded bustling cityscape that we imagine is typical of the Mediterranean town. The best recorded town-plans – those of Caerwent, Silchester, Verulamium and Wroxeter – suggest that the townscape was dominated by a fairly small number of large aristocratic houses. This picture is beginning to appear in other towns too, as archaeological investigation continues.[39] The towns were certainly built with a good deal of enthusiasm and expense, in the late first and through the second century. In the third and/or early fourth century, they were provided with town walls, again at some expense. Yet, even at that time, they seem to have been declining in importance. It has been common to contrast what is happening here with the picture on the Continent. And the British experience may well be different from the experience of the Mediterranean town. But if we look at towns in northern and western Gaul, we can get a very similar picture to what we see in Britain. We must not be misled by the fact that throughout Gaul, towns continued to exist through the late Roman period and into the early Middle Ages, while in Britain, after the collapse of the Western Roman Empire, every town ceased to exist as anything more than a pile of ruins, inhabited if at all by a few farmers. It is quite possible that it is only the survival of the *Church* in Gaul which allowed the town to survive, even if the town was no more than a concentration of clerics, monks and nuns, with a lay population which serviced them and the rural population who visited for baptism, or cures at the shrine of the local saint. Long before the sixth century, towns in parts of Gaul, particularly the north, were a pale reflection of their second-century glories. Over most of Britain, the Church perished as well as the Roman town.

The archaeological problem is that while it is relatively easy to date the establishment of a building, it is very much more difficult to know when it has fallen into disuse or simply fallen down. And that problem is compounded if one is looking not at one building, but at a whole assemblage of buildings, underneath a modern town, where it is seldom possible to do more than take a few more or less random samples. It may be possible to find a building in Verulamium, for instance, which appears to have been built *c.* 380, and which then underwent repairs and modifications, presumably into the fifth century; but that does not prove that town-life went on into the fifth century, merely that there was life in a town. It does seem, from excavation after excavation (in Gaul as well as in Britain), that whole areas within the walls of towns ceased to be occupied in the late Roman period, and that public buildings and amenities were not maintained. As we shall see in the next section, this is not the result of a general collapse in Roman society and economy (villas were flourishing economic centres in the fourth century), but of the changing nature of Romano-British society and economy.

The evidence has suggested to some that Britain did not need towns by the second half of the fourth century; perhaps it never really had. But are Roman towns actually emptying, or are we misinterpreting the evidence? Some of this depends on our interpretation of the phenomenon we have already met in London: dark earth. 'Dark earth' is found in many Roman towns – and some places which are not towns, such as Pevensey Castle, one of the Saxon Shore forts – and is a much-debated feature, which plays a crucial role in the debate about what is happening to towns in later Roman Britain. The dark earth layer occurs above the earlier Roman deposits, and above the dark earth are to be found the earliest Anglo-Saxon layers. The dark earth itself is charcoal-rich, and includes late Roman and sometimes Anglo-Saxon material. Four theories have been offered to explain it.[40] It is an accumulation of soil on a derelict site; it is soil dumped to create suitable conditions for horticulture; it represents rubbish dumped from neighbouring sites; it is all that remains of turf- or mud-walled or timber-framed buildings, and thus may represent intensive occupation rather than dereliction. If the last hypothesis is the truth (as Dark and Dark think), then the population may not have declined in the late Roman period, but it might have changed in social makeup; perhaps towns became places where relatively large numbers of low-status people (artisans?) lived.

Whether towns were ever major producers of goods, however, is a matter for debate: the small-scale workshops which constituted the manufacturing base in Roman Britain were apparently not usually in the towns. We may thus contrast the Roman town with the medieval town. The Roman town, as far as we can see, brought rents and produce from the countryside; it was a centre for consumption rather than production, and it probably depended for its survival on the presence of administrative officials and the local aristocracy (and in some places the army) who constituted the consuming class. The usual developed medieval town on the other hand had, by the twelfth century, an established urban class engaged in commerce and manufacturing, who were separated by law and/or social status from the landed aristocracy. There was a clear legal and economic distinction between town and country, and a psychological one as well, in the feudal world, summed up in the German phrase 'town air makes one free'. Did such distinctions actually exist in the Roman mind? We need to look at the other side of the equation.

The countryside

For a long time, the Romano-British countryside meant the ultimate symbol of Romanisation: the villa. About a thousand of them are known in Britain.[41] These were the homes of the elite, the most heavily Romanised and presumably Latin-speaking aristocracy. Where the bulk of the inhabitants of Roman Britain actually lived was a matter for speculation and hypothesis. Aerial photography for a long time did little to clarify matters, with a continued concentration on military sites: a 1987 survey of aerial reconnaissance work spent forty pages discussing military sites – 'military gunge', as Richard Reece would call it[42] – and just two discussing rural settlement. But the results are coming in. A 1970 survey of the Fenland revealed the extent of the Roman impact on the landscape; an aerial survey in East Anglia, in the area of Colchester and Ipswich, showed that settlements were extended much more evenly over the landscape than had hitherto been thought; and the droughts of the mid-1970s discovered nearly 300 hitherto unknown Roman sites in North Cumbria, showing Carlisle in the context of its *vici*, roads and farmsteads.[43] It was as a result of these aerial surveys, primarily, that estimates of the population of Roman Britain have gone up from a few hundred thousand to three or four million. Suddenly, the silent, or invisible, majority had been revealed.

It is clear that settlement types within the rural landscape were very varied. The basic distinction was between the 'lowland' and 'highland' zones, which has also been expressed as the 'Civil Zone' and the 'Military Zone'; recently Dark and Dark have suggested 'villa landscape' and 'native landscape'.[44] None of these pairs of terms is wholly satisfactory, but together they suggest some of the range of contrasts which we can see. In the 'lowland' or 'villa' landscape there were enclosed farms, often with demonstrable pre-Roman origins, consisting of timber buildings in a ditched or embanked enclosure; unenclosed farms, which seem more common in the later Roman period; dispersed settlements; and nucleated settlements, or villages. In the 'highland' or 'native' landscape, villages and dispersed settlements were much more rare. Roman-period settlements have been found on old hill-forts and promontory forts, and enclosed settlements of various kinds were more common. In the south-west the Cornish name of 'rounds' are given to the commonest form of enclosed settlement: round or oval houses set within a circular earthen bank, not unlike the 'raths' which are the most frequent type of rural settlement known from first-millennium Ireland. These small farms were not necessarily low in status in this part of Roman Britain (a region with only one town, Exeter, and almost no villas): imported amphorae and high-quality glass-ware have been found in them, for instance.[45]

The study of the rural landscape has shown perhaps the greatest advance within the field of Romano-British archaeology, but there has been much fruitful work on villas too. *Villa* is a somewhat problematical word: it is a Latin word that means a country-house, and not necessarily a farm, but in Romano-British archaeology it has tended to mean 'a Romanised country-house and estate-centre', which at one extreme will mean a large stone-built complex, with a plan perhaps derived from Mediterranean models, with under-floor central heating, a heated bath-house, floors decorated with mosaics, and so on. But when does a native British farm-house become a 'villa'? The term 'villa' in fact covers a large range of settlement types, and merges in with the category of the farmsteads that continued for a long time along pre-Roman lines. Villas used to be studied largely as an aspect of 'Romanisation'. Their mosaics, and the occasional sculptures, were compared to their Roman models, in a sense in order to give them marks for quality of imitation. But villas are now being viewed in their landscape, rather than as individual pieces of Italy set in a foreign land.

The distribution of villas is extremely uneven, although it does reflect the distribution of major towns, suggesting a strong social or economic link between the two. To begin with, there are hardly any villas in much of the north and west, in the 'highland zone'. The reasons for the contrast are not easy to understand. There is no reason to think that villa-style agriculture could not have been carried out in some parts of the 'highland zone'. Breeze has suggested that the lack of villas in the 'Military Zone' was the result of the army acting as an economic depressant, creaming off money and acting in effect as the local aristocracy.[46] Variations can be found within the 'villa landscape' too. There are very few villas in the West Country (especially Somerset and Gloucestershire) before *c.* 200, for instance. Thereafter we have a high level of 'Romanisation': sculptures are greater in quantity and quality there, and half the sumptuous villas of Roman Britain are to be found in that area. Branigan has suggested that the area may have been a massive imperial estate in the early days after the Conquest, and that it was parcelled out in the third century, possibly to wealthy refugees from Gaul, fleeing the barbarian attacks of that time. There are signs of villa abandonment in north Gaul at that time; there are also a number of dedicatory inscriptions to Gallic gods in the West Country.[47] There is another explanation for the late appearance of villas elsewhere in the country: not the arrival of outsiders, but the gradual growth in wealth of native landowners, who at some point adopted Roman building methods. Pre-Roman farmsteads are frequently found adjacent to or underlying villas, and there are signs that villas are gradually enlarged or upgraded: all signals, perhaps, of continuity of landowning, and the slow growth of prosperity, which may eventually be expressed in some kind of 'Romanising' activity.[48] Small-scale farms in the north went through a similar process: a move from timber to drystone walling in the early Roman period, and a move from the traditional rounded houses of the Iron Age period to more 'Roman' rectilinear buildings in the mid-Roman period. On the whole the most prosperous villas are to be found situated around the most prosperous towns; but there are exceptions, with the relatively poor Dorchester (Dorset) being associated with numerous villas, while Exeter is not associated with villas at all.[49]

Parts of the Roman landscape show signs of the considerable effort and organisation undertaken in order to feed more people. On the Wentlooge level of south-east Wales, not far from the Second Legion's headquarters at Caerleon, a seawall 12 km long was constructed, the salt-marsh drained, and 325 km^2 of arable land created.[50] The large-scale reclamation of land in the Fens of eastern Britain has been associated with Hadrian: it is possible that he wanted to increase the productivity of a large imperial estate (confiscated from the Iceni after Boudicca's revolt, perhaps) in order to supply his new units on the northern frontier.[51] Car Dyke, in this theory, would be a canal, linking the farmland of the Fens to the sea, so that the army could be supplied. On the other hand, rural surveys in the north suggest that this region may have been capable of supplying most of its own agricultural needs; the Fen reclamation may have been much more of a piecemeal process, and Car Dyke a drainage ditch, or means of local transport.[52]

The villas of Roman Britain were flourishing as never before in the mid-fourth century. But there is little to suggest much survival into the fifth century. Although the population may have survived in the same place over much of Roman Britain, the agricultural enterprises sustained by the aristocracy seem to have collapsed in the early fifth century, certainly over most of the eastern part of Roman Britain. An example of how this may have happened on the ground comes from work on the Upper Thames Valley. In the Lechlade area of Gloucestershire there were late Romano-British settlements along the riverside at around 1 km intervals, farming thanks to a drainage system that had been in operation since long before the coming of the Romans. By the middle of the fifth century most of those drainage ditches had silted up, and the settlements had disappeared. The land seems still to have been used, however, but as pasture; ploughing continued further away from the river, on a gravel terrace where the Roman villa of Roughground Farm had been. Nearby, the small villa of Barton Court Farm was demolished some time in the fifth century, and farmers occupied the ground, constructing timber buildings in the area. Judging from the bones, sheep began to be more important than cattle and horses. There was continuity, in a sense, but there was also an abandonment of large-scale enterprise.[53] It was as if Romanisation was an experiment which had had its day.

Industry and trade

As with towns and the rural economy, much of the debate about industry and trade in Roman Britain has centred on questions of Romanisation, and the nature of the economic relationship between Britain and the rest of the

Roman Empire. Did Britain gain or lose from the 'balance of trade' between itself and the continental Empire; for that matter, did Rome gain economically from its possession of Britain, or was it, as Strabo had warned (above, p. 28), more expensive than it was worth? This is no doubt not a question which could be answered in the same way throughout the period. Britain emerged from the political and economic problems of the third century in a much better condition than other provinces, for instance. At the very end of the third century, a panegyric to the Emperor Constantius claimed that Britain was a province that the state could not afford to lose, since it was 'so rich in harvests, with such abundant pasture, shot through with so many seams of ore, a lucrative source of so much taxation, girded round with so many ports.'[54]

In the pre-Roman period, the imports were largely luxury items, most notably wine, the import of which was probably controlled or monopolised by the elite, and used to support their own status. Even so, the quantity was probably not large: the most prolific site, at Hengistbury (Dorset), yielded just over one thousand sherds of amphorae, which could represent as little as thirty vessels, imported over a span of fifty years.[55] The quantity increased after the conquest, but so did the range of the imports. Even so, pottery predominates in the finds, because of its durability. Occasionally barrels are found, mostly from the Rhineland, but the Mediterranean amphorae, containing olive oil and *garum* (fish sauce) as well as wine, predominate in the record, even if Mediterranean imports themselves did not necessarily predominate. There was also large-scale importation of fine table-wares in the early Roman period, most notably of the ubiquitous Samian ware: a pottery with decoration produced in a mould, which was not actually, by the imperial period, produced on Samos, but in Italy and, above all, Gaul. Even so, local wares were also produced – indigenous types, often using Roman forms.

In the later Roman Empire there was a drastic reduction in the quantity of imported pottery, which may or may not reflect changes in the patterns of trade in other more perishable items (for which the pots were containers) as well. There are all kinds of possible explanations for this decline. It could be that much more wine was being imported in barrels; or, indeed, that a British wine production had been established by the Romans. Grape-pips are known from a range of archaeological sites, although these could come from imported raisins; possible evidence for vineyards has come from North Thoresby (Lincs) and Wollaston (Northants).[56] The decline in olive oil and fish sauce may reflect the decline of the number of Roman soldiers of Mediterranean origin in Britain, which may have resulted in a change of diet. Over the long term it is possible to detect the growth of indigenous industry in Britain, notably in the countryside. In the late Roman period, the scale of pottery production increased very considerably in Britain, and the production seems to concentrate in fewer but larger clusters of kilns. Nene Valley ware, for instance, was produced at Alice Holt and at Water Newton

(Cambridgeshire): in both places, massive waste tips have been found around the kilns, and at the latter site the kilns stretch for several kilometres from the small town. North of Water Newton there is a large palatial villa: some have compared it to a 'stately home', but we might better think of it as an equivalent of the mansion of a nineteenth-century industrialist.[57]

Even more impressive are the remains of the Roman iron-working industry. This is, of course, fairly restricted geographically, but where it is found – in the Weald, in the Forest of Dean, in the East Midlands – it can be on a very large scale. Some of the slag-heaps in the Forest of Dean were so extensive that they were themselves mined for ore in the Industrial Revolution. At Laxton in Northamptonshire there were slag-heaps for several hundreds of metres around the furnaces, and a 100-metre wide river valley nearby was filled with iron slag.[58] Elsewhere in Britain there are the remains of gold-mining, lead-mining, stone-quarrying and other industrial activities as well. All in all, Roman, and particularly late Roman, industrial activities were extensive. What is uncertain is how these industries were organised. It is known, for instance, that the Roman army maintained its own factories for the production of pottery, weapons, and other military essentials; one does not know the extent to which the archaeological record of industrial activity relates to imperial-run enterprises, or whether it is more a question of private enterprise. This relates closely to the problem of the Roman economy as a whole. Was the Roman economy an 'embedded economy'? – that is, an economy where exchange was embedded in social and political concerns, and not run in terms of profit and loss – or a free market. It has been suggested that what was happening in the later Roman Empire was a breakdown of the embedded economy: the liberation of exchange and the consequent growth of the economy.[59] This development might also be seen in the increased usage of lower denomination coins, which shows a greater use of the market by ordinary people. The evidence of the growth of industry might suggest that this 'freed' economy was allowing the emergence of an entrepreneurial class in Roman Britain: a few tentative steps, which were not to be retraced until the seventeenth and eighteenth centuries, at the beginning of the Industrial Revolution.

Language, culture and identity

Wondering about how Roman Britain might have developed economically had the barbarian invasions of the fifth century not interrupted the course of affairs is no doubt a fruitless occupation. But comparing how the barbarian invasions affected Britain and the continental Empire can tell us something significant about Roman Britain. The greatest difference is a linguistic one. The barbarian invasions of the fifth century had only a marginal linguistic effect south of the Channel. Although Germanic dialects became predominant in former Latin-speaking areas located just inside the frontiers – a few miles west of the Rhine, in what is now Germany and the Low Countries, and a few miles south of the Rhine and Danube, in Switzerland or Austria – the bulk of the inhabitants of the former Roman Empire on the Continent still speak a language derived from Latin: Italian, Spanish, French, Occitan, Catalan, and so on. Yet in Britain Latin was wiped out within a matter of decades, surviving only as the language of the Church.

It is instructive to compare Britain specifically with modern Romania. This area, to the north of the Danube, was the last major conquest made by the Roman Emperors: it was added to the Roman Empire, some sixty years after the conquest of Britain, by Trajan in 106, and became the province of Dacia. It was lost to the Roman Empire by the invasion of the Goths, in the middle of the third century. It was part of the Roman Empire for just 165 years. Geographically it would appear to be in the Greek-speaking eastern half of the Empire. But it was conquered by the Roman army, for whom Latin was always the main official language. It acquired the name Romania, 'the land of the Romans', centuries after the Roman armies were driven out. And even today its language, Romanian, is as close to Latin as Italian is. It is of course possible, as some argue, that the Vlachs, or Wallachians – the name given by Germanic-speakers to the Latin-speaking foreigners: 'Welsh', in fact – moved into Dacia from south of the Danube at a later date: this is still a hotly disputed matter. Nevertheless, Britain remained in the Roman Empire some three times longer than Dacia. Yet by the sixth century, there is no sign that Latin was a spoken language at all, except among the clergy (who learnt it as a second language on joining the Church). In the eastern part of Britain, Old English, the language of the Anglo-Saxon invaders, came to predominate (though how quickly is uncertain); in the west and north, in the parts of Roman Britain which were not overrun by barbarian invaders, various versions of Brittonic (later Welsh), the language of the pre-Roman peoples of Britain, were spoken. Britain seceded from the Latin world: one of the most momentous developments of the middle of the first millennium.

The standard explanation of this is that, despite what happened in Dacia, Latin never really took root in Britain. The British aristocracy no doubt spoke Latin, along with the army, and probably many townspeople; but it never really penetrated the countryside, and that was where the bulk of the population lived. If one takes stone inscriptions as evidence of Latinity, the distribution is very suggestive.[60] The army are responsible for a great proportion of the surviving inscriptions: they come from the legionary fortresses, and in great numbers from Hadrian's Wall and its associated forts. Some towns produce almost no inscriptions, and the countryside is almost devoid of them. With the disappearance of the army and of town-life, in the fifth century, the society that produced inscriptions disappeared as well.

It is possible that this standard explanation is not taking sufficient notice of the very different histories of Britain and Gaul. It may be that other reasons exist than 'level of Romanisation' for the fact that French is spoken in France today. (French is, of course, derived from Latin; Frankish, the Germanic language of the Frankish invaders, was the ancestor of modern Flemish and Dutch.) To begin with, in Gaul the Frankish invaders had for a long time had close relations with Gaul; they were close neighbours, and indeed some Franks had been allowed to settle in the Empire, west of the Rhine mouths, in the mid-fourth century. Franks had served in the Roman army in Gaul (and elsewhere), and Frankish leaders had almost certainly become bilingual. Their takeover of northern Gaul in the late fifth century was very smooth, and was assisted by the Gallic bishops and the Gallic aristocracy: they basically filled a vacuum left by the shrinking authority of the Roman Emperors. Even so, it may only have been between the fourth and fifth centuries that Latin started penetrating the countryside. There were Gauls in central Gaul still in the sixth century who spoke Gaulish, a Celtic language related to Welsh. It is noticeable that even in the most Roman parts of Gaul, such as Aquitaine, there are few Latin inscriptions which are very far from towns. Perhaps Gaulish was used as widely in the Gallic countryside in the third and fourth century as Welsh was in the British countryside. It may be that it was Christianity that served to bring Latin to the countryside; after all, churchmen made an effort to communicate with peasants, which Roman landowners have never really needed to do, since they could use bilingual bailiffs. Crucially, however, Frankish kings and aristocrats, over almost all Gaul, seem to have used Latin – already, perhaps, well on its way to becoming French – as their first language. Gregory of Tours, a Latin-speaking cleric who is our main source for sixth-century Gallic history, had plenty of dealings with Frankish notables, and never seems to have needed an interpreter. So, thanks to the Church and the pro-Roman attitudes of the Franks, Latin survived in Gaul.

The situation in late Roman Britain was probably very different. Christianisation was barely under way when the structure of Roman government collapsed, which may have meant that Latin was still largely a language restricted to towns, the great aristocratic estates and the army. The incoming Angles and Saxons had not been neighbours of the Romans for centuries, as the Franks had been. Their takeover of eastern England was more violent. The aristocracy and, probably, the leaders of the Church, fled from the east; town-life disappeared; the Roman army disappeared. The Angles and Saxons dealt with the Romano-British as lord to servant, unlike the Franks, who had to deal with the surviving Gallo-Roman elite as equals. The Anglo-Saxons had no incentive to learn Latin; there were no institutions, either of aristocratic or ecclesiastical tradition, to preserve the memory of Latin; and the leadership of the independent British passed to westerners and northerners, who came from among the least Romanised parts of Britain.

In short, the disappearance of Latin tells us more about the very considerable disruption of the fifth century than it tells us about the level of

Romanisation in Roman Britain. But much of this depends on speculation. Knowing what the spoken language was like is one of the most difficult tasks for any historian: written language need not correspond to spoken language, and written language was almost always Latin and not any Celtic language. There are graffiti surviving, which suggest that for some artisans, Latin was the obvious language. 'Australis has been wandering off on his own every day for a fortnight' was scratched onto an unfired tile in London by some irritated workman; lines from Virgil's *Aeneid* were found on a tile from Silchester.[61] It has often been said, ever since the classic work by Kenneth Jackson,[62] that the Latin spoken in Britain was an archaic, formal Latin: not a living, developing language in the same way as in Gaul or elsewhere on the Continent. This idea is dependent on the analysis of Latin loan-words found in medieval Welsh: a technical matter, on which only a handful of specialists can pass judgement.[63] Subsequent to Jackson it has been suggested that the available evidence shows in fact that a whole range of levels of Latin can be detected, ranging from the formal to the vernacular and even, perhaps, the regional dialect.[64] It cannot be said that the issue has been decided. But it is important to underline that there are many Latin loan-words in Welsh. Some of these words are late, coming from Christian Latin rather than classical Latin, but it does suggest that, as one might expect, bilingualism was common in Roman Britain. One must assume not just that there was a range of Latinities, dependent upon class and region, but also a whole range of cultures, ranging from the purely Latinate to the largely indigenous. The culture of the elite in the south-east was probably barely distinguishable from elite provincial culture anywhere in the western Empire, strongly influenced by the literary culture of the Latin educational system. On the other hand the culture of those in the highland regions of Wales or the Pennines may have been little different from that of those living outside the Roman Empire, in lowland Scotland. Although the Welsh poetry ascribed to sixth-century bards such as Aneirin and Taliesin may only be of ninth-century date or later, it would be rather implausible to imagine that a tradition of poetry sprang from nowhere in the post-Roman period, or to argue that the Celtic poetic tradition mentioned by Diodorus Siculus and Strabo had disappeared among the Britons with the Roman occupation, to be 'reinvented' in the early Middle Ages. It had been a purely oral tradition in pre-Roman times, and perhaps remained so right through the Roman occupation and early Middle Ages, until embraced by monastic scribes late in our period.

The first Latin writer actually writing in Britain (excluding those who produced inscriptions or graffiti) was Gildas: a monk usually thought of as living in western Britain in the mid-sixth century (though see below, pp. 97–8). It is interesting that his historical account of Roman Britain always thinks of 'the Romans' as being an external force, who occasionally cross the Channel to help out the Britons. Gildas was writing several generations after the collapse of Roman Britain, and may simply have forgotten that since 212 all those in the Roman province were legally Romans. But he may be reflecting or remembering a genuine feeling of identity that took little account of the legal niceties. Even in Gaul and elsewhere on the Continent, Romans did not immediately identify themselves as 'Romans' first and foremost. Gauls, for instance, identified themselves as Gauls in the context of the Empire, when comparing themselves to inhabitants of other regions, such as Syrians or Egyptians: each group had their own ethnic stereotypes (Greeks were effeminate; Gauls gluttonous). But within Gaul they thought of themselves as Arvernians, Toulousains or Poitevins: citizens of *civitas*-territories, but also members of the pre-Roman peoples (the Arverni, Tolosates or Pictavi) whose territories had become the Roman *civitates*. Even in the sixth century this was the main mode of self-identification in Gaul. A near contemporary of Gildas, Gregory of Tours (d. 594) boasts of his senatorial ancestors, but like Gildas does not think of himself as a Roman: he only uses that word in a contemporary context when referring to the city of Rome, or to those Christians who follow the Roman and orthodox line.[65] He was an Arvernian, from the Auvergne. It is easy to think of this merely as a term denoting geographical origin, as 'Mancunian' or 'Brummie' are used today of the proud citizens of Manchester and Birmingham; but it is probably better to think of it in terms of ethnic identity. No amount of Romanisation, in Gaul, appears to have eradicated that basic identity in Gaul; we may assume (but in the absence of evidence) that things were no different in Britain. As in Gaul, it may have been the emergence of new indigenous political institutions in the wake of the collapse of the Empire which did more to bring about new forms of identity than several centuries of Roman rule had done.

4

Religion in Roman Britain

Of all the aspects of Romanisation, one is probably more important than any other, in terms of the long-lasting nature of its impact. Although many modern British towns are built on the same site as Roman towns, there was (as we shall see) little real continuity, save in the continued presence of ruins. Roman roads continued to be used in many parts of Britain, and Roman fortifications were also reused and rebuilt, and in that sense Rome survived, but only as a collection of monuments in the landscape, to be used or discarded at will. Many aspects of Roman culture – an appreciation of secular Latin literature, or the towering achievement of Roman law – had to be reintroduced at a later date. But in their introduction to Britain of Mediterranean religions, Rome made a permanent contribution to British culture. The worship of Jupiter or of Mithras may have vanished, but, in part of Britain at least, Christianity remains the state religion. It was through that Roman religion that Rome survived as a real presence in Britain in the second half of the first millennium. It was a different Rome: a papal Rome, a location of spiritual authority and, above all, of the relics of saints, those passports to salvation. But with this Rome one communicated in Latin, providing a crucial link with the imperial past. It was an imperial past which still had great resonance. It was an Anglo-Saxon, a contemporary of Bede, who came up with the memorable thought that 'While the Colosseum stands, Rome stands; when the Colosseum falls, Rome falls; when Rome falls, the world falls.'[1]

Christianity was only able to make headway in Roman Britain in the very last decades of Roman rule, as the last of a whole series of Mediterranean cults which had come to Britain in the Roman period. It was the only one which would eventually replace the old pre-Roman forms and objects of worship, largely for the very simple reason that it was the only one (apart from Judaism, whose presence in Roman Britain is uncertain) which refused to tolerate any other religion. Christians dismissed all other forms of worship (apart from Judaism) as 'paganism': the religion of *pagani*, or peasants.

(Modern French has two words deriving from *paganus*: *païen*, pagan, and *paysan*, peasant.) 'Heathen' has a similar dismissive etymology in Old English, meaning 'from the heath' or 'from the backwoods'. In most parts of the Roman Empire in the fourth and fifth centuries, Christianity was predominantly urban, and had barely begun to penetrate the countryside, so that designation was, at that point, fairly accurate. But to use the word 'paganism' (as St Augustine of Hippo, AD 354–430, the probable originator of the Latin word *paganismus*, did) is not only an insulting term, if applied to everything from rustic nature worship to the higher forms of Greco-Roman philosophy, but also misleading, in that it does imply that there was one single form of non-Christian religion. Although within the Roman Empire there was a great deal of interchange of ideas between one cult and another, and one system of ideas and another, paganism was not a coherent system. To treat paganism as a unity is no more sensible than to think that one can understand Christianity in late antique or medieval times by reading the New Testament. Beneath the smooth surface lurks immense variety.

The Romanisation of the pre-Roman gods

The Romans tolerated a great variety of religious practice, but they drew the line somewhere. They did not like religions which preached intolerance, and which expressed contempt for the cult of the Emperor-gods (something which seemed akin to treason): for these reasons they were suspicious of, or hostile to, Judaism and Christianity. They also did not like those religions which offended against their own standards of humanity or civilisation in some way. The Druids of Gaul and Britain fell into that category. Caesar is our most detailed source for Druidism, and, as in other respects, we cannot know how trustworthy he is. He tells us that 'the Druidic doctrine is believed to have been found existing in Britain and thence imported into Gaul; even today those who want to make a profound study of it generally go to Britain for the purpose'.[2]

Druids, said Caesar, acted as judges and as teachers: they instructed the young in astronomy and philosophy as well as religion. They formed a unified body among the Gauls, and had a 'national' assembly each year in the centre of Gaul (in the territory of the Carnutes, whose centre was Chartres), where they made judgements in legal disputes. (Pliny added the detail, familiar to us from the *Astérix* comic books, that one of their rituals was the cutting of mistletoe with a golden sickle.)[3] They believed in the ability of the soul to survive death: 'they think that this is the best incentive to bravery, because it teaches men to disregard the terrors of death'.[4] So far, this resembles other descriptions of barbarian religions: Romans were quite inclined to attribute wisdom to the priests of exotic peoples, just as many people in the West are today. But Caesar wished to paint the Druids as peculiarly barbarous:

> As a nation the Gauls are extremely superstitious; and so persons suffering from serious diseases, as well as those who are exposed to the perils of battle, offer, or vow to offer, human sacrifices, for the performance of which they employ Druids. ... Some tribes have colossal images made of wickerwork, the limbs of which they fill with living men; they are then set on fire, and the victims burnt to death. They think that the gods prefer the execution of men taken in the act of theft or brigandage, or guilty of some offence; but when they run short of criminals, they do not hesitate to make up with innocent men.[5]

Such barbarities, of course, must be eliminated; their existence is a moral justification for the conquest of Gaul and, ultimately, the conquest of Britain. Suetonius notes that Claudius abolished the 'savage and terrible Druidic cult' in Gaul,[6] which before had only been forbidden to Roman citizens, and Pliny (adding an extra enormity to Caesar's account) records that

> It is impossible to estimate the debt which is owed to the Romans, that they have swept away these monstrous rites, in which to kill a man was held to be the highest religious duty, and to eat him was held to be most beneficial.[7]

It has been common practice, among British scholars, to dismiss these claims of Druidic atrocity, quite reasonably, as Roman propaganda. But we must not underestimate the standards of Roman morality, or the possibility that human sacrifice did indeed exist. Most pre-Roman religious sites yield quantities of pig bones, and bones of other domestic animals, including horse. But human bones 'turn up with macabre frequency':[8] pieces of skull from Hayling, limbs and a torso from a pit at Danebury, a dismembered child from Wandlebury. Sacrifice is impossible to prove, however: trophies of war (head-hunting was known), or executions of prisoners or of criminals, could be responsible for the remains.

Caesar said that the god whom the Gauls venerated most was Mercury: 'the inventor of all arts, the god who directs men upon their journeys, and their most powerful helper in trading and getting money'; after him came Apollo, Mars, Jupiter and Minerva, 'about whom they have much the same ideas as other nations'.[9] Caesar was doing in Gaul what Romans would do in Britain: making rough and ready comparisons between their Roman gods and the gods worshipped in the newly conquered province. If a god was an inventor and at the same time the god of trade, then he must be Mercury, and the king of the gods must be Jupiter, regardless of the name that was used by the provincials. It was in this way that the Romans had themselves assimilated Greek myths, recognising Jupiter in Zeus, Mercury in Hermes, and so on. This attempt to impose a pantheon on the gods of a conquered people gives paganism within the Roman Empire a superficial uniformity, and it also to a large extent conceals from us the traditional beliefs and practices of the provincials. We might to some extent be able to reconstruct something of Celtic mythology by referring to the traditions written down, centuries later, by monks living in Ireland; it is possible, for instance, to relate some of the pagan gods of Irish tradition to some of those mentioned in Gallic or British inscriptions, which does suggest that there was some commonality across the Celtic-speaking world. But it is also likely that many gods and goddesses, and the religious practices associated with them, were very local in nature; and that the relevance of this later Irish material has been exaggerated.

In Romano-British inscriptions – themselves symptoms of Romanisation (as well as of social status), we must remember, and thus not representative of the population at large – it was common to add the name of the local god to the Roman equivalent. Thus we have Mars Belatucadrus, especially on the Wall (where inscriptions are frequent, and where soldiers are likely to adopt the cult of the god of war), or Mars Nodens, worshipped at the shrine of Lydney, on the Severn, or Apollo Maponus, or dozens of other variations, some of which are apparently so local that they only occur on one site. Minerva was equated with the native goddess of Sulis: the hot springs at Bath, *Aquae Sulis*, were called *fons Minervae* by the Roman writer Solinus, while inscriptions name the goddess either Sulis or Sulis Minerva. Henig calls Bath 'the most extreme case of Romanisation': Roman architects transformed the spring into an elaborate pool, enclosed by a building decorated with statues, and next to it was an elegant Mediterranean-style colonnaded temple, a suite of baths and a theatre, the latter probably for both entertainment and worship.[10] But the whole was probably the result of an assimilation of a pre-Roman cult.

Sometimes gods imported from elsewhere in the Empire are given the same treatment. Thus a Germanic god, Mars Thincsus, is honoured at Housesteads, on the Wall, and a Gallic god, Mars Toutates, is recorded in more than one place. That sometimes this pairing is not done with any ethnic distinctions in mind is suggested by curse-tablets at the shrine of Uley, which couple the names of two Roman gods: Mars-Silvanus and Mars-Mercury.[11] This conflation did not always happen, however. There are plenty of examples of cults of native gods and goddesses, some of which have a local distribution. There is the goddess Brigantia and her consort Bregens, for instance, evidence for whom comes from the northern and southern boundaries of the territory of the Brigantes.[12] Some deities seem to be personifications of local features like rivers or streams. Sometimes it is not certain whether the gods named in dedications are local ones or not. We can presume that Viredecthis, Ricagambeda and Garmangabis were Germanic deities, partly because dedications were set up by soldiers from Tungrian and Suebian cohorts.[13] But a shrine of Coventina, a water goddess like Sulis, was established at Carrawburgh (Northumberland), and she was thought to be a local British cult until a dedication to her was found in Galicia, in north-west Spain. The Matres, the mothers, depicted in sculpture normally as three goddesses, may have been the focus of a pre-Roman cult in Britain, but were possibly imported from north-east Gaul. There are some twenty known statues of the three from southern Britain, with the possibility that there were cult centres at London and Ancaster; in the north there are some sixty dedicatory inscriptions to the Matres, almost all from the area of the Wall.

The archaeological investigation of temples has found a similarly skewed distribution: over sixty Romano-British temples of native type have been discovered, all but a tiny handful in the south. There seems to be a remarkable continuity of site, if not of type, with pre-Roman times, suggesting that the Romans may have introduced new techniques – building with masonry, most notably – but made few other innovations to native religion. There is, for instance, a circular temple built of stone, over 13m in diameter, within a rectangular stone enclosure, at Hayling Island (Hampshire): this temple, built early in the Roman period, replaced a rather smaller but still circular wooden temple, based on the round hut typical of late Iron Age dwellings, which had been placed inside a palisaded enclosure. The only votary for which an inscription survives at Hayling is that of a soldier of the Ninth Legion. A native cult continued into the Roman period; its buildings were enhanced; it attracted foreign adherents. There was one change, however, which corresponded to a change in life in Britain that we have already noted. In the pre-Roman period there were pits by the temple containing numerous offerings of weapons and cavalry equipment. The ban on the civilian use of arms (and the fact that military weapons belonged to the State, not to the soldier) put a stop to that particular religious practice. A rather similar story can be told about Uley temple, on the western edge of the Cotswolds overlooking the Severn estuary. It began its career early in the Iron Age, and before the Roman conquest had a palisade added, to replace the ditches which previously had formed its sacred boundary. There was a pit containing offerings of weapons, as at Hayling Island. But in Uley the memory of this tradition suggested a compromise with Roman law: offerings of small *model* spears were made on the site. (The gods did not apparently object to substitutes for the real thing: at Hayling there were also offerings of what looked like standard gold coins, which turned out to be base metal, gilded.) Later in the Roman period these wooden buildings at Uley were replaced by a stone-built temple, and a number of other ancillary buildings, two of which contained votive offerings and others which may have housed visitors to the shrine.

The fate of Uley temple is clearer than for most. It was demolished in the last quarter of the fourth century, at about the time that the Emperor Theodosius declared public pagan worship illegal. The cult statue of Mercury was destroyed, although, interestingly, the head was carefully preserved within a construction of stone slabs. New buildings were put up, one of which had the base for an altar and a rounded apse – presumably a church. Worship continued on the same site where it had carried on for nearly a thousand years.

Mediterranean cults

Britons were introduced to various new deities taken from across the Channel; given the close connections between Britain and Gaul, they may have been familiar with some of these before the Roman conquest. But the Romans also introduced cults which must have appeared very exotic to the British, such as the cults of Isis and her consort Serapis from Egypt, and Cybele and her eunuch consort Atys from Asia Minor. The orientalised cult of the Roman god Bacchus can probably be included with these. The epigraphic evidence for these cults, mostly of east Mediterranean origin, comes very largely from the militarised area around Hadrian's Wall – the area in which the largest number of newcomers to Britain must have congregated. But there is evidence of other kinds from the south: a graffito of a pot from London indicating the presence of a temple to Isis; heads of Serapis from London, Silchester and a grave in Wiltshire; statuettes and depictions of Atys in London and elsewhere; and, in the Thames at London, a highly decorated implement which, it has been suggested, was the instrument used for castrating initiates to the cult of Cybele[14] (this aspect of the worship of Cybele had caused it to be banned by Rome for over two centuries, until finally legalised by Claudius).

The best known of the Oriental cults (apart from Christianity) is the cult of Mithras. Mithraism was an offshoot of the Persian religion of Zoroastrianism (which still survives among the Parsees of India). Mithras represented light, in perpetual struggle against the evil forces of darkness, and was often associated with the Sun God. He was not the creator-god (who was Ormazd, or Ahura Mazda), but was sent by that god to save the world: being born, some said, on the shortest day, the day at which the sun seems reborn – December 25th. Salvation is associated with his sacrifice of a bull, which is often represented in sculpture: or in those pieces of sculpture which partially survived Christian acts of demolition in the fourth century. There are examples from the mithraea in London and in York, and fragments from sites by the Wall, such as Carrawburgh, Housesteads and Rudchester. His worship required utter commitment by his followers, and there were complex ceremonials, such as those of initiation into the various grades of worshipper.

The similarities between Mithraism and Christianity ought to be obvious, and indeed seemed so at the time: Christians regarded Mithraism as a demonic parody of their own faith.[15] But in fact all these oriental cults, the so-called 'mystery religions', had things in common with Christianity: or, to put it another way, Christianity was the most successful of the mystery religions. They were cults with initiation rituals (such as baptism), in which some of the ceremonies were secret and restricted to those who had been initiated. (The Latin word for Mass derives from the phrase at the start of the ceremony when those who had not been initiated were dismissed from the church.) Their theologies placed the worshippers in the context of cosmological dramas, known through the revealed word of the deity, giving them a sense of purpose and of certainty about the universe and its destiny (something which the traditional Greco-Roman religions had not been good at). Salvation after death was promised by more than one: the miracle of resurrection is central to the cult of Isis and of Atys. These cults also fostered a sense of community among their worshippers, strengthened by their participation in sacred meals as part of their ceremonial. The ritual eating and drinking of bread and wine by Mithraists was another aspect of Mithraism which Christians regarded as obscene parody, but worshippers of Bacchus and of Atys engaged in similar meals. There may have been even more similarities: but no sacred books of the other cults survived the triumph of Christianity, and a good deal of what we know about these cults, particularly Mithraism, comes from the very hostile pens of Christian writers. Did all these cults have elaborate moral codes, for instance? There is no reason why not. But as ever we are hampered by lack of evidence of the daily lives of the adherents of most cults. What does seem to be true, however, is that Mithraism never went out of its way to attract converts: women were not admitted, and the mithraea are small, and largely associated with the military. Christianity did not have those limitations: indeed, as a religion which preached anti-military virtues it may have appealed precisely to those elements of the population that felt excluded, alienated or oppressed by the increasingly militarised establishment. Most mystery religions were small and exclusive; Christianity, which may have begun that way, had become a vigorous missionary religion by the fourth century.

Religion in Roman life

It is important not to confuse mythology with religion – that is, not to confuse beliefs about the gods with public or private ritual practice. Roman religion was much more about communal and individual practice than it was about adherence to any particular dogmas about the supernatural world. Indeed, it is important not to confuse mythology and belief, and to ask the question Paul Veyne used as a title of a book: 'Did the Greeks believe in their myths?' After all, it was common to refer to myths as 'the lies of poets'.[16] There were certain assumptions made, however, probably by all except the most determined philosophical sceptics: that there were a multitude of powers affecting the lives of men and women, and that these powers needed to be placated in order to avoid disaster, and might be appealed to if disaster (illness, loss of property) had already struck. These generalities probably apply to all Roman religions, and they certainly apply to Christianity: Christians too believed in a multitude of powers (angels, saints, demons), who could intervene in men's lives, for good or ill. Christians too (and this become much more developed by the fourth and fifth century) might well prefer to appeal to a saint, particularly a local saint – a bishop, say, who had looked after his flock while alive – than to a powerful god. Jupiter, or God the Father, were both far too imposing and remote to be appealed to directly. In this way attitudes to the divine in the early centuries of the first millennium mirrored people's understanding of the way in which the world worked. Only the great – senators or generals – would approach the Emperor directly. Lesser mortals used intermediaries in order to reach the imperial ear: the senators, for instance. The system of patron and client which lay behind Roman social and political relations operated on the spiritual plane too: hence the later Christian concept of the 'patron saint' – someone in heaven who would listen to your problems and take them to the much more distant and forbidding figure of Almighty God.

The spiritual patrons of ordinary Romans were probably normally the local gods – or, later, for the Christians, the local dead bishop. But as befitted his status, the Roman Emperor's public religious rituals usually involved the most elevated of the Roman gods: Jupiter, Juno and Minerva. That trio of what some have called the State gods might vary according to circumstance: at Chichester, for instance, Neptune, the god of the Ocean, had a temple alongside that of Minerva (and possibly Jupiter), appropriate for a coastal town. At the end of the third century it was the Emperor who led the cult of Sol Invictus, the Unconquered Sun: again associating himself with the most powerful god. This was a cult begun by Aurelian (270–75), and it remained the chief deity of the State until the time of Constantine (306–37). Constantine was a sun-worshipper too, as his early coins attest, and his first divine vision (in 307) was of the Sun God Apollo; when he had what he interpreted as a vision of the Christian god, in 312, what he said he saw was a sign in the heavens, above the sun. For some time after his 'conversion', the Sun God loomed much larger on his coins than the Christian Chi-Rho symbol, which denoted the first two letters of Christ's name in Greek. The equation continued to be made. The birthday of the Sun God was 25 December, which was adopted as the birthday of Christ by the fourth century; a common fourth-century representation of Christ was modelled on the traditional iconography of Apollo. The triumph of Christianity might best be regarded as the end-product of the imperial tendency towards the worship of one all-powerful God, which progressed through the cult of Jupiter, through the Sun God, to the best-organised monotheistic cult of all, Christianity.

The close association of the Emperor with the most powerful of the gods led to the idea that some emperors were actually received in the afterlife into the companionship of the gods. Vows were never made to these god-emperors: in that sense they were not 'real' gods. But temples were built to them, and the cult of the god-emperors was particularly important in the army. The most notorious of the imperial cult-centres in Britain was at Colchester, where a temple to the Divine Claudius was inaugurated very soon after his death. Tacitus said that Boudicca and her rebels had particular hatred for this building: they thought that

> the temple erected to the Divine Claudius was a blatant stronghold of alien rule, and its observances were a pretext to make the natives appointed as its priests drain the whole country dry.[17]

It was here within the temple that the Roman garrison of Colchester tried to hold out, and there that they were massacred. The temple was rebuilt after the rebellion was suppressed: all that survives now is its huge podium (32 by 23.5 metres), which served as the foundation for the Norman castle.

There were other cults that were closely tied up with the institution of the Empire, and which were in a sense cults which allowed loyalty to the Empire and the Emperor to be shown. The goddess Victoria was an obvious one; her altar in the Senate House was the occasion of one of the most celebrated debates in Roman history, in 391, when the pagan intellectual Symmachus pleaded for its retention and Saint Ambrose, Bishop of Milan, argued for its removal. Symmachus clearly thought of Victoria as a very real personage, and one whose cult had been vital in the secular success of the Roman people. Like Victoria, the goddess Fortuna was also often linked to the live Emperor. Fortuna would protect the Emperor, and thus the Empire and its individual inhabitants. She might even protect imperial property: provisions for the campaigns of Septimius Severus were sealed by lead bearing the image of Fortuna and the inscription FORT[UNA] AUG[USTAE]: to the Fortune of the Emperor.[18]

Neglecting these gods who protect the Empire might be a sign of treason. An example of Roman attitudes may be found in a later Christian story – probably largely legend – about the martyrdom of St Alban at Verulamium (now St Albans). He was executed because he refused to make an offering to a god in the forum. Romans might themselves disagree about the powers of such-and-such a god, or the merits of paying respect to *this* god rather than *that* god, but they would almost all be agreed that deliberately insulting a god (and by extension insulting that god's worshippers) was not only socially disruptive, but also potentially dangerous. The gods did have the potential to bring indiscriminate punishment to those who insulted them: not just to the individual, but to the whole community. By the early fifth century, as the Empire slid from one setback to another, traditionalists were complaining that the gods were punishing the Roman Empire for allowing Christians to gain the ascendancy, while Christians argued that God was punishing the Roman Empire for allowing pagans to continue to worship. For both, the health of the state was bound up with correct worship; for Christians the solution was to worship one God in just one way, while for non-Christians the answer was, as an insurance policy, to placate all possible gods in all the traditional ways. After all, the piety of the good old days had allowed the Romans to dominate the known world; could it possibly be coincidence that Rome's problems began with the rise of 'atheism' (as non-Christians perceived Christianity)? It was to answer this charge that St Augustine of Hippo wrote *The City of God*, one of the great works of

Christian theology and one of the most fascinating products of the Roman mind.

We can know something of the role of religion in the State, and of the public piety involved in the dedication of altars by individuals. But it is much more difficult to know of the role religion played in daily life. Our evidence mostly comes from times of crisis in people's lives. We have the bones which are the remains of sacrifices, for instance: goat and chicken at Uley (animals associated with Mercury), or pig at Hayling Island.[19] We have little surviving of the 'sacrifice' of wine – libation, or the pouring of wine from a dish or jug onto the ground – although sometimes the dishes are found, dedicated to a god and sometimes themselves deposited as an offering. Personal crisis brought visits to shrines. Christians, on the whole, seem to have gone to shrines mainly to seek cures; the evidence from Roman Britain about the desires of pagans seems weighted towards justice than towards healing. 'The god is expected to perform like a celestial hybrid of Sherlock Holmes and Gilbert and Sullivan's Lord High Executioner, not only discovering the perpetrator of the crime but also exacting a fitting punishment.'[20] Two great stores of evidence survive, from a temple room at Uley, and from beneath the waters of the spring of Sulis at Bath. These consist of metal plaques inscribed with a request to a named god to perform a particular service. They are couched in pseudo-legalistic language, and indeed are not that different in form from the letters addressed to imperial officials.[21] They are sometimes called curse-tablets, because of the often rather lurid punishments which the supplicant calls on the deity to visit on the criminal:

> Docilianus, son of Brucerus, to the most holy goddess Sulis. I curse whoever stole my *caracalla* [hooded cloak], whether man or woman, slave or free, that the goddess Sulis inflict death on him, and not let him sleep now or in the future until he brings my cloak to the temple of her divinity.[22]

Occasionally, at Bath and elsewhere, there are 'proper' curse-tablets, in which someone calls down a curse on someone without asking for any intervention by the god. Often the god is promised some reward for helping the supplicant, such as in a tablet from Caistor-by-Norwich, where the victim has lost fifteen denarii, a wreath, bracelets, a suit of clothes, a mirror and ten pewter vessels. 'If you [Neptune] want the pair of leggings, they shall become yours at the price of his [the thief's] blood.'[23] Acknowledgements of the god's help also survive: no pairs of leggings, but inscribed metal plaques, bronze letters which presumably were nailed up in the form of inscriptions on a wooden board, plaques in the shape of leaves or masks, and gifts of all kinds. As in Catholic and Orthodox countries today, votive offerings in the form of representations of the parts cured were also presented to shrines: breasts carved on a piece of ivory, bronze arms from Lydney, legs from Uley, and pairs of eyes at Wroxeter.[24] There are buildings at some of these shrines which, by analogy with examples from elsewhere in the Empire, may have housed pilgrims. At Lydney and at Nettleton there were long buildings which may have been for 'incubation' (sleeping overnight while awaiting dreams sent by the gods), or were perhaps used to house the sick who visited the god for cures.

It is possible to argue that for most people religion *is* about crisis management. At times of deprivation or illness, one goes to the gods. In order to get through the day Romans made small offerings or prayers to the household gods, the *lares* of Roman tradition, and they wore amulets and charms in order to protect themselves from evil spirits. And religion was invoked to cope with the greatest crisis of all: the deaths of members of one's family. There was no single concept of the afterlife in the Roman world, and it is not easy, or safe, to relate specific burial rituals to specific afterlife beliefs. It is possible that cremation, the most common form of disposal of the dead in the early Empire, was designed to speed the spirit on its way to the afterlife; it is less certain that inhumation, which became more and more frequent from the second century onwards, throughout the Empire, had anything to do with a changed attitude towards the afterlife. It is true that Christians had an aversion to cremation; but the change from cremation to inhumation occurred far too early for Christianity itself to have had anything to do with it. It is possible that there was a general change in attitude to the treatment of the dead, shared by all kinds of different people within the Empire, including Christians. It is also possible that it was a response to changes in society and the environment which had nothing to do with religion. Incinerating a body to ashes is a prolonged process, which consumes immense quantities of wood and thus costs a good deal; inhumation, even with a stone sarcophagus, might actually have been cheaper. However, it was possible to devise elaborate monuments – carved sarcophagi, preserved above ground – to contain the body, and thus to preserve the memory of the dead person; those without such resources could have an inscribed gravestone above the inhumed body.

Changes in burial practice – the move from cremation to inhumation, the development of different kinds of tomb or grave-marker, fashions in the objects that were actually placed in graves – seem to have occurred in Britain at roughly the same time as on the Continent. As elsewhere in the western Roman Empire, archaeological traces occur of the meals that would have taken place around the graveside on the day of burial. As elsewhere, there are occasionally traces of the meals that used to take place above the grave on the anniversary of the death: a cremation burial at Caerleon has a lead pipe connecting with the surface, and tile channels or pipes have been noted at Chichester and Colchester, all of which were for pouring wine onto the remains of the dead, as a way of linking the dead with the living family. This custom was at the origin of saints' days, on which Christians remembered the dead martyr or holy person on the anniversary of the death. It is with the veneration of the body of the saint, however, that Christians introduced a major innovation in the treatment of the dead. Romans regarded the dead body as polluting, physically and spiritually, and would place cemeteries at some distance from the living: typically the major Roman cemeteries are along the main roads that lead from a town, at some distance from a town's walls. When Christians started venerating the bodies of saints, they built churches over the bodies of those saints, within the Roman cemeteries. On the Continent, where Christian traditions were not disrupted in the fifth century as they were over much of Britain, settlements often arose around these extramural churches, so that the living were effectively intermingled with the former Roman cemetery. At the same time, the bodies of saints were often being removed from the extramural cemeteries and reburied within the walls of towns; churches, whether inside or outside town-walls, themselves became prized burial-places, and churchyard burials began. It was a change of attitude which in Britain, ultimately, led to the overcrowded urban cemeteries of the early nineteenth century, where semi-decomposed bodies had to be removed before new burials could take place. In the 1820s and 1830s there were a series of condemnatory reports from reformers, worried about cholera and other dangers to public health, which led to the foundation of out-of-town municipal cemeteries – on the model of those of the pagan Romans.

Christianity in Roman Britain

Of all the conspicuous invasions of Britain which are touched on in this book – such as those of the Celts, the Romans, the Anglo-Saxons, the Vikings and the Normans – none had such a profound effect as the 'invasion' of Christianity. Christianity was not only the most long-lasting cultural import of the period, it was also the one which most profoundly linked Britain to the rest of Europe. The ecclesiastical links which were set up with the coming of Christianity lasted until the Reformation and beyond; the cultural world of Europe, as it exists today, is much more a creation of Christianity than it is of Rome. Or, to put it another way completely: it is through Christianity that Rome had its most profound influence upon Britain and Europe. Britain was still part of the Roman Empire when, in the 390s, the Emperor Theodosius ordered all pagan temples to be closed and all public pagan worship abandoned. Christianity effectively became the state religion. Soon afterwards Britain ceased to be a part of the Empire, but the new imperial religion survived and continued to win converts.

Those other invasions were conspicuous: that of Christianity was not. When Bede wrote his *Ecclesiastical History* in the early eighth century he noted that Lucius, a king of Britain, wrote to Pope Eleutherius (*c.*175–89) to be made a Christian; this neatly paralleled the way in which Christianity came from Rome once again in 597, when St Augustine arrived to begin the conversion of the Anglo-Saxons. King Lucius suited Bede's didactic purposes, but his source (the *Liber Pontificalis*, the official collection of papal biographies) had it wrong: Lucius was a king of Edessa in Syria, who had a fortification called Britium, and had nothing whatsoever to do with Britain. In fact we do not know when Christianity first arrived in Britain; but we can be sure that it did *not* arrive through official channels. Like other Mediterranean cults, it must have first reached Britain through the chance arrival of soldiers, merchants, or other travellers.

Optimistic reports on the Continent spoke of the early successes of Christianity in Britain. Tertullian wrote *c.* 200 that 'the parts of the island inaccessible to Rome have been subject to Christ',[25] and Origen, forty years later, claimed that Christianity was a unifying force among the Britons.[26] But our earliest native record of Christianity may be in the *Passio* of St Alban, which records the death of a Briton in one of the official persecutions of Christians, perhaps in the early third century: the place of his burial was later believed to be at the site of the great medieval abbey of St Albans, outside the Roman city of Verulamium. The only other martyrs recorded are Julius and Aaron, both of whom were executed at Caerleon, probably in the mid-third century. The name of Aaron has suggested to some that the earliest British Christians may have been Jews; certainly Christianity spread first and most rapidly within the scattered Jewish communities of the Empire. From the third century too, possibly, comes the spectacular silver hoard of Water Newton, found by a metal detector in 1975 within the small Roman town of *Durobrivae*, near Chesterton (Cambridgeshire): the hoard is certainly Christian, and it has been suggested that it is the church plate of a community, buried, perhaps, to escape confiscation during a time of persecution. If it is from the third century, it is the earliest church plate in the Empire;[27] but other opinion inclines firmly to a fourth-century date.

When Constantius I, who had not been an enthusiastic persecutor of Christians, died in 306, near York, his troops acclaimed his son Constantine I ('the Great') as Augustus in his place. It took Constantine nearly twenty years to secure control over the whole Empire, and even longer for him to accept baptism within the Christian Church, as the first Christian Emperor. But persecution of Christians stopped long before that, and it is no coincidence that the Church in Britain emerged from obscurity at this time: three British bishops are recorded as being at the Council of Arles in 314. The text is corrupt: we may doubt that the first known bishop of York (in Latin *Eboracum*) was actually called Eborius (though our doubts are not as profound as those we have when we read in the *Annales Cambrenses* that Ebur died in 501, aged 350).[28] Restitutus of London is certain enough; Adelfius was probably from Lincoln. We do not know how many bishops there were in Britain in the early fourth century; we do not know which towns had Christian communities large enough to elect a bishop. We can assume, however, that by the end of the fourth century, after nearly a century of rule by Christian Emperors, the Church in Britain expanded at the same rate as elsewhere in the Empire. If the Continental pattern had been followed, there would have been bishops in each town, and the bishop of each provincial capital would have been a metropolitan, having seniority and some authority over the other bishops within his province. One possibility is that the five ecclesiastical provinces, with their capitals, would have been *Maxima Caesariensis* (London), *Britannia Prima* (Cirencester), *Britannia Secunda* (Lincoln), *Valentia* (York) and *Flavia Caesariensis* (Carlisle).

The archaeological evidence for early Christianity in Britain is quite extensive, but scattered, and in almost every case presenting problems of identification and function. There are various silver hoards of apparently Christian nature (though none so extensive as the Water Newton hoard); objects with Christian inscriptions or motifs (including a number of lead tanks or cisterns, which may possibly have been used as fonts); and, of course, a number of churches, the clearest possible record of past Christian communities – if their identification as churches is certain. There seem to be some churches within Roman towns, such as at Lincoln (Flaxengate) and Silchester, and some extra-mural cemetery churches, at Canterbury (St Pancras and possibly St Martin's), and some possible estate churches. One of the latter may be seen at Hinton St Mary, a Roman villa which is also the classic example of a Christian mosaic. The mosaic, 6 by 9 metres, is well known; it is prominently displayed in the British Museum. The central roundel shows the head and shoulders of a fair-haired and beardless young man, with the Chi-Rho symbol that forms the first two letters of Christ's name in Greek behind his head. If it is a portrait of Christ, it is one of the earliest in Europe, and certainly the only one susceptible of being trodden on. Other elements may have Christian meaning: Bellerophon on Pegasus, killing a monster, may be Good triumphing over Evil; four persons in the spandrels could be the Four Winds, or the Four Evangelists. A tree might be the Tree of Life. Or just a tree. It has been suggested that the villa-owner may have been a deliberately cautious man, choosing motifs that would appear Christian to a fellow-Christian, but not necessarily to a pagan;[29] or perhaps he was simply someone who had adopted Christianity for the sake of convenience, but saw no reason to abandon traditional images.

The bulk of the rural population in much of Gaul was only just beginning to receive baptism by 400, and it is highly unlikely that the process was happening more quickly in Britain. Many may have accepted the power of the Christian God; but if we accept as the definition of a Christian someone who has received baptism *and* renounced the worship of all other gods, then the number of Christians may have been small. Interestingly, however, there seems to be a good deal more archaeological evidence of Christianity in the British countryside than in the Gallic countryside in the late Roman period, and one wonders whether this suggests a real difference between the two areas. There is also archaeological evidence of paganism, however, continuing until the time, in the fifth century, when most archaeological evidence of recognisably Roman type disappears. There are pagan monuments being restored, as at Cirencester, and dedications made at the shrine of Lydney, both of them possibly in the 390s, when public worship of the old gods has been made illegal. As Britain slipped away from Roman rule in the first decades of the fifth century, some may have taken that as license to return to their old religious ways, and even, perhaps, to see the newly-arrived pagan Saxons as a useful counter to the Christianity of the British authorities who inherited power from Rome. Neither the historical nor the archaeological evidence survives to enable us to give any substance to speculation.

Pelagianism

It is likely, however, that it was during the dying throes of the Roman Empire in Britain that the Church made the greatest progress among the Romano-British populace. We can tell the story of British Christianity in the fifth and sixth centuries through a handful of known individuals: notably Pelagius, Germanus, Palladius, Patrick and Gildas. Pelagius was in some ways the most interesting of all of them: the only known early British theologian, and the only major heretic to emerge from Britain until John Wycliffe in the fourteenth century. Nothing is known of his time in Britain. He presumably gained his first education there, but he is visible first of all as a law student in Rome in the 380s. He abandoned his studies to join the Church, and in the mid-390s his writings and sermons began to become known in Rome and beyond. He was an impressive figure: according to a hostile source he was 'a most monstrous great Goliath of a man', who 'confronts one, head-on, with his great solid neck and his fatness'.[30] His opinions impressed too, particularly among the groups of monks who were increasingly found in the West, imitating the Desert Fathers of Egypt and Syria, devoting their lives to asceticism and prayer, and increasingly portraying themselves as the *true* Christians, who were giving up everything for Christ, as He had demanded. Pelagius argued that man had free will, and could by his own actions – prayer and good works – achieve salvation and the kingdom of God. It was a natural enough creed for a monk: this is what many had joined a monastery for. But Pelagius's main opponent, St Augustine of Hippo, saw that this doctrine was divisive, potentially creating an elitist group within the Christian community, and he argued strongly for the supreme importance of God's grace, which could not be 'bought' by pious deeds, and which could nevertheless be given to any Christian. Some of Pelagius's ideas were eventually declared heretical in 418, even though his ideas could be found lurking in many Mediterranean monasteries in the early Middle Ages, in a disguised form that theologians call 'semi-Pelagianism', and would crop up again and again in the subsequent history of Christianity.

Pelagius the Briton would thus seem an interesting aside in a history of Britain, were it not for an odd and as yet inexplicable fact: that Pelagianism seems to have become more deep-rooted in Britain than elsewhere in the Empire. According to Constantius, who wrote his *Life of St Germanus* in about 480, his hero Germanus, an ex-Roman soldier who had become bishop of Auxerre in central Gaul on his retirement, had been approached some fifty years earlier by a deputation of British clergy. They reported that Pelagianism was rife in Britain, and that the British Church needed outside help. Germanus went to Britain in 429, and combatted the Pelagians by preaching and miracle-working. He seems to have had wide popular support in Britain; but his opponents are portrayed by Constantius as powerful men. These 'teachers of perverse doctrines ... came forth flaunting their wealth, in dazzling robes', and had crowds of hangers-on, including at least one man of high military rank.[31] As one would expect in a life written to glorify a saint, Germanus was spectacularly successful: the heresy was wholly destroyed.

There may have been political reasons for his visit: he apparently led an army against marauding barbarians (p. 94). Although later sources tell us nothing about continuing heresy in Britain, we may doubt that Germanus was quite as successful as his *Life* claims. It seems likely that the orthodox members of the Church in Britain really were worried about the spread of the heresy, and that so were their neighbours in Gaul, and even the pope. It is instructive to look at what a contemporary Gallic chronicler, Prosper of Aquitaine, writes about this episode:

> Agricola the Pelagian, son of the Pelagian bishop Severianus, corrupted the churches of Britannia by his underhand ways. But at the instance of Palladius the deacon, Pope Celestine sent Germanus, bishop of Auxerre, to act on his behalf; and having put the heretics to rout he guided the British back to the Catholic faith.

Some have seen Palladius as a Roman deacon, a member of the papal household, and the inspiration of this papal initiative; but he could simply have been the messenger that Germanus had sent to Rome. But it is intriguing that it is this same man whom Pope Celestine sends to Ireland, in 431 according to Prosper of Aquitaine, 'to those Irish who believed in Christ, as their first bishop'. Prosper congratulates Celestine on freeing Britain from the plague of heresy, and doing rather more: 'while he was careful to keep the Roman island Catholic, he also made the non-Roman one [*barbaram*] Christian'.[32] It is possible he did not wholly succeed, however. Works by Pelagius were known in England and Wales in the seventh and eighth centuries, and also in Ireland.[33]

Patrick

We do not know whether Prosper was better informed about Palladius' mission than we are: apart from this hint, we have no information that Palladius ever got to Ireland, let alone had a successful mission. It is worth noting that he was not sent primarily as a missionary to convert the heathen.

As with other bishops sent outside the Empire in the fourth and fifth century, he was specifically sent to be bishop to Christians already there. Indeed, we probably know the name of one of those Christians: a boy called Patrick, who had been captured from his home in Roman Britain by Irish raiders and enslaved. The Christians in Ireland may have consisted not just of captives (though Patrick said that thousands were taken with him), but merchants and other travellers who had perhaps met Christianity in Britain or on the Continent and taken it home with them. A community without a bishop was obvious prey to heretic preachers; it was not surprising that Celestine should choose to send a bishop to Ireland, as part of the mission against Pelagianism. Nevertheless, later Irish tradition did not celebrate Palladius as the apostle of Ireland, but Patrick. Some scholars have speculated that Patrick and Palladius might be the same person, or, in order to reconcile contradictory Irish traditions, that there were two St Patricks. 'Two Saint Patricks?' said the heavenly vision of St Augustine in Flann O'Brien's comic novel *The Dalkey Archives*: 'We have four of the buggers in our place, and they'd make you sick with their shamrocks and shenanigans and bullshit.'[34] Perhaps so, but the Patrick of history is not the Patrick of Irish tradition: he is the only fifth-century Romano-Briton about whom we know much at all.

Patrick's *Confessio* is a unique document in early British history. Apart from being the first extended text in Latin surviving from the pen of a Romano-Briton writing in these islands, it is also an extremely rare autobiographical document. Not only is it our only reliable source for the conversion of Ireland, but it also tells us, indirectly, more than any other source we have about the church in fifth-century Britain. It is not possible to date Patrick's life with any precision. The traditional date for his return to Ireland as a missionary, after he had escaped captivity and returned to Gaul and/or Britain for some years, is 432: that is rather suspiciously close to 431, the year of Palladius's mission. It is as if a later Irish writer, who knew that Palladius had been the first bishop in Ireland, decided to place Patrick as close as possible without usurping his position. In fact, it is likely that Patrick's career began in mid-century. Another set of traditional dates may be the correct ones: arrival in Ireland in the early 460s and death in the early 490s.

Patrick wrote his *Confessio* in order to counter the complaints of some bishops in Britain. The complaints were various, and related not only to what he was doing in Ireland, but also to his earlier career: they had heard about an unnamed sin that he had committed and confessed, to a close friend, when he was fifteen years old. He claimed that he had always been honest with the pagan Irish among whom he lived; that he had always refused gifts from those he had converted, and had taken no money for baptism or when consecrating priests: this would have been the heinous sin of simony. (In the next breath he says that he gave presents to kings, and to the sons of kings who travel with him – a sign of his high status in Irish society, according to early Irish law-tracts – and it is not clear where he acquired his money, if he did not accept gifts.) But his most frequent defence was that 'I never had any cause, except His gospel and His promises, ever to return to that people from which I had previously escaped with such difficulty.'[35] It was the voice of God which called him to preach to the Irish, and to take heed (the first missionary apparently to do so) to Christ's words in Matthew 28, 'Go now, teach all nations': it was not his own personal desire to increase his status and his wealth. The fact that he protested so loudly suggests that there was some irregularity in his mission, and the most obvious possibility is that it was only God's voice which had sent him on this mission: he had not been properly consecrated as bishop. In his *Letter to the Soldiers of Coroticus*, the only other writing from his pen, he starts: 'I, Patrick, a sinner, yes, and unlearned, established in Ireland, put on record that I am bishop. I am strongly convinced that what I am I have received from God.'[36] This is an odd statement from someone secure in his episcopal status.

It is not impossible that the complaints against Patrick came to a head after his publication of the *Letter to the Soldiers of Coroticus*. Coroticus was a Christian king in Britain who had led a raid which had captured and enslaved Irish Christians. It is a letter glowing with righteous indignation and fine Latin invective. Patrick had sent a message to Coroticus with one of his Irish priests, whom he had taught from early childhood, asking for the baptised to be returned; the priest was met with jeers. Now he told the king and those that were with him that they are estranged from God: excommunicated. He compared Coroticus to the Christians in Gaul: 'they send suitable men to the Franks and other peoples with so many thousand solidi to ransom baptised captives; whereas you kill them or sell them to a foreign people which does not know God'.[37] He spoke of Coroticus's allies as being '*Scotti*, Picts and apostates'. Coroticus must be a British king somewhere in western Britain; the foreign people to whom he sells slaves are presumably the Picts, while the *Scotti* are perhaps those Irish who have already settled in Argyll. If Coroticus was a British Christian king, of course, he must have been in one diocese or another, and have his own bishop. This kind of interference by one bishop in the internal affairs of another diocese – not just any interference, but the excommunication of the ruler – was something that would have angered any British bishop, and may thus have led the British bishops to call for Patrick's return to Britain to stand trial. He refused to come: it was God's will that he remain in Ireland. That the British church was organised enough in the late fifth century to have synods, and unified enough too (despite the fact that Britain, left to its own devices by the Roman Emperors, was now ruled by perhaps as many as a dozen different kings) is of considerable interest.

The fifth and sixth centuries may well have been the period during which the bulk of the people in the western part of Roman Britain converted to Christianity, but next to nothing is known of this process, and we are reduced to clutching at the kind of straws which Patrick offers. At one time historians used to accept the idea that the fifth and sixth centuries were the great age of the saints in Wales, and to use the eleventh- and twelfth-century *Lives* written of saints like Cadog, David and Illtud as a reflection of sixth-century realities. The church dedications to St Cadog (in south-west Wales) or St Teilo (in south-east Wales) were seen as a record in the landscape of the careers and travels of these early saints. But it is now recognised that the *Lives* and the church dedications tell us more about eleventh- and twelfth-century Wales than of the early heroic days of Christianity; church dedications to those two saints, for instance, probably represent those churches owned or claimed by the main houses of Cadog and Teilo – Llancarfan and Llandeilo Fawr.[38] The many *llan-* place-names may well record the presence of early monastic houses of some kind: *llan* means 'enclosure', but seems to have been used largely of 'ecclesiastical enclosure'. The problem is that it is impossible to date the foundation of these 'enclosures'. Was Wales as active in the promotion of early monasticism as the *Lives* suggest? Certainly the seventh-century *Life of St Samson of Dol*, a Breton saint, shows that its author thought that had been the case just a century before his time: St Samson himself had been at the monastery of Llantwit, moved to Caldey, and had dealings with other monasteries, and subsequently his family had founded other monasteries in South Wales.[39] There are very few early charters from Wales, but those later preserved in the cartulary of Llandaff again suggest that Wales was well endowed with religious houses at an early date. Roman Christianity continued to flourish in at least one part of the former Roman province of Britain. St Gildas, one of the sixth-century saints with an especial reputation for sanctity and learning – if he was indeed the author of *The Ruin of Britain* (see below, pp. 94–9) – thought that the church in Britain was so flourishing and prosperous that it had become corrupt.

Evidence for post-Roman Christianity in other parts of Roman Britain is even more difficult to interpret. There are the oft-cited 'Eccles' place-names, which are to be found in Lancashire and in West Yorkshire, in the territory of the sixth- and early seventh-century British Christian kingdom of Elmet, but also in East Anglia and in Kent. They are thought to be evidence of a British Christian community surviving within Anglo-Saxon society: *eccles* derives from **egles*, the British form of *ecclesia*, the Greek word for 'church', also used in Latin. (Oddly, Anglo-Saxons used *cirice* for 'church', derived from the Greek *kyriakon*; the Scots got their *kirk* from the same ultimate source, but via the Vikings.) There are cemeteries such as Cannington (Somerset) and Poundbury (Dorset), which may have been used by post-Roman communities of Christians. There are also hints that these Christian communities in Britain may have been sustained by contact with Continental Christianity. There are now many post-Roman sites in western Britain which have yielded sherds of Mediterranean pottery, and items such as stoppers from Byzantine water-jars. The pottery may have contained olive oil, or wine (essential for the celebration of Mass in Christian communities of any kind). Early Latin epitaphs in Wales also show hints of connections with Gaul and even with North Africa; there is one example of post-consular dating – dating by using the number of years after the last Roman consul known in the West (Justinus, AD 540) – which otherwise is only known from the Rhône valley near Lyon. Ecclesiastical contacts with Gaul may have been through the British colony in Brittany (see below p. 106); but the British Church may also have had more direct links with the Mediterranean world.

Nynia and the southern Picts

The Romano-British Church not only survived; it may also have become a missionary church, taking Christianity beyond the frontiers of the Empire, even though it may have done so after the collapse of that Empire. There is no evidence that Christianity had penetrated into the territory north of Hadrian's Wall by the early fifth century, at which time the Roman Empire lost control not just of that frontier, but of the whole province. The question of the conversion of what is now Scotland is one of the most obscure in the whole of these darkest centuries in post-Roman history.

There are two figures who have been credited with the title of 'Apostle of the Picts' or 'of Scotland': there was even heated public controversy about this in 1997, when St Columba's death in 597 was remembered, and when a rival group of supporters urged acceptance of the date of 397 for Nynia's arrival in Scotland.[40] Both saints make their appearance in the same chapter of Bede's *Ecclesiastical History*:

> In the year of our Lord 565, when Justin II took over control of the Roman Empire after Justinian, there came from Ireland to Britain a priest and abbot named Columba, a true monk in life no less than habit; he came to Britain to preach the word of God to the kingdoms of the northern Picts which are separated from the southern part of their land by steep and rugged mountains. The southern Picts who live on this side of the mountains had, so it is said, long ago given up the errors of idolatry and received the true faith through the preaching of the Word by that reverend and holy man Bishop Nynia, a Briton who had received orthodox instruction at Rome in the faith and the mysteries of the truth. His episcopal see is celebrated for its church, dedicated to St Martin, where his body rests, together with those of many other saints. The see is now [731] under English rule. This place which is in the kingdom of Bernicia is commonly called Candida Casa, the White House, because Nynia built a church of stone there, using a method unusual among the Britons.[41]

Although much more is known now about the site of Candida Casa, translated into Old English as *Hwitærn* (Whithorn), because of the excavations conducted there between 1984 and 1991, this passage in Bede is almost all that is known about Nynia, and the passage raises more questions than it answers. When did Nynia live? The reference to St Martin of Tours (who died in 397, already a widely renowned holy man) is not as helpful as it might be, because Bede does not actually say that St Nynia dedicated it himself. Had Nynia really been trained at Rome, or does that simply mean 'in Roman ways', in contrast to the Irish St Columba who is the main subject of this chapter of Bede's history? Who were the southern Picts? The peoples of this part of south-west Scotland were British, the descendants of peoples such as the Novantae and the Damnonii in the west, the Votadini in the east and the Selgovae between them: the Picts in this period are not generally thought to have lived further south than the line between the Clyde and the Forth. Did Nynia travel from his somewhat inappropriate base at Whithorn to convert these Picts? And was he also responsible for beginning the conversion of the British peoples north of Hadrian's Wall, who certainly became Christian sometime between 400 and 600?

It has been suggested that Coroticus, or one of his predecessors, had been one of those converted from Whithorn. If so, Patrick's letter suggests that not all had progressed smoothly: he refers to Coroticus's allies as being '*Scotti* and Picts and apostates', the last normally referring to those people who have been baptised and have then reverted to their old religion: perhaps some of the British peoples north of Whithorn (if Coroticus was indeed a northern king, rather than someone from the south-west). Sadly, anyone interested in the conversion of those living immediately to the north of the Wall – let alone of the southern Picts themselves – is reduced to clutching at straws in this way. The wheel-made Roman pottery in the lowest levels at Whithorn suggests that the community may have been established in the late fourth century; the six mid-fifth century Latin inscriptions in and near Whithorn support Bede's idea that Nynia had links with the Continent rather than with the nearby diocese of Carlisle.[42] If so, then he was possibly the last missionary from the Continent until St Augustine of Canterbury arrived from Rome at the end of the sixth century, to begin a new phase of the history of Christianity in Britain.

5

The migration period

Migrations and/or invasions

The fall of the Roman Empire in the West is usually blamed on internal decline, or barbarian invasion, or a complex mixture of both. Any theory based on ideas of internal decline has to explain why the Roman Empire in the East, usually known as the Byzantine Empire, carried on until the Ottoman Turks captured Constantinople (or Byzantium) in 1453. The Byzantine Empire went through many of the same problems as the West was facing in the fourth and fifth century, yet it did not collapse. The reasons for this are indeed complex, but they do suggest that we should be looking at the barbarians just as closely as we look at 'decline'. And if we look at 'decline' carefully enough, we see that what is happening is, in fact, a process of change in many aspects of Roman government, economy and society. To categorise all these as 'decline' is hardly helpful, particularly when one of the most important of those changes is the 'decline of traditional religion' – a process more popularly known as 'the conversion to Christianity'. Peter Brown once suggested that the Roman Empire could be likened to a flower vase. In one theory a cat (the barbarians) knocked it off the mantelpiece, and it shattered; in a second theory the cat brushed against it, but, since it was all so cracked already, it fell into pieces on the mantlepiece. But what *really* happened, Brown said, was that the vase 'changed ineluctably into a tea-pot'.[1]

One of the major differences between East and West was, in fact, the very different nature of the barbarian threat. The Roman Empire formally and finally split into Western and Eastern parts in 395, when the two surviving sons of Theodosius the Great each inherited one half. The division north of the Mediterranean ran south from the Danube frontier, between the provinces of Illyricum and Dacia. Thus, the Eastern Empire faced barbarians along a relatively small frontier in Europe, along the Middle and Lower Danube; in Asia its frontier was with relatively stable monarchies such as those of Armenia and Persia, and further south with what seemed to be a series of minor barbarian peoples known collectively as the Arabs. No one in the late Roman Empire could have imagined that the Arabs, in the seventh century, would prove the most serious threat ever faced by the Roman Empire, conquering some of its richest provinces in the course of a generation. In the fourth or fifth century, the Persian Empire would have appeared the most obvious danger: it was a well-ordered centralised state, with a formidable army, the only people the Romans knew of outside the Empire whom they did not see as barbarians. But, by chance, the Eastern Roman Empire had mostly friendly relations with the Persian Empire in the fourth and fifth century. If any unfriendly barbarian power in the north tried to invade across the Danube, the Eastern Emperors were wealthy enough to pay them off, or persuade them to move westwards.

The Western Roman Empire was faced with a very different set of problems. The land frontier, running along the Rhine and the Danube, was over 2500 miles long; the Atlantic and Channel coasts were open to seaborne raiders, and even harder to defend. The threat from the barbarians had been very serious in the third century: of the western provinces, only Britain emerged largely unscathed. In Gaul, for instance, there were major barbarian attacks right into the heart of the province, forcing the authorities into a large-scale programme of fortification and military reorganisation. In the fourth century, the traditional raiding and counter-raiding continued, but on a much smaller scale. Most Emperors were far more worried about the threat of usurping Roman generals than they were about invading barbarians. Indeed, individual barbarian peoples were as often allies as they were enemies. Emperors and generals paid them to defend the Empire by fighting other barbarians; they paid them to support their attempts to usurp the imperial title, or to support their claim against other usurpers. As we have already seen (p. 49), some barbarians reached exalted positions within the Roman army, and thus wielded considerable power within the Empire. Barbarians themselves had neither the desire nor the ability to derail this gravy train. The Empire was a hugely wealthy employer – it was, after all, a tax-producing machine constructed for the purpose of paying taxes to its soldiers – and vastly more powerful than any individual barbarian people.

'Barbarian', for the Greeks, meant anyone who did not speak Greek, whose speech was a meaningless 'barbar' sound. For the Romans it meant anyone from outside the Roman Empire, including the Irish (whom Romans called 'Scotti') and the Picts, both peoples who spoke Celtic languages, as well as the Arabs, and the Berbers of North Africa, the only non-Roman people still to have the Roman *barbari* as their name. But most of the barbarians with whom the Romans had dealings spoke one of the Germanic languages. We call them 'Germans', after the Latin word for the inhabitants of the Rhineland region, but the Romans did not see all these peoples as related in any way, nor did the various German peoples themselves. It was only nineteenth-century philologists who discovered their relationship – and who invented 'the Celts' at the same time. The languages of the Germanic peoples were not all mutually comprehensible: there was a considerable difference between East Germanic languages like Gothic, West Germanic languages like Frankish and Old English, and North Germanic languages like Old Norse.

Peoples speaking Germanic languages faced the Romans across the entire length of the European land frontier in the fourth century, from the Franks at the mouths of the Rhine to the Goths at the mouths of the Danube. But there were also Germanic-speaking peoples further into the interior of Germania, who had little direct contact with the Roman Empire. These included the Saxons in the area between the Weser and the Elbe, the Angles from the angle between Germany and the Jutland peninsula of what is now Denmark, and the Jutes of Jutland itself. All three peoples were very familiar with the northern seas; it was as sea-borne raiders, Vikings four centuries before their time, that the Romans of Gaul and Britain were most likely to encounter them. Latin and Irish sources refer to all these raiders indiscriminately as 'Saxons'. We shall see later how these peoples, once settled in Britain, came to think of themselves as 'Angles' or 'English', although in Welsh and Irish the newcomers are still called 'Saxons', or Sassenachs.

It was in the second half of the fourth century that the Romans met for the first time another barbarian people whom they would regard as archetypical barbarians: that is, the antithesis of all the characteristics of civilisation. They had no letters, no constitution, no laws (so the Romans thought), no agriculture, no towns, not even any settled dwelling place. They were a nomadic people, who had come from the steppes of Central Asia: the Huns. Had the Huns not entered the Roman world, it is quite possible that the western Roman Empire would not have fallen. They overwhelmed the German peoples whom they came across, forcing some whole peoples into the Empire, and thus precipitating a crisis which neither Germans nor Romans could resolve. The Ostrogoths, who lived by the western shores of the Black Sea, were the first to be defeated and conquered by the Huns; their neighbours, the Visigoths, elected to take refuge within the Roman Empire, and crossed the Danube in 376. The Romans did not know what to do with the Visigoths: Emperors in turn fought them, and allied themselves with them. After defeating and killing the Emperor Valens in 378 and sacking Rome in 410, the Visigoths were eventually settled in south-west Gaul in 418, after agreeing to help defend the Empire in return for their settlement. The kingdom they eventually founded in Spain lasted until the Arab conquest of the peninsula in 711.

After precipitating the Visigoths into the Empire, the Huns moved westward. The 'invasion' of the Vandals, Burgundians and other Germanic peoples across the Rhine in 407 was almost certainly more of a flight of refugees from the Huns than a real invasion. The chaos that ensued forced the Romans to withdrew all the troops they could from Britain and, in 410, caused the Emperor Honorius to write his famous letter telling the British *civitates* to look to their own resources. The Burgundians were eventually settled in south-east Gaul (part of which we now call Burgundy) under terms similar to those used with the Visigoths; the Vandals moved through Spain (through Andalucia, which on one theory originated as 'Vandalusia'), across the Straits of Gibraltar, and took the rich Roman province of Africa (roughly modern Tunisia) by force in 431.

The Huns reached the height of their power under Attila, in the mid-fifth century. Some historical atlases depict most of Europe east of the Rhine and north of the Danube at this time as one massive territory labelled 'Hunnic Empire'. This implies rather more organisation and centralisation than could have been the case. The centre of Hunnic power was probably the Hungarian plain; from there the Huns and their Gothic associates (the very name 'Attila' is a Gothic word, suggesting the closeness of their collaboration) enforced the payment of tribute from as many of the Germanic and Slavic peoples of central Europe as they could, and launched raids on the Roman Empire, the main goal of which was probably the extortion of yet more piles of gold. The Roman alliance with the various barbarian peoples settled in Gaul seems to have proved its worth: a combined force of Visigoths, Burgundians and Franks put together by the Roman general Aëtius pushed back Attila's attack on Gaul in 451.

The 'Hunnic Empire' disappeared with Attila's fatal nose-bleed in 453. But the legacy of Attila's Empire was itself fatal to the Western Empire. The Emperors had lost most of their authority. In some western provinces the kings of the Visigoths, Burgundians, Franks or Vandals seemed more powerful than the Emperors, and more competent as protectors of their Roman subjects. Crisis came not long after Attila's death. In 455 the Emperor Valentinian III was murdered, and the Vandals sailed across the Mediterranean and sacked Rome; in 456 the Visigoths imposed their own Emperor on the West, a Gallic aristocrat called Avitus. Although the year 476, when the German general Odoacer deposed 'his' puppet Emperor, has traditionally been taken as the end of the Western Empire, the Anglo-Saxon historian Bede perceptively noted that the Roman Empire really came to an end a generation earlier, not at the hands of the barbarians, but as the result of its own internal factions. 'Valentinian was murdered by the followers of the patrician Aëtius whom he had put to death, and with Valentinian the western Empire fell.'[2]

The relevance of these cataclysmic events to Britain is not necessarily direct. We might hypothesise that the Angles and Saxons could actually have been persuaded to take to their ships by the Huns. One source tells us that the Huns extended their extortionate tentacles as far as the 'islands in the Ocean', which, if accurate, does not mean Britain (as Mommsen thought), but just possibly the Baltic: if so, then their power must have reached the homeland of the Angles and Saxons.[3] But ships from these Germanic peoples had been raiding Britain for long before the Huns arrived on the frontiers of the Western Empire, and there may well have been other reasons for the migration to Britain, as we shall see.

The events described briefly above have, by French historians, often been called 'les Grandes Invasions'; German historians call the process 'die Völkerwanderungen', the migrations of peoples. Those in northern Europe have frequently followed the German lead, and the whole period from the fourth to the sixth century in northern Europe is often called 'the migration period' ('die Völkerwanderungszeit', or VWZ). Clearly the difference is one of interpretation, and of political perspective. French historians evolved their ideas in the wake of the Franco-Prussian war, a new Great Invasion; German historians continued to develop *their* ideas while they were searching for more *Lebensraum* in the 1930s and 1940s. Nationalism but particularly racialism have had a deep influence on the way in which the end of the Roman Empire has been described. Blond virile Aryans bring a welcome end to the empire of the effete Latins, debased through miscegenation with degenerate orientals (and, for some, weakened by its adherence to pacifist Christianity); or, alternatively, primitive barbarians from the Germanic forests mindlessly destroy the achievements of the Grandeur That Was Rome and imperil Christianity itself.

Inevitably, the whole process seems much more complex now, and we have a better grasp of just how much of it we do not understand. To what extent was it really an 'Age of Migrations'? Did whole peoples actually migrate, and if so, how? How did the Visigoths migrate right across Europe, from the Black Sea to the shores of the Atlantic, or the Vandals from central Germany to North Africa? Nowadays it is usually thought that when the sources refer to the Visigoths on the move, we are not to imagine an entire people, men, women, children and property, moving like nomads. What Romans called 'the Visigoths' was an army, and thus a political grouping; by the time they settled in Gaul and Spain they were probably made up from half-a-dozen different Germanic peoples, together with dissident Romans and escaped slaves. For many impoverished Roman peasants, for whom the Roman tax-collector was the real enemy, the arrival of a barbarian army in their area might well have seemed a liberation. It has been very difficult for twentieth-century historians to come to a post-colonial perspective on the collapse of the Roman Empire. It is an interesting legacy of the classical education that we enjoyed in the West until well into the twentieth century, or, in Britain, of our ambiguous feelings about our own imperial past, that we are still expected to assume that the collapse of a bloated, corrupt, exploitative and tyrannical Empire was a disaster when it happened in the fifth century, but a triumph when it happened to the Soviet Union in 1991.

The lessons of recent research on the Migration Period over the last generation are several. Firstly, that the ethnic labels used by our written sources are not biological groupings, but political or even military ones. Secondly, that the cultural groupings discovered by archaeologists in terms of similar material cultures (as measured in metalwork types, pottery, etc) do not necessarily correspond to either ethnic groups *or* the labels that are used in the written sources. And thirdly, that not all movements of peoples were either 'migrations' *or* 'invasions' in the strict sense of those words, but had many different forces working on them, maybe all at the same time. Some were refugee movements, and only the experience of the twentieth century, perhaps, can inform us about the massive human suffering which remains largely unrecorded in the surviving sources. Some may have been movements of settlement and colonisation, into areas wide open to such immigration by dislocation and by the collapse of the Roman landowning class. Some were genuine conquests, led by military leaders; others were opportunist raids, which evolved into something else as opportunities expanded. Even within Britain, we will not easily find the movements of peoples easily categorised.

The end of Roman Britain

Barbarian attacks on Britain had probably been occurring throughout the fourth century. How often is a matter of conjecture, since it may not be coincidence that the first serious attacks we know about coincide with the beginning of the surviving portion of our best narrative source for the Roman Empire in the fourth century. This is the *History* of Ammianus Marcellinus, who was born in Antioch but wrote in Rome in the 380s. His narrative begins in 353; in 360 'the wild tribes of the Scots and Picts broke their undertaking to keep peace, laid waste the country near the frontier, and caused alarm among the provincials, who were exhausted by the repeated disasters they had already suffered'.[4] This is our first mention of that pair, Picts and Scots, who so frequently appear as a pair in our fourth- and fifth-century sources. 'Picts' is a word used from the early fourth century to refer to all the northern peoples, hitherto called 'Caledonian'. The Scotti are the inhabitants of Ireland, who, as we shall see, were by the fifth century not just raiding Britain, but settling in parts of it.

If Ammianus is not merely trying to exaggerate the problems faced by Valentinian and Valens at the beginning of their reigns, the Picts and Scots attack again, together with the Saxons and the Attacotti, in 364. The Attacotti only appear in our sources on two or three occasions: Ammianus said that they were a belligerent people, and St Jerome claimed that they were cannibals;[5] it is assumed that they too are from northern Britain, but one can hardly say that even their existence is proved. Finally, in 367, Valentinian heard of the most serious disturbance of all: not just a series of random attacks, but a *barbarica conspiratio*, a barbarian conspiracy, that had 'reduced the provinces of Britain to the verge of ruin'.[6] The Picts, Scots and Attacotti attack from the north; the southern coasts were attacked by Franks and Saxons, who apparently threatened London itself. One Roman general, in command of coastal defences, was killed; numerous Roman soldiers deserted. The Saxon Shore defences – a line of fortresses along the south-east British coast from Brancaster in Norfolk to Portchester in Hampshire, which faced a similar line of defences on the north Gallic coastline – had clearly not worked.

It has been customary to assume that Ammianus was not exaggerating, and that there really was a *conspiratio*, an alliance between the various barbarian peoples, from Ireland to northern Germany. Not only is this inherently unlikely, but there was a good reason for Ammianus to exaggerate the scale of the disaster. He was writing during the reign of Theodosius the Great, and it was the emperor's father, Count Theodosius, who had been sent to Britain to restore order. Count Theodosius was, according to Ammianus, outstandingly successful, and 'left the provinces [of Britain] dancing for joy'.[7] Claudian's panegyric to the Emperor Honorius also talked of the victories of Count Theodosius (Honorius's grandfather), with little attention to geographical or (probably) historical exactness: 'The Orkneys were drenched with slaughter of the Saxons; Thule was warm with Pictish blood; and icy Ireland wept for the heaps of Scottish dead.'[8]

Archaeological traces of destruction and of rebuilding have often been assigned to the disaster of 367 and the reconstruction of Count Theodosius, mostly more as a result of wishful thinking than anything else. Indeed, it has also been suggested that there is in fact no real evidence for destruction at all:[9] perhaps Ammianus really did exaggerate the danger. And if Theodosius did restore order, and to some extent restore the defences, he did not end the barbarian threat. An attack by Picts and Scots in 382 was mentioned in a fifth-century chronicle, for instance; there were no doubt others, records of which do not survive.

Barbarian raids were not the only activity which helped to weaken the Roman hold on Britain. On either side of the year 400 there were also usurpations, which may have damaged Britain even more than the rest of the Empire. In 383 a Spanish soldier who had served with Count Theodosius was proclaimed Emperor by the troops in Britain. His name was Magnus Maximus, and despite his Spanish origins he played a role in later British legend: as Maxen Wledig (the Welsh form of his name) he appears as the ancestor of the kings of Dyfed. He left for the Continent, possibly withdrawing British troops, and did not meet defeat until he met the Emperor Theodosius's forces in North Italy in 388. In 406, the British army elevated Marcus as Emperor, and after his death they chose a Briton called Gratian, who like Marcus lasted only a matter of days or weeks. Finally, Constantine III was proclaimed Emperor by the troops in Britain – almost exactly a century after Constantine the Great had himself been proclaimed Emperor in Britain – and immediately moved to take control of Gaul. Constantine III survived to threaten the legitimate Emperor Honorius until 411, but by then Britain was effectively no longer a part of the Roman Empire.

It is always assumed that Constantine III withdrew troops from Britain, mainly because it is difficult to see him establishing his power in Gaul without doing so. But the significant comment to make on these usurpations –

those of Maximus, Marcus, Gratian and Constantine – is that they show that the troops in Britain thought of themselves still as very much part of the Roman Empire. Their object was not to declare independence, the better to defend Britain from its enemies, but to unite the western Empire. Indeed, the last three usurpations, of 406 and 407, were very likely reacting to the state of affairs on the Continent – the attacks on Italy and Gaul by various groups of barbarians, which left those provinces in a state of turmoil. Constantine III was not actually very effective in his efforts to restore order in Gaul; but nor was the Emperor Honorius. It might be argued that these usurpers saw Gaul as more important to defend than Britain, and were prepared to sacrifice the latter. But there is actually no reason to believe that they thought Britain was a province about to be lost. Even in 410, when Honorius told the British to defend themselves, there was not necessarily any reason to think that a future expedition might not be sent to Britain, as it had been under Count Theodosius or Stilicho. The British were still requesting such aid a generation or more later.

However, there is one puzzling but intriguing comment on these events from the Greek historian Zosimus, writing in the early sixth century but using earlier written sources, in a passage describing the events after the barbarian invasion of 407:

> [The barbarians] reduced the inhabitants of Britain and some of the Gallic peoples to such straits that they revolted from the Roman Empire, no longer submitted to Roman law, and reverted to their native customs. The Britons, therefore, armed themselves and ran many risks to ensure their own safety and free their cities from the attacking barbarians. The whole of Armorica and other Gallic provinces, in imitation of the Britons, freed themselves in the same way, by expelling the Roman magistrates and establishing the government they wanted.[10]

It was shortly after this (although in the context of a discussion about military problems in Italy, which has led some people to think that it is *Bruttium* – Abruzzi in southern Italy – that is being referred to, and not Britain) that Zosimus reported that the Emperor Honorius wrote to the British *civitates* telling them to look to their own resources.[11] This might indicate that the Britons and Gauls, when they 'expelled their Roman rulers', were actually expelling the supporters of Honorius's enemy, the usurper Constantine III. And there are inexplicable comments in the passage quoted above, which may simply suggest that really Zosimus did not know very much about Britain. Could Britain really have been affected by the barbarians who came across the Rhine: the Burgundians, the Vandals and others? This seems highly unlikely. Or was it that Britain was coincidentally attacked by other barbarians (Saxons?) at that same time? And, finally, did the Britons, at this point, really 'throw off Roman rule and live independently, no longer subject to Roman laws' like some Gauls?

We have to remember that Zosimus was writing in the East, far from Britain, and at a time in which the Britons certainly *were* living independently: he may merely have been trying to offer a date as to when this began. But Edward Thompson, and others, have seen this as a possible reflection of the activities of the Bacaudae in Britain. This is the word (Celtic in origin) which Latin sources use to describe local rebellions, which were particularly serious in Gaul in the second and fifth decades of the fifth century. Thompson (a Marxist historian) would think in terms of 'peasant rebels', engaged in social rebellion; Halsall and others would rather see these people as 'local gentry', illegally taking up arms to protect themselves from barbarians, and perhaps from Roman tax-collectors.[12] Zosimus suggests to us that the end of Roman Britain might have been a process hastened on by British resentment at Roman exploitation, or indeed that there might have been pro-Roman and anti-Roman groups in Britain; but it is fragile evidence on which to build a hypothesis.

Gildas and the end of Roman Britain

Our main problem is that after 410 there is very little mention of Britain in continental sources. There is the *Gallic Chronicle of 452*, which has two significant (and possibly genuine) entries: that in 410 or 411 Britain was devastated by the Saxons, and that in 441 Britain fell under Saxon dominion. Later in the century there is the *Life of St Germanus of Auxerre* by Constantius, which refers to the visits of the saint to Britain to combat the heresy of Pelagianism, during one of which he defeats the Picts and Saxons by organising the British army to shout 'Alleluia' at them. We also have various indications from Continental sources of British emigrants to Gaul. Most of these were clerics, but there was also a military leader called Riothamus, who had an army of Britons in the Loire area *c.* 470; presumably he was part of the exodus which turned Armorica into *Britannia*, or Brittany.

But for the history of Britain for the centuries immediately following 410 we are largely dependent on insular sources: and for over a century this means just one text, *De Excidio Britanniae* (*The Ruin of Britain*), ascribed to Gildas. We could start by asking the five questions we should ask of any text (see above p. 12): Where was it written? When? By whom? Why? And where did the information some from? We do not know where Gildas wrote; we do not know when; we cannot be certain that we know by whom; and we do not know where the information came from. It is fairly clear why he wrote, however. He wanted to lament the sins of the present, and to warn that God's punishment would inevitably follow if there was no moral reform. It was written at a time of peace: that, for Gildas, is part of the problem. Peace brings prosperity; prosperity brings luxury; luxury brings vice. And vice, ultimately, will bring God's punishment, which typically comes in the form of enemy attack.

Gildas addresses five people by name in the course of his diatribe: five British kings, 'Constantine, tyrant whelp of the lioness of Dumnonia', a murderer and adulterer; 'Aurelius Caninus, lion-whelp', a parricide and fornicator; 'Vortipor, tyrant of the Demetae', rapist; Cuneglasus, 'despiser of God'; and Maglocunus, 'first in evil, mightier than many both in power and malice'. Three of these kings can possibly be identified with kings who figure in the Welsh king-lists (with their names in their Welsh form): the most certain of these is Maglocunus, Maelgwn of Gwynedd. But the Welsh king-lists do not give us dates by which we might fix Gildas's text more accurately.[13] After very specific charges against the kings, Gildas complains in more general terms about the British clergy, who are fools, liars, and hypocrites, and 'who have church buildings, but go to them for the sake of base profit'.[14] Gildas quotes frequently from the Bible, particularly from the Old Testament prophets (on whom he is clearly modelling himself); his prose style, once thought of as being obscurely provincial, is now thought of as being as skilled and complex as anything produced by someone trained in the secular schools of Gaul or northern Italy in the later fifth century.

Gildas is not valued today for what he says about the sins of his contemporaries, although that for him was the whole purpose of his book: he is quoted for the twenty-two chapters (out of 110) which offer an historical sketch of the end of Roman Britain. It is a somewhat infuriating sketch, probably based largely on oral information, and offering nothing in the way of dates. Apart from a reference to the Roman patrician Aëtius, 'three times consul', his only 'date' is the reference to a great battle between the British and the Saxons at Mount Badon, 'pretty well the last defeat of the villains, and certainly not the least', which he locates by saying 'That was the year of my birth; as I know, one month of the forty-fourth year since then has already passed'.[15] However, the Latin of that sentence is obscure. When Bede read it, perhaps using a text of Gildas that was better copied than ours, he seems to have thought that Gildas was saying that the battle of Mount Badon was forty-four years after the arrival of the Angles and Saxons in Britain.[16] Ian Wood has suggested that the passage might mean 'From that time until the year of the siege of Mount Badon, the most recent and certainly not the least slaughter of the trouble-makers, the forty-fourth year begins, as I know, for it is the forty-fourth year since my birth; and now a month has passed [since Badon].'[17] Not only do we not know when Gildas was born, we cannot even be sure of the significance of Mount Badon, the only named military encounter in Gildas's text: and, of course, we do not know where Mount Badon is.

That there are no dates to help us in Gildas's text is not to offer any complaint against Gildas as an historian. There could have been no agreed dating system in Britain in Gildas's day. Romans had used the names of the consuls elected for the year for the dating of official documents, but this required the keeping of consular tables and was cumbersome. Romans also used the number of years since the founding of the city of Rome (753 BC in our system), and there were some local systems in some provinces (year 1 in both Spain and Africa was the date of the foundation of the Roman province). It is probable that individual kingdoms in Gildas's day used the regnal years of their king, but, as we have seen, Gildas was writing for the subjects of at least five British kings. The BC/AD system was not used by any historian until Bede, in the early eighth century. In short, Gildas had little choice but to be vague.

Let us run through the story as Gildas tells it. The recurring theme is that 'ever since it was first inhabited, Britain has been ungratefully rebelling, stiff-necked and haughty, now against God, now against its own countrymen, sometimes even against kings from abroad and their subjects'.[18] The British were unwilling to submit to Rome; they were lacking in enthusiasm for the new religion of Christianity. As soon as Christianity became the religion of the Emperor, they opted for heresy and treason. When Maximus rebelled, Gildas said, he withdrew the whole army, leaving the land to be ravaged by Picts and Scots. The British called for help: the Romans sent troops, told the British to build a wall, and left. The British, being leaderless and irrational, did build a wall from sea to sea, but it was of turf and thus no good. The Picts and Scots came again. The Romans again responded to the British plea, and this time they built a stone wall, and also forts on the south coast (the first hint that the Saxons might be a threat too). But the Romans had had enough: they said that the British should defend themselves. They gave the British stirring advice, and left them *exemplaria instituendorum armorum*, which Winterbottom translates as 'manuals on weapon training'.[19]

The gross error that Gildas makes in dating Hadrian's Wall and the Antonine Wall (if those are the walls he is referring to) have led some to dismiss him as a serious historian. But if he was writing in southern Britain in the late fifth century or later, how could he have discovered the dates of the walls? – indeed, it is only since the nineteenth century that we have known that the main wall was built by Hadrian. It is interesting that Gildas always treats the Romans as a foreign people who come occasionally to help the British. Whenever it was Gildas was writing, he has lost the concept that the British – his own ancestors – had themselves been Roman citizens. The end of Roman Britain must have come somewhere between 410 and Gildas's own time, because the end of Roman Britain really came when the British no longer felt themselves to be Romans.

As soon as the Romans left, Gildas wrote:

> there eagerly emerged from the coracles that had carried them across the sea-valleys, the foul hordes of Scots and Picts, like dark throngs of worms who wriggle out of narrow fissures in the rock when the sun is high and the weather grows warm. They were to some extent different in their customs, but they were in perfect accord in their greed for bloodshed: and they were readier to cover their villainous faces with hair than their private parts and neighbouring regions with clothes.[20]

The Picts and Scots seized everything north of the Wall, and the country to the south fell into disorder and chaos. The Britons appealed to 'Agitius, thrice consul', who is usually assumed to be the patrician Aëtius (who achieved his third consulship in 446). The appeal went unanswered, but affairs improved on their own, the Picts and the Scots refraining from further attacks. Peace was restored, and with peace came luxury and vice.

The British, under 'the proud tyrant', convened a council to determine how to deal with future attacks, and they decided to invite in the Saxons to help them. Three *cyuli* arrived (Gildas's transliteration of the English *keel* into Latin); and then more came. They asked for supplies, 'falsely representing themselves as soldiers ready to undergo extreme dangers for their excellent hosts'.[21] They asked for more; when it was refused they rebelled, and laid the island low, tearing fortifications down, butchering the inhabitants even in the mountains. After much suffering, the British rallied, under their leader Ambrosius Aurelianus, a son of those who had worn the purple (?) and grandfather to Gildas's contemporary kings. Victory went to the British, and then to their enemies, until the siege of Mount Badon. To this day, Gildas wrote, the towns remain 'deserted, in ruins and unkempt', and 'people daily rush headlong to hell'.[22]

It is a powerful story, told in vivid and memorable language. Bede used it as the basis for most of his account of the collapse of the Roman Empire, and he delighted in the story that it told: a story of sinful Britons, on the verge of greater punishment by God when they proved deaf to Gildas's pleas. Bede despised the Britons of his day; for Bede the Saxons (or, as he would have said, Angles) had been the instruments of God's punishment on the Britons.

But it is a story which raises enormous numbers of problems. It is possible to reconcile it with most other written sources, such as Bede's *History* or the *Anglo-Saxon Chronicle*, but that is largely because the *Chronicle* depends on Bede, and Bede was almost totally dependent on Gildas. Bede did do his best to date Gildas's account. He noted that the invitation to the Saxons came not long after the appeal to Aëtius, which he seems to date to the very year of Aëtius's third consulship (446), rather than, properly, to any of the years between that and his assassination, during which Aëtius could be described as 'three times consul'. But in his chronological recapitulation at the end of the *History* he has the entry:

> 449 Marcianus and Valentinianus ruled as co-Emperors for seven years. In their time the English came to Britain on the invitation of the Britons.[23]

Thus we have what remained until the twentieth century the orthodox date for the *adventus Saxonum*, the coming of the Saxons: 449. It was a date derived from Gildas by Bede's ingenuity, and it enabled him to provide a date for Mount Badon as well, forty-four years after the *adventus*, thus around 493. Since Gildas seems to say that he wrote forty-four years after this, we come to our traditional date in the 540s for Gildas's work.

Not only is this a precarious edifice to raise on just one assumed date (the letter to Aëtius), but it certainly does not fit in with other evidence. Gildas's notion that the Picts and the Scots were the scourge *before* the letter to Aëtius, and the Saxons the scourge *after*, has been the major problem for anyone trying to make sense of Gildas's story. Bede believed it totally, for he used it to redate, wrongly, the visit of St Germanus to Britain: he thought that St Germanus's meeting with hostile Saxons showed that the visit must be *after* 449, while nowadays historians would use the *Life of St Germanus* to demonstrate that Gildas and Bede were wrong, and the Saxons were in Britain long before 449. Indeed, as we have seen, the *Gallic Chronicle of 452* thought that the Saxons had been a serious threat to the British since at least 410, and that they had subjected most of Britain by 441. Molly Miller suggested that Gildas in fact offers two narratives, one of invasion from the north and one from the south, and that these should be read as happening contemporaneously rather than consecutively. This reading involves using the 'meanwhile' which begins chapter 22 (near the end of Gildas's historical sketch) to mean, in practice, 'now, let us go back fifty years and see what has been happening in the south of Britain'.[24] The appeal to Aëtius would thus be an appeal to a Gallic general to help the Britons against attacks by Saxons in the south, rather than against Picts and Scots in the north, which does make rather more sense. It may be that Gildas found it easier to construct a clear narrative if he wrote first of Picts and Scots, and then of Saxons. Most modern commentators have not accepted Miller's neat solution, however; perhaps its very neatness is suspicious.

The question of dating in Gildas is made much more difficult by the support that has been growing over the last decade or so for the idea that Gildas did not write in the 540s, but fifty years earlier, in the late fifth century. The earlier date would please the Latinists, for it is not easy to see how Gildas could have acquired his particular Latinity as late as the sixth century. It would mean abandoning the identification of the author with the St Gildas who seems indeed to have lived in the mid-sixth century, and relocating the kings he mentions some two generations earlier; but these are not insuperable problems.

The above discussion may seem involved, and inconclusive, and indeed it is. So much of the history of Britain in the fifth and sixth centuries has been written from Gildas's account, that it is important to realise what a problematical text it is. Can we draw anything conclusive from it at all? We can assume that the kings Gildas writes for did exist; and it is unlikely that Gildas invented Ambrosius Aurelianus or the siege of Mons Badonicus. There is no reason to reject the idea that Saxons were invited in to help defend Britain against the Picts and Scots (or other Saxons): this was perfectly in line with Roman thinking elsewhere in Europe, as we have seen. Indeed, Gildas uses some of the technical language used of such treaties with barbarians. The process by which an armed group of barbarians moves slowly from paid mercenaries to political authority over the subjects of their former employers happened again and again on the Continent. In each case on the Continent the transfer of authority happened for two reasons: the Emperors were unable to exert their command over a distant province, and there was sufficient will on the part of the provincials – aristocrats and others – to favour this transfer, as offering better protection for their property and lives than a distant and impotent Emperor. The difference between Britain and the rest of the Western Empire may be that the Saxons took over without any local good will. The transfer of power to barbarians on the Continent resulted in little disruption to local power structures or to the basics of Roman life; in Britain that disruption appears total.

The Arthurian gap

Gildas provides us with our best contemporary evidence for the fifth and sixth centuries. Otherwise we have the dry names in king lists and the very dubious records of the *Anglo-Saxon Chronicle* and the much later compilation known as the *Historia Brittonum*, and other annals, such as the *Annals of Ulster* and the *Welsh Annals*. All these were compiled at a later date, and we do not know to what extent the contemporary realities of the authors' times were read back into the past. We have already seen (p. 12) the likelihood that the fifth and sixth century entries of the *Anglo-Saxon Chronicle* were largely fictions: or, to put it more generously, were attempts by the ninth-century chronicler to explain the present through the past.

Bede himself, famously, adds just a few facts to what he finds in Gildas and the *Life of St Germanus*. He tells us that Gildas's Saxons were in fact Angles, Saxons and Jutes, who came from three different parts of the northern Germanic world. He tells us that Gildas's 'proud tyrant' was called Vortigern (though this is arguably merely a translation into Welsh of 'proud tyrant'), that the two Saxon leaders whom Vortigern invited were called Hengist and Horsa, and that Horsa's monument was still to be seen in Kent. But that is all. Did Hengist and Horsa – words meaning 'stallion' and 'horse' – really exist, or are they figures of legend? Bede knows only four dates in British history between 449 and the sending of missionaries to the English in 596: the solar eclipses of 538 and 540, the beginning of the reign of Ida, king of the Northumbrian Angles, in 547, and the arrival of St Columba in Iona in 565. The only date relevant to the history of the English is thus Ida's kingship: Bede almost certainly worked out Ida's date from a list of Northumbrian kings with their regnal years. He probably placed one king's reign after another, ignoring the possibility of joint rules or gaps in the kingship. The only dates which can actually be checked externally are the solar eclipses. He got those right.

If there is a Dark Ages in British history, this is it. And it is in the dark heart of this Dark Ages that tradition has placed King Arthur. There is a gap, into which Arthur fits perfectly. There have basically been three approaches to Arthur: to regard his existence as certain; to regard it as possible; and to regard it as an unnecessary hypothesis. At one extreme lies John Morris, whose book *The Age of Arthur* constructed a complex political history for Britain in the fifth and early sixth century, building hypothesis upon hypothesis with enormous ingenuity, imagination, and wishful thinking, and making Arthur's reign of central importance. Somewhat more cautious was Leslie Alcock, the excavator of the hillfort at South Cadbury (Somerset), which one sixteenth-century antiquary had identified with Camelot; Alcock's *Arthur's Britain* does examine the evidence for Arthur in some detail, but like Morris concludes that Arthur may well have been the really significant figure that tradition suggests. At the other end of the spectrum is Nicholas Higham, whose recent book *The English Conquest* has concluded not only that Arthur is fictional, but that the political context in which he has generally been inserted is equally fictitious.

There is one event above all others that is normally associated with Arthur, and that is the siege of Mount Badon, *mons Badonicus*. The *Welsh Annals* (perhaps compiled as late as the tenth century) date this battle to 516, 'in which Arthur carried the cross of our Lord Jesus Christ for three days and three nights on his shoulders, and the British were the victors';[25] it also says that Arthur and Medraut (the Mordred of later romance) fell at the battle of Camlann in 537. The ninth-century compilation known as the *Historia Brittonum* lists the twelve victories of Arthur, of which Mount Badon was the last: 'and in it nine hundred and sixty men fell in one day, from a single charge of Arthur's, and no one laid them low save he alone; and he was victorious in all his campaigns'.[26] It is not difficult to fit the origins of these fantasies into Gildas's story. Gildas seems to think that the siege of Mount Badon was important; he doesn't mention the name of the victor – any more, as Kenneth Jackson argued, than a Victorian would need to specify that it was Wellington who won Waterloo.[27] Thus we have numerous histories which imagine that Arthur turned the tide of the Saxon advance, and established a generation or more of peace for the British kingdoms in the west of the island. Some imagine that this is a local south-west British matter: they associate Badon with Bath or Badbury Rings (Dorset); others take their cue from the twelve battles of the *Historia Brittonum*, and have Arthur ranging the length and breadth of Britain. The fact that there are sites and monuments named after Arthur from Scotland to Cornwall and Brittany has also suggested to some his wide-ranging political power.

It has been quite common for historians to subscribe to the 'no smoke without fire' theory of Arthur, even though the smoke is very thin, and indistinguishable from highland mist. The *Historia Brittonum* appears now to be the earliest written reference to Arthur: the Welsh poem known as *Gododdin*, which talks about the bravery of a warrior, 'though he was no Arthur', used to be seen as sixth-century, but that particular passage is now generally agreed to be later than the *Historia Brittonum*. Even if it is based on early tradition, Richard Barber has suggested that the Arthur referred to in the poem may not be 'our' Arthur, but our earliest certain Arthur: Artuir, the son of King Aedan of Dalriada, the Irish colony in south-west Scotland.[28] He was killed, probably fighting the Picts, sometime around AD 600. There is another candidate for an historical Arthur, too: Lucius Artorius Castus, *praefectus* of the Sixth Legion at York, who led two legions from Britain against the Armoricans of north-west Gaul, AD *c.* 200: we know about him from the memorial in his native Dalmatia. 'He is at least a war-leader of eminence and has the right name,' wrote Oliver Padel.[29]

Padel and Higham have both argued, in their different ways, that a British war-leader called Arthur did not exist at all as an historical figure, let alone an historical figure in a specific sixth-century context. Padel compares the earliest known legends about Arthur, from chapters 56 and 73 of the *Historia Brittonum*, with the similar legends in Irish tradition, which centre around the folk-hero Finn. Stories about Finn and his warband (the Fenians) are to be found all over the world where *q*-Celtic was spoken, just as Arthurian legends are to be found throughout the *p*-Celtic world: Finn was protector of his land, he too has a list of battle honours, and so on. The stories about Arthur in the *Historia Brittonum* have a folkloric element about them which is quite different from the stories usually recorded of historical personages, such as the *Historia*'s story of Arthur's dog Cabal, who impressed his footprint upon a stone which can still be seen today. Like Arthur, Finn was brought into reality by being inserted into an historical context – in Finn's case, twice: his death was recorded in 283 in one set of annals, while another tradition had him defending Ireland from the Vikings in the ninth century.

Higham does not speculate about the possible folk origins of tales of Arthur. He concentrates on the sixth century, arguing that it is Gildas's words concerning Mount Badon which have led to the necessity for Arthur, by allowing readers to conclude that Mount Badon was a significant victory, and therefore needed a significant leader. Higham argues that even Gildas implies that Mount Badon was a very temporary victory; he believes that, far from living in a kingdom which, thanks to Arthur's legacy, still preserved its independence, Gildas lived in Wiltshire or Dorset, in an area which was already paying tribute to the Saxons. The British may have wished for a folk hero like Arthur to rescue them from the Saxon yoke, as they did down to modern times; but there was no Arthur forthcoming.

I wrote this section in May 1998, in the week in which a challenge was launched on BBC Radio 4's *Today* programme, offering £10,000 to anyone who can prove that Arthur was not from north of the Scottish border. The money seems safe; proof in these matters is an impossible dream.

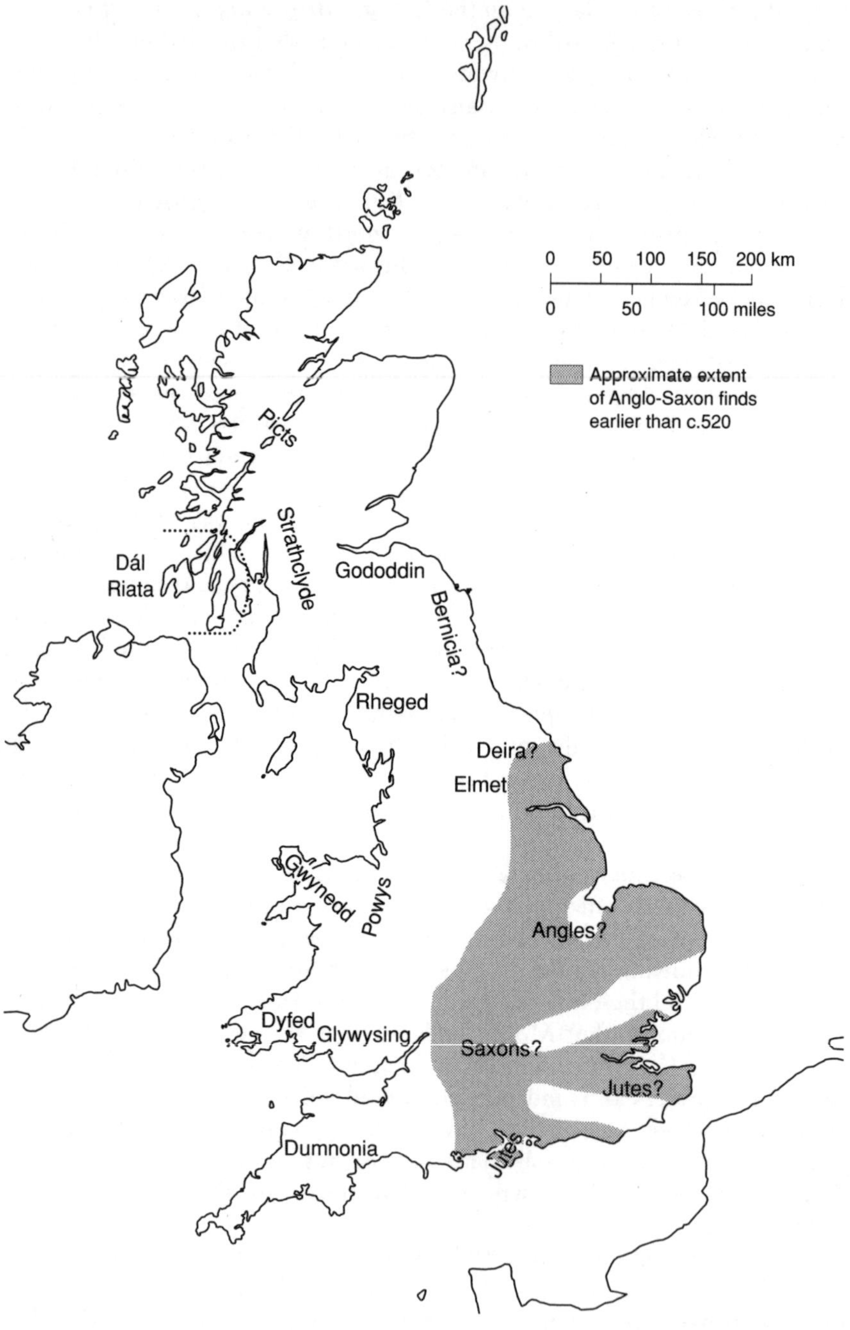

Map 3 Britain in *c.* 500

Migrants and settlers, 1: the Picts and Scots

Not all those involved in raiding the Roman Empire actually turned from raiding to establishing permanent settlements. It could be that becoming a settler either involved force – the Huns forcing the Visigoths into the Roman Empire – or a social structure that allowed for or encouraged mobility. The activity of the Normans in the eleventh century, who settled not only in Britain but also in southern Italy and Sicily, certainly had something to do with inheritance customs, whereby eldest sons inherited the whole property and younger sons had to fend for themselves. The *inactivity* of the Picts in the fifth or sixth centuries – active raiders who did not seem to colonise – may likewise have been something to do with their own society: some form of partible inheritance or kinship ownership would not have offered the same encouragement to move into new areas. It seems unlikely to be anything to do with the alleged matrilineal system of the Picts, which nowadays is treated rather sceptically.

The settlement in Britain of the *Scotti* from Ireland was likewise of a fairly limited nature, compared to the settlements of other barbarian peoples, but it certainly involved more than just what we call 'Scotland'. The exact nature of those settlements is quite unknown. We know from the *Confessio* of St Patrick that the Irish made slave-raids on western Britain, and some of the settlements may have been an extension of these armed raids. It may also be, as Myles Dillon imagined, that some Irish in western Britain were welcome *foederati*, troops invited by the British to defend them against the Saxons.[30] For some areas we have virtually no evidence. The fact the Manx language is closely related to Irish, as well as a large number of Irish place-names in the Isle of Man, shows that the island (which had never been treated as part of *Britannia* by the Romans) was thoroughly settled by the Irish. There is a certain amount of debatable evidence, from later church dedications for instance, that there were Irish settlements in West Cornwall.[31] But the bulk of the evidence for settlement relates to Western Wales and to south-west Scotland.

The route from Antrim across to Galloway was obviously the shortest route from Ireland to Britain, but the route from Leinster to Anglesey was probably as well known then as it is for travellers from Dublin to Holyhead today. North-west Wales has traces of an Irish presence in place-names, above all in those which reflect the Irish word for Leinster and Leinstermen: the Lleyn peninsula itself, which juts out into the Irish Sea, and names such as Mallaen and Dinllaen. There are also Irish personal names on inscriptions in this area. There is rather more substantial evidence for south-west Wales (for the area which began to be known as Dyfed in the early Middle Ages, from the name of the pre-Roman people of the Demetae), but it is fiendishly difficult to know precisely what this evidence means. Later traditions in both Wales and Ireland suggest that Irish took over territory here. The *Historia Brittonum* reports on the Irish:

> Later came the Kindred of Eight and lived there with all their race in Britain until today. Istoreth son of Istorinus held Dal Riada with his people. Bolg with his people held the Isle of Man and other islands about. The sons of Liathan prevailed in the country of the Demetians, and in other countries, that is Gower and Cydweli.[32]

The 'sons of Liathan' is an exact translation of 'Uí Liatháin', the Irish people who lived in the Cork area, on the southern coast of Ireland. An Old Irish text, *The Expulsion of the Déisi*, apparently from the eighth century, claims that it was the Déisi who went, under their leader Eochaid: the list of his descendants given in the text matches in a number of cases the later Welsh list of the kings of Dyfed.[33] The Déisi, or Déisi Muman, were neighbours of the Uí Liatháin, living between Cork and Waterford. The easiest way of reconciling these two sources (if it is not dangerous to think that reconciliation of such late sources is at all possible) is to imagine that both groups contributed to the settlement in Dyfed.

There is, however, much more substantial evidence for the Irish in south-west Wales than these late sources. There are place-names which appear to be of Irish origin, particularly in north Pembrokeshire, and there are inscribed memorial stones. Thomas has broken the early inscriptions (up to AD *c.* 700) down into four types. Type (a) have inscriptions wholly in ogam script, that is, in a script developed in Ireland in which the letters are made up of groups of straight or diagonal lines, normally cut onto the edge of a stone (but initially probably devised for wood). Type (b) are the 'bilinguals', with the Irish inscription in ogam repeated in Latin with the Latin alphabet; type (c) has a full Latin inscription, but with only the name repeated in ogam; and type (d) is solely in Latin, with one of the standard Christian formulae, such as HIC IACET . . . (Here lies . . .). Thomas suggests that these types may in fact be in chronological order:[34] in other words, that the inscribed epitaph, such as are found in numbers in south-east Ireland, was an introduction by the Irish settlers, which were gradually taken over by those more used to Latin ways. Some of the stones show not only bilingualism, but biculturalism. For instance, there is a stone from Clydai with the two inscriptions ETTERN[? MAQI VIC]TOR in ogam and ETTERN- FILI VICTO[RIS], in Latin characters, meaning that a family with the very Roman sounding Aeternus son of Victorius thought it worthwhile erecting a stone with that name translated into Irish and ogam. These Irish immigrants seem to have considerable social status, and are able to introduce new cultural elements – the funerary inscription, the ogam alphabet and the Irish language – into south-west Wales. Are they allies of the British leaders, or their conquerors? In either case, judging on the evidence of the inscriptions alone, their influence dies out in the seventh century.

The most long-lasting and certain contribution of the Irish to the mainland was their settlement in western Scotland. Place-name evidence, above all the appearance of names beginning in *Kirk-*, *Kil-* and *Slew-*, show that there was an Irish influence of some kind in the far south-west of Scotland, in Galloway, although all in an ecclesiastical context. But the most significant event was the establishment of the kingdom of Dál Riata (also called Dal Riada or Dalriada) in the far west, in Argyll, stretching from Kintyre north to Ardnamurchan, and including islands such as Jura, Islay and Mull. It was here that the Irish language established itself, eventually spreading northwards through the Highlands and Islands and beyond, ousting British and Pictish dialects, and establishing Gaelic as the language of northern and western Scotland; this development probably happened simultaneously with the spread of English, following the Anglian conquest of the eastern seaboard in the seventh century. Those who cherish Gaelic as the native language of Scotland have decided to adopt the language of one invading people of the early Middle Ages rather than that of another; the language of the indigenous people, the Picts, has disappeared altogether.

The early history of Dál Riata is very uncertain. Archaeology is of no help at all: without the historical sources and place-names we would not suspect an Irish colonisation at all. The evidence is thus late, not contemporary. Tradition had it that the first king of Dál Riata was Fergus Mór mac Eirc, around 500, but this did not necessarily mean the beginning of Irish settlement in the region, merely the emergence of a king. Initially settlement may have been from several different kingdoms on the north-eastern coast of Ireland, but Fergus Mór himself was from the Antrim kingdom of Dál Riata, which gave its name to the better known kingdom in Scotland. In a meeting at Druim Cett (Co. Derry) in 575, the constitutional position of the Irish kingdom of Dál Riata was agreed by the two great kings of the area, Aédán mac Gabráin of the Scottish Dál Riata and Aéd mac Ainmerech, the powerful king of Ulster. He came from the Uí Néill, the descendants of the semi-legendary figure Niall of the Nine Hostages, whom later Irish tradition remembered as a king who had raided Roman Britain. Mediator at Druim Cett was a figure whom we shall be meeting again: St Columba. Columba's credentials were ideal. He was abbot of the monastery of Iona, in Aédán's kingdom and under Aédán's patronage, and indeed, if we are to believe his hagiographer Adomnán, it was Columba who had been ordered by an angel to ordain Aédán as king the previous year. But he was also himself a member of the Uí Néill dynasty, a cousin to Aéd. The compromise reached at Druim Ceatt seems to have been that the Irish Dál Riata were to pay tribute to the king of the Scottish Dál Riata, but were to be regarded as subjects of the Uí Néill king.

Migrants and settlers, 2: the British

The British too contribute to the movement of peoples in late Antiquity, with one possible migration, and two much more certain migrations. The possible one, and still much disputed, is that of Cunedda and the Votadini.

Later tradition had it that Cunedda and his sons came down from the kingdom of the Votadini (Gododdin: Lothian in Scotland), to settle in north Wales; the kings of Gwynedd would later trace their descent from him. It has been thought that this may represent one type of migration known elsewhere in the Roman Empire: the virtually forced removal of a people by the Romans for strategic reasons, in order to defend a significant area. But scholars are generally agreed now that this tradition is almost certainly an invented one, without any historical substance: the purpose for which it may have been invented, however, remains obscure.

There is no doubt that the migration of Britons to Armorica, the north-west peninsula of Gaul, happened, even if there are serious problems about the details. Gildas says that the British were fleeing the Saxons, but if many of them were coming from south-west Britain and south Wales, as most think, then it is rather more likely that they were fleeing the raids of the Irish. The movement certainly began in the fifth century, and one of the most significant figures is a man called Riotimus or Riothamus. Jordanes, a Gothic historian of the sixth century, said that Riothamus came across the sea in the 460s with an army of 12,000 men, to help the Emperor Anthemius against the Visigoths, a Germanic people who were by then settled in south-west Gaul. He failed; he was defeated in the area of Bourges. A letter of the Gallo-Roman grandee Sidonius Apollinaris survives, in which he apologises profusely to Riothamus for raising the matter of the rumour that the British immigrants were enticing slaves away from their Gallo-Roman masters.[35] We can say little more about him, although twentieth-century historians have tried. The Breton scholar L. Fleuriot has argued that 'Riothamus' should be read as 'Rigotamos', a title meaning 'great king', and that Riothamus was actually Ambrosius Aurelianus, the British leader mentioned by Gildas, while the Arthurian enthusiast Geoffrey Ashe has suggested that Riothamus was the 'original Arthur', and that the traditions preserved in Geoffrey of Monmouth of Arthur's campaigns in Gaul preserved a memory of Riothamus and his British Expeditionary Force on the Loire.[36] We must discard such fantasies: most of the 'traditions' preserved in Geoffrey of Monmouth actually stem from his own fertile imagination in the 1130s, and were probably intended as some obscure comment on the Continental ambitions of his contemporary Anglo-Norman kings.

Riothamus is not the only named Briton in Gaul in the fifth century. Apart from some British ecclesiastics who clearly took refuge in southern Gaul, there are some others who can be associated with the British 'colony' in Armorica, such as Mansuetus, 'bishop of the Britons', at the church council in Tours in 461. By the late sixth century, in the writings of Gregory, bishop of Tours (in whose ecclesiastical province Armorica lay), we can see that the Church in Armorica was quite independent of the rest of the Gallic Church, and the British warlords or kings, whom Gregory calls 'counts' (as if they really were officials of the Frankish kings), were conducting their own private wars and raids without reference to the rest of Gaul. Gregory's contemporary, the poet Venantius Fortunatus, referred to the Roman town of Rennes as 'Redones Britanniae', 'Rennes in Britannia': the first indication that usage had changed the name of the north-west peninsula of Gaul from Armorica ('the land of the sea') to Brittany (*Britannia*).

There is a good deal of dispute about the nature of the impact of the British emigrants on Gaul: there are still some Breton scholars, in particular, who would argue that the Celtic language which still flourishes in the province owes as much or more to the survival of Gaulish than it does to the importation of British/Welsh. Many scholars, on the other hand, believe that a British elite imposed its culture and identity upon the Gallo-Romans of north-west Gaul as successfully as the Angles and Saxons imposed theirs on south-west Britain. Cultural links were set up between Brittany and south-west Britain that lasted for centuries; the self-awareness of the Bretons that they were a separate people allowed them to preserve their effective political independence from France until the end of the Middle Ages, and their separate identity from the French until the twentieth century and beyond.

Some British refugees ended up further afield than Brittany. There are several distinguished British clerics who found themselves a home in the relative peace of southern Gaul, the most distinguished of whom – best known for his theological writings – was Faustus, who became abbot of the elite island monastery of Lérins and then bishop of Riez. The farthest flung refugees, however, are the ones we know least about: the ones who went to north-west Spain. Present at the Council of Braga in 572 was a bishop with the Celtic name Mailoc, who came from the *ecclesia Britonensis*, the British church. But a document from the same period specifies that there was a *sedes Britonorum*, a see of the British, in Spain and talks of 'the churches which are among the British' in that see. That see eventually became Mondoñedo, 70 km north of Lugo. The phrase seems to suggest that only Britons lived in that see: even if this is an exaggeration, the dominance of the Britons within this very extensive territory strongly suggests that it was more than just a few immigrants from Britain who came to Spain.[37] The bishops of Mondoñedo use the title *episcopus Britoniensis* down to the end of the eleventh century; and not far from that town is the place-name Santa Maria de Bretoña.

Migrants and settlers, 3: Angles, Saxons and Jutes

For Bede, the migration of the Germans to Britain was a relatively neat thing: the Jutes came to Kent, the Isle of Wight and parts of Hampshire, presumably from Jutland, the Danish mainland; the Saxons came from Old Saxony into the territories occupied by the South Saxons, East Saxons and West Saxons; the Angles came from *Angulus* (*Angeln* in German), between the homeland of the Jutes and Saxons, and became the East Angles, the

Middle Angles, the Mercians and the Angles to the north of the Humber. '*Angulus* is said to have remained deserted from that day to this.'[38]

There were other peoples involved, according to other documents. The Greek writer Procopius mentions Frisians, coming from what is now the Netherlands. Bede himself, elsewhere in his *History* (V.9) seems to say that the Angles and Saxons in Britain derive their origin from many peoples in Germania (from which their neighbours the Britons call them *Garmani*): these include the Frisians, Rugians, Danes, Huns, Old Saxons and 'Boructuari' (who are known in Continental sources as the Bructeri, one of the groups that made up the Franks). The archaeology seems on the whole to confirm this variety, and even to extend it. It is quite likely, for instance, that those bodies dressed like Franks who have been found in Kentish cemeteries from the sixth and seventh centuries actually *were* Franks – people from the area ruled by the Frankish kings – rather than Jutes wearing imported clothes. (Quite a lot of the problems associated with using archaeology to determine the nature and extent of migration and settlement in this period is related to the question of whether people in this period used costume and jewellery deliberately and in a precise way as a badge of ethnicity.) There are people in East Anglia in the fifth century who were burying the ashes of the cremated dead in urns which are almost identical to those used in cremation cemeteries in northern Germany; and it has been suggested that the evidence shows that potters migrated along with their decorative stamps. Jutes in Kent in the sixth century were using pottery which is very similar to that found in Jutland, and nowhere else. Rather more surprisingly, as John Hines has shown, there were women in eastern and northern England who are being buried wearing wrist-claps of a type which is only otherwise known in Norway: a relic, almost certainly, of a migration across the North Sea in the late fifth century which has no reflection in the documentary sources. It is even possible that at least one group of immigrants – or one military leader and his followers – came to East Anglia from Sweden: they had the custom of burying their elite in ships, under mounds of earth, a custom well-attested in the Stockholm area but rare elsewhere in Europe, and in one of those ship-burials, at Sutton Hoo (Suffolk), were found a Swedish helmet and shield.

The evidence for the participation of some of these peoples in the migration is fairly tenuous: wrist-clasps for Norwegians, one word in Bede for the Rugians of the Baltic Sea coast. A recent analysis of the evidence for the Frisians by Rolf H. Bremmer[39] suggests that lack of communication between scholars in different disciplines can make tenuous evidence seem more substantial just because each scholar derives support from supposed evidence from other disciplines. The literary evidence for the Frisians is weak, he argues: Bede's list at V.9 in context is probably a list of unconverted peoples on the Continent rather than of the ancestors of the English, and Procopius is notoriously ignorant of western European affairs. The archaeological evidence for the Frisians is slowly disappearing: neither the 'Anglo-Frisian' pots nor 'Frisian' combs now appear typically Frisian. Place-names which seem to have the element *Fris* (as 'Friston') are in forms which suggest that they are later than the Migration Period, perhaps from the eighth or ninth century, when there is plenty of evidence for the activity of Frisian merchants in England. And finally, the most crucial element of all: the Frisian language. It has long been pointed out that Frisian is closer than any other Germanic dialect to English, but it is now thought that this may have been the result of both Frisian and English – neighbouring dialects in the Continental homelands – being insulated from changes that were occurring in other dialects of Continental Germanic.

Perhaps the most interesting archaeological confirmation of documentary evidence concerns Bede's statement that the homeland of the Angles still remained deserted since the Migration Period. There are several dozen cemeteries between the Elbe and the Weser from the fourth and fifth centuries which exhibit aspects of the material culture which is to be found in the fifth century in Britain, particularly in East Anglia. Those cemeteries all seem to come to an end in the later fifth century. It is possible that there was a change to a type of burial which is undetectable archaeologically, but this is unlikely. It looks as if Bede may be right; that the bulk of the population of that one small part of northern Germany did indeed decamp and move to Britain. This did not happen in Saxony and Jutland, where settlements continued into the early Middle Ages, which again confirms Bede's point: that it was the Angles who came over in such numbers as to empty their own homeland. 'Such numbers', of course, is relative: we are talking only of an area barely larger than Kent, and an area that was very probably less densely settled than Kent in the Roman period.

Although the migration was no doubt in part an opportunistic one, perhaps taking advantage of the position which a few Saxon *foederati* in Britain had won for themselves, one possible reason for the migration was a geophysical one. The landmass of Scandinavia, relieved millennia before of the weight of the ice cap of the last ice age, was still continuing to rise slowly; the landmass of North Germany was slowly sinking. Combined with a possible equally slow rise in the sea-level, this meant that in the late Roman period there seems to have been frequent flooding of the very flat North Sea coastal areas of Germany from which the Angles and the Saxons came. One solution to this was to live on artificial raised mounds, above the flood plain; these mounds, called *terpen*, can still be seen. But it was not an ideal solution; flooding by sea-water was hardly good for arable soils. A simpler solution was to migrate; this may have been the reason for the emptying of Angeln which Bede describes. In this model, the English were as much economic refugees (or, in the official language of Britain in 2000, 'bogus asylum seekers') as invaders: it is possible that some of them moved into eastern Britain even before the collapse of Roman rule.

There is no doubt about the Anglo-Saxon migration to Britain. It was not solely a military settlement: it is easier to imagine that Anglo-Saxon men, women and children came over the North Sea than that Anglo-Saxon warriors came over loaded with quantities of feminine jewellery and persuaded Romano-British women to have themselves buried wearing it. Nor indeed was Britain the only area to which these Angles and Saxons migrated. Anglo-Saxon brooches have been found in cemeteries in Picardy and Normandy, as have typically Anglo-Saxon place-names, which shows that there was actual settlement by Angles and Saxons in northern Gaul. British tourists driving south from Calais may well find themselves going through places which have an oddly English ring to them: Alincthun and Audincthun (both Pas-de-Calais) are barely disguised Gallicisations of Allington and Oddington. Such place-names are easier to date in Gaul, where they appear as a rare alien intrusion, than they are in Britain, where they came almost totally to displace the native and/or Roman place-names, particularly in the eastern half of Britain. But the cemetery evidence offers a reasonably clear guide to the areas to which the earliest settlers came, and to the rough dates.[40] The earliest Anglo-Saxon sites, up to *c.* 450, are to be found scattered between the Thames and the Humber: although there are some close to the eastern coasts, there are other sites in the Upper Thames valley and elsewhere far inland. By 475, the settlement map has begun to fill in, with the western boundary of Anglo-Saxon settlement (as measured by recognisable cemeteries) running from York down to the Salisbury region. By the 520s settlement had moved further westwards towards the Severn valley, and further northwards into North Yorkshire, but there are still areas in the east – the counties immediately to the north of the Thames, including Suffolk, and also the Weald of Kent and Sussex – where there is little evidence of settlement. Even by the 560s, although there are by then some cemeteries in Suffolk, there are still areas which seem deprived of cemeteries with typically Anglo-Saxon material. Were it not for the notoriously unreliable quality of the *Anglo-Saxon Chronicle* for this period (see above p. 12) one would be tempted to associate these gaps with surviving British enclaves within Anglo-Saxon territory: the *Chronicle* reports that in 571 the Anglo-Saxons captured four 'towns' from the British – Limbury, Aylesbury, Bensington and Eynsham – none of which were in fact far from Anglo-Saxon settlements founded more than a century earlier.

It is impossible for us to know exactly how the Angles, Saxons and Jutes transferred themselves from their homeland to Britain. But it is almost certain that they did not do it in the neat way described by Bede, for whom they all moved in organised fashion into the Anglian and Saxon kingdoms, or into the Jutish territories of Kent and Hampshire. What actually happened was that new ethnic identities were formed within the territories and/or political units that were created in the course of the sixth and seventh centuries. This is most obvious in the case of the Saxons: it is apparent that the South Saxons, the East Saxons, the Middle Saxons and the West Saxons could not have emerged as separate peoples until they had established themselves on the map of southern Britain. But it is also clear in the case of the

Jutes, the bulk of whom came to be called the Cantwara: the men of the Roman territory of Cantium (Kent). Archaeology may offer clues about the process of self-identification. The Saxons and Angles were distinct groups on the Continent, but archaeologically it is the Saxons who present the clearest evidence of a consciously distinct material culture, in particular with a series of brooch-types which concentrate in their homeland, between the Lower Elbe and the Weser: the supporting-arm brooch (which developed into the equal-armed brooch), and the saucer brooch. These were brought over to Britain, but not just to the southern areas which were eventually to become 'Saxon', but up to the Humber and beyond. They continued to be made in particular in the southern Midlands, in what would become the Anglian kingdom of Mercia. The Anglians did not seem to have such distinctive dress-elements, but, argues Hines,[41] adopted the Norwegian-style wrist-clasps in the course of the sixth century to create a distinctively Anglian form of costume for women. At the same time in Kent, dress-styles change with the adoption of some Scandinavian forms, such as small square-headed brooches and D-bracteates, which are small gold disc pendants with highly stylised ornament (probably derived from pagan religious iconography), but using them on a costume which is much closer to Frankish tradition. It is not impossible that Kent was under Frankish overlordship in the sixth century; it was certainly under Frankish cultural influence, adopting jewellery set with the semi-precious garnet, and Frankish-style belt-buckles. Finally, Saxons too in what became the Saxon kingdoms developed their own distinctive features, such as the developed saucer brooch, and the disc brooch (which may derive from Romano-British originals). These dress-distinctions become much less noticeable later in the seventh century, but they may offer a physical representation of the search for new identities in the sixth century, as mixed communities of Angles, Saxons and Jutes take on the identity of 'Angle', 'Saxon' or 'Jute', depending on the territory in which they lived, and perhaps led by a ruling class who identified with one ethnic group rather than another. By the time we get into the historical period, as Bede's *History* begins to dominate our picture of England, the memory of Saxon settlers in Anglian territory, or vice versa, has been erased from the memory.

Almost all that we can surmise about the physical settlement of the Angles, Saxons and Jutes in Britain comes from cemetery archaeology, as we have seen: cemeteries clearly demonstrate the former existence of a community, whose size and age and gender distribution may be determined by full excavation, and cemeteries also provide the material evidence, above all the pottery and the metalwork. It was a growing custom in many parts of western and northern Europe during the fifth century to bury the dead fully dressed, and sometimes with pottery and other vessels, and with other items of everyday use or symbolic value. This was a custom which has provided the archaeologist with an enormous quantity of artefacts, many of which were discovered in construction works in the nineteenth century, and are consequently without much archaeological context. We cannot be certain that the distribution which we have is actual, or a result of historical accident. How much of the relatively dense concentration of early Anglo-Saxon cemeteries in the regions of Oxford and Cambridge has to do with the numbers of interested antiquaries and archaeologists in those towns in the nineteenth and twentieth centuries?

There are two assumptions made by many people about the custom of burying items with the dead in the Migration Period: that it is a pagan custom, and a Germanic custom. Now, there are burial customs which are certainly pagan, above all the custom of burning the dead on a funeral pyre. In the Roman Empire inhumation was in fact replacing cremation even before Christianity was becoming significant, but cremation did survive among some Germanic peoples in the North. The burial of cremated ashes in funerary urns was a custom brought over to Britain, and is found above all in East Anglia: the classic site is Spong Hill (Norfolk), where some 2000 cremations were excavated.[42] Cremation seems to have died out early in the sixth century, several generations before the Christian mission to the Anglo-Saxons started (according to the accepted historical story, at least); inhumation with grave-goods of various types then continued until it gradually died out by the eighth century. It has been customary to relate the decline of the custom of 'furnished burial' with the spread of Christianity into the English countryside. But in fact comparisons with the Continent suggest that there is nothing inherently non-Christian about the custom of burying the dead fully dressed (with jewellery in the case of women, and weapons for men). Among the Franks, just across the Channel, the custom only took off among the aristocracy in the very same generation in which they converted to Christianity; some of the most lavish burials, with weapons, armour, jewellery, bronze and pottery vessels and so on, are those of the aristocracy buried underneath Cologne Cathedral or the abbey-church of St-Denis. Churchmen were not worried about the custom at all; there was no attempt to ban it.

If we cannot use changing burial customs to trace religious change, we should also think carefully about using them to chart the settlement of Germanic groups in the former Roman Empire. The custom of burying the dead fully dressed with their personal effects was not an inherently Germanic custom. The Franks adopted the custom long after many of them had come into the Roman Empire, and it was exported by them back into the Germanic lands east of the Rhine. Its spread through northern Gaul and beyond is probably more to do with the spread of Frankish lordship and the influence of the Frankish ruling and military class than with the colonisation of parts of Roman Gaul by immigrating Franks. We have documentary evidence for the way in which Romans took Frankish personal names, as a way of identifying with the ruling class; along with this probably went Frankish styles of dress, and – although we cannot prove it – the new burial styles that leading Franks had adopted. If we transfer this model across the Channel, we ought to wonder whether so-called 'Anglo-Saxon cemeteries' necessarily represent communities of incoming Germans. The apparent expansion of the Anglo-Saxon community in the late fifth century may not represent a new influx of immigrants from Germany, but an adoption of Anglo-Saxon customs by British communities. Conversely – and this is even more significant – we ought to wonder whether some communities of immigrants might have rapidly adopted native British burial customs: which, given that they do not leave any clear distinguishing features except a skeleton, are largely invisible archaeologically, except where the cemetery can be dated by some chance factor. There are relatively few typically 'Anglo-Saxon' graves in Northumbria, for instance, above all in the northern kingdom of Bernicia; yet this was the most powerful of the Anglo-Saxon kingdoms in the seventh century. Was Northumbria a largely British kingdom with a small Anglo-Saxon military elite, or is the archaeological evidence misleading?

This suspicion of ethnic interpretations of the burial evidence has the weight of some two decades of opinion behind it. Guy Halsall has argued forcefully for a *social* explanation of burial customs rather than a religious or ethnic explanation. For him, the taking up of the custom of furnished burial has to do with the social turmoil and extreme social mobility of the fifth and early sixth century. Grave-goods are a way of establishing status and position within a community. It is not a question of grave-goods *reflecting* social realities, so that one could count up the number of weapons or items of jewellery and come to some notion of actual rank within the community. 'Rather than being a passive mirror of social organization, it is an active strategy in the creation of social reality, an act of "social theatre".'[43] As Halsall comments, if a cemetery shows evidence of a great deal of stratification between rich and poor, and an associated settlement shows very little, with all the houses being roughly the same size, this need not be regarded as an anomaly. If one family *does* begin to dominate the community and establish itself in a house that is much larger than the rest, then actually it no longer needs to compete with its neighbours by 'fighting with grave-goods'.

Ethnic explanations have not totally disappeared, however, and are perhaps due for a revival. It has been suggested that DNA analysis of skeletal material may one day resolve the question of the biologically ethnic makeup of the population of early English cemeteries. It is even possible that simple measurement of skeletons may reveal something. Phyllis Jackson has suggested that the shape of English feet may have been different from those of the native population.[44] Heinrich Härke has shown from a study of those buried in several Anglo-Saxon cemeteries that those males buried with weapons (and usually with a richer assemblage of grave-goods altogether) are on average between 2 and 5 cm taller than men without weapons. This could obviously correlate with the fact that a warrior elite would tend to be better nourished than their social inferiors; but in fact both groups suffer from the same malnutrition-related defect in tooth-enamel, which suggests that both groups were in fact subject to the vicissitudes of famine and shortage. When correlated with the fact that the males in these cemeteries were on average 4 cm taller than those from earlier Romano-British cemeteries, there is the possibility that 'Anglo-Saxon' cemeteries contain the bodies of a dual population: Anglo-Saxon warriors and Romano-British peasants. The possibility of an ethnic distinction is strengthened when we look at what lies behind this simple word 'warrior'. A 'warrior-grave', for an archaeologist, is a grave containing weapons. But some of the 'warriors' were as young as twelve months, and as old as sixty. There was no correlation between fitness and strength and the possession of weapons: grave 110 at Berinsfield (Oxon), for instance, was of a man with spina bifida, yet equipped with shield and spear. For 'warrior', therefore, read 'Anglo-Saxon', for whom weapons were a symbol of status and superiority rather than something necessarily to be used in battle.[45]

The *number* of immigrants is clearly the most problematical aspect of all. If we are to judge just by what are generally regarded (before Härke's hypothesis) as the typical 'Anglo-Saxon' graves, we are dealing with quite small numbers: an estimated 30,000 excavated graves and 35,000 excavated individuals (allowing for the fact that cremation burials often contain more than one individual), over a period of 300 years.[46] The allowance we make for undiscovered burials is largely guesswork. Estimates for the number of Anglo-Saxons who came to Britain in the fifth century thus range from 10,000 to 100,000: but recently the consensus seems to be moving towards the lower end. Would such tiny numbers – and put alongside the consensus that the Romano-British population, at least at its height, may have been four million or more – be enough to account for the crucial change: that the language of the Anglo-Saxons, Old English, replaced the language of the indigenous people. Many scholars have given this more weight than the evidence of material culture:

> Thousands of folk of impeccable Romano-British pedigree might have gone over to living in sunken huts, wearing Germanic costume and burying their dead in cremation urns, but they would not so readily have changed their language.[47]

The impact of the Anglo-Saxons over most of southern England was more profound, in that sense, than that of the Romans, or Vikings, or Normans. Not only did they bring in a new language, but they renamed almost all features of the landscape, and almost all the settlements. Does this mean that numerically their immigration was very much stronger than the archaeology would suggest? Or is it just that the incoming Germanic peoples replaced the former social elite and were able to impose their cultural norms over a very much larger but demoralised and disorganised population? Härke's hypothesis about warrior-graves may suggest the latter.

It is to be hoped that archaeologists will come to clearer ideas than this about the relationships between the incoming Anglo-Saxons and the settled population. This is likely to be a question of looking closely at local landscapes. A hint comes from Martin Welch, in his study of Anglo-Saxon Sussex, where the earliest Anglo-Saxon cemeteries are in the restricted area between the Ouse and Cuckmere rivers, where there are few Roman villas, and well away from the most Romanised part, around Chichester. This suggests that there was some sort of accommodation between the two groups, or indeed that the Romans were able to control where the Saxons settled.[48] But, as we have already seen, there is a real problem in identifying the different ethnic groups, and there is also a very real problem in identifying *clearly* British sites in Anglo-Saxon areas. There are few recognisable British artefacts, in either pottery or metalwork. British sites of this transition period in western Britain are best identified and dated when imported Mediterranean pottery is found on them: we may be missing sites of this period altogether if that recognisable pottery is not present. Jones has pointed out a nice irony in a comparison of two archaeological type-sites: South Cadbury (Somerset), a reoccupied British hill-fort (much touted as a possible Arthurian 'Camelot' at the time of its excavation), and Chalton (Hampshire), a 'typical' Anglo-Saxon village. The British site produced only two easily identifiable metal objects, both of which were Anglo-Saxon, while the Anglo-Saxon village produced only one distinctive metal object: a disk from a British hanging-bowl.[49]

6
The post-Roman kingdoms

What was a king?

The early medieval political world, both inside and outside the former Roman Empire, was full of rulers, distinguished by various words in various languages, most of which we translate as 'kings'. We derive our English word 'king' from the Old English *cyning*, 'a man from the kin', although most other peoples in western Europe used a word derived from the same Indo-European root: in Latin *rex* (pl. *reges*), in Gothic *reiks*, in Irish *rí*, in Welsh *ri* (although the usual word was *brenhin*). Even in Old English the territory a *cyning* rules is a *rice* (like modern German *Reich*). Personal names incorporating this Indo-European root are common throughout Europe among barbarian royal families: there is Theodoric the Great, of the Ostrogoths; Childeric, Chilperic and others among the Franks; and even among the Anglo-Saxons there are names like Æthelric, Cynric, and Osric. For the Romans *reges* were either the rulers that they themselves used to have in the dim past, before they were thrown out by the first republicans, or else the kind of rulers that suited barbarians. But kingship was the norm for barbarians, and, once converted, they discovered support in the rhetoric of the Old Testament. With the Bible's assistance, the clergy developed new ideas of kingship in western Europe in the centuries immediately following Roman rule. It was possibly the Irish who first revived the Old Testament idea of inaugurating a king by anointing with holy oil; but it was an Englishman who combined that with crowning, when Bishop Boniface, a West Saxon, inaugurated the first Carolingian king of the Franks in 751.

The world not only had kings, but it had an Emperor too. Barbarians recognised that *imperator* or *Augustus* was a title reserved for the Emperor in Constantinople. Indeed, on the Continent, most barbarian kings for a long time recognised the Emperor as their legitimate overlord, at least to the extent of abiding by imperial rules about placing the Emperor's head, and no-one else's, on their gold coinage. It was only at the very end of the sixth century – a couple of generations before the minting of gold coins ceased in the West – that barbarian kings in general started usurping this imperial privilege. Even so, no barbarian claimed the title of Emperor until the very end of the eighth century. Something of the prestige of the Roman Emperors had disappeared by then. Barbarians had devised new ways of thinking of the Roman Emperors: they were effeminate Greeks, or they were descendants of the Romans who persecuted Christians. Sooner or later most barbarian peoples devised myths to place themselves as equals to the Romans: most commonly, they claimed that they, like the Romans themselves, were descended from Trojan princes who escaped the Greeks at the end of the siege of Troy. Thus Francus was the progenitor of the Franks, and Brutus of the inhabitants of Britain. Barbarians thus claimed ethnic equality with the Romans, and, indeed, by then 'Romans' were indeed just another of the ethnic varieties of western Europe: they were the inhabitants of central Italy (part of which is now called 'Romagna'). Nevertheless, the concept of emperorship meaning 'rule over several different peoples and different kingdoms' did survive. Bede uses the term *imperium* of powerful Anglo-Saxon rulers; and the Englishman Alcuin uses the word in several letters to Charlemagne, king of the Franks, in the late 790s.[1] In 800 Charlemagne took the decisive step and had himself crowned Emperor: he was ruler over numerous territories and peoples, but possibly in his own mind the crucial fact that there was, at that time, no Emperor in Constantinople – indeed, it was far worse than there being no Emperor, in terms of the natural order of the world, since a *woman* – Irene, the previous Emperor's mother – had seized the throne and ruled as Emperor.

Kings were rulers of peoples, not territories, in the early centuries after the collapse of the western Empire: their titles were *rex Francorum*, king of the Franks, not *rex Franciae*, king of Francia or France; *rex Nordanhymbrorum*, king of the Northumbrians, not *rex Nordanhymbriae*, king of Northumbria. The question, then, is not so much 'what was a king?' but 'what was a people?' The Saxons were a people; but so, by the seventh century, were the South Saxons of Sussex, the Middle Saxons of Middlesex, the East Saxons of Essex and the West Saxons of Wessex. There was in fact no king of the Saxons or of the Angles; there were kings of new peoples, who had been created during the process of migration and settlement in different parts of Roman Britain. Indeed, most of these peoples were patently new. There could have been no sub-group of the Angles known as the Northumbrians until Angles settled north of the Humber (indeed, the first appearance of this people was as the *Humbrenses*, when they were living *by* the Humber, rather than north of it); there could be no South Saxons until other Saxons had established a kingdom to their north.

A document known as the 'Tribal Hidage' survives to give us some hints about what 'peoples' were in the early Anglo-Saxon England. The Tribal Hidage was basically a tax or tribute record, listing the taxable value of each of the peoples of England in terms of the number of 'hides'. (Bede says that a hide was 'land of one family', but it was basically a tax unit rather than an economic unit.) The West Saxons were assessed at the highest rate: 100,000 hides. The South Saxons and East Saxons were each assessed at 7,000. But of the thirty-four listed assessments, the bulk relate to the Angles of central and eastern England. The East Angles and the Mercians were by far the largest of these, both assessed at 30,000. The rest were small peoples, the existence of most of which would not have been known if the Tribal Hidage had not survived: the East and West Wixna, the Noxgaga, the Ohtgaga, and so on. Some can be located, like the *Cilternsæten* of the Chilterns, the *Pecsæten* of the Peak District, the *Hwicce* of Worcestershire, but not all of them can. The Angles of Northumbria are the only people omitted, which has led to a suggestion that the document may have been compiled originally by the Northumbrians themselves around the mid-seventh century, when they were the dominant people in Anglo-Saxon England, or indeed in the whole of Britain, and indicated how they expected to profit from the situation.[2] There was clearly a great deal of difference between the West Saxons, assessed at 30,000 hides, and the *Wihtgara*, men of the Isle of Wight, assessed at 600. Bede regarded the ruler of the former as worthy of the Latin word *rex*, but would never have granted such a title to the leader of the Wihtgara. It is not at all unreasonable to imagine that the Wihtgara, like all these peoples in the Tribal Hidage, once had their own *cyning*, but that some *cyningas* were more equal than others.

Our sources for the most part do not tell us about the small kingdoms, but about the 'super-kingdoms', which for the most part were probably put together by an amalgamation of several smaller peoples. By the mid-seventh century at the latest, a small number of 'super-kingdoms' had emerged among the Anglo-Saxons: what used to be called the Heptarchy, made up of (from the north in an anti-clockwise direction) the Northumbrians, the Mercians, the West Saxons, the South Saxons, the *Cantwara*, or men of Kent, the East Saxons and the East Angles. Our two main narrative sources, Bede's *History* and the *Anglo-Saxon Chronicle*, treat this situation as if it was one of long standing. Only a few hints survive that the political structure may have been very different in the sixth century, or for that matter in the early part of the seventh. It is only outside these sources, for instance, that we clearly see a lower rank of king. One of our earliest surviving charters, witnessed and approved by the king of the Mercians in around 672, is in the name of Frithuwald, the *subregulus* of the men of Surrey.[3] While it is quite possible that the king of the Mercians treated Frithuwald as his 'sub-little-king' (to translate the Latin literally), it is very likely that those in Surrey thought of him as their king. There are similar charters from the 'sub-kings' of the Hwicce. Bede mentions several times the district of Lindsey (Lincolnshire), which is sometimes under the domination of the Northumbrians and sometimes under that of the Mercians. Nothing in Bede's account suggests that the men of Lindsey have their own king: yet a genealogy of their kings (from the sixth to the eighth centuries) survives, and the last, Aldfrith, may have witnessed a charter at the time of Offa, well after Bede's death. We may even see many of the kings of the Tribal Hidage peoples engaging in battle alongside Penda of Mercia against King Oswiu of the Northumbrians in 655. Bede talked of 'thirty *duces regii*' taking Penda's side.[4] 'Royal war-leaders' is an odd phrase, and may unwittingly reveal that Bede knew perfectly well that more people in England partook of royalty than he normally let on. He tells us too of *principes*, important regional figures, who might also have thought of themselves as *cyningas*. The Church was on the side of the larger kingdoms; it was not part of Bede's agenda to offer comfort to those small peoples who had become absorbed by the larger.

This process whereby 'super-kingdoms' emerge from a voluntary or enforced amalgamation of several smaller peoples can be found on the Continent too. The Franks were a federation of smaller peoples, such as the Chamavi and the Bructeri, each under their own kings, who frequently acted together during the fourth and fifth centuries. At the very end of the fifth century, one Frankish king, Clovis, managed to wipe out all rival dynasties, and unite the Frankish people properly. No rival kings emerged to challenge the dynasty he founded, the Merovingians, for two and a half centuries, and the existence of those smaller peoples seemed to have been forgotten. Yet in the time of Charlemagne, three centuries after Clovis, a law-code was issued for the Chamavi. A sense of independent identity had survived after centuries of total invisibility; the situation might have been very similar in England.

The idea of a hierarchy of kingship that we can detect in England can also be found elsewhere. We can see it in Ireland, a land barely touched by Rome, let alone the German world. There the most basic political unit was the *túath*, normally translated as 'tribe' (but possibly better as 'people'): there were some 150 of these in Ireland in the sixth or seventh century. They were ruled by the *rí túaithe*, the smallest in scale of any known European kings at this period, in terms of the size of their kingdoms. Those kings who were powerful enough to exact tribute from the *rí túaithe* were the *rí ruirech*, the 'kings of kings'; over them were the *rí coicid*, literally the 'kings of the quarter', that is, kings of the four main provinces of Ireland (Ulster, Leinster, Munster and Connacht). The respective duties and responsibilities of each are laid down in Irish law tracts such as *Críth Gablach*. In part, the neatness probably relates more to the lawyer's mind than to political reality, but there certainly is some substance to the structure that the texts reveal. There is almost no substance, however, in the peak of the pyramid, the *ard rí*, or high king, or the *rí Érenn*, or king of Ireland. There were kings who claimed this position, and who were inaugurated at Tara, the hillfort at the heart of the central fifth province of Meath, but 'no Irish king ever managed to make it a reality, and most law-texts do not even provide for such a possibility'.[5]

There was no equivalent among the Anglo-Saxons, as far as we know, of an inauguration into high-kingship, but there certainly was a similarly recognised position, that had rather more of a political reality. Bede listed the seven kings whom he reckoned to have had a similar *imperium* over other kings,[6] though with perhaps typical Northumbrian patriotism he does not think that any of them ruled north of the Humber, but simply held sway over all the southern English kings. The exceptions were three Northumbrian kings, who held much of Britain, according to Bede: Edwin (616–33) even apparently held Anglesey and the Isle of Man (one of those few hints that Anglo-Saxon kings actually had significant navies well before the time of Alfred the Great, 'the founder of the Royal Navy'). Oswald (634–42) held similar territory, and Oswiu (655–70) made tributary the Picts and the Irish who lived in Scotland. We shall look at those claims later. Here it is worth pausing on the word which the Old English translator of Bede's Latin text used of these kings: *bretwalda*. Some have thought to translate this simply as 'broad-ruler', but it is generally accepted now that it means 'ruler of Britain'. For most kings that remained no more than a distant aspiration, but that it should be an aspiration at all is interesting. The Welsh too, of course, long preserved the idea that all *Prydain* was rightfully theirs, and the Welsh too had this idea of hierarchical rule, with phrases in Latin running from *magnus rex* to *reguli*, and a much wider range of ruler-words in Welsh.[7]

It used to be thought that peoples produced kings; increasingly it is being seen that kings can create peoples. This is a process which was happening on the Continent as well. In the fourth century, the Franks were a barbarian people living outside the Roman Empire by the mouths of the Rhine. By the fifth century, the Franks were major military supporters of the Romans in northern Gaul, and effectively took over authority from the Romans when the Roman Empire in the West collapsed. By then many of them had been living within the Empire for a century; they spoke Latin, and soon became Christians. Their kings ruled Franks and Gallo-Romans alike. By the time Gregory, bishop of Tours, writes the history of his times, up to 592 – a history which *he* never called the *History of the Franks* – the distinction between 'Frank' and 'Roman' has been lost. All those over whom the kings of the Franks ruled, at least in northern Gaul, thought of themselves as Franks. A new people had been created out of two groups with very different origins and cultures: this new people came to share a culture, to some extent, but what bound them together ultimately was the political rule of the Frankish kings. By the eighth century, neither Franks nor Burgundians could understand how the Romans had disappeared from the territories they controlled: they imagined that their ancestors had killed them all.[8]

Similar processes must have been happening in England, and in Britain as a whole. Indeed, it explains the fate of the British who had been living in eastern Britain. Bede always thought of the British as the people who lived in the West, and without actually saying so he allowed the reader to think that the fate of the eastern British was that of the British described in a passage he borrowed from Gildas:

> Some of the miserable remnant were captured in the mountains and butchered indiscriminately; others, exhausted by hunger, came forward and submitted themselves to the enemy, ready to accept perpetual slavery for the sake of food . . . some fled sorrowfully to lands beyond the sea; while others remained in their own land and lived a wretched existence, always in fear and dread, among the mountains and woods and precipitous rocks.[9]

In fact, most British must have carried on living in eastern Britain; it is probable that the majority of the population of all the Anglo-Saxon kingdoms were made up of descendants of the British, and almost certain that the majority in Northumbria, Mercia and Wessex were. Almost all of these British, except those who lived in places like Walton (= 'settlement of the Welsh'), leave no historical trace behind them. Some of them may indeed have been oppressed and subjected – it is presumably no accident that the word used of the British in Old English, *wealh*, meant both Welshman and slave – but others may have taken new ethnic identity and have prospered in the new kingdoms, and may even have played a part in their creation. It is interesting that the originator of the West Saxon dynasty, Cerdic, has a name which appears to be British – indeed, the same as that of the ancient British hero who resisted the Roman invasion, Caratacus – and that a later West Saxon king has the same name, in Bede's spelling, as an earlier British king of Gwynedd: Cædwalla. Relations between the British and the Anglo-Saxons were certainly not always as hostile as Bede likes to imply. As we shall see (p. 158) the hostility Bede felt towards the British church appears to have been reciprocated by British churchmen, but there were alliances between the English and the British, and exiled English kings took refuge at British courts. According to the hagiographer Felix, St Guthlac had himself been in exile among the British, and there learned 'to understand their sibilant speech'.[10] Thanks to this earlier education, we are told, he was able to understand the demons he later encountered in the Fens. Perhaps this story was a case of the hagiographer literally demonising those surviving British in the Fens who were hostile to Guthlac; perhaps it was an Anglo-Saxon making the assumption that the agents of Satan would speak Welsh; perhaps, indeed, it was a joke. Humour is the most perishable of all human creations. Sadly, therefore, we cannot take this story as evidence of the language spoken in the Fens in the late seventh century, although there is nothing implausible about the survival of Welsh-speakers within Anglo-Saxon areas at this period. The position of inferiority suffered by the eastern British, and the status conferred by the ability to speak to Anglo-Saxon lords, must be the answer to 'the obscurest question in the whole of English history', which is 'Why aren't we [the English] speaking Welsh?'[11]

'Celtic' and 'Germanic' society

That we have come to think of 'Celtic' and 'Germanic' societies in Britain as irreconcilable opposites has something to do with Bede's hostility to the British, something to do with the much more recent history of nationalisms in these islands, and something to do with the nature of our sources. We know a reasonable amount about the Anglo-Saxons, precious little about the British or the Picts, and a very great deal about the Irish: indeed, there is more source material in the vernacular from Ireland in the period before 1100 than from the rest of Europe put together. The Irish have thus stood as the representative 'Celts' in these islands. The traditional view of Celtic scholars has been that the Irish society that we learn about through these vernacular sources shows that Ireland was like a living fossil, preserving features of early Indo-European societies that have disappeared everywhere else except at the other end of the Indo-European world, in the ancient Sanskrit world of northern India.

This is probably most obvious when dealing with ideas about kingship. With Germanic kingship, scholars have 'stressed the centrality of active and predatory war-leadership',[12] but have recognised that, with the settlement in the Empire and the injection of Christian ideology, Germanic kingship in the early Middle Ages was in a state of rapid and dynamic change. The early Irish king, on the other hand, was seen as static and unchanging, a prehistoric survival, a symbolic and sacral figure-head, who left legal matters in the hands of jurists and engaged in ritual warfare which made little political difference. He was 'a priestly vegetable'.[13] He was hemmed in by various arcane *geisi* or 'taboos', and on his moral state depended the welfare of the kingdom. If the 'sovereign's truth' prevailed, there would be peace, stability, good weather, and fertility; with the 'sovereign's lie' comes strife, pestilence and famine.[14] This idea, which accompanies some idea of a direct link between king and divinity, through priesthood or some other mechanism (such as divine descent), is usually called 'sacral kingship' for short. And it is found in an Anglo-Saxon context too. William Chaney notes that Alcuin wrote to King Æthelred of Northumbria in the 790s reminding him that 'in the king's righteousness is the prosperity of the whole folk, victory of the army, mildness of the seasons, abundance of the land, the blessing of sons, the health of the people'; Chaney sees this as evidence of the continuity of ideas of sacral kingship into the new Christian era.[15]

Our problem comes with determining the origin of these ideas. In this particular case, however we can be clear. Chaney did not translate the first words of Alcuin's sentence: 'We read that ...': Alcuin was not putting ancient Germanic pagan ideas into Christian guise, but was commenting, as Bede had before him, on 'Samuel's great speech on kingship to the Israelites, in which the prophet emphasized that the king's good deeds would bring success to his people.'[16] How far are the ideas we find in the early medieval sources part of an archaic past, or part of a deliberate attempt to use the Old

Testament as a model for kingship? In Ireland there is certainly a mass of legal material, and sagas such as the *Táin Bó Cuailnge* (The Cattle Raid of Cooley), which, although written down only in the twelfth century, seem to offer, in Kenneth Jackson's words, 'a window on the Iron Age'.[17] If Celtic society was different from Germanic society, it was perhaps in the existence of a learned class who could preserve such traditions – the *filid*. It used to be imagined that the *filid* continued to exist in Ireland in Christian times as a kind of pagan underground, preserving the old traditions in opposition to, or at least with the disapproval of, the Christian priesthood. Many of the products of secular learning in the early Middle Ages, however, are fully imbued with Latin and Biblical learning; it is likely that the *filid* shared with their more spiritual colleagues a training in the monastery. Kim McCone's study of this question concludes that what the learned class in early medieval Ireland were doing, for law as well as for history, was to construct a past and a set of traditions for themselves that could accommodate their traditions with the current Christian religion and with the current political situation. We should not imagine objective historical scholarship, if such a thing is anyway possible. If in saga, he suggests, we find Irish *filid* extolling the ancient custom of the decapitation of defeated enemies, this is possibly because it was still done; indeed, it had Old Testament sanction. If one moves from works of scholarship, which tell us how scholars and jurists thought kings ought to behave, to the world of real Irish kings (in so far as we can perceive it), we may suspect that Irish kings were not so very different from other western European kings. The provincial kings, in their political manoeuvrings, were not unlike the kings of the Mercians or of the West Saxons (and had, by the seventh century, perhaps achieved the same kind of dominance over lesser kings, *subreguli* or *ríg tuaithe*); the role of the king in the creation and administration of the law may have been much more significant than the Irish lawyers thought that it ought to be.

If the Irish and the Anglo-Saxons are beginning to look more like each other, this is even more true of the British and the Anglo-Saxons. In fact, there are many things which they had in common, as has been pointed out most cogently by Peter Sawyer.[18] One might point to common Indo-European origins, or a lack of influence from the Roman past (the common absence, for instance, of such Roman institutions as towns or coinage), to explain this. Certainly it is not just a matter of a level of interaction and cultural borrowing between the two peoples, at least not in the British Isles, since some of these characteristics are to be found among Germanic peoples on the Continent, and indeed among the Celtic-speaking Irish. It would probably be idle to comment that the Germans on the Continent too had populated many areas formerly controlled by Celtic-speaking peoples, and to postulate a Celtic background. It may just be that similar circumstances produced similar societies; it may also suggest that in Wales and in the area on either side of the Wall, pre-Roman ideas about social organisation survived right the way through the Roman period, just as the Celtic language did.

Britons and Anglo-Saxons were both ruled by kings, who owed their power primarily to their abilities as warriors and warlords. Unlike in the more institutionalised monarchies of the Franks or the Visigoths, on the Continent, it was not (it seems) acceptable to choose a king who was below the age at which he could exercise those functions, and it was certainly not acceptable to choose a queen (as it had apparently been, for instance, among Britons around the beginning of the millennium). Kings were normally chosen from royal families – relationship to the previous king was important, but need not necessarily be close – and thus descent was important. Early Welsh genealogies often traced descent from the fifth-century leader Cunedda, while English genealogies usually traced royal descent from the god Woden. (After the conversion to Christianity several more stages are inserted into the genealogy, putting Woden in his place by making him a distant descendant of Adam.) It has been suggested that the extant genealogies preserve a fossilised record of a time, in the seventh century, when dominant Northumbrian kings impose a pattern on the divine genealogies. All the Anglian kingdoms claimed descent via a different son of Woden; the Kentish kings share, with Deira, descent from Uegdæg, and the West Saxons share, with Bernicia, descent from Bældæg.[19] Genealogies were frequently fabricated and manipulated, and sometimes one can discern the political structures that lie behind the later fabrications.

The family celebrated in the genealogy is a fundamental element of both British and Anglo-Saxon life. It was the family or kin who defended an accused person in law; it was the threat of force from the family (the threat of feud) which brought the accused person to court, and helped enforce the verdict. If a member of the kin was murdered, the value of that person – *wergeld* in Old England ('man-money') and *galanas* in Welsh ('honour-price') – was paid to the kin by the guilty party. That price was determined by social status, for insular society was very hierarchical. In the earliest English laws of Kent, from the seventh century, the wergeld of an ordinary freeman or *ceorl* (pronounced 'churl') was 100 shillings: initially, at least, the value of 100 Frankish gold coins, for at the time of the earliest Kentish laws (those of Æthelberht, d. 616) the Anglo-Saxons did not have a coinage of their own. An *eorlcunde* man – that is, a man born to the status of an *eorl* or noble – was worth 300 shillings. In the law of Ine of the West Saxons (c. 690) the values were double: 200 shillings for a *ceorl*, and two higher grades, 600 and 1200. The difference in value is probably related to a change in coinage, rather than any difference between Kentish and West Saxon society.

Social status was expected to go along with a certain amount of land. In the laws of Ine there was provision for men of *gesith* (noble) status who had three, ten or twenty hides. One hide was thought to be normal for a *ceorl* and his family; indeed the earliest meaning of the word *hid* was 'nuclear family' rather than 'land'.[20] The laws of Ine offered a set of corresponding values for the Welsh in his kingdom of Wessex (which was rapidly expanding westwards, into Wiltshire, Dorset and beyond), which show that a hide was the property qualification for a freeman, and five hides for a noble. A hide of land probably meant more than average wealth: we must not imagine that the *ceorl* was necessarily the average adult male. A *ceorl* was perhaps more 'farmer' than 'peasant'. There are indications in the Kentish laws, for instance, that the average *ceorl* or freeman's 'family' might well include slaves and semi-free dependents: his *hlafæta* – his dependants, or literally his 'loaf-eaters' – which meant that he was their *hlaford*, or lord. If this lord should prosper, as one later Anglo-Saxon text has it, 'so that he possessed fully five hides of land of his own, a bell and a castle-gate and a special office in the king's hall, then was he henceforth entitled to the right of a thegn'.[21] There was an ethnic difference in Ine's Wessex: an Englishman might earn the status of a ceorl or a thegn by acquiring property, but he does not necessarily lose this status if he loses the property, whereas a Welshman does.

Thomas Charles-Edwards first pointed to the similarities in the system of the hide which can be found right through these islands: they suggest to him common Indo-European origin, but suggest to me that the English might have inherited it from the British with whom they shared the land. The early Irish knew a similar system. The most detailed Irish law tract dealing with these matters, the *Críth Gablach*, said that a lord of the lowest grade had five free households subject to him, which is exactly equivalent to the idea of thegnly status coming with five hides. A group of five farms was known in Irish as *coictreb*, while the Irish colony in Scotland, Dál Riata, seems to have divided up the kingdom into *cét treb*, or 'hundred farms'. This had its equivalent in the Welsh *cantref* and in the English 'hundred', which originally stood for 'hundred hides', and became a basic subdivision of the shire.

An individual did not *own* land. The head of the family held it on behalf of the family, and had certain rights in it; other people, from kings down to serfs, may have had rights of different kinds over that same piece of land. Inheritance was determined by custom, and not according to the whim of an individual: land went to the surviving family – normally the sons – in strict proportion. Giving land to someone outside the family was equivalent to disinheriting the legitimate heirs, and was not therefore possible. If kings wished to reward their followers with land, as opposed to movables such as gold, he could do this by conquest, or he could loan estates to followers for one lifetime or more (and leave the problem of actually recovering it again to his successor). This conflicted with the ideas which the Church had about property: once land was given to the Church it could not be alienated. Churchmen in the seventh century were thus responsible for introducing a new legal idea to the English, drawn from Roman law (where an individual had much greater power of ownership): we shall look into this more below (p. 207).

Not all would necessarily be protected at law by their family. Slaves, legally speaking, had no family: they had owners, and their owners would protect them as they would any other property. Others deprived by circumstance of suitable protection might seek a lord who would substitute for a family leader. Such protection might actually be a valuable asset for a lord, which is one reason why later medieval kings were jealous of their duty to protect widows and orphans: they could exploit their estates. Lordship was an important institution in British and English society, and one which might at times have conflicted with the ties of kinship. Both lordship and the kin were perceived as a threat to central power, once kings became more ambitious. In the tenth century, in the newly created kingdom of England, we find King Edmund legislating against feud, and King Æthelstan complaining about the kin being so powerful in some areas that royal troops have to move in to a district to catch a thief.

Lords were expected to bring their men along to support the king's army in time of war: which might, in the immediately post-Roman centuries, be a regular, if short-lived and seasonal occupation. There is much debate about the size of early medieval armies, and hence the status of the men who served in them. The general consensus seems to be that they were small, and made up largely of kings, their aristocrats and their retinues. A much-quoted passage from the laws of Ine of Wessex (*c.* 690) is not easy to interpret. It said that a group of seven men are to be defined as thieves, between seven and thirty-five is a band, and over thirty-five is an army. We are not to conclude that an army is somehow more legitimate than a war-band (or band or marauders): Ine went on to lay down penalties for those taking part in the activities of both.[22] We may presume that not all military activity was regarded as legitimate by the king, and that there were opportunities for free enterprise. This is borne out by the story of St Guthlac's youth, from almost the same year as Ine's law, as related by his hagiographer Felix.

> A noble desire for command burned in his young breast, [and] he remembered the valiant deeds of heroes of old, and as though waking from sleep, he changed his disposition and gathering bands of followers took up arms; but when he had devastated the towns and residences of his foes, their villages and fortresses with fire and sword, and, gathering together companions from various races, had amassed great booty, then as if instructed by divine counsel, he would return to the owners a third part of the treasure collected.[23]

Guthlac did this between the ages of 15 and 24; and then, starting to worry about the state of his soul, he joined the monastery of Repton.

There is a wonderful story in Bede which tells us a good deal about the nature of Anglo-Saxon society as well as of the customs of war. There was a battle in 679 between Æthelred of the Mercians and Ecgfrith of the Northumbrians, in which Ecgfrith's brother Ælfwine was killed. The Archbishop made peace between them, and it was agreed that 'no further lives [be] demanded for the death of the king's brother, but only the usual money compensation which was paid to the king to whom the duty of vengeance belonged'.[24] During the battle, Imma, one of Ælfwine's soldiers, was struck unconscious: when he woke up, he was lying among the dead. He was captured by one of the Mercian king's close followers: Bede says *comes*, 'companion' (later 'count'), and we may assume that this meant that he belonged to what Latin writers called the *comitatus* of the king, that is, the king's retinue or warband. The captured Imma was afraid to admit that he was a *miles*, a soldier: he declared that he was a poor married peasant, who had come to the army to help with the supplies. But after he had been imprisoned for some time (an annoying prisoner, for his bonds kept miraculously falling off), his captors realised 'by his appearance, his bearing, and his speech', that he was not an ordinary poor man, but a noble and a *minister regis*. The *comes* said that if he had not given his word, he would die, as vengeance for the death of his brothers and kinsmen in the battle. Instead, the *comes* sold Imma to a Frisian slave merchant based in London. The merchant had no more success in keeping him in bonds than Æthelred's *comes*; the bonds would slip off each morning at nine. The merchant let him go to the king of Kent, who had once been *minister* to his aunt, King Ecgfrith's wife Æthelthryth; Imma received the money for his ransom, and sent it to the merchant. When he returned home to Northumbria, he discovered that his brother, a priest, had believed him dead, and had said masses for his soul each morning at nine.

This story is revealing in all kinds of ways. A noble could be distinguished by his speech and bearing (or Bede was at least prepared to believe that this was possible). Imma was a *miles*, a soldier, and tried to pretend he was a peasant. The Old English translation of Bede's *History*, from the ninth century, translated both *miles* and *minister regis* as *þegn* (thegn: as in Shakespeare's Thane of Cawdor), and translated the phrase 'a young man from the *militia*' as *sum geong cyninges þegn*, 'a young king's thegn'. For him, then – and we might assume him to understand the niceties of status better than we – a soldier and a thegn, a member of the royal retinue, were equivalent, and pretending to be a peasant would convince someone that they were not in the army proper. It may be reading too much into the text, but it is also interesting that Imma insisted that he was a *married* peasant: it seems likely that the king's retinue was made up of unmarried men, who would only marry and settle down on land granted by the king when they retired, at the age of 25 or so. War was a young man's occupation. Æthelred's *comes* – Æðelredes gesið in the Old English translation – treated Imma well, as long as he knew him to be a peasant; if he had known he was a noble, he would have killed him in revenge. Instead, keeping his oath to spare his life, he sold Imma into slavery; it took a merchant to realise that a noble's ransom would be worth a lot more than the slave cost. It is also interesting that Imma thought he could presume on the king of Kent's relationship to Queen Æthelthryth of Northumbria, as her former *þegn*, in order to acquire the ransom money.

The world of honour and vengeance this story reveals is not just restricted to the Anglo-Saxons. The *Gododdin* is a Welsh text, whose date and origins are hotly disputed. Is it actually a poem composed by the sixth-century Welsh poet Aneirin, or reworked later, or indeed wholly composed later? It is a poem in praise of the *comitatus* of the king of the Gododdin: the people known to Romans as the Votadini, whose main royal stronghold was on the castle rock at Edinburgh. The *comitatus* is the *gosgordd* in Welsh. Its members live in the royal household, and are bound to the king by a solemn contract, which involves serving him in war. They boast of what they will achieve in war, and if they fulfil their boasts they will have fame, and will have immortality in poetry. Central to the value system espoused in the poem are 'honour and shame, fame and disgrace'.[25] In this they are no different from the warriors who serve Hrothgar and Beowulf in the Old English poem *Beowulf* (which is just as problematical in date and thus historical value as the *Gododdin*). Indeed, both poems, and Bede, show one reason why these values should be so widespread: kings attract to their *comitatus* warriors from other kingdoms than their own. Bede talks of how King Oswine of Northumbria was 'beloved by all because of the royal dignity which showed itself in his character, his appearance, and his actions; and noblemen from almost every kingdom flocked to him to serve him as retainers'.[26] A generous king who seemed on the ascendant attracted retainers; the death of that king could cause a very rapid turn of fortune for the kingdom, as those same ambitious young men left for another court. There is every reason to think that these young men could be from British or Irish kingdoms as well as from other English kingdoms. At the aristocratic level, at least, loyalty was to the king as individual, not to the people.

We have got to the heart of what is often called 'the heroic age'. It has proved to be very easy to romanticise it, rather than see it for what it is: a system of exploitation which gives free rein to the propensities of adolescent males for bonding, status-seeking and mayhem. A very specific example of romantic interpretation relates to the presumed Germanic heroic ideal of the warrior who preferred to die with his lord rather than to surrender or to outlive him. This, Tacitus tells us, was a characteristic of Germanic warriors in the first century; it is also found, almost a millennium later, in the celebrated Anglo-Saxon poem *The Battle of Maldon*, which depicts the tragic defeat of the English in the face of a Viking attack in 991.The real problem is that we do not find this ideal expressed one single time in the intervening period. This has not stopped some Germanist scholars from seeing it as an essential part of the warrior ethos throughout the early Middle Ages. Questioning this view, Roberta Frank has argued recently that *The Battle of Maldon* is not an *archaic* poem, but a very up-to-date one, not espousing the values of barbarian heroism, not peering 'backward through the mists to Germania, but just around the corner, to an eleventh-century Europe in which the profession of warrior was a way of achieving religious perfection and a martyr's crown.'[27] Not the barbarian, therefore, but the knight.

Assembling a band of young warriors from a multiplicity of kingdoms – not unlike a Premier League football club signing a team-full of international soccer players – was something that presumably added to a king's prestige.[28] We can see a material analogue to this in the famous royal graves of Sutton Hoo. All of the burial mounds have been robbed out except Mounds 1 and 17, but enough survives to suggest that this was a royal cemetery for the East Anglian dynasty. It is close to Rendlesham, which Bede describes as a royal site, and also to Ipswich, which was already being developed as a port in the seventh century, and which might have been used by the kings in order to acquire prestige items with which to display their generosity. Mound 1 contained a large ship, in which the burial and the grave-goods were placed: a custom known particularly in Sweden, but in Britain only in East Anglia. The wonderfully crafted gold jewellery may well have been produced in East Anglia itself, although it used imported garnets, possibly from Bohemia, and gold, probably melted down from imported Frankish coins; but most of the surviving contents were very obviously, and deliberately, prestige items from abroad: a quantity of fine silverware from Byzantium, a shield and a helmet from Sweden, a hanging-bowl from western Britain, and gold coins from Francia (which date the grave to the late 620s at the earliest).

The kingdoms of the north

In these last two sections, I shall try to sketch out the broad political developments in Britain in the post-Roman period, up to the coming of the Vikings in the eighth century. This has been done largely by ethnic division in the past: that is, there have been studies of the Picts, of the Scots, of the Welsh and, above all, of the various Anglo-Saxon kingdoms. On the whole, nineteenth- and twentieth-century historians have probably been more obsessed by racial and ethnic division than people were in the early Middle Ages, and the development of kingdoms within these different 'ethnic' groups did not happen in isolation, but in constant interaction with each other. It has seemed to be more interesting to look at developments in terms of 'international relations' in Britain within two very broad geographical areas: north of the Humber and Ribble and south of those rivers. Although the Northumbrians themselves, especially in the seventh century, were often involved in affairs south of the Humber, the main focus of their interest was on the north and west, while the eyes of the kings south of the Humber and Ribble, whether in the Welsh or English areas, seldom strayed northwards. To a large extent these two halves of Britain did operate as separate polities, at least up until the Viking period, when both the English and the Scots begin to move towards 'governments of national unity'.

As we have seen, there were basically four ethnic groups in the north in the sixth and seventh centuries: the Picts in the far north, the Irish newcomers in the west of Scotland, the surviving independent British, both north and south of the Wall, and finally the Angles, who had established the

Map 4 Major and minor kingdoms in *c.* 700

kingdoms of Bernicia and Deira (north of the Tees and between the Tees and Humber respectively) by the late sixth century. By the tenth century those four groups had been reduced to two – the English and the Scots (although the Viking onslaught had added a fifth ethnic group, and created new political entities). The complex process by which this happened can hardly be said to be understood clearly. For much of the period the sources are either Northumbrian or Irish – above all Bede's *History* and the *Annals of Ulster* (which originated in annals kept up at the monastery of Iona, off the Scottish island of Mull) – and we thus know about the political life of the Picts and the British kingdoms only from the outside.

Between the sixth and eighth centuries there was not only a great deal of interaction between the various kingdoms of northern Britain, but between Britain and Ireland as well. As we shall see, the frequency of exile was one of the elements of this interaction; others were marriage alliances, and the practice of fostering sons at foreign courts. All these were high-level interactions, of course. More common, no doubt, was interchange among clerics, who might study abroad, or travel for business or pilgrimage. It was an 'age of migrating ideas', as the title of a book on the early medieval art of the north puts it.[29] As an example of those 'migrating ideas' in practice, we may take the case of the Book of Kells. This masterpiece of book production, now in Trinity College Dublin, was in the monastery of Kells in the Middle Ages. Kells (County Meath) was given to Iona at the time of the Viking raids, and there is little doubt that the Book came to Kells from Iona. But there is a great deal of controversy about where it was actually produced: in Iona itself, the island monastery off Mull, which was a great intermediary between Ireland and Scotland, or in Northumbria, or even in Pictland. Each of those possibilities has been canvassed. The unifying factor, of course, is the Irish church: as we shall see, Irish missionaries brought Christianity to the Northumbrians and the Picts. But the cultural traffic was by no means all one way: Pictish animal art is represented in the highly sophisticated repertoire of the Kells artist(s), as is the interlaced animal art which has its origins in the northern Germanic world of Scandinavia and England. Art historians sometimes speak of 'Hiberno-Saxon art', to categorise such much better provenanced items as the Lindisfarne Gospels: but there are two other northern peoples, the British and the Picts, who may also have contributed to the Book of Kells, not just the English and the Irish. It is a truly international product of the northern world in the eighth century – though the tourist industry which has grown up around 'Hiberno-Saxon art' in Ireland and Britain today thinks of it all as 'Celtic'. (There is nothing quite so guaranteed to make an Anglo-Saxon archaeologist or historian irate as the sight of modern reproductions of Anglo-Saxon animal ornament, sold on tourist items throughout these islands, labelled as 'Celtic art'.)

One of the mechanisms which led to both alliance and hostility between the various northern kingdoms was the system of royal succession, whereby kingship did not necessarily go from father to son but where there may be several claimants with equal rights to kingship. Unsuccessful claimants would go into exile to the courts of neighbouring kingdoms, there to plot for their return. One of the strangest such exiles, about which we would dearly love to know more, was when a palace coup forced the infant Dagobert II, king of the Franks, to go into exile in 657: he was brought to Ireland, and there he stayed until, in 673, Bishop Wilfrid of York was involved in bringing him home, and back to the Frankish throne. But exile is something that, on a more local level, was commonplace in the history of Northumbria in the seventh century, and it is there that it is convenient to start.

The kingdom of the Northumbrians was made up of two kingdoms with very separate histories: Deira, roughly the eastern part of Yorkshire, and Bernicia, the land to the north of the Tees. These two kingdoms had been united, at the end of the sixth century, by the Bernician king Æthelfrith. What the united kingdom was called is uncertain: the way in which Bede explains, on several occasions, what 'Northumbrian' actually means, suggests that he may in fact have invented the word; a seventh-century document refers to the kingdom of the *Humbrenses*. The unity of the kingdom was clearly quite fragile for a long time, and the vicissitudes of Northumbrian history in the seventh century can partly be explained by the antagonism between Deira and Bernicia, fuelled by the hatred of exiles. In 603 the king of Dál Riata, Aédán mac Gabráin, attacked Æthelfrith of Northumbria, and suffered a disastrous defeat at the unidentified site of Degsastan. 'From that time no king of the Irish in Britain to this day had dared to make war on the English,' wrote Bede.[30] But Northumbrian politics may have been behind the attack: the *Anglo-Saxon Chronicle* said that Hering, son of Hussa, had led the army. Hussa appears to have been a predecessor of Æthelfrith, and Hering was thus using the alliance with the Irish in Britain to further his claim to the Northumbrian kingship. He may have been in exile in Dál Riata since Æthelfrith's accession in 592. Hermann Moisl, piecing together much Irish material of varying degrees of reliability, suggests that with him was another Northumbrian, Ælfred, whose son Osric married a daughter of Aédán mac Gabráin.[31]

Ælle had ruled Deira before Æthelfrith, and Ælle's son Edwin spent his exile during Æthelfrith's reign in the southern kingdoms, at the courts of Cadfan of Gwynedd, Rædwald of the East Angles and Æthelberht of Kent. He persuaded Rædwald to send an army north to defeat Æthelfrith and install him as king; when this plan succeeded, the sons of Æthelfrith went into exile among the Irish and the Picts. One of them at least, Oswald, was in Iona, for there he and his thegns were converted to Christianity. He and his fellow exile Osric (according to Moisl) may have fought on the Dál Riatan side in a battle in Ireland in around 628. When Edwin was killed in battle by Penda of the Mercians and Cadwallon of Gwynedd in 633, Eanfrith, one of the sons of Æthelfrith, returned from exile among the Picts to become king in Bernicia; he must have married a royal daughter of the

Picts, because years later Eanfrith's son Talorcan becomes king of the Picts (one of the few facts which suggests that Pictish succession may indeed have been matrilineal, as Bede said). Edwin's nephew Osric became king in Deira, but reigned as briefly as Eanfrith. Both were killed in 634 by the Welsh king Cadwallon, and Æthelfrith's other son Oswald reunited Northumbria. As David Kirby has pointed out,[32] there are enigmas here. What was the king of Gwynedd doing campaigning near the eastern end of Hadrian's Wall? How was it that two sons of Æthelfrith were close at hand to take power when Edwin was killed? Were Eanfrith and Oswald, in exile among Picts and Irish respectively, dependent upon the military support of Picts and Irish? What were the precise aims of Cadwallon and Penda, and what was the nature of their alliance? We have no answers: but the series of events do clearly show the way in which exile helped shape events and relations between kingdoms.

Like Edwin, Oswald died in battle against the pagan Penda – who thus conveniently created a pair of Christian martyrs for the Northumbrian dynasty – and he was succeeded by a third son of Æthelfrith, Oswiu (or Oswy). Bede delicately states that he had 'a partner in the royal dignity',[33] Oswine: the latter was actually of Edwin's family, and thus a member of the rival Deiran dynasty. It is not impossible that he owed his succession to Penda himself, and Oswiu – who also had to contend during his reign with the hostility of his own son and of the son of his brother Oswald – eventually had him murdered. The monastery of Gilling was built to atone for this sin, at the orders of Oswiu's wife Eanflæd – herself, as the daughter of Edwin of Deira, a relative of the murdered king. The murdered Oswine was the last Anglo-Saxon to be an independent king of Deira.

Edwin, Oswald and Oswiu were, successively, the most powerful Anglo-Saxon kings of the middle third of the seventh century. Each of them is on Bede's list of those who held *imperium* over the southern kingdoms: the so-called *bretwaldas*. Edwin, Bede tells us, even brought Anglesey and the Isle of Man under English rule. When the king of the West Saxons plotted to assassinate him, Edwin took his army south and 'either slew all those whom he discovered to have plotted his death or forced them to surrender'.[34] Oswald maintained Northumbrian power in southern England; Bede says that Oswald and the West Saxon king together gave Dorchester-on-Thames to the first bishop in Wessex, which suggests strongly that Oswald was the overlord of Wessex. For a few years after Oswiu overthrew Penda of the Mercians in 655, he too was able to enjoy a similar kind of domination in the south, while at the same time he 'overwhelmed and made tributary even the tribes of the Picts and Irish who inhabit the northern parts of Britain'.[35]

It was indeed north of the Humber that these three kings, and Oswiu's son and successor Ecgfrith (670–85), had their greatest successes and ultimately, in 685, their greatest disaster. Between them they extended English power throughout the north more rapidly and to a greater extent that any later English kings, and were (briefly) to have more success in

Scotland than any English king before Edward I's equally brief career in the north.

Edwin, the Deiran, and hence the southern Northumbrian king, was more concerned with consolidating the southern part of the kingdom. If his success in Anglesey was no doubt temporary, he did strengthen Deira considerably, by taking over the Christian British kingdom of Elmet. This kingdom had extended from the Pennines eastwards beyond Leeds, and perhaps as far as York; it is remembered still in such placenames as Sherburn-in-Elmet (North Yorks). We can only guess as to the impact on the Northumbrians of the incorporation of this British kingdom; indeed, the relationship between the Britons and the Anglo-Saxons north of the Humber is a matter of considerable controversy. Bede gives a clear impression that the Britons are the enemy, and that they play no role in the development of the Northumbrian kingdoms. Archaeology perhaps suggests something different. Edwin's palace at Yeavering, north of Hadrian's Wall, is mentioned by Bede, but he does *not* mention (or, probably, know) that it had been a British political centre before the arrival of the Angles in Bernicia. This, at least, is what Brian Hope-Taylor seems to have shown in his excavation of the site, although the dating does depend on his estimate of the average life of a timbered building on the exposed heights of Yeavering. What he found also, however, was that near Edwin's great hall was a building which seems to be a grandstand, constructed in wood but modelled on a Roman theatre, intended for seating over 300 people, and that Edwin's timber hall had been plastered on the outside, with the plaster scored to represent masonry. This architectural imitation of the Romans is one with Bede's description of Edwin progressing through his peaceable kingdom behind a 'standard which the Romans call a *tufa* and the English call a *thuf*'.[36] It is possible to construct an early history of Deira and Bernicia which shows them as basically British or Romano-British kingdoms which have been taken over as working entities by an Anglo-Saxon elite, which still respects (or pays lip-service to) their Roman past. Bernicia and Deira are the only two Anglo-Saxon kingdoms to have British names.

Historians are divided over how the Northumbrians took over Rheged – the important British kingdom to the west of the Pennines, in Cumbria and parts of south-west Scotland. The 'pacifists' have associated it with the later tradition that Oswiu, before marrying Edwin's daughter Eanflæd, had been the husband of Rhiainfellt (or Riemmelth), the granddaughter of Rhun, king of Rheged – who, again according to late Welsh tradition, had baptised Eanflæd and Edwin. Neither of these traditions is mentioned by Bede. The marriage may have been contracted before 633, when Oswiu was in exile; it may have led the way to a peaceful incorporation of Rheged. But there is no hint in British or other Celtic tradition that a kingdom might pass to another dynasty via a marriage alliance. A passing comment in Eddius Stephanus's *Life of Wilfrid* in a passage concerning the foundation of the church of Ripon in the 670s, suggests that the takeover was far from peaceful: the bishop stood before the altar and read out a list of places which the kings had given him, and 'also a list of the consecrated places in various parts which the British clergy had deserted when fleeing from the hostile sword wielded by the warriors of our own nation'.[37] The places mentioned include Yeadon, in Elmet, but also three places across the Pennines, in Rheged; Eddius Stephanus makes the conquest sound quite a recent event, in which case it might well have happened under Ecgfrith. Alfred P. Smyth has suggested that this may be tied in with the appearance of British exiles in Ireland: the *Annals of Ulster* record 'that British warbands were active along a 160-mile stretch of the east coast of Ireland from 682 until 709'.[38] They may have taken over the Isle of Man for use as a base.[39] If these are British warriors who had fled from Rheged following its capture by Ecgfrith, this gives some context for an event which even Bede finds no explanation for:

> In the year of Our Lord 684 Ecgfrith, king of the Northumbrians, sent an army to Ireland under Duke Berht, who wretchedly devastated a harmless race that had always been most friendly to the English, and his hostile bands spared neither churches not monasteries. The islanders resisted force by force so far as they were able, imploring the merciful aid of God and invoking His vengeance with unceasing imprecations.[40]

It was the first attack of the English on Ireland; and the last known until Strongbow's attack in 1169. If seen as a warning to the Irish not to aid British exiles in any attempt to recover Rheged, it makes a good deal of sense.

Rheged south of the Solway Firth may have been Anglicised fairly quickly; but Anglian forces only moved slowly westwards into Galloway. It was not until 731 that they felt strong enough to establish a bishopric there, at Whithorn; and the dearth of English place-names in that region suggests that the conquest was not followed up with much settlement. The two great stone crosses of Ruthwell and Bewcastle may have been erected around 700 by the Northumbrians as a symbol of Anglian power, and of the power of an orthodox church, in what was still a frontier region.

The situation was rather different on the east coast. The centre of power of Bernicia was far to the north on that coastline: the royal seats Bamburgh and Yeavering and the monastery and episcopal see of Lindisfarne were all some fifty miles north of Hadrian's Wall, and thus in territory that had been part of an independent British kingdom for centuries. It was from that base that Angles began to move into Scotland in some numbers. We have already noted the defeat of the king of Dál Riata, Aédán mac Gabráin, in 603 at the unidentified site of Degsastan, from which time, according to Bede, no king of the Irish in Britain dared attack the English. If Degsastan was in Lothian, as some think, what may have happened is that the Irish and the Angles were disputing between them control over the British kingdom of Gododdin (the former territory of the Votadini). If so, the English under Æthelfrith won Degsastan, and dominance over Gododdin; under Æthelfrith's son Oswald, in 638 (according to the *Annals of Ulster*) they besieged the main stronghold, Edinburgh. East Lothian may already have become Anglian by that date; some would argue that Anglian place-name types there, such as Whittinghame and Haddington, are of early date. Oswald's reign not only coincides with the influx of Irish ecclesiastical influence (as we shall see in the next chapter), but also the decline of the power of Dál Riata: their king Domnall Brecc was killed by the Britons of the kingdom of Strathclyde in 642. Edinburgh must have fallen in the mid-seventh century, if not in 638, as the Anglians felt strong enough by around 681 to found the bishopric of Abercorn, on the Firth of Forth opposite Dunfermline, west of Edinburgh. It may not have been the Northumbrian king himself who spearheaded this advances: we have hints of the existence of a powerful aristocratic Anglian family who may well have been based in Lothian. Beornheth is described as a *subregulus*, who aided Ecgfrith against the Picts in the 670s; he was probably the father of the *dux* Berht, who had led Ecgfrith's expedition against Ireland, who in turn seems to have been the same person as the *dux regius* ('royal duke'?) Berhtred, who died fighting the Picts in 698. Judging by his name, another member of the family was Berhtfrith, who was in charge of a campaign against the Picts in 711, and was described by the *Life of Wilfrid* as 'a leader second in rank to the king', *secundus a rege princeps*.[41]

From 685, the main opponents of the English in Scotland were not the Scots/Irish, but the Picts: Dunfermline and the whole area north of the Forth was probably under Pictish control. Under Oswiu, however – and here we only have Bede as authority – the Northumbrians apparently acquired overlordship over the Picts. The evidence comes in a series of bald statements, all of which tell the same story: 'Oswiu subjected the greater part of the Pictish race to the dominion of the English' and he 'overwhelmed and made tributary even the peoples of the Picts and Irish who inhabit the northern parts of Britain'.[42] When Bede describes the power of Bishop Wilfrid, *c.* 670, he said that he 'administered the see of the church at York and of all the Northumbrians and Picts, as far as Oswiu's power extended'. This was the same Wilfrid of York who, at Pope Agatho's synod in Rome in 680–1, had taken it on himself to speak on behalf of the 'whole northern part of Britain and Ireland, together with the islands inhabited by the English and British peoples, as well as the Irish and Picts'.[43] In *c.* 671, perhaps taking advantage of the death of Oswiu, the Picts had thrown out their king Drest, who had been under Oswiu's thumb; the following year Oswiu's successor Ecgfrith had led an army into Pictland and inflicted a terrible defeat on them. This resulted in the rise of a new and powerful leader among the Picts, Bridei, and the next time Ecgfrith intervened there was a very different result. Ecgfrith attacked the Picts in 685, met their army at Nechtansmere (Dunnichen Moss in Forfar, far into southern Pictland), and was heavily defeated. Ecgfrith was killed; his new bishop of Abercorn fled south to Whitby; the Angles were pushed back south of the Forth and possibly east of Edinburgh. Bede shows no surprise; it was God's justice, the result of the curses of the Irish for the unprovoked attack that Ecgfrith had made on them the previous year. But his exact words are interesting:

> The Picts recovered their land which the English had formerly held, while the Irish who lived in Britain and some part of the British nation recovered their liberty, which they have now [i.e. in 731] enjoyed for about forty-six years.[44]

The Picts recovered their land: perhaps land north of the Forth which had been won by Oswiu and Ecgfrith. The Irish – the kingdom of Dál Riata – and parts of the British nation – the British kingdom of Strathclyde, with its main fortress at Dumbarton(?) – recovered their liberty. What kind of subjection had they suffered before 685? Perhaps 'liberty' means freedom from tribute. Bede's estimates of the size and/or wealth of territories in terms of 'hides' comes from some Northumbrian record of hidage, made for the purposes of collecting tribute, such as the extant Tribal Hidage. It has been suggested that when Bede wrote that the island of Iona, in the far west of Scotland, was about five hides in size, he may have been consulting a document from around the mid-seventh century, when even Iona paid tribute to Northumbria.[45] In the early eighth century, Adomnán, abbot of Iona, certainly retained memories of Northumbrian power when he claimed that Oswald had been 'ordained by God emperor of all Britain'.[46]

What can we know about the kingdoms which the Northumbrians were trying to dominate? When we turn to look at the history of the 'Celtic' peoples of Scotland, we are hampered by a severe shortage of written sources,[47] and by a strong tendency to look for origins. Because of this, perhaps, the history of Scotland in the early Middle Ages has often been seen in terms of 'Picts, Gaels and Scots', to use the title of Sally Foster's volume for 'Historic Scotland'.[48] The Picts supplied the political power; the Gaels (i.e. the Irish) supplied a national language; the Scots, the nation that had emerged by the end of the first millennium, are the result of the fusion of the two. Marjorie Anderson's invaluable *Kings and Kingship in Early Scotland*, to take another example, deals only with Irish and Picts. It is almost as if there is a conspiracy to forget the role of the Angles and Britons in the history of Scotland. It was rumoured that a planned volume to precede Barbara Crawford's *Scandinavian Scotland*, to be called *Anglian Scotland*, had to be abandoned, because of the hostility with which this title was greeted in Scotland. But *British* or *Welsh Scotland* has not even been conjectured: perhaps there is the feeling that Welsh-speakers have no business north of the border. More to the point is that they were absorbed, and then largely forgotten. But they were in fact very significant in the first post-Roman centuries. The British kingdom of Goddodin, as we have seen, probably succumbed to Scottish and Anglian pressure in the first half of the seventh century, but the British kingdom of Strathclyde was a significant power, which continued in existence until the tenth century.

The height of the power of the Strathclyde Britons was probably in the mid-seventh century. As we have seen, the king of Dál Riata, Domnall Brecc, was defeated and killed in 642 by the Strathclyde Britons, under their king Owain, son of Bili. A Welsh poem celebrated the event, describing a raven gnawing at the head of the dead Irish king. The death of Domnall fulfilled the prophecy of St Columba, said Abbot Cumméne of Iona (d. *c.* 669), and 'from that day to this the family of Aédán [the royal descendants of Aedán mac Gabráin] is held in subjection by strangers, a fact which brings sighs of sorrow to the breast'.[49] Are those strangers the Britons of Strathclyde, or the Angles of Oswiu and Ecgfrith, or even the Picts? Domnall Brecc's defeat by Owain – at Strathcarron in Stirlingshire, which might seem to be outside either of their territories – had not been his only political setback. He had suffered two defeats by the Picts, which may have lost him territory in the north, and was defeated by the king of the Uí Néill in Ulster, and thereby lost control of the Irish kingdom of Dál Riata. The long political decline for Dál Riata was also a product of internal divisions which manifested themselves after Domnall Brecc's death; the group over which he was king, the Cenél nGabráin, lost their dominance over the other three peoples of Dál Riata, and the Cenél Loairn began to supply some of the kings.

The power of the kings of Strathclyde was partly determined by the balance of power with their Irish neighbours, but also tied up with their relations with the Picts: as tangled a problem as anything else concerned with the Picts. Without getting embroiled in the problems of the annals and genealogies, one can summarise this situation by saying that between 631 and 653 we seem to have three Pictish kings of British descent; that between 653 and 685 Pictland was under the domination of the Angles (the phrase 'puppet kings' is often used); and that the Picts who defeated the Angles at Nechtansmere in 685 were led by someone with the closest possible British connections: Bridei (or Bruide), the brother of Owain of Strathclyde. In the eighth century the Picts seem to have been largely independent, except for a brief period between 750 and 752 when Teudubr, king of Strathclyde, was overlord of the Picts; at times between 789 and 839 the Picts seem to have been ruled by the kings of Dál Riata; finally, as we shall see in Chapter 9, in 942 a king of Dál Riata, Cináed mac Alpín (Kenneth mac Alpine), definitively united the Picts and the Scots in a new kingdom of Scotland.[50] One of the many 'problems of the Picts' is how it was that this powerful and relatively unified people could have been dominated so frequently by various of its southern neighbours.

Picts have been thought to be a 'problem' for many years. This is partly because their language was at first unknown (but now thought to be a variant of British/Welsh), and because they disappeared as a people before actually producing any written documents that survive, which means we know about them only from Irish or English sources. The most characteristic Pictish monuments also add to the air of mystery. These are the Pictish 'symbol stones': dressed and undressed stones (and in a few cases rock outcrops and cave walls) decorated with accomplished incised ornament depicting humans and animals, but also with strange abstract symbols. These have been given equally strange names by modern archaeologists, such as 'V-rod' and 'Z-rod' or 'swimming elephant'. There are some fifty symbols altogether, some of which seem to be representations of high-status objects such as swords, cauldrons, armlets and so on. The symbols are usually in pairs, and in over 20 per cent of cases accompanied by representations of a mirror and comb. Nearly three hundred stones are known, almost all from the east coast of Scotland north of the Tay; this is roughly the same area which produces place-names with the *pit* element, which are presumed to be Pictish (although those are also found in some numbers between the Tay and the Forth).[51] The symbols have been found on metalwork too, such as the massive silver chain (neck ring) from Whitecleugh (Lanarkshire). It is thought that the symbol stones were produced over a long period, possibly from *c.* 500 to the early eighth century. What the symbols might mean has occasioned much debate, and much of it highly fanciful (but none the less possibly correct). The symbols may represent clans, or ranks, or components of personal names; the monuments may be memorial stones, signs of ownership, witnesses to marriage or other alliances, or they may be non-Christian religious monuments of some kind.

Whatever the symbol stones might mean, they seem to be evidence that the Picts had a very distinctive culture, bound up perhaps with the development of its kingship from the sixth century onwards. The Picts were, it is often said, the first people in these islands to attain national unity with a single kingship; as Sally Foster says, it is very tempting to see these stones 'as a form of political statement – even an expression of Pictishness – reflecting the strength of royal authority'.[52] It seems that the earliest of the stones are to be found in the north – north of the Mounth, the mountain range which narrows the eastern coastal plan just south of modern Aberdeen, and which seems to have been a natural barrier separating northern and southern Picts. At the time of St Columba (see p. 149) in the late sixth century, the centre of royal authority seems to have been north of the Mounth, and both north and south of the Moray Firth. By the seventh century and thereafter, it seems to have been the southern Picts, in the area between the Tay and the Mounth, who were dominant; and it is there that the later symbol stones are mainly found.

The problem of Pictish kingship, and the attempts to make sense of king-lists in order to draw up dynasties and thus attempt to write an inordinately sketchy political history for the Picts, is all bound up with the question of matriliny among the Picts. This supposedly made them different from all the other peoples in Britain and Ireland, all of whom were Celtic in language and culture, and thus making the Picts mysteriously 'pre-Celtic'. Even those who reject the idea that the Picts were not 'Celtic' sometimes cling to the matrilinear thesis. It is dependent on an Irish legend of the origin of the Picts, which Bede knew, which told how the Picts received their women from the Irish on condition that their kingship descended through the female line, and on the facts that two kings of the Picts definitely had foreign fathers: Talorcan (653–7), son of Eanfrith (king of Bernicia, 633–4), and Bridei (*d.* 695), son of Bili of Strathclyde. Origin legends are rarely renowned for historical accuracy, and the fact that we know the names of no royal Pictish women, and in the sources kings are always referred to as sons of their fathers rather than their mothers, suggests that this origin legend is as implausible as most.[53] The question of how foreigners managed to impose themselves on the Picts has to be explained in other ways. Nor were Talorcan and Bridei necessarily the only examples. John Bannerman suggested that Gartnait, king of the Picts at the end of the sixth century, was a son of the Dál Riatan king Aédán mac Gabráin; Marjorie Anderson thought that Gartnait and Drest, Pictish kings in the mid-seventh century, may have been sons of Aédán's grandson Domnall Brecc. In 750, Teudubr of Strathclyde became king of the Picts, when he defeated Óengus mac Fergusa, the powerful king of the Picts – who may have been a Scot . . .

All this evidence suggests that there is something different about Pictish kingship, which is nothing to do with matriliny. It might lead us to question the idea that the Picts had a unified kingship at all: that these named kings are not Pictish kings so much as overlords. There are indeed infrequent references in the sources to the seven provinces of the Picts, such as Cait (Caithness and south-east Sutherland), Fife and Fortriu: it is not impossible that these provinces frequently or always had their own kings. The 'kings of the Picts' may have been overlords, coming to the fore, like bretwaldas among the English, by their ability and talent – or by the powerful allies that they had among the southern neighbours of the Picts. It is interesting that in early Irish records the 'kingship of Fortriu' seems to have had a double meaning: either the kingship of this province, roughly the districts of Strathearn and Menteith, or synonymous with the kingship of the Picts as a whole, or at least of the Picts south of the Mounth.[54] This is rather like the usage of the 'kingship of Tara' among the Irish: kingship of a small territory in Meath, or a phrase used of the high-kingship of all Ireland. Fortriu is the southernmost and westernmost of the Pictish provinces: relatively easy to dominate by powerful kings of Angles, Britons or Irish. It is possible that some of the so-called 'kings of the Picts' were actually kings of Fortriu, imposed on the Picts by their neighbours. It is also possible that sometimes the Picts themselves chose foreigners: leaders chosen because of their military prowess to act as overkings and defenders of the Picts from external aggression (which is mostly going to come through Fortriu). Given how unlikely it is that further documentary evidence will come to light, it will never be possible to be certain. But we certainly ought to avoid falling into the trap which nineteenth-century nationalism (and, to some extent, Bede) prepares us for: imagining a sense of national feeling that simply was not there. We have already seen the international careers which warriors could pursue; and the frequency with which royal courts would harbour foreign exiles.

Most of this section has concentrated on the seventh century, partly because Bede gives us at least some information, and partly because that is the period of Anglian aggression, which, until 685 at least, dominates northern politics. Ecgfrith's defeat and death in 685 was clearly a major setback to Northumbrian expansion in central and northern Scotland, but does also usher in a period of greater stability. In the short run, too, better relations were established between Northumbria and her northern neighbours: Ecgfrith was succeeded by his half-brother Aldfrith (685–705), who in 685 was in exile in Iona – 'studying', Bede says discreetly, reminding one of modern actors 'resting' (although Aldfrith was indeed a genuine scholar: one of the very few English kings of whom this could be said). He was the son of Oswiu and Fín, the daughter of the northern Uí Néill king; later Irish sources call him 'Flann Fína', and say that he was the pupil of Abbot Adomnán of Iona. The relations between the two were certainly close. Adomnán persuaded Aldfrith's Irish relations to give money for the ransom of the Irish whom Ecgfrith had captured in 684; Aldfrith persuaded Adomnán to abandon the traditional Ionan method of calculating Easter – and to attempt to enforce that on his monks. The Angles held on to East Lothian, probably as far as Edinburgh, and to Berwickshire, but the bishopric of Abercorn was never re-established. In the south-west of what is now Scotland, however, the English advance still continued. There is an English bishop of Whithorn throughout the eighth century (the succession comes to an end with the coming of the Vikings), and place-names suggest some settlement in what is now Dumfries and Galloway; but the history of the Northumbrian control of this part of south-west Scotland is a hazy one. Almost the only event one knows about, however, is a story of English advance: in 750, Eadbert of Northumbria took over the area of Kyle in Ayrshire. The place-names in south-west Scotland are a fascinating palimpsest of different periods of occupation: English, British/Welsh, Irish and Viking. It is possible that English settlement was more intense than current maps indicate. Kenneth Jackson argued that in Cumbria there was an advance of Welsh (or, as he puts it, Cumbric) place-names, as the kingdom of Strathclyde expanded into that area in the tenth century, after the Vikings had shattered Northumbrian power.[55] But another of Jackson's judgements is worth remembering too:

> The rule of Northumbria continued unshaken until the latter part of the ninth century, and the English language must have impressed itself profoundly, especially in the east and south. Here it must have become the regular language, probably in most places the only one, although one cannot tell to what extent Cumbric may have lingered as the speech of the peasantry in remote areas.[56]

The history of 'Anglian Scotland' has yet to be written; but the arrival of a northern dialect of the English language (what became called, confusingly for outsiders, 'Scots') must be seen as its major legacy.

The kingdoms of the south

The picture in the north, complex as it may be, is somewhat more clear than that of the history of the southern kingdoms. As we have seen, the Tribal Hidage suggests that the original political map of England was much more fragmented than would be thought from the simplified picture drawn by Bede for the early seventh century. That picture, which presumably reflects the political realities of Bede's own lifetime, gives a picture of a number of smaller kingdoms in the East: the kingdom of the men of Kent, of the South Saxons, of the East Saxons, and of the East Angles, and two larger kingdoms in the West, the kingdoms of the West Saxons and of the Mercians. Charters show us kings of Surrey and of the Hwicce in the later seventh century, whom their overkings (in Latin, at least) call *subreguli*: charters do not exist to show us whether any of the numerous small peoples of the Tribal Hidage also had their own *subreguli*, but it may well be so. There is one revealing political episode recorded by Bede, which occurred on the death of Cenwealh, king of the West Saxons, around 672: '*subreguli* took up the kingdom of that people, and dividing it up among themselves they ruled it for about ten years'.[57] Earlier, under 626, one version of the *Anglo-Saxon Chronicle* said that Edwin of the Northumbrians killed *five* West Saxon kings to avenge their plot against him. To what extent and for how long was the king of the West Saxons merely holding together a loose confederation of smaller kingdoms? For that matter, when did the 'kingdom of the West Saxons' emerge at all? As Bede tells us, the earlier name for the people was 'the Gewissa' and it was perhaps only in the later seventh century that 'West Saxon' became current; later, in the eighth century, the kings were referring to themselves as 'kings of the Saxons'. The picture that Bede has bequeathed to later generations of historians, of several largish political entities in southern England, may be a picture that simply does not apply before the mid- to late-seventh century.

The first kingdoms to emerge in the post-Roman south were, presumably, Roman rather than Anglo-Saxon anyway. This is not quite unique in the western Roman Empire: there is a king of the Romans in North Africa in the fifth century, and a leader in Gaul was also called *rex Romanorum*. But it is in western Britain that the direct political descendants of the last emperors of the Romans survived, until their independence was snuffed out by Edward I in the thirteenth century. Presumably, at some point in the fifth century, there were several British kingdoms in eastern Britain as well as those in the West, which survived longer. We have already seen the kingdom of Elmet, which existed in Yorkshire until the early seventh century. We have already noted the possibility of a British kingdom north of the lower Thames, between London and St Albans, in an area remarkably devoid of early Anglo-Saxon cemeteries, which may have lasted into the later sixth century. Signs of sub-Roman settlement in London, including fifth-century imported amphorae, may reflect such a continuation; major timber-framed buildings replacing the masonry villa at Latimer (Bucks) may relate to this horizon.[58] What we do not know is whether any of the new Anglo-Saxon kingdoms were not newly constituted kingdoms so much as Romano-British states taken over wholesale by the Anglo-Saxons. We have already noted that Deira and Bernicia, in the north, with their Celtic names, may have been political entities before the Angles; perhaps Kent or others of the southern kingdoms were too. The *-sæten* people-names like the *Pecsæten* of the Peak District and the *Cilternsæten* of the Chilterns may once have been small kingdoms: indeed, Somerset and Dorset may have been independent Romano-British territories until taken over by the West Saxons, some time in the seventh or early eighth century. It has been suggested that the Anglo-Saxon diocese of Worcester, which included Gloucester, Cirencester and Bath, preserved the boundaries of the seventh-century kingdom of the Hwicce, which itself may have been reproducing the territory of the Romano-British kingdom that preceded it.

We are on slightly firmer ground when we move further west. We have, to start with, the names of the five kings mentioned by Gildas (p. 95): Constantine of Dumnonia, Aurelius Caninus, Vortipor of the Demetae, Cuneglasus, and Maglocunus, 'dragon of the island'. Constantine was king of Dumnonia: Devon and Cornwall. In Roman times Cornwall – a remote territory with no towns and no villas – seems to have been a full part of the *civitas* of the Dumnonii, and thus administered from Exeter. Tintagel has been mooted as a possible royal centre for the post-Roman kings of Dumnonia. (Cornwall may not have been an independent entity until the ninth century.) Vortipor was the king of the Demetae, in Welsh 'Dyfed': the south-west province of modern Wales. A memorial stone stands in Casteldwyran churchyard (Carmarthen) inscribed in Latin MEMORIAE VOTEPORIGIS PROTICTORIS (and in Irish ogam script simply VOTECORIGIS), which may well relate to Gildas's king, remembered in Welsh as Gwrthefyr.[59] He seems to have taken the title, or simply the description, 'Protector': which, if he was the rapist of his own daughter, as Gildas alleges, might have afforded the monk some bitter amusement. This part of Wales, as we have seen, seems to have been subject to a considerable amount of Irish settlement at this time; perhaps Vortipor's kingdom owed its origins to the assistance of Irish warriors. The final king mentioned was Maglocunus, usually associated with Maelgwn, king of Gwynedd, known from other sources. 'Dragon of the island' may reflect his association with Anglesey. Gwynedd, Venedotia in Latin, was not associated with a particular pre-Roman people, like the Dumnonii or the Demetae: it is possible that Maelgwn or another from his dynasty displaced the king of the Ordovices, the centre of whose power was further south (and preserved in names such as Orddwy, in Merioneth). A stone at Penmachno (Caernarfonshire), perhaps from the fifth or sixth century, preserves the memory of a *civis Venedotis*, 'a citizen of Gwynedd', who was the cousin of a *magistratus*.[60] One must not assume that a kingdom with no obvious Roman origins did not in fact have very real awareness of its Roman background. It is easy to think of the British kingdoms as 'Welsh', while perhaps we should be thinking of them as 'Romano-British'.

Where would the two other kingdoms, those of Aurelius Caninus and Cuneglasus, have been? If there was a geographical logic to the order in which Gildas mentions the kings, then Aurelius Caninus might have been the king of Gwent, in southern Wales, a name which derives from the Latin word for the chief town of the Silures, Venta Silurum, or Caerwent. Cemeteries recently excavated at Caerwent suggest that it was a centre of some sort in the fifth and sixth centuries. And, finally, Cuneglasus may have been the king of Powys, the territory in central Wales, between Dyfed and Gwynedd, but also possibly extending into what is now the West Midlands. The former Roman town of Viroconium (Wroxeter) would seem, from Philip Barker's excavations, to be an important centre still in post-Roman times, and perhaps it belonged to the kingdom of Powys. That name, it seems to be generally agreed, comes from the Latin word *pagenses*, or 'country people'. There were other smaller kingdoms too, particularly in southern Wales, such as Ergyng and Brycheiniog: how much can be said about them in part depends on one's view of the authenticity of the early charters in the twelfth-century Book of Llandaff.[61]

Very little is known about these early Welsh kingdoms, about their internal politics, external relations, or even extent. We probably should not think in terms of 'boundaries' so much as 'spheres of influence', and those spheres may be reflected in the evidence of church dedications. Each dynasty seems to have supported the cult of a particular local saint, and dedicating a church to that saint may indicate some kind of act of political allegiance: thus we have St Beuno in Gwynedd, Sts David and Teilo in Dyfed, St Garmon in Powys, St Brychan in Brycheiniog, and Sts Cadog and Illtud in Gwent. The evidence does suggest that Gwynedd emerged in the sixth century as the most powerful of the kingdoms, and it was Gwynedd which supplied the kings who appear as the great enemies of the English in the pages of Bede: it was Cadwallon of Gwynedd who occupied Northumbria for a year after the death of Edwin (633–4), according to Bede.

Ironically, perhaps, it was Cadwallon's ally Penda of Mercia (?632–55) who was to help create the most powerful kingdom of the English in the south. He twice defeated the Northumbrians, killing Edwin in 633 and Oswald in 642, before succumbing himself to a coalition of forces led by Oswiu in 655. Bede, the Northumbrian patriot, by extolling the power of the Northumbrians in southern England under those three kings, does tend to hide the fact of Penda's prolonged power, and the fact that not long after Penda's death his son Wulfhere managed to establish himself in an equally powerful position. Wulfhere had been hidden by some Mercian aristocrats after his father's death, during a period in which the Northumbrian Oswiu seems to have controlled Mercia, and he not only recovered all Mercia, but managed to impose some kind of overlordship over most of southern

England. It was Wulfhere who arranged the baptism of the first Christian king of the South Saxons, Æthelwealh, and who was in a position to reward him with two provinces which the West Saxon king would have regarded as his own: the Isle of Wight and part of Hampshire (both, interestingly, territories which Bede regarded as Jutish).

From the time of Wulfhere (658–75) onwards, the Mercian kings were among the most powerful in England: in particular Wulfhere's brother Æthelred (675–704), and, above all, two descendants of Penda's brother Eowa: Æthelbald (716–57) and Offa (757–96). Partly because of Bede's hostility to the Mercians, there is a good deal that we do not know about the early history of Mercia, and hence about the reasons for its success. One reason, however, was undoubtedly its situation as a frontier territory: a *mearc* or March, from which derives its name Mercia. Although Hunter Blair argued that the frontier in question was with Northumbria – the disputed area of North Derbyshire, North Lincolnshire and South Yorkshire – it is rather more likely that it was the frontier with the Welsh that was important. To begin with, Penda may have been a junior partner of the king of Gwynedd: perhaps it was thanks to Cadwallon that he held his kingdom against the claims of his brother Eowa. But it was probably already in his reign that the Welsh lands of the West Midlands – Herefordshire, Shropshire and Cheshire – were incorporated into his kingdom. Whether this was by conquest or by some other means is quite unknown. It is possible that he created the sub-kingdom of the Magonsæte (Herefordshire and southern Shropshire) for one of his sons, who took the name Merewalh ('famous Welshman') as a compliment to his subjects; it is also possible that Merewalh was indeed a Welshman, ruling the territory in close alliance with Penda.[62] It is possible that the Hwicce, in Worcestershire and Gloucestershire, also came under Mercian domination at the time of Penda. The origin of this kingdom, and the role of the Anglo-Saxons in this largely Welsh area, as with the Magonsæte, is quite uncertain. But even if Mercian involvement was achieved by accommodation rather than by conquest, it must have resulted in the Anglicisation of the area: although there were many Welsh-speakers in the western Midlands right down to the thirteenth century, the place-names were almost entirely anglicised. More importantly, expansion must have afforded the Mercian kings ample opportunity to reward their followers with estates, a prerequisite for continued political power.

The culmination of the Anglicisation of the west came under King Offa, whose Dyke is probably the greatest feat of linear engineering in Britain between the Antonine Wall and the canals of the eighteenth and nineteenth century. Having said that, it is not at all clear that the work was carried out exclusively in the reign of Offa, as later tradition said, and there are other problems with the earthwork which archaeological work has not been able to resolve: needless to say, it is hardly possible to excavate a 150-mile frontier in its entirety. About eighty miles are preserved, and it is now generally thought that there were originally no gaps, except where rivers (above all the River Wye, to the south) themselves provided adequate obstacle. In origin, the earthworks were some 60 feet wide, with a ditch some 6 feet deep on the Welsh side, and a rampart rising some 25 feet above it. In parts there was a stone wall at the top; in other parts, perhaps, a wooden palisade. It was presumably intended to stop the constant raiding, and cattle-raiding, from the West, as well as being an impressive reminder to the Welsh of the power of the Mercian kings. It was a very near contemporary of the Danevirke, the earthwork built by the Danish kings to defend the Jutland peninsula from attacks from Germany, and dated by dendrochronology to the year 737. As Patrick Wormald has pointed out, we must not see Offa's Dyke as 'the first great public work of English government':[63] it was in fact perhaps the last in a long series of linear defences built in Britain since the Bronze Age. That prehistoric tradition may be found elsewhere in Anglo-Saxon England, such as in the two Wansdykes ('Woden's dykes') and other earthworks of Wessex, which may relate to temporary borders established between the English and the Welsh in the sixth century.

The advantage which the West Saxon and the Mercian kings had – building their power by extending their territories further and further West, into British territory – was denied the smaller kingdoms in the East. Bede thought that Ælle of the South Saxons had held *imperium* over the southern English in the sixth century, and that Æthelberht of Kent had succeeded him in this position near the end of that century, while Rædwald of the East Angles succeeded Æthelberht in the 610s. But those kingdoms had had their day. Sussex – separated from kingdoms to the north by the apparently sparsely inhabited Weald – was so much a backwater that it was the last of the English kingdoms to be converted to Christianity. Kent and East Anglia did profit from their ability to trade with the Frisians and the Franks across the sea. Mound 1 of Sutton Hoo witnesses to the overseas connections of the East Anglian royal house, to Scandinavia, Byzantium and Francia. But the buried wealth of Kent in the seventh century is even more impressive, in that it is spread through dozens of graves in numerous cemeteries. At Sarre, for instance, near the Wantsum Channel which separated the (then) island of Thanet from the mainland, was a cemetery with a very high proportion of rich 'warrior' graves, but also several graves with sets of scales, as well as imported pottery, and coins from Francia and from Byzantium. Perhaps these warriors were protecting the trading settlement; perhaps the weapons were a sign of status acquired by wealth. Kent, at any rate, had close links with northern France. It was from there that King Æthelberht acquired his Frankish princess, Bertha, in the late sixth century; it was to there that the first missionaries to the Anglo-Saxons sailed in 597.

7

The missionary Church

We have seen in an earlier chapter how Christianity came to Roman Britain, and from there to Ireland with St Patrick and to parts of Scotland with St Nynia. The *Confessio* of St Patrick is evidence that in his day (probably the second half of the fifth century) the Church was still operating in the British kingdoms, as an organisation controlled by bishops and capable of having councils where bishops from more than one post-Roman kingdom could meet together to take decisions. By the later sixth century the Church seems to be thriving in Ireland and in the western parts of Roman Britain. But such evidence as we have suggests that it had virtually died out in those parts ruled by the Angles and Saxons. One has to say, however, that the evidence is hardly conclusive. There are certainly no records of bishops operating in Anglo-Saxon England in the sixth century; but absence of evidence is not conclusive. Our own picture is dominated by Bede's *Ecclesiastical History of the English People*, which is keen to point out how the English derived their Christianity direct from the bishop of Rome, the Pope, and not from the British. As we have seen (above, p. 83), it is possible that Christian worship continued, with or without bishops, in the territory controlled by the Angles and Saxons. But, for Bede and for any churchman, Christianity without bishops was even worse than no Christianity at all: an ecclesiastical structure was more important than a belief system, because only such a structure ensured correct belief and worship, and hence the salvation of souls. The missionaries who reintroduced that structure to Roman Britain, and carried it to places which had never been reached by the Romans, were the heroes of Bede's narrative.

Columba

The first named missionary in Bede's account was Nynia, the apostle of the southern Picts (see above, p. 84). We do not know where Bede found his

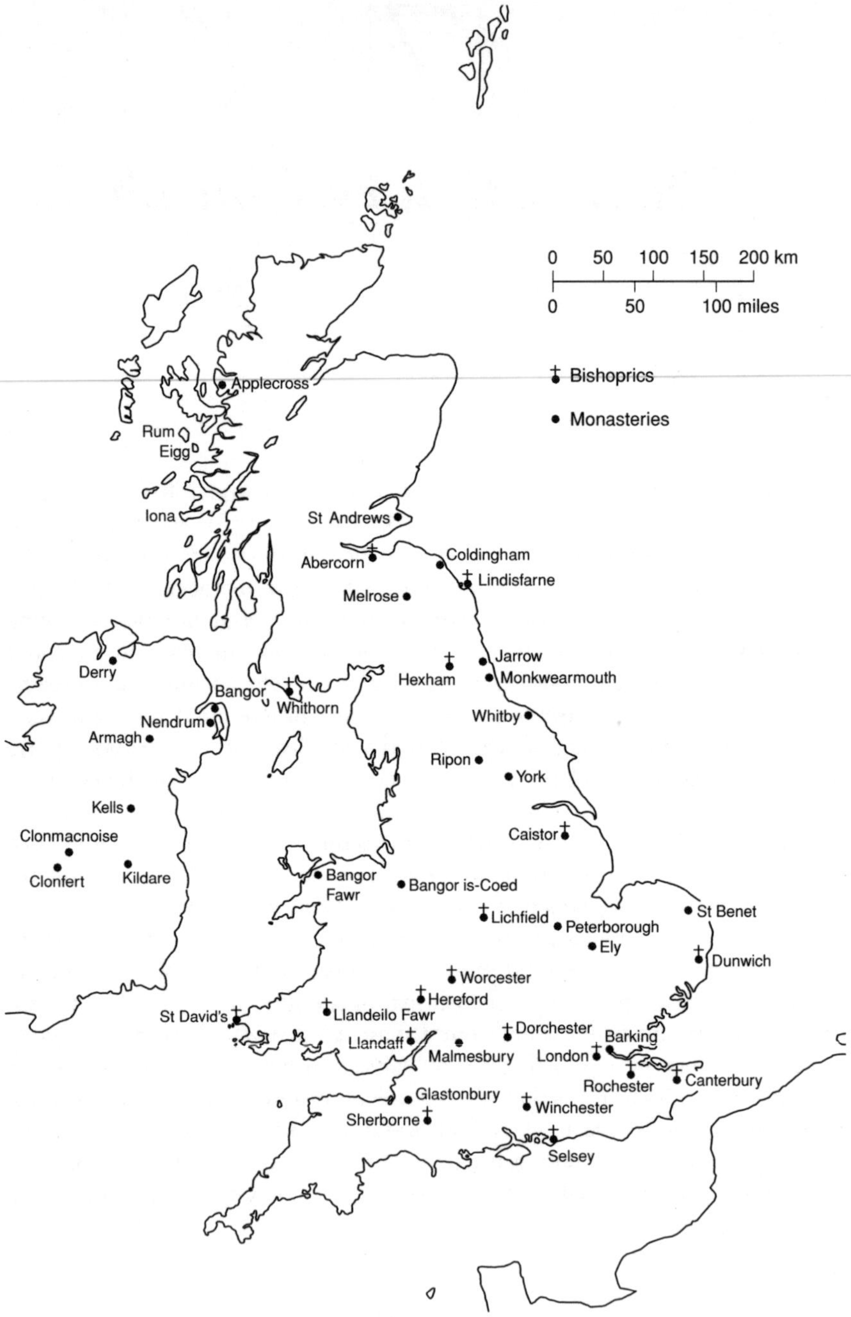

Map 5 Major ecclesiastical sites in pre-Viking Britain

information about Nynia of Whithorn. He probably knew Pehthelm, who became the first Anglian bishop of Whithorn in around 710, several decades after that part of Britain had been taken over by the Anglian kings of Northumbria. But Bede was also capable of getting information from the Picts themselves. Whatever the source, it is possible that the information was tainted or influenced by political factors: Nynia, said Bede, came straight from Rome (the *correct* route for missionaries, in Bede's view). Most of the Picts had been led astray, in religious terms, because they had received their Christianity, several generations after Nynia, via St Columba and his monastic community at Iona.

There is much better information on Columba than there is on Nynia: an extensive *Life* of St Columba was written by his eighth kinsman to succeed him as abbot of Iona, Adomnán (628–704). The sole manuscript of this *Life* is now lost: but it was copied in 1621 by the scholar who first located it, in the library of the island monastery of Reichenau, in south-west Germany. Many Irish monks came to live in the monasteries of Francia in the eighth and ninth centuries; it is by no means the only case of a text that does not exist in Britain at all, but survives as a result of the travels of British and Irish monks abroad. It was a manuscript that had been copied by a scribe called Dorbbéne, who is known to have been a senior monk of Iona when he died in 713. The *Life of St Columba* is thus one of the rare early medieval texts whose manuscript might actually date back to the time of the author himself. We do not have to worry about mistakes or scribal editing, as we do with so many other crucial texts. But we do still have to worry about Adomnán's reliability. Any *Life* of a saint in this period may be as much about how the saint *should* have lived as it was about the saint's actual life, and, if it was written many years after the saint's actual life (as in this case), it may reflect the ecclesiastical and political concerns of a later age, using the saint's life to justify actions or to invent claims.

According to Adomnán, Columba studied with an abbot in Leinster, and, in his forties, 'sailed away from Ireland to Britain choosing to be a pilgrim for Christ'. There is nothing terribly unusual about this in the early Irish Church. In the *Life* of his namesake Columba the Younger (usually known as Columbanus), it is said that the saint first chose the 'lesser pilgrimage', leaving his family and province to go into another province, as a pious act of self-denial; he then chose the 'greater pilgrimage', leaving Ireland altogether: voluntarily severing his life from its roots and choosing the same fate as was imposed on rapists and parricides.[1] Pilgrimage, for the early Irish, was not a question of going to a holy place, but of leaving kin and country for the sake of God, like the three Irishmen who were found drifting in the open sea in an oarless boat at the time of King Alfred.[2] It is often suggested that Columba *had* to leave Ireland because of his involvement in a battle on the side of his kinsmen, the Uí Néill, or because of his excommunication by a synod for the offence of copying a manuscript without permission. These things may have contributed to his decision, but perhaps only in the sense that he could not lead a holy life with those kinds of distractions. He sailed north, to a small island off the western coast of Mull, and there founded perhaps the most famous monastery in early medieval Britain. The island was called Hy, but this was Latinised as Iona: the word seemed divinely inspired to the medieval mind, since 'Columba' was the Latin version of the name of the Hebrew prophet 'Jonah' (also meaning 'dove'), which itself could be Latinised as Iona.

Bede, who probably did not understand the Irish idea of pilgrimage but understood very well the Christian duty to convert the pagan, thought that Columba 'came from Ireland to Britain to preach the word of God in the provinces of the northern Picts', and that he received the island of Iona from the Pictish king Bridei.[3] This is perhaps what the Picts in Bede's day remembered. But it is likely that Iona was in fact part of the territory controlled by the Irish who had settled in Scotland in the previous century, the kingdom of Dál Riata, and that the conversion of the northern Picts did not begin immediately, and perhaps not until the time of Columba's successors. Columba did visit the fortress of King Bridei, north of Loch Ness – and even encountered the terrifying Loch Ness monster on one occasion – but although Adomnán refers to the saint's encounters with the king's 'wizards', he does not claim that the king had actually been converted by Columba. What is certain is that over the century that separated Columba's death in 597 and the time of Abbot Adomnán, the influence of Iona was exerted right up the western seaboard of Scotland and very probably across the mountains to the east coast, which, as we have seen, was the heart of the Pictish kingdom. Even in Columba's lifetime Iona had become an 'international' monastery, with British and Pictish monks, and even two Englishmen. Daughter houses were founded in the Hebrides, and on the Scottish mainland. By the early eighth century, the Pictish kings were Christian and, moreover, many of the churches in Pictland were dependencies of Iona. Thanks to Adomnán and Bede, we think of Columba as an Apostle to the Picts, but his successors may have been rather more active and successful than Columba himself. Indeed, some important missionary work was being done by Irishmen who were not actually connected to Iona at all: we know little about them, because their work was not celebrated by an equivalent of Adomnán. Donnán of Eigg, for instance, apparently not only founded churches in south-west Scotland, south of Iona, but also north of Skye, beyond the influence of Iona altogether. That the missionary effort was not without its enemies is also suggested by the brief report in the *Annals of Ulster* of 'the burning of Donnán of Eigg with 150 martyrs' on 17 April 617, presumably at his monastery of Eigg, an island nearly forty miles north of Iona. Even more important was Maelrubai, who sailed directly from Ireland in 671, and shortly afterwards founded the monastery of Applecross: this was on the mainland, east of Skye, closer to the centres of Pictish power than the foundations of Columba or Donnán. The church dedications to Donnán and Maelrubai in north-west Scotland are in much the same area, and that is an area that does not overlap with the churches connected with Iona. Maelrubai was still alive when Adomnán wrote his *Life of Columba*, but is not mentioned once by Adomnán: perhaps the Ionan abbot was all too well aware of the importance of Maelrubai in the north, and wrote the *Life* partly to counter that power and to reestablish the waning influence of Iona.

Another shadowy missionary figure in the North is St Kentigern, for whom our knowledge is almost entirely dependent on *Lives* written as late as the twelfth century, hundreds of years after his death. According to this tradition he was British, from Lothian, and his mother was associated with Traprain Law, an ancient hill-fort of the Votadini (see p. 37). Kentigern himself was said to have been brought up in a Christian community among the southern Picts, north of the Forth, and was then established in Glasgow by King Rhydderch Hen, the British king of Strathclyde in the late sixth century. In the twelfth century it was said that Rhydderch Hen had been baptised in Ireland; but Adomnán of Iona claims that he was in contact with St Columba and Iona. The king apparently needed Kentigern to strengthen Christianity in Strathclyde. One later *Life* says that Kentigern came across a cemetery in Glasgow that had been founded long before by Nynia; it may be that Nynia's proselytising effort in this area needed to be revivified by a second generation of missionary activity.

Were there other British bishops involved in conversion in Britain at the time? Bede categorically denies that they had any role in the conversion of the *English*, but we may doubt Bede on this point, and the British may have been involved as missionaries elsewhere. Patrick was certainly not the only British missionary in Ireland. He had contemporaries, like Auxilius and Secundinus, who may have been British, and he had successors, such as Maucteus (Irish 'Mochta') and Uinniau, who certainly were. From the seventh century onwards Irish hagiography celebrated the way in which British ecclesiastics founded churches and monasteries in Ireland, and how Irish saints were the pupils of British saints. Better evidence of such activity comes from a problematic text (from between the fifth and seventh centuries), the *Synodus episcoporum*, which prohibited the ministry of British clerics who arrived in Ireland without letters of introduction, and from linguistics and phonetics, which suggest that ecclesiastical words arrived in the Irish language via the British.[4]

Augustine

The undoubted achievement of the monks of Iona was to do more than anyone else to convert the Angles and Saxons. Even Bede admitted that. But Bede was careful to point out that the influence of Iona only began to be felt on the English after the Roman mission led by Augustine. He may have been wrong; Adomnán believed that there were two English monks at Iona before the arrival of Augustine in England.[5]

Bede's account of the end of Roman Britain and the origins of Anglo-Saxon England in the *Ecclesiastical History* is, as we have seen, confused and sketchy. He says almost nothing about the sixth century. In Book I. 22 the century is summarised in about fifteen lines, which emphasise how British society collapsed into disorder and sin. He ends the chapter noting that among all the unspeakable crimes of the British was this: 'that they never preached the faith to the Saxons or Angles who inhabited Britain with them. Nevertheless God in his goodness did not reject the people whom he foreknew, but he had appointed much worthier heralds of the truth to bring this people to the faith.' Chapter 23 introduces Gregory (Pope between 590 and 604) and his decision to send a group of monks to England, under Augustine (who was prior of Gregory's own monastery of St Andrew's in Rome). This was the crucial event in the ecclesiastical history of Britain, as far as Bede was concerned. Fifteen out of the next sixteen chapters are devoted to Gregory, Augustine and their mission, chapters which continue to dominate our understanding of the events.

We cannot always know the sources of Bede's information for Augustine's mission. In the Preface to the *History* he specifically mentions Abbot Albinus of St Augustine's in Canterbury as his major helper, and the man who persuaded Nothelm, a London priest, to bring Bede much information collected in Canterbury. Later, that same Nothelm (who became archbishop of Canterbury in the year of Bede's death) went to Rome and in effect acted as Bede's research assistant, going into the papal archives and copying down the papal letters that seemed relevant to him. He may even have provided Bede with the *Libellus Responsionum*, which did *not* exist in the papal archive – St Boniface complained about that in the 740s – but which did circulate as an independent manuscript, or 'little book', at the time, purporting to contain Pope Gregory's answers to a number of questions sent to him by Augustine.

There may have been Northumbrian sources of information available too. Certainly the nun (or possibly monk) at Whitby who wrote the first ever *Life of Gregory the Great* had some sources of information. Bede did not himself know this *Life*, but he shares one story with it: the famous story of Pope Gregory the Great meeting his first Englishmen. This is almost certainly a Northumbrian story, possibly even a Whitby story, since it foregrounds Deira, the southern kingdom of the Northumbrians. Gregory saw slave-boys in the market-place in Rome, along with other merchandise. They stood out because of their fair complexions and fine hair. He discovered to his distress that they were pagan, and that they were called *Angli*. 'They have angelic faces, and belong with the angels in heaven.' They are from Deira. 'Good! They will be snatched from the wrath (*de ira*) of Christ.' Their king is Ælle (who according to the *Anglo-Saxon Chronicle* began to reign around 560). 'Ælleluia! The praise of God will be sung in those parts.'

Bede did not seem to know the other story in which Gregory is again shown displaying a love of puns, which is in Chapter 10 of the anonymous *Life*. The author tells how Gregory himself decided to go on a mission to save the poor heathen English, despite the pleas of many people in Rome. He left; but papal messengers were sent to bring him back. Gregory knew the messengers were following, since their message was sent to him in advance by God: a locust settled on him as he was reading a book. *Locusta* = *loco sta*: 'Stay in your place.' He ignored the divine order, interestingly, and set off northwards again; but the papal messengers caught him and persuaded him to return to Rome. These stories are hardly likely to come from the Canterbury tradition (nor are they terribly likely to be true). On the other hand, the anonymous author of the *Life did* know things that Bede apparently did not know; she knew that the name of Gregory's mother was Sylvia, for instance. Whitby, like Canterbury, must have had its sources of information.

Gregory did not go to Britain himself, but sent Augustine. Bede relates that Augustine arrived in England, having persuaded his reluctant companions to carry on with the journey; he landed together with some forty monks, and some Frankish interpreters. He meets the most powerful English king at the time, Æthelberht of Kent, in the open air, because Æthelberht apparently thought they might work magic against him if they met inside a building. Did these foreigners with long flowing robes remind Æthelberht of magicians? There is at least one Anglo-Saxon grave, from Portway (Hants), which is apparently that of a man buried in a dress, with brooches and a necklace, and a large lump of flint on his chest, which has been interpreted as the grave of a magician.[6] Æthelberht could hardly have been ignorant of Christianity, however: he had a Christian wife. Bede says that the king was not interested in conversion immediately, but he did not hinder the work of the missionaries. Augustine established a base in a former Roman church, dedicated to St Martin, and thereafter built new churches, and restored other Roman churches. It is not clear from Bede how much communication there was with the Papacy. It was only in 601 that more missionaries are sent out, together with some of the things the new Church needed: vestments, church furnishings, the vessels needed for the Mass, 'and many books'. This was three years before Gregory's death. Inserted after Gregory's death, and thus presumably happening in the last years of Augustine's life, Augustine met the British bishops in a diplomatically disastrous encounter; and also began to consecrate other bishops for the English.

It was not really until the 1960s that historians began to dig into this account, and into the other sources, to see whether Bede's version is in any way misleading. If one looks at Sir Frank Stenton's classic *Anglo-Saxon England*, written in the 1930s, one can see that his account of Augustine is written entirely from Bede; he worries over some of the details, but does not subject Bede to any serious criticism. Nowadays we are a little less reverent; but we have also advanced further; and it is interesting to see how it has happened. There are three main areas where we have made advances. The first is in the realisation that our primary source for Augustine's mission is *not* Bede, but the surviving letters of Gregory the Great. The second is the deepening of our knowledge of Bede's own preoccupations and interests, and hence deepening of our understanding of the ways in which he might be distorting the picture. And the third is the understanding that this is not just a problem for English historians: to see how Augustine's mission operated, we need to understand how to place it in its full continental framework.

We have come to realise that Bede was not a dispassionate and neutral historian – indeed, that there *are* no dispassionate and neutral historians. Bede wrote history for a reason, and the patterns he saw in history reflected those reasons. Christianity proceeds from Rome. The Britons received it from Rome, but they fell into disorder and sin; the English have received it from Rome, and they too, by Bede's own day, were falling into disorder and sin. Bede wrote his *History* in large part to call the sinful English Church and people back to God, in case they too were punished, as the British had been by the invasions of the Angles and Saxons. Just over fifty years after Bede's death, another Northumbrian, Alcuin of York, who may well have read every word of Bede's extensive writings, argued that the coming of the Vikings was indeed the punishment for the sins of the English. It is important to note that Bede had several agendas, and is certainly not telling us everything he knows; and may be putting things he does tell us into a particular light.

The first place to start must be the only contemporary evidence: the surviving letter collection of Gregory the Great (which confirms that the Gregorian letters Bede included in his *History* were accurately copied). Bede's 'research assistant' Nothelm found some of the letters relating to the English, but only those actually addressed to the missionaries or to English royalty. He missed, for instance, the earliest relevant letter, which Gregory wrote to Candidus, *rector* of the papal estates in Gaul, in September 595, urging him to buy Anglian slaves and place them into monasteries.[7] It has suggested to some that Gregory was already planning a mission; it was, or became, missionary practice to train slaves to serve in missions to their countries. It is also interesting for its use of 'Anglian'. As we have seen, all other writers at the time, on the Continent or in Celtic-speaking areas, refer to the Germanic settlers in Britain as 'Saxons' or 'Sassenachs'. Gregory was consistent in using 'Angle', and Bede follows him in this. It is arguably thanks to Gregory that I have written this book in 'England' rather than 'Saxony'. The terminology took a long time to catch on. A century after Gregory, the writer of the *Life of St Wilfrid* refers to his hero returning to Yorkshire, solid Anglian territory, and calls it *Saxonia*. It was confusing terminology: there was (as there still is) a Saxony in North Germany as well. The word 'Anglo-Saxon' was probably coined in the eighth century by the

English missionaries in Germany, specifically to distinguish the Saxons in England from the Saxons in Germany.

The next relevant letter was written to Theuderic and Theudebert, kings of the Franks, on July 23 596, announcing that the Angles had expressed a desire for conversion, and asking them to protect Augustine on his voyage through Gaul since they would clearly wish all their subjects to be converted.[8] Theuderic and Theudebert had both come to power that year, on the death of their father. Their ages in 596 are unknown, but it is unlikely that the eldest was more than twelve; they were under the regency of their grandmother Brunhild. Three interesting things emerge from this letter. The initiative for the mission seems to have come from the English themselves, rather than from the Pope, which is what Bede and the Whitby author assumed. The Frankish kings are particularly involved because of their duty to convert *their subjects*. Even if Bede or his research assistant had read this letter, they might not have realised that in the sixth century the Frankish kings did in fact claim to be overlords of the south of England: indeed, there is some evidence that their claims to overlordship may have had some reality in fact.[9] The third interesting point is that Gregory complains that the English had been asking for priests *e vicino* – from nearby – without success; in another letter Gregory asks Brunhild to send priests *e vicino*, so they are likely to be Frankish priests, not British ones.

All this immediately puts a rather different gloss on Augustine's mission. It was not a papal initiative: very few things were in the early Middle Ages. The popes had no international bureaucracy; their main attention was on Rome itself and the estates of the church of Rome in Sicily and elsewhere, and external affairs usually only impinged on them when an appeal was made to them. Augustine's mission was also something tied up very closely with Frankish politics. There had been a Frankish bishop, Liudhard, at the Kentish court, ever since Æthelberht had married Bertha, who was Theuderic and Theudebert's aunt. In the nineteenth century the discovery near St Martin's church in Canterbury of a gold medalet inscribed LEUDARDUS EPS (= *episcopus*) proved his existence. It is not impossible that Æthelberht wanted a replacement for his wife's bishop without being beholden to the Frankish kings or having his new bishop under the authority of the Frankish Church. But Gregory was relying on the Frankish kings, or the regent queen, to ensure the conversion of the English. His requests in that matter are tied up with what Gregory wanted from the Frankish Church; he complained about their lack of response to the English request for priests in the same tones as he complained about corruption within the Frankish Church.

The next letters relating to England in Gregory's register are to various Gallic bishops, repeating the request to assist Augustine in his journey through Gaul. These too were all written on July 23 596. Those who want to imagine that the saintly Gregory was deeply involved with the conversion of England should note that Gregory's direct involvement with the mission took him little more than two days: twenty-three of the twenty-nine relevant letters were written on either July 23 596 or June 22 601, and only one of the six others, the very last, to Abbot Mellitus, was actually concerned with the mission directly rather than simply mentioning it as an aside. Gregory's response to the news that the English wanted to be converted was in fact rather cautious. He sent a group of monks under Augustine, who at first was their prior, and then their abbot, and only much later was consecrated bishop.

Gregory's uncertainty about the mission lasted until the very end. On June 22 601 he wrote to King Æthelberht urging him to destroy all temples and to root out paganism by force. The second group of missionaries, under Abbot Mellitus, left Rome bearing this letter. A month later, on July 18, Gregory sent post-haste a letter designed to catch up with them along the way, saying that he has spent a lot of time thinking about the mission – that is, some three weeks – and he is now suggesting a different missionary strategy.

> The idol temples of that race should by no means be destroyed, but only the idols in them. Take holy water and sprinkle it in these shrines, build altars and place relics in them. . . . When people see that their shrines are not destroyed they will be able to banish error from their hearts and be more ready to come to the places they are familiar with, but now recognising and worshipping the true God.[10]

Their animal sacrifices should not be stopped; they should be converted into the slaughter of animals for food on the feast-days of saints: 'It is doubtless impossible to cut out everything at once from their stubborn minds.' What Æthelberht thought when he heard of this contradictory advice coming from Rome is not recorded. Nor does it seem, from current archaeological knowledge, that many churches were in fact reused temples: although there is a possible example at the Northumbrian palace of Yeavering. However, there is corroborative literary evidence: in *c*. 700 the cleric Aldhelm writes to a monk who had spent several years studying in Ireland, and thanks God for the fact that among the West Saxons Christian learning is now taking place in buildings 'where once the crude pillars of the same foul snake and stag were worshipped with coarse stupidity in profane shrines'.[11]

Gregory's problem may have been considerable ignorance about conditions in Britain. There is clearly more communication going on than the surviving letters reveal: by 598, for instance, Gregory has somehow heard that 10,000 Angles have been converted on Christmas Day 597. But the communications may not have given him much information about the state of affairs in what he probably thinks of as the Roman province of Britannia. On June 22 601, he advises Augustine to set up episcopal sees for Britain in the cities of London and York: he knows from his archives that London and York are the main Roman cities in Britain, but does not realise that this hardly corresponds to the political and social realities of seventh-century

England. Not only were London and York not at the centres of kingdoms in 601, but each was probably a largely uninhabited labyrinth of Roman ruins. Gregory wants to set up urban sees on the Continental model in a country which has no use for towns at all. Ironically, of course, the establishment of the Church in empty ruined Roman towns had the effect, eventually, of bringing some semblance of urban life back to most Roman cities in Britain. But, as we shall see, Irish missionaries viewed the situation differently: their sees, like Lindisfarne or Lichfield, were on rural sites.

Gregory's unpreparedness for the mission seems like nothing when compared to Augustine's, if the *Libellus Responsionum*, recorded in Bede's *Historia Ecclesiastica*, does indeed contain a genuine set of questions from Augustine together with Gregory's responses. 'How should bishops live with their clergy?' or 'Even though the faith is one are there varying customs in the churches?', the first two questions, are matters that one would have thought Augustine should have been sufficiently prepared for. The sixth question, 'Whether a bishop may be consecrated without other bishops being present', elicited the justifiably irritable reply: 'In the church of the English of which you are as yet the only bishop, it is not possible for you to consecrate a bishop otherwise than alone.'[12] Other questions relate to knottier problems, and in one case at least Gregory refers to information he has received from England: that many, while pagans, had married their widowed step-mother or their brother's widow. These people (who probably thought they were charitably protecting their kin – or their family property) were now to be told that they should remain celibate in these sinful marriages. The longest answer relates to the ritual uncleanness of pregnant and menstruating women, and of men after sexual intercourse. Some of these answers may well have come as a shock to newly converted Anglo-Saxons.

Gregory's letters seem to show that the Franks had a good deal to do with the success of Augustine's mission. Gregory gives the honour of the *pallium* – the woollen scarf which has rested on the tomb of St Peter overnight and thus acquired the power of a relic – to Syagrius, bishop of Autun, for his help, unspecified, with the mission; he tells Brunhild that she has done more than anyone else, apart from God, to convert the English. It may well be that this is mere flattery, and that Gregory hoped to cajole Brunhild into reforming the Frankish Church. But it could be that the Frankish Church provided much more assistance to the early missionaries than Bede tells us, or knew about.

If Brunhild did more than anyone after God to convert the English, where does this leave Augustine? He is still an enigma, to a large extent. We know that he worked miracles: several of Gregory's letters make mention of those (and warn him against pride). But the *Libellus Responsionum* suggests he may have been an ill-prepared and naïve man, and if Bede's story of his meeting with the British bishops is accurate, he was perhaps also a somewhat arrogant and impolitic one. Augustine met them, Bede says, at a place 'still called in English' *Augustinæs Ác*, or 'Augustine's Oak', on the borders of the Hwicce and the West Saxons: this was territory that may have been within Æthelberht's sphere of influence, as a king who had power over other kings in southern England (see p. 146). The meeting shows that Augustine was taking seriously his position as an ecclesiastic who had been told by Gregory in a letter of June 22 601 to have under his subjection all the bishops of the English 'but also all the bishops of Britain'.[13] Augustine wanted the British to give up those customs which were at variance with those of Rome, in particular their method of calculating Easter, and he wanted them to join with him in the conversion of the English. Augustine tested his powers against the British bishops: he healed a blind Englishman, where they had been powerless to do so. (This is presumably a symbolic story: Augustine is the man to whom God has given the power to cure the English from their pagan blindness and to show them the light.) The British bishops go away to confer, and a hermit tells them to return to Augustine's presence, and, if Augustine does not rise from his chair when they enter the room, they will know him for an arrogant man. He does indeed remain seated, the British refuse to conform to his demands, and Augustine curses them, and threatens them with death at the hands of the English. Bede records, apparently complacently, that Æthelfrith, the pagan king of the Northumbrians, slaughtered an army of the British at Chester, including some twelve hundred clerics who had come to aid the British with their prayers. 'Thus the prophecy of the holy Bishop Augustine was fulfilled.'[14] It is interesting that Bede himself relates this story which, to our eyes, tells against Augustine. But Bede may have been writing for an Anglo-Saxon audience who detested the British and was unable to feel any sympathy for them. The detestation may have been mutual. According to Bede's Anglo-Saxon contemporary Aldhelm, the British clergy refused to eat with the English, and insisted that all vessels used should be scrupulously cleaned before re-use, and demanded that any Saxon who visited them had to do forty days' penance before they would allow him to speak with them.[15]

In the eyes of Gregory and Bede, Augustine did at least have some success in converting the men of Kent, and in beginning the mission to other kingdoms. He ordained two of his monks as bishops, Justus as bishop of Rochester in Kent, and Mellitus as bishop of London, in the kingdom of the East Saxons. Bede points out that it was the overlord of the East Saxon king, Æthelberht himself, who actually built St Paul's in the Roman city of London, as Mellitus's church. That much had depended on Æthelberht's own personal authority was shown when he died, *c.* 616. Mellitus was expelled from London by the East Saxons, who returned to their paganism (if indeed they had ever been baptised in any numbers); Rædwald, king of the East Angles, who had been converted in Kent when Æthelberht's power was at its height, reverted to paganism; and Æthelberht's son, himself a pagan, was clearly not worried when Augustine's successor Laurence decided to abandon the mission and return to Gaul with Mellitus and Justus. Laurence changed his mind only at the last minute, but even so the mission seems to have been halted in its tracks; when Mellitus returned, after a year's absence, the pagans of London refused to allow him back.

The last convert-king to accept baptism as a result of Æthelberht, if only indirectly, was Edwin, king of the Northumbrians. He married Æthelburh, Æthelberht's daughter, and brought her north to his kingdom, together with her bishop, Paulinus, one of those Italians who had joined the mission in 601. If Bede is to be believed, it took her a long time to convert her husband, but eventually he did accept baptism, in York, the new ecclesiastical capital of the north, possibly in 627. The dates are problematical, but so, even, is the fact. A later Welsh source claims that Edwin and many of his men were baptised by Rhun, son of Urien, the British king of Rheged, 'and for forty days on end he went on baptising the whole nation of the thugs' [i.e. the English].[16] Edwin, like so many of his royal colleagues, had spent much time in exile in Christian courts, British, Irish or Pictish, and such a connection is not impossible. However, Bede mentions none of this; Paulinus is the hero.

> So great is said to have been the fervour of the faith of the Northumbrians and their longing for the washing of salvation, that once when Paulinus came to the king and queen in their royal palace of Yeavering, he spent thirty-six days in the task of catechising and baptizing. During these, from morning till evening, he did nothing else but instruct the crowds who flocked to him from every village and every district in the teaching of Christ.[17]

The Northumbrians were much more enthusiastic, apparently, than southerners had been, and there may be a reason for this. The bulk of the population of Northumbria, particularly in the north (Yeavering was north of Hadrian's Wall), must have been British in ethnic origin, and may already have been nominal Christians, looking forward to their first sight of a bishop for several generations. Paulinus baptised these people in the river Glen, but he might have preached to them in the grandstand, discovered on the palace-site on the hill above in the excavations of Brian Hope-Taylor (see above, p. 134).

Paulinus also baptised in Lincoln (the small kingdom of Lindsey was subject to the Northumbrians at the time). An abbot in that district told Bede that an old man had told him that Paulinus was 'tall, with a slight stoop, black hair, a thin face, a slender aquiline nose . . . at the same time both venerable and awe-inspiring in appearance'.[18] It is the first description of an inhabitant of post-Roman Britain which we have. It is also a portrait of a rather intriguing and enigmatic character. Bede tells the story of Edwin wandering in exile, trying to keep one step ahead of his rival Æthelfrith's assassins, and coming to the court of Rædwald of the East Angles. Edwin learnt that Rædwald was planning to hand him over to the assassins. He sat up one night, fretting over his fate, when a stranger suddenly appeared before him in the night, and gave him advice. Edwin promised to follow the one who would help him escape the assassins; the stranger placed his hand on Edwin's head and said that this sign would remind him. Upon which he disappeared; and Bede gives the impression that it was a heavenly spirit. The anonymous *Life of St Gregory the Great*, however, identifies the stranger as Paulinus; both sources relate that years later it was Paulinus who came to Edwin, now the king in place of Æthelfrith, and made that same gesture. Edwin was convinced by Paulinus' arguments; and so were his counsellors, and his high-priest Coifi profaned the temple at Goodmanham (East Yorks) by leaping onto his stallion and throwing a spear into the shrine. Richard North has recently shown how complex Bede's narrative is at this point, weaving ideas from Virgil's *Aeneid* together with folkloric motifs and stories about Woden; he suggests that this 'venerable and awe-inspiring' (or 'terrifying') man was actually mistaken for Woden, as St Paul was once mistaken for Woden's Roman analogue Mercury (in Acts 14:7–9), and that it was he who was 'the hooded one' (*coifi*) who first threw the spear, just as Woden did in his war against rival gods.[19] True or not, it is a reminder of how complex and artful Bede's text can be. Bede, after all, before becoming an historian, had become Europe's leading exponent of Biblical criticism, of teasing out the often very well hidden and allegorical meanings of sacred texts.

In 633 Edwin was defeated and killed in battle at the hands of what Bede regarded as an unholy coalition between Penda, the pagan king of the Mercians, and the British king Cadwallon of Gwynedd. Paulinus fled south to Kent, with Queen Æthelburh and most of Edwin's family, and although at least one priest stayed behind, Northumbria's kings briefly reverted to paganism again. Paulinus was given the bishopric of Rochester, since its previous occupant had drowned in the Mediterranean on his way to see the Pope. Christianity in England, at least in terms of an organised Church, was again restricted to Kent alone. Bede put a brave face on it in his account, but effectively, after thirty-five years, the Roman missionaries had made very little headway at all.

The second mission to the English

After a year of paganism in Northumbria – a year which Bede intriguingly said was later censored from existence 'by those who compute the dates of kings'[20] – Oswald, the son of Æthelfrith, took the kingdom and drove out his enemies' British allies. He himself, with his war-band, had been in exile among the Irish, and had been baptised there, and he sent to Iona for a bishop. Bede reports the story that at first the monastery had sent a hardline preacher, who made no headway at all, and returned to Iona reporting that the English were impossible to convert. A monk spoke to him, in effect repeating Pope Gregory's thoughts to Abbot Mellitus (see above p. 156), saying that missionaries have to start gently with the milk of simple teaching, and wean their listeners slowly to the solid food of God's word. Everyone turned to look at him and, as is the way of committees, suggested that if it was such a good idea, he could try it himself. The monk was Aidan, who, far more than Augustine or Paulinus, is the true hero of the conversion of the English in Bede's eyes.

King Oswald gave Aiden Lindisfarne on which to establish his see and his monastery: like Iona, an island a short distance from the mainland (although, unlike Iona, nowadays only an island twice a day). It has been customary for people in modern times to wax lyrical about the romantically remote places in which the Irish established their monasteries: Skellig Michael, on a rock in the Atlantic; Iona; and Lindisfarne, now known as Holy Island. But most Irish monasteries were in fact on the mainland, surrounded by many acres of prime agricultural land. Skellig Michael was probably just a seasonal hermitage (like the hermitage established by St Cuthbert on Inner Farne, an island some three miles east of Lindisfarne); and Iona and Lindisfarne were in fact very well placed indeed, in an age when boat was much swifter and easier than horse, cart or foot, to keep in touch with the surrounding areas. However remote and romantic Lindisfarne looks today, it was actually within sight of Oswald's fortification of Bamburgh, one of the most important centres of power, and thus was at the very heart of the political machine in Bernicia.

Thanks to the Irish, who flocked to Lindisfarne under its bishop and abbot Aidan, and thanks to the power of the Northumbrian kings, which was at its height under Oswald (633–42) and his successor Oswiu (642–70), the stalled mission began to move again. The political and military successes of these two brothers was a major factor in the spread of Christianity, as we can see in the first new royal conversion mentioned by Bede, in which the Irish were not mentioned at all. The West Saxons under King Cynegils received Christianity through the preaching of Birinus, an Italian ordained by the archbishop of Milan at the orders of the Pope. He was given the Roman town of Dorchester-on-Thames, near Oxford, for his see: and he was given it by Cynegils and Oswald of Northumbria. Oswald stood as godfather at Cynegils's baptism; subsequently he married Cynegils's daughter. We must assume that Oswald was using his position as Cynegils's overlord to impose this new relationship on him: according to the laws of Ine of the West Saxons, a godson had the same relationship of subordination to his godfather as a man had to his lord.[21] The political move did not have a long-lasting result; Birinus had no more success than other Italian missionaries. But it shows the way in which political realities could encourage the spread of Christianity.

Ireland was not the only source for missionaries in the mid-seventh century: there was also Gaul. But the first of these to be mentioned in Bede shows that we cannot make a neat contrast between Irish and Franks (as the inhabitants of Gaul, or at least northern Gaul, were called by the seventh century). Gaul, a mostly Christianised country by the sixth century, had itself received its own Irish mission in the late sixth century. Columba the Younger, usually called Columbanus to distinguish him from Columba of Iona, had arrived in Gaul in 590. He had not come as a missionary, but as a 'pilgrim', an exile for God, together with, apparently, a symbolically twelve disciples, and he settled in the remoter parts of eastern France. He eventually founded three monasteries there, in Burgundy, the most famous of which was Luxeuil, and before his death in 615 he had also founded Bobbio, in north Italy. Luxeuil became a source of inspiration for many religious people in Gaul, and monasteries modelled on Luxeuil, and using a modified version of Columbanus's rule, were founded throughout the seventh century, above all in north-east Gaul. A clue to Columbanus's success comes when one looks at these monasteries. They are very different from the Gallic monasteries of the fifth century, many of which were urban and under the close control of the bishop; these tended to be small in scale, and, because of their relative poverty, many of them barely survived the death of the holy man who founded them. Nearly all of these monasteries operated according to rules laid down, not necessarily in writing, by their founder. Columbanian monasteries tended to be founded by wealthy aristocrats with the help of large grants of land, in the countryside, and lived by a written rule, which often, in terms of the procedures laid down, owed much more to St Benedict's *Rule* than to Columbanus's.

We shall look at the role of the monastery in the life of the Church in Britain in the next chapter. Here it is just worth noting that the new style of Frankish Christianity which was emerging in the wake of Columbanus – in which the rural monastery was becoming an important counterweight to the urban bishopric in the religious life of the nation – offered a useful model for the new English Church. And it had many points of similarity to the Irish church, which must have been strengthened as more Irish clerics arrived in Gaul. The question of what Columbanian practice owed to Ireland is a debated one. Clearly Ireland had had to adapt before Gaul to the problem of how to introduce Christianity, with all its urban institutions, into a country with no towns, and it may be that there were Frankish clerics going to Ireland to learn, as well as Irish coming over to Gaul. We know of one, thanks to Bede. Agilbert came from a noble Frankish family in the Paris region, and, after 'spending a long time in Ireland for the purpose of studying the Scriptures',[22] he was appointed as bishop to the West Saxons. He was in Wessex for a number of years, until King Cenwealh grew tired of his inability to speak Old English properly, and without consultation divided his diocese in two and gave the southern part, with Winchester as the see, to Wine. Wine had been consecrated in Gaul, and may indeed have been Frankish, but he could at least speak English. Agilbert retired to Gaul in disgust, and ended his amazingly international career as bishop of Paris. He was buried in one of the most imaginatively carved sarcophagi surviving from the seventh century, still to be seen in the crypt at Jouarre (the Columbanian nunnery whose abbess was his sister). Given its quite exceptional nature in seventh-century Gaul, some have suggested that he imported a sculptor from Britain; others that it was Gallic sculptors who were responsible for founding the flourishing sculptural schools in Britain.

Other Frankish clerics played a role in the conversion of the English, most notably the Burgundian bishop Felix. Sigeberht of the East Angles had been baptised while in exile in Gaul, and when he returned to be king 'he at once sought to imitate some of the excellent institutions which he had seen in Gaul, and established a school where boys could be taught letters.'[23] Felix was there, with his see at Dunwich, from around 630 until the late 640s. For the recently converted southern English Gaul was an obvious source of Christian inspiration. Bede, writing of the reign of Eorcenberht of Kent (640–64), the first English king to order all idols to be destroyed in his kingdom and to order the observance of the Lenten fast, noted that the king's daughter became a nun at Faremoutiers in Gaul:

> at that time, because there were not yet many monasteries founded in England, numbers of people from Britain used to enter the monasteries of the Franks or Gauls to practise the monastic life: they also sent their daughters to be taught in them and to be wedded to the heavenly bridegroom.[24]

Even though Bede describes Felix as a man who brought teachers to the kingdom of the East Angles, he does not depict him as an evangelist. The man who in East Anglia 'converted many both by the example of his virtues and the persuasiveness of his teaching, turning unbelievers to Christ and confirming believers in His faith and love'[25] was Fursa, an Irishman. He founded a monastery in East Anglia, within the Roman walls of a Saxon Shore fort at Burgh Castle, before travelling on to Gaul: his body was later venerated at Péronne, known as late as the tenth century as *Perrona Scottorum* because of the many Irish who came there.

There were Roman and Frankish missionaries in England, then. But in fact rather more permanent successes were credited by Bede to the Irish, or those trained in the Irish tradition. It may just be that Bede regarded the early Irish as better evangelists; but it may be that he sees the Irish missions, which were mostly from Lindisfarne, as part of the Northumbrian imperialism of which he, as a Northumbrian, heartily approved. The list of Lindisfarne successes is quite long. Peada, king of the Middle Angles and son of the powerful pagan king of the Mercians Penda, was baptised by Bishop Finán, Aidan's Irish successor at Lindisfarne: it was the condition for being allowed to marry King Oswiu's daughter. When Penda died and Oswiu took over the Mercian kingdom, Finán consecrated the Irishman Diuma as the bishop of both the Middle Angles and the Mercians; he was succeeded by the Irishman Cellach, who, when he returned to Iona, was succeeded by Trumhere, 'a pious man trained in the monastic life, who though of English race was consecrated bishop by the Irish'.[26] At the same time, Sigeberht of the East Saxons was persuaded by Oswiu to convert, and he was baptised at a royal estate by Hadrian's Wall. He was given a Northumbrian as his bishop, an Englishman called Cedd, who had been a monk at Lindisfarne. Cedd founded monasteries at Bradwell-on-Sea and Tilbury, ordaining priests to help him in his work of conversion, still finding time to visit Northumbria frequently and to assist in the running of the monastery he established there, at Lastingham on the North York Moors. Technically he was bishop of London, the first since Augustine's colleague Mellitus was thrown out some forty years earlier, but it is more correct to say that he was bishop of the East Saxons.

Cedd was not the last of the missionary bishops trained at Lindisfarne, even if by the 650s these were increasingly English rather than Irish. Cedd in fact had three brothers, all of whom became priests, and one of whom, Chad, was asked for by the king of the Mercians as bishop of both Mercia and Lindsey (which had by now transferred from Northumbrian rule to that of Mercia). He set up a monastery at Barrow in Lincolnshire, and his see at Lichfield. The last kingdom to be converted, the kingdom of the South Saxons, was also converted by a former Lindisfarne monk. Bishop Wilfrid, the first bishop of the South Saxons (with his see at Selsey), had been bishop of York previously, and would be bishop of Hexham, when he finished his troubled career. Because he was the champion of the Roman cause at the Synod of Whitby in 664 (see below), standing up against Colmán, the bishop of Lindisfarne, it is rather easy to forget that Wilfrid was a Lindisfarne old boy too. Not only did he convert the last English kingdom to Christianity, he also led the first English mission to the pagans on the Continent. The number of early Anglo-Saxon dioceses which had a Lindisfarne monk as their first bishop is an astonishing tribute to the legacy of missionary enthusiasm inherited from the Irish monastery of Iona.

The myth of the Celtic Church

In 664 a synod was called at *Streanæshealh*, the nunnery run by Abbess Hild: it is traditional to identify this as Whitby, although as an important royal monastery it might be more sensible to locate it at Strensall, a few miles north-east of York. The 'Synod of Whitby' was summoned in order to settle the differences over the question of how to calculate Easter, although there were other matters dividing the Church in the north too, such as different styles of tonsure. The differences were particularly obvious, and embarrassing, at the Northumbrian court. Oswiu was loyal to his Lindisfarne teachers, and followed their practices; his wife Eanflæd came from Kent, and followed Roman practices, as did Oswiu's son Alhfrith, who had been instructed by Wilfrid, the eventual spokesman for the Roman party at Strensall. Bede said that one year the court was due to have two Easters, with the king celebrating Easter while the queen was still observing the Lenten fast. In the end, in Bede's account, it was Oswiu who made the decision about the calculation of Easter (rather scandalously, since it was a wholly ecclesiastical matter), declaring that he would rather be on the side of St Peter, who held the keys to heaven, than on that of St Columba.

This difference of custom is often seen as a manifestation of a much wider division between the 'Celtic' and 'Roman' Churches. Our traditional image of the 'Celtic Church' comes from Bede. Indeed, he introduces the matter in the same chapter in which he talks about Nynia and Columba. Columba's monasteries of Iona and Durrow were both very influential, wrote Bede:

> From both of these sprang very many monasteries which were established by his disciples in Britain and Ireland, over all of which the island monastery in which his body lies held pre-eminence. This island always has its abbot for its ruler who is a priest, to whose authority the whole kingdom, even bishops, have to be subject. This unusual arrangement followed the example of their first teacher, who was not a bishop, but a priest and monk. [...] It is true that [his successors] used tables of doubtful accuracy in fixing the date of the chief festival, since they were so far away at the ends of the earth that there was none to bring them the decrees of the synods concerning the observance of Easter; but they diligently practised such works of religion and chastity as they were able to learn from the words of the prophets, the evangelists and the apostles.[27]

We find here all the elements of the myth of the Celtic Church: the holy and apostolic life of the monks, the dominance of abbots over bishops, and the fact that they did not use the correct formulas for calculating the date of Easter. Bede clearly admires the Irish monks he describes, as 'saints and scholars', and as missionaries to the English; but he invariably berates them for calculating Easter at the wrong time (and for wearing the wrong kind of tonsure). He berated Welsh monks as well: not only had they done nothing to convert their English neighbours, but they too stubbornly resisted the correct Roman method of calculating Easter, as, until 721, did the Picts, who had of course learnt their Christianity largely from Iona.

Nothing that Bede says is necessarily wrong, so why do I speak of the 'myth' of the Celtic Church? The 'Celtic Church' is a term that has been fondly used by several generations of historians, in these islands, and has passed into popular usage. It has often carried associations that are foreign to the historical reality. In the nineteenth century it could be imagined that the Irish, Welsh and Pictish resistance to Christianity as it was taught by Rome was a heroic resistance to centralisation imposed from Rome, a proto-Protestant desire to live an apostolic life without interference from a self-styled head of the Church. That answered, for some, the problem of how and when it was that a primitive, holy, apostolic (and hence 'proto-Protestant') Church became Roman Catholic and Papist: in these islands it happened when uniformity of Roman practice was enforced upon the Celtic peoples of Britain. That is clearly an anachronistic way of looking at the past. In the twentieth century it has been replaced by a hazily romantic idea of the Celtic Church, which was somehow more pious, spiritual, and attuned with nature than the Church in England or elsewhere: this is an image which can be accepted by evangelicals or charismatics, and even by New Agers, who can happily believe that the Celtic Church in the early Middle Ages preserved some authentic traits of the wisdom of the druids. There is a hint of racialism in all this too: the Celts are a people who are more spiritual, natural, poetic and child-like than their Germanic neighbours, who are practical, rationalistic, utilitarian and philistine.

These modern concerns distort our view of the past, and obscure some home truths. The Celts are in a real sense the invention of nineteenth-century linguists, who were the first to realise that the Welsh and the Irish (and the Picts, Cornish and Bretons) spoke related languages: this concept of relatedness was unknown in the ancient and medieval worlds. If we want to talk about relatedness in a biological sense, the French (largely descended from the 'Celtic' Gauls) and the English (who are almost certainly descended from a largely British, and hence 'Celtic', stock) are, of course, almost as Celtic in terms of descent as their western and northern neighbours, while the Irish and the Welsh, indeed, may be largely descended from the pre-Celtic peoples whom Celtic-speaking warriors forced to speak their own Celtic languages (which survive as Gaelic, Welsh and Breton). But other objections to the idea of the 'Celtic Church' as a concept with any meaning for the seventh-century historian are more significant. Resistance to Rome was not ideological in any sense: in most areas Christians were happy to accept the bishop of Rome as the senior figure in the western Church. Even the bishop of Rome was happy for local churches to have their own customs in areas such as liturgy (as Gregory the Great made clear to St Augustine in the *Libellus Responsionum*). But some Irish in the seventh century thought that the methods of Easter calculation which they had received from Rome in the fifth century had earned the approval of Saint Columba, and ought not to be displaced by new-fangled methods. Rome had indeed refined its method of caclulating Easter in the early sixth century: and Bede, as someone who actually understood the complicated mix of Biblical and astronomical knowledge which allowed one to work out when Easter ought to be, knew that this was better than that which Columba's followers adhered to. The question of the tonsure may have been related: initially it was a result of Ireland being far from the centres of Christianity, and inclined to follow its own customs (something that was, on the whole, accepted in the fifth or sixth centuries). Perhaps, as some believe, the Irish tonsure, whereby clerics shaved the back of their neck up to the crown of the head, was some remnant of druidic practice. But, as the lines hardened in the seventh century, it may have become some badge of loyalty, as opposed to the 'Petrine tonsure' (a circular shaved patch on the crown of the head, as in traditional depictions of St Peter), which became the badge of the

Romanist party. What was at stake was not so much ideology, as loyalty to communities and to patron saints. And the struggle was not between 'Celts' and 'Romans', at least by the time of the Synod of Whitby, in 664, when King Oswiu settled the issue in Northumbria. Most of the Irish Church had by then already adopted the Roman Easter: indeed, Bede says that the 'most violent' *supporter* of the Roman Easter was an Irishman, Ronan. It was only the devotees of St Columba, in the territories under the influence of Iona, who preserved their old traditions, together with the Welsh.

Ironically, it was the Englishman Bede who was responsible for the myth of the Celtic church, in that it is in his pages that we first find this image of Ireland as the 'land of saints and scholars', which has so pleased the Irish to this day. But if we look at Bede's *Ecclesiastical History* carefully, we can see that Bede wants to present us with Irish saints of great holiness, like Aidan, who came from Iona to Lindisfarne, to convert the Angles of Northumbria, because he wanted to present his readers with models of ideal behaviour safely in an ideal past. It was difficult for people living in eighth-century Northumbria, used to a wealthy, aristocratic church, closely connected with royalty, to imagine churchmen behaving like good austere monks. Would the 'Celtic Church' have appeared quite so exceptionally holy to us had Bede not had a desire to reform the English church of the mid-eighth century?

The 'Celtic Church' is, however, known not only for its involvement in the Easter controversy and its holiness. As Bede noted in the passage quoted at the beginning of this section, the Irish Church was also known for the unusual nature of its organisation, or, rather, he says of Iona: 'This island always has its abbot for its ruler who is a priest, to whose authority the whole kingdom, even bishops, have to be subject.' Bede added that 'this unusual arrangement followed the example of their first teacher, who was not a bishop, but a priest and monk.' The idea of abbots having power superior to bishops is something that is often taken as a characteristic of the entire 'Celtic Church', and the origins have nothing to do with Columba. It was certainly the case that when Bede was writing the important churches in Ireland and in Scotland were monastic churches; often abbots of an important monastery, like Iona, would control other dependent churches in their confederation or *paruchia*. The abbots were the powerful figures in the Church, not the bishops. What the origins of this 'unusual arrangement' were, however, is another matter.

At one level the solution is simple. It was a result of the accommodation of the Church to the structure of Irish society, which was quite different from that found elsewhere within Christendom in the fifth or sixth century. The Irish Church was the first church to be established outside the former Roman Empire in the Latin West. Everywhere in the Roman Empire there was a uniform ecclesiastical structure, based on the Roman secular administrative system. The basic secular units in the Empire were the *civitates*, the city territories, each with a town at its administrative core; the *civitates* were grouped together into provinces, each of which had its *metropolis*, or provincial capital. It was easy to accommodate the Church to this structure. Each *civitas* was to have a bishop, with his see (derived from the Latin for 'seat') in the town: the bishop's church in the town was the cathedral (derived from the Greek for 'seat'). The bishop of each provincial capital was the senior bishop of the province, the metropolitan bishop, with a certain amount of authority over the other bishops within the province, notably at times of episcopal elections or of episcopal misconduct. Episcopal incomes derived from land given to the episcopal churches in their *civitas* or elsewhere, and from donations from the faithful in kind or in cash.

How could such a system have been transported to Ireland, or any other territory outside the Empire, where there were no towns? The first missionaries, like Patrick, certainly tried. But at some uncertain point the episcopal system was overtaken and dominated by abbots and their *paruchiae*. Kathleen Hughes saw the replacement being a slow one, with two rival systems, episcopal and monastic, in conflict with each other until the eighth century, at which time the monastic system won. Certainly there are ample signs of an episcopal system working in the sixth century (when a synod of bishops met to excommunicate Columba), and in the seventh century (when according to the *Letter of Cummian* a synod met to discuss the question of the calculation of Easter), while by the eighth century the monastic *paruchia* seems indeed to be dominant. But it has more recently been suggested that it was not so much a victory of the *paruchia* system over the episcopal system as a breakdown of the diocesan structure and of the attempt by bishops to create *episcopal paruchiae*.[28] Ultimately the question is probably an economic one. It is likely that the diocese was in most cases the territory controlled by one Irish king: each king had his bishop. The income of a bishop was, as on the Continent, largely dependent on the size and wealth of his diocese. In seventh-century England, where some very large territories were being conquered by kings, the power and wealth of an individual bishop could be enormous: early in the time of Bishop Wilfrid of York, his diocese (the kingdom of Northumbria) was possibly as large as the whole of Ireland. But in Ireland itself, where there might have been as many as 150 kings at one time, the size of the average diocese and its income was tiny. On the other hand, abbots could found churches or acquire them as dependencies anywhere in Ireland: they could build up a *paruchia* that extended over many kingdoms and many dioceses. The only way in which bishops could hope to rival abbots in wealth, and hence status, was to try to expand their influence outside their own diocese, and to create their own *paruchia*. The classic example of such an attempt was that made by Armagh, in northern Ireland, whose bishops were by the seventh century claiming in the *Liber Angeli* to be the heirs of St Patrick and controllers of a *paruchia* that ought to contain every church in Ireland that was not in a monastic *paruchia* and every seat of a territorial bishop. Many parts of Ireland rejected Armagh's primacy, and abbots preserved their dominance. Monasteries might well possess their own bishop, who had full episcopal rights (to consecrate priests, for instance), but who was a member of the monastic community and therefore subordinate to the abbot.

By the seventh century, the abbacy of Irish monasteries was quite normally regarded as the possession of a particular family, as it was in Iona; and by the eighth century at the latest it was quite common for monasteries to have become embroiled in secular politics. There were reasons other than simple piety which led men like Columba and Columbanus to forsake their country and to found a monastery abroad. But when they did, they not infrequently took Irish ideas about Church organisation with them. It is interesting that the only two seventh-century popes who communicated with Ireland were also responsible for giving the first known papal privileges to two monasteries founded by Columbanus on the Continent.[29] These privileges exempted the monasteries from the burden and trial of episcopal visitation, effectively making them independent of bishops. Rome and Ireland were not necessarily on different sides: 'the popes may well have realized better than some modern commentators that the bureaucratic city-based model for the church was not necessarily the best one at all times and in all places.'[30] Ironically, perhaps, the Irish recognised the Pope's importance by calling him the *abb* (abbot) of Rome.

Ireland was the first country outside the Latin Empire to convert to Christianity and to have to face the problems of fitting an urban institution into a rural society. But there was another problem which it was forced to address, which would also have repercussions in Britain. The Irish were the first people to be converted to Christianity who were not Latin-speaking. That is a statement which needs some qualification. The British in Roman Britain were probably not, mostly, Latin-speaking, nor were the provincials in other parts of the Latin West (such as the Berber- and Punic-speaking populations of North Africa). But everywhere but in Ireland, the Church was run, and conversion carried out, by a Latin-speaking elite. Indeed, it is possible that in some parts of the Empire, it was only with the coming of Christianity, which brought the educated classes in contact with, and preaching to, the peasantry, that Latin began to make headway against the deeply-rooted languages of the countryside. But what happened in Ireland, where Latin was virtually unknown?

For the first time, the Church had to become an important educational institution. All those who joined monasteries or the secular clergy had to be taught Latin, and thus monasteries became schools in a way in which they were not (in the fifth or sixth centuries) in Europe. School-masters had to be trained, and school books written; Latin grammars designed for Teaching Latin as a Foreign Language (TLFL?) had to be devised. In the seventh century, ambitious churchmen came to Ireland to learn the basics; they came from England, which was equally non-Latinate, but they came from Francia too, since many there had German as their first language, and even those who spoke Latin were finding that their Latin had evolved so far from literary and classical Latin that they were beginning to be forced to treat it as a foreign language. One such was Agilbert, as we have seen, the well-connected Frank from the Paris region, who studied in Ireland, became bishop to the West Saxons in England, came to the Synod of Whitby and ended up as bishop of Paris. If for most people Irish monasteries were like primary schools – a place to acquire basic literary skills – for others they were like universities, where the classics of Latin pagan and Christian learning could be studied. Aldhelm of Malmesbury, whose own Latin was influenced by the flowery and obscure language developed by Irish scholars, said that in Ireland one could learn 'grammar, geometry and physics', and above all Biblical exegesis, or, as he put it, 'the fourfold honeyed oracles of allegorical or rather tropological disputation of opaque problems in aetherial mysteries.'[31]

The mission at home

Bede gives us a picture of the ideal pastoral bishop in Aidan. He served as a moral example to all his clergy. He did not care for worldly possessions, but handed over any gifts he received to the first poor man that he met, or else would ransom captives and make them his disciples and priests. He walked, rather than rode on horseback, and talked to all he met on his travels, trying to convert the unbeliever or encourage the believer. He was always busy, engaged in study or in prayer. He did not keep silent about the sins of the rich, and never gave them money. He did not feast or carouse with the king. There is just one sentence that suggests that Bede wanted his readers to make comparisons with the Church of his own day, the 730s: 'Aidan's life was in great contrast to the slothfulness of our own times.'[32]

We realise that the whole description of this heroic holy man is constructed as a criticism of the Church of his own day when we compare it with Bede's letter to Egbert of York, which he wrote in 734, a year before his death and a year before Egbert became the first archbishop of York.[33] Egbert had been a pupil of Bede's at Monkwearmouth-Jarrow, which might explain the frankness. He starts by apologising for that frankness, suggesting that it would have been better to say these things in person rather than on parchment; but his weak health prevented him from travelling to York in 734, as he had done in 733.

Bede urged Egbert not to gossip or to disparage others, and ironically said that 'it is rumoured' that certain bishops spend their time with drunkards and bon viveurs rather than with men of religion and continence. When Bede wrote, in November 734, there were only three other bishops in Egbert's province: Bede's own bishop and friend Acca of Hexham had been expelled in 731 but had been replaced only two months previously by Frithoberht; there was also Æthelwald of Lindisfarne and Pehthelm of Whithorn. Anyone reading the letter must have known very well to whom Bede was referring.

Bede was worried about the salvation of bishops' souls, but he was also worried about the souls of Northumbrians in general. His first point was that dioceses were too large for bishops to travel around and preach: priests ought to be ordained whose task it was to preach and to baptise in the countryside. Those with no Latin ought to be taught the Lord's Prayer in their own language: not just laymen, but clerics and monks too. Those clerics who receive earthly reward without preaching will have committed a great crime.

> For we have heard, and it is rumoured, that many villages and hamlets of our people are situated in inaccessible mountains and dense woodlands, where there is never seen for many years at a time a bishop to exhibit any ministry or celestial grace; not one man of which, however, is immune from rendering dues to the bishop.[34]

And he adds that accepting money from those who listened to preaching had been forbidden by Christ, and gives advice on the reform of monasticism and the Church in general. What we might find rather startling is that, despite the lack of sufficient priests for preaching and baptism, Bede expressed not a single worry about the possibility of surviving paganism. He was writing almost exactly a hundred years after Aidan had arrived in Northumbria; had pagan practices really been successfully replaced by Christian ones, in Northumbria and elsewhere, and if so, how had this been accomplished?

Hitherto we have followed Bede, in recounting the history of the conversion. But it will have been seen that for Bede conversion was primarily a question of the conversion of kings. This may indeed have been the crucial element; conversion from the top was not only politically sensible, it may also have been the only practical course of action, when the missionaries were so few. A Christian king would have done his best to create a Christian aristocracy; those aristocrats would have been reluctant to allow their own men to continue in pagan customs. Bede himself notes that King Eorcenberht of Kent ordered the destruction of the idols in his kingdom, and the earliest surviving English legislation does indeed show that kings were not averse to imposing Christianity by law. The laws of Wihtred of Kent from 695 order the Christian observance of marriage; fine a lord who orders his dependent to work on Sundays; and decree heavy fines for a freeman who works on Sundays, or who offers sacrifices to devils (i.e. to the pagan gods).[35] The very first law of Ine of the West Saxons from *c.* 690 fines those who do not have their child baptised within thirty days of birth: if a child dies before baptism, then the father shall be dispossessed of all property. Failure to pay church tax by Martinmas (November 11, after the harvest) incurs a 60 shilling fine and the obligation to pay the original tax twelve-fold.[36] Bede's comment about paying tax even if you never see a preacher seems all too likely.

Kings were prepared to enforce Christianity, perhaps persuaded by clerics that the welfare of their kingdom depended on it. However, we cannot know how efficiently such laws were carried out, and it is clear that it took a long time before the Church was able to put in place the necessary mechanisms for imparting the Gospel to ordinary Anglo-Saxons. Part of the Church's ultimate success may have been the relatively calm way in which it dealt with paganism. It is as if it was indeed following the advice of Pope Gregory, as given to Abbot Mellitus, not to root out paganism, but slowly to Christianise pagan practice and gradually to teach people of the truth of Christianity. Thus, the pagan names for the days of the week were not abolished, as some early medieval missionaries demanded: indeed, only in Portuguese did that happen. The English were allowed to keep Woden's Day and Thor's Day, just as the French have kept Mercury's Day and Jove's Day. English kings carried on celebrating their descent from Woden (even if the Church discreetly placed Woden in a genealogy going back to Adam, thus emphasising his status as a mere human). A healing charm against poisons, from the *Lacnunga*, a medical text in a manuscript from around 1050 – the very end of the Anglo-Saxon period – still recalls Woden:

> Then Woden took nine glory-twigs
> smote then the adder, that it flew apart into nine.[37]

Woden appears only once, however; more significant is the fact that these charms preserve a whole thought-world which, if largely expressed in Christian terms, must have its origins in pre-Christian folk-belief. It is in a sense equally impressive (though perhaps less so when we remember that the manuscript was produced in a monastery) that these charms have been almost wholly Christianised, by the introduction of invocations to God or his saints. Although sources such as penitentials (lists of sins with their appropriate penances) and the records of decisions made in church councils do show that the Church is worried about the survival of pagan practices (even among the clergy), actual pagan *worship* does not seem to be a problem.

How did the Church get its message across to the vast mass of the population, who lived in scattered settlements throughout the countryside? A good bishop, Bede would have said, spent much of his time travelling around, preferably on foot rather than on horseback (so that he did not present himself as proud and aristocratic), preaching wherever he found an audience; but, as Bede also said, there were many bishops who were not good. And even a superhuman bishop like Aidan could hardly have visited every settlement in a large diocese. The first bishops may have had problems: they were, of course, all people who arrived with no knowledge of the English language, whether they were Italians, Irish or Franks. The greatest of all the early archbishops of Canterbury, who was a major figure in the reorganisation of the ecclesiastical structure in England during his episcopate (668–90) was Theodore: born in Tarsus in Syria, a refugee from the Muslim invasion, who presumably spoke Greek and Syriac and had learnt some Latin during his time in Italy. But we only hear of interpreters twice: Augustine had Frankish interpreters, and King Oswald was himself able to interpret for Aidan, for he had learnt Irish when in exile. Early bishops perhaps depended as much for their success at conversion on such theatre as healing as on preaching. The first English-born bishops, however, were at pains to use the English language to the best possible advantage. Bede himself, on his death-bed, completed his translation of the Gospel of St John into English, and recited an Old English poem (perhaps of his own composition) on the departure of the soul from the body. In his *History* he tells the story of Cædmon, a cowherd on the estates of the monastery of Whitby (with an apparently British name), being given an angelic vision, after which he was able to put Biblical stories into epic English verse. That story also shows the importance of song and verse in the lives of English people, even cowherds; it was vital to supply people with new Christian themes, which might supplant their accustomed pagan fare.

Although the word of God could eventually reach large numbers through such means, more permanent institutions were needed, to ensure the salvation of as many souls as possible. The ultimate answer to this problem was the parish, a subdivision of the diocese which was small enough that one church and one priest could cater for all its needs. The average English rural parish, as it was eventually established, consisted of only a few score or hundred souls; the average urban parish, at the end of the Middle Ages, might only consist of two or three streets of houses. But that parish system was really only fully in place by the twelfth century. The question of how the parish system developed, and how the Church coped with pastoral care in earlier centuries, has been a matter of some controversy in recent years, and has centred on what has become known as the 'Minster hypothesis'.[38]

The Old English word *mynster* was simply the Anglicisation of the Latin *monasterium*. 'Minster' has been favoured by some as a word, rather than 'monastery', on the grounds that 'monastery' reminds us of the world after the tenth-century Reformation, when monasteries were contemplative institutions without pastoral functions, in which monks lived a strict life according to a rule. In the early English church, this argument goes, *monasterium* was a word which was used of a much wider range of institutions, and in particular was used of communities of priests whose primary function was pastoral. The 'Minster hypothesis', to simplify it considerably, is that by the eighth or ninth centuries pastoral care was in the hands of communities of priests, in a network of 'minster parishes', which covered the country. The extent of these 'minster parishes' can sometimes be detected in the affiliations between later parish churches: a 'mother church' may be distinguished, whose jurisdiction over other parishes is a remnant of its former role as a minster. From the ninth or tenth centuries onwards the minster parishes fragmented, until, eventually, we reach the well-known parish geography of the later Middle Ages. In a sense the minster parish 'system' was not a system: it varied from one part of England to another, and given that the minsters themselves varied from large royal monasteries down to a community of half-a-dozen priests or fewer it was inevitable that on the ground the type and level of pastoral care provided was uneven. Critics of the hypothesis have pointed to the lack of uniformity of terminology in the texts, and to evidence that not all monasteries were involved in any pastoral work. All that suggests is that there was indeed no uniform 'minster system'; it does not refute the idea that pastoral care was often exercised by communities of priests over a much wider area than later parishes. Bede may well have been right in his *Letter to Egbert* that there were far too few bishops to carry out the work of preaching properly: some of the dioceses were as large territorially as several dozen dioceses in North Africa or Provence. But the minster system was an imaginative way to cope with this problem, and to harness the institution of monasticism to the work of the missionary.

The mission overseas

Bede wrote his letter to a former pupil, Egbert, who in the year of Bede's death became the first Archbishop of York, with a *pallium* sent from Rome. But there is another Egbert in Bede's world who is much more interesting. This other Egbert embodied the internationalist spirit of the early English church. He first appeared in Bede's *History* at III.4, when he came to Iona in 715, and finally persuaded the monks to abandon their own method of calculating Easter and accept the Roman method. He had by that stage lived in Ireland for many years, as an 'exile for Christ'. Bede gradually reveals more about him. He was one of 'many in England, both nobles and commons, who, in the days of Finán and Colmán [of Lindisfarne], had left their own country and retired to Ireland, either for the sake of religious studies or to live a more ascetic life.'[39] He had gone with Chad, the Northumbrian who later became first bishop of Lichfield. He was in the (unidentified) Irish monastery of Rathmelsigi, when it was struck by plague. Egbert made a vow never to return to Britain, and to recite the psalter in its entirety every day, if he recovered. He did recover, and lived a fiercely abstemious life until 729, when he died on Iona, aged 90. He may have been an ascetic, but he did not withdraw himself from the world: he kept a careful eye on what was going on in the affairs of kings and bishops. In 684 he warned King Ecgfrith of the Northumbrians not to attack the Irish, who had never done him any harm; as a punishment for ignoring him, Ecgfrith died at Nechtansmere, with much of his army, in battle against the Picts. Some ten years after this, Egbert hatched a great scheme.

> He planned to bring blessing to many peoples by undertaking the apostolic task of carrying the word of God, through the preaching of the Gospel, to some of those nations who had not yet heard it. He knew that there were very many peoples in Germany from whom the

> Angles and Saxons, who now live in Britain, derive their origin ... Now these people are the Frisians, Rugians, Danes, Huns, Old Saxons, and Bructeri; there are also many other nations in the same land who are still practising heathen rites to whom this soldier of Christ proposed to go, after sailing round Britain, to try if he could deliver any of them from Satan and bring them to Christ.[40]

He prepared himself and his companions for the voyage. But a monk from Melrose told him that he had had a vision of his former abbot telling him that Egbert should go to Iona, not to the Continent. Egbert decided that this must indeed be the will of God. But, nevertheless, Egbert's scheme was the impetus behind some at least of the missionary effort which brought Christianity to the peoples beyond the Rhine. One of his companions, Wihtberht, another Englishman in exile in Ireland, preached to King Radbod and his Frisians, but to no avail. Egbert then apparently sent Willibrord, who arrived in Frisia at a time when the Franks had thrown Radbod out; with Frankish help he converted many Frisians. (Wilfrid of York, during one of his periods of exile from his see, had earlier gone to Frisia as a missionary, but had achieved little success.) Two other Englishmen left Ireland in Willibrord's wake, both called Hewald, and after the colour of their hair dubbed Black Hewald and White Hewald. They went to Saxony to preach, and were put to death by the Saxons, who perhaps suspected that they were agents of the Franks (as Willibrord had been). It was Pippin, the leader of the Franks, who buried them with great honour at Cologne, and who supported the mission of another Englishman, Swithubert, in his attempt to convert the Bructeri, a Frankish group east of the Rhine. Swithubert eventually founded a monastery at Kaiserswerth, on the Rhine. Willibrord and, later, Boniface were the most important Anglo-Saxon missionaries, however; between them they converted and/or organised the Church in a large territory east of the Rhine.

Willibrord was trained at Wilfrid's monastery of Ripon, and by Egbert in Ireland, and set off for the Continent in 690, with eleven followers. The first thing he did was to proceed to Rome, to ask for papal blessing for his mission; he went again five years later to receive the title of archbishop. This recognition of papal authority was natural enough in a product of Ripon; Wilfrid himself had travelled twice to Rome appealing for papal intervention in his struggles to regain his diocese. It must have surprised the Popes, however; they were not on the whole accustomed to being treated with such deference. A reverence for the Papacy was one of the most important legacies of the mission sent by Gregory the Great to England, and because of the influence of the English abroad, throughout the eighth century, it arguably had a considerable impact on papal self-confidence and on the general status of the papacy within Francia and Europe as a whole. Willibrord was supported in his mission by the most important of the non-royal aristocratic families in Francia, the Pippinids (who later in the century, as the

Carolingians, took over both kingship and Empire). Pippin II's mother-in-law gave him land for the building of a monastery at Echternach (in modern Luxembourg), on the site of a very grand Roman villa (parts of which may well still have been standing when Willibrord moved in). From there Willibrord moved on to Frisia, under its pagan king Radbod; even though it must have been transparently obvious to Radbod that Willibrord's mission was tied up with Pippinid ambitions to control Frisia, he did allow Willibrord to operate in his kingdom. Willibrord, with papal approval, set up an archiepiscopal see at Utrecht, and consecrated bishops to help him. He visited the court of the Danish king as well – the first attempt to bring Christianity to Scandinavia – although he had no success; he also moved across the middle Rhine into Hesse and Thuringia, into areas where Christianity was by no means unknown.

There would be something in the argument that no Englishman has ever played a more important role on the Continent than Boniface; his only rival for this position is probably his younger contemporary Alcuin of York. Yet his reputation (like that of many other historical figures) has been steadily whittled away by historians in recent years. It is no longer possible to see him as 'the Apostle of Germany', for instance. In almost every area in which he was active there had been missionary work before. Some of this had been done by Frankish bishops, working across the Rhine in areas where ecclesiastical structures had never been set up by the Romans; some by Columbanus and by his various Irish followers and successors. (If this book was about Ireland as well as Britain there would be much greater stress on the impact that the Irish had on the Continent between the seventh and ninth centuries.) Although he was inspired by the missionary ideal, and was eventually martyred for its sake, Boniface was actually much more important as a reformer and organiser.

Wynfrith, as he then was, entered the monastic life in Exeter, but moved to the monastery of Nursling, near the port of Hamwic, where he may well have met Frisian merchants. He went to Frisia and tried his hand at missionary work; the political circumstances were far from ideal, since Pippin II had just died, and the Frisians were taking advantage of this to break free from Frankish domination. Two years later he tried again, and this time followed Willibrord's footsteps to Rome. The new pope was Gregory II, who had taken his name in honour of Gregory the Great: it was the beginning of the rehabilitation of Gregory I's reputation in Rome itself, which may have caused the Pope to look kindly on Anglo-Saxon missionaries. Wynfrith received a commission from the pope to act as a missionary beyond the Rhine; he also received a new name, which had been borne by five previous Popes: *Bonifacius*. At first, Boniface worked with Willibrord, but he does not seem to have wanted to be under tutelage: he got Gregory II to consecrate him as bishop in 722, and he was taken under the protection of Pippin II's son Charles Martel, the first Carolingian. For fifteen years he worked in Hesse and Thuringia, establishing monasteries at Amöneburg, Fritzlar and

Fulda, and then, moving further south, at places like Ochsenfurt and Tauberbischofsheim in Franconia. He brought numerous Englishmen and women with him: Wigbert, abbot of Fritzlar, Burchard, bishop of Würzburg, Leoba, abbess of Tauberbischofsheim, Willibald, bishop of Eichstätt, and so on. The numerous manuscripts in Anglo-Saxon hands which survive in German libraries, some imported into Germany from Anglo-Saxon monasteries, but many written by Anglo-Saxons in Germany, are material witness to the enterprise started by Willibrord and Boniface.

Boniface himself was deeply annoyed that his sense of the urgency of the mission was not shared by Frankish bishops. It was natural that his missionary impulse should spill over into a desire to reform the Frankish Church itself. He held five reforming councils in Francia in the 740s; as Archbishop of Mainz, from 745 onwards, he was himself a leading ecclesiastic in Francia. The reform movement was something which could be supported by the Carolingians. Charles Martel and his son Pippin III were keen to extend their power; and their main enemies were the entrenched local aristocratic families of northern Gaul. By insisting on following the rules of the Church, concerning the election of bishops, or the separation of the clergy from the laity, the Carolingians could undermine the power of the aristocracy who then controlled the Church; through their support of the reforming Church they could in their turn control it.

Alongside the organisational reform of the Church, and the extension of this into territories east of the Rhine like Alamannia and Bavaria, went a renewed interest in clerical training. Latin had to be the language of the new multiethnic Frankish Church: and it had to be the Latin of the Vulgate Bible, and not the evolved Latin spoken every day over most of Francia, which was much closer to French than to Latin. So divergent had Latin become from the spoken language, that scribes were committing numerous errors even in making copies of the Bible. Boniface was horrified to discover a priest in Bavaria who was baptising people *in nomine patria et filia et spiritu sanctu*: 'in the name of the fatherland and the daughter and the Holy Spirit': Pope Zacharias reprimanded him for believing that a second baptism of these people was necessary in order to save their souls.[41] In Boniface's concern for the word we can discern the first traces of the so-called Carolingian Renaissance, which was at its heart an educational reform carried out, partly by Anglo-Saxon clergy, above all during the reigns of Charlemagne and his son Louis the Pious.

The acts of the first reforming council of 742 are the earliest document dated by the Anno Domini system of dating rather than by regnal dating. Regnal dating was impossible; the previous Merovingian king had died, and another had not yet been found and installed. It thus proved very convenient to adopt the new system which the Northumbrian historian Bede had been the first to use as a universal dating system, and we may be confident that it was Boniface who suggested it. It may even have been Boniface who suggested that Pippin III write to the Pope for permission to depose the last

Merovingian king and become king in his place. The Carolingian mayors were acting as kings; that is what they should be. From a distance it looked as if that is what had already happened; the Northumbrian monk who wrote a continuation to Bede's *Chronicle* in one of the two earliest manuscript copies of Bede's *History* noted Charles Martel's death in 741, 'Charles, king of the Franks, died.'[42] It may have been Boniface too who introduced the rituals of anointing and coronation to the Frankish ceremony of royal inauguration (see below, p. 192). Two years later, in 753, Boniface went into northern Germany, to preach to the pagan Saxons and Frisians. The Continuator to Bede's *Chronicle* noted: 'Boniface, also known as Wynfrith, bishop of the Franks, with fifty-two others won the martyr's crown.'[43] He and his followers were cut down by a group of sea-borne pirates; there is a book in the library at Fulda, said to be the one with which he tried to ward off the blows, which still bears two deep sword-cuts in it.

The Anglo-Saxon mission did not end with Boniface's death. Nor did the policy adopted under Willibrord and Boniface of linking the conversion of pagans with the extension of Carolingian power end with Boniface. The forced 'conversion' of the Saxons carried out by Charlemagne was one of the most horrific events in European history; the capitulary which he issued for Saxony laying down death as the penalty for, among other things, refusing to be baptised, for cremating the dead, and for eating meat during Lent, is one of Europe's, and Christianity's, most chilling documents. It is to the credit of Alcuin of York (see below, p. 184) that he disapproved of Charlemagne's policy with regard to the Saxons: after Frankish armies had defeated the Avars (an Asiatic people who had migrated to Hungary), he wrote asking him not to make the same mistakes: 'You should consider in your wisdom whether it is right to impose the yoke of tithes upon a simple people who are beginners in the faith.'[44] But before the English can congratulate themselves for being nicer than the Franks, it is worth bearing in mind that Boniface's successor as archbishop of Mainz, Lul, was an Anglo-Saxon. Even if he may not have advised on Charlemagne's brutal policy, as has been suggested, he did compose Latin verses in 786 celebrating Charlemagne's 'success' in Saxony. In the middle of the ninth century, it was believed that the Anglo-Saxon missionary Leofwine (Latinised as Lebuinus) had preached to the Saxons in the 770s, saying that if they did not convert

> there is a king in a neighbouring country who will invade your land, who will despoil and lay waste, will tire you out with his campaigns, scatter you in exile, dispossess or kill you, give away your estates to whomsoever he wishes, and thereafter you will be subject to him and to his successors.[45]

Fulda, which still housed many Anglo-Saxon monks, was probably the main base for the missionary work in Saxony, which followed closely behind Charlemagne's armies. Willehad was a Northumbrian who worked in Saxony and who very narrowly avoided martyrdom there after a Saxon revolt against the Franks; after studying at Echternach (then under the abbacy of the Englishman Beornrad, who went on to be archbishop of Sens) he returned to Saxony, and in 787 was consecrated bishop of Bremen. Just as Englishmen in the seventh century went to Ireland to be trained, so some north Germans went to England. Liudger was a Frisian who went to York in 767 to study with the master of the cathedral school, Alcuin; like Willehad he had to flee Saxony in 782, and after spending some time in Rome and Monte Cassino he eventually returned to Saxony and founded a monastery at a place now known simply as 'the Monastery': Münster. He became bishop there in 804.

The English mission is an fascinating phenomenon, and nor is it restricted to the late seventh and eighth centuries: in the eleventh century Englishmen like Sigfrid, from York, played a major role in the conversion of Sweden. In his account of the English missionaries abroad, Bede emphasised the importance of the feeling of kinship which the English had for the north Germans: this was their homeland. Their success may have been partly due to the ease with which they could communicate with the north Germans. But their success was primarily a result of the patronage of the Carolingians, who perhaps found them, as outsiders, devoid of political ambitions in Francia, easier and safer to work with than fellow-Franks.

8

Eighth-century achievement

The Northumbrian Renaissance

Historians have discovered numerous renaissances now, each of which was doing something like the much more self-conscious Renaissance of the later Middle Ages: rediscovering the classical past, and remoulding art and literature accordingly. The Twelfth-Century Renaissance was the first to be rediscovered; then the Carolingian Renaissance of the late eighth and ninth centuries. The Northumbrian Renaissance is perhaps insignificant compared to these others, and perhaps other names for the phenomenon would be more appropriate. But it does signal how remarkable the achievement of Northumbria was. From roughly the late seventh century through to the middle of the eighth there was a flourishing of learning, literature and art in Northumbria that had no parallels in contemporary Continental Europe at all: the nearest rivals to Northumbria in terms of cultural achievements at this time were in Ireland and in southern England (particularly in the circle of Theodore of Tarsus, Archbishop of Canterbury from 669 to 690), and possibly even in Pictland. Much survives from Ireland; relatively little from southern England; and nothing from Pictland except a magnificent array of sculptures. We may thus be misled, yet again, by the accident of survival, but possibly not. Northumbria was in a unique position. Its 'Renaissance' was built upon the influx of books that came from Ireland and the Continent in the course of the seventh century; it was sustained by the enormous wealth accrued by the kings and aristocrats in the middle part of the seventh century, when Northumbria was the most powerful kingdom in Britain; and considerable talent could be found in its monasteries.

One of the largest monasteries in Britain was the monastery in Northumbria in which Bede himself lived, founded by Benedict Biscop on 70 hides of land donated by King Ecgfrith in 674 and standing on two sites at Monkwearmouth and Jarrow. It was a centre of learning, but also of economic exploitation: as has often been noted, the three great Bibles which

Bede's abbot Ceolfrith ordered to be produced at the beginning of the eighth century would have required the skins of some 1500 healthy cattle. One of these Bibles still survives, in Florence: it was intended as a gift for the pope, but did not quite reach its target. It is called the Codex Amiatinus: a magnificent book, of 1030 sheets of calf-skin, each some 69 by 51 cm in size, and 25 cm thick: in Rupert Bruce-Mitford's memorable words, 'with its protective wrappings and travelling case and original covers it must have weighed a good 90 lb, practically the same as a fully grown female Great Dane.'[1] The Codex Amiatinus was such a fine copy of Italian script and book production that for long it was not recognised as a product of Anglo-Saxon England at all. It illustrates how determined Northumbrian monks were to be part of the Latin world: their zeal extended not just to copying the art and script of Italy, but to writing in the language advocated by the ancient Latin grammarians.

The Lindisfarne Gospels illustrate another aspect of the Northumbrian Renaissance. The strength and originality of that Renaissance rested on the fact that Northumbria had been the missionary ground of two separate traditions, the Roman and the Irish. The Roman links had been revived at the time of Bishop Wilfrid of York, by Wilfrid himself, but also by Benedict Biscop, who made five trips to Rome and to Gaul, mostly for the purpose of collecting books for the library of Monkwearmouth-Jarrow. But the connection with Ireland had not ceased with the Synod of Whitby and with the subsequent departure of various disgruntled Irish churchmen. So close were the connections and thus the cultural contacts between the Northumbrian and Irish Churches that there has been serious disagreement about the original provenance of some of the most famous manuscripts. The Book of Durrow – 'a national symbol of Ireland, showing up on merchandise ranging from travel posters to dish towels in Shannon airport'[2] – has been claimed for Northumbria; so has the other great treasure from the library of Trinity College Dublin, the Book of Kells. Some good reasons have been advanced on this; other arguments smack rather more of racial prejudice. This is what the great palaeographer E.A. Löwe, wrote: 'I confess that the Book of Durrow has always seemed to me a book apart among the group of early Irish manuscripts now in Dublin, and the suspicion woke in me that perhaps English workmanship accounted for the orderliness of its script and the balance and sobriety of its ornamentation.'[3] But there is prejudice in the other direction as well: the lack of recognition that the animal interlace ornament found on many works of Irish art does actually have a 'Germanic' rather than a 'Celtic' origin. Even if the books of Durrow and Kells may be Irish, perhaps from Iona, artists resident in Northumbria were just as capable of similar work as they were capable of imitations of the Italian. The Lindisfarne Gospels were undoubtedly produced in Lindisfarne, yet the manuscript bears many of the characteristics of Irish manuscripts. A tenth-century note in Old English says that the book was written (though *writan* means 'draw' as well as 'write') by Eadrith, bishop of Lindisfarne from 698 to 721); bound by Æthelwald, bishop from 724; and decorated on the outside with precious metals and gems by Billfrith, a hermit. The distribution of the internal illumination follows the model of books like Durrow, with a carpet page – a page of unbelievably complex geometrical and animal interlace – and an Evangelist's portrait preceding each Gospel, and with the first page of each Gospel dominated by an elaborately decorated initial letter. There is spiral decoration, as on Irish metalwork, and a plethora of animal interlace, as on Anglo-Saxon metalwork, while the Evangelists' portraits may have Mediterranean models. This manuscript, perhaps the most sumptuous in the British Library's holdings, is symbolic of the three main artistic currents which meet in Northumbria.

The Franks Casket, in some ways, is an even more astonishing cultural object. It was found in central France in the nineteenth century, and bought by Sir Augustus Franks, who donated it to the British Museum; the right side of the box was eventually found in a private house, and ended up in the Museo Bargello, Florence, only a few hundred metres from that other monument of the Northumbrian Renaissance, the Codex Amiatinus. It is made of whalebone, as its runic inscription in Old English proclaims, and is only some 22 cm long. It is the curious juxtaposition of motifs that makes the Casket such an enigma. The front depicts the Virgin and Child adored by the Magi, next to a rather gruesome scene from the Anglo-Saxon legend of Weyland the Smith, where he presents to the king a cup made from the skull of the king's son; the damaged lid shows a figure labelled as Ægili besieged by soldiers in his house or fort (possibly Egil the archer, Weyland's brother); the left side shows Romulus and Remus being suckled by a wolf; the back shows the sack of Jerusalem by the Roman general Titus (here the inscription is partly in Latin); and the right side has an enigmatic scene with a monster facing a warrior on the left, a stallion in the middle, and three hooded figures on the right – even the three-line inscription in runes (the pre-Christian writing system of the Germanic world) does not help to identify the scene, although it almost certainly has to be explained in terms of Germanic mythology surrounding death: 'the scene is a promise of heroic death, as yet unfulfilled'.[4]

Much ingenuity has been expended by scholars trying to unravel the meaning of the Casket as a whole: entirely suitably, for, as Old English poetry shows us, the Anglo-Saxons themselves loved complexity and riddling. One should probably approach the Franks Casket just as someone like Bede would have approached a story in the Bible: it contains not just a literal meaning, but symbolic and allegorical meanings as well. Thus, Romulus and Remus, the twins who founded Rome, may remind an Anglo-Saxon of Hengist and Horsa, who were the founders of the Anglo-Saxon kingdoms; but the wolf might be seen as the Church, suckling the faithful. It might have a clearly political meaning too: when Æthelberht of the East Angles tried to escape Mercian domination in 794 he issued a coin with the same scene on it. He was executed by Offa of Mercia. Near a church dedicated to him (the church of the martyr St Æthelberht at Larling in Norfolk), was found, perhaps totally coincidentally, a fragment of whalebone with the wolf and twins on it, normally dated to the late eighth century.[5] Each panel may comment in some way on the other panels: the salvational interpretation of Romulus and Remus echoes the representation of the Virgin and Christ, while even the scene of Weyland may have such an interpretation, since the child born to the king's daughter after she had been raped by Weyland was Widia, a hero and saviour of his people. Exile is also a common theme in every scene except the lid (so far as we know). But it is also particularly striking that each scene appears to contain some reference to the concept of good and bad rule, again shown through contrasted examples from Judaeo-Christian and Germanic tradition.[6]

The Ruthwell Cross is the fourth and last of our examples of material culture from the Northumbrian Renaissance. The idea of erecting wooden or stone crosses goes back to the earliest days of the Northumbrian Church; sometimes these crosses are erected within monastic precincts, but in the days before there were many churches they were also placed in the open countryside, to create a place where Christians could gather to pray or to listen to sermons. They were often carved with scenes drawn from the Bible or the stories of the saints; but none has such a complex iconographical scheme as the Ruthwell Cross. Ruthwell is in Dumfries, in an area probably only conquered by the Northumbrians in the mid-seventh century (although there was a tradition that it was moved there from Priestwoodside on the Solway Firth); the cross is usually dated to the first half of the eighth century. The stone shaft is over 5.5 m high. Beneath the figures of Christ and the evangelists, on both sides, were scenes from the Bible and the early Church, each identified and described in Latin inscriptions. Meyvaert has argued that it may originally have stood in the nave of a monastic church, separating the area reserved to the monks from the area used by the lay congregation: the face seen by the monks consisted of scenes representing the monastic life, while scenes of more general Christian significance were viewed by the laity.[7] On each side, framing panels of flora and fauna, were inscribed lines from the Anglo-Saxon poem (preserved also in a tenth-century manuscript), 'The Dream of the Rood': the crucifixion from the point of view of the Cross. This inscription was in runes, which may have been more familiar to the laity than the Latin alphabet. The whole ensemble was like a book in stone: and a complex book, at that, with much for both clergy and laity to contemplate.

If two books, an ivory casket, and a stone cross give some idea of the richness of the Northumbrian Renaissance, Bede himself is its greatest spiritual and intellectual product: a man who drew on the resources of a library assembled by Benedict Biscop and others, that was probably the largest in Britain (although still sadly deficient compared to the greater libraries of the Mediterranean world) to produce Biblical commentaries and various didactic works that would be used for centuries, as well as a *History* which is not only an invaluable source (as can be seen from this book), but a great work of literature.

Bede was not the only scholar of the Northumbrian Renaissance, nor necessarily the most influential. That latter distinction must go to Alcuin. He was educated in York; his first master was Egbert, Bede's own pupil. But he regarded the founder of the York school to have been Ælberht, with whom he travelled on the Continent in search of books. When Ælberht became archbishop, in 767, Alcuin was put in charge of what was now a very considerable library.[8] He became the main master of the cathedral school, and from that position he was headhunted in 781/2 by Charlemagne, king of the Franks, to run the palace school at Aachen. Most of his surviving writings – three hundred letters, 220 poems, twenty-five treatises on various academic subjects, editions of liturgical and Biblical texts, and the various decrees he drafted – were produced after he emigrated to Francia, at nearly fifty years of age. He is generally reckoned to be a crucial figure in the Carolingian Renaissance, and in the formulation of Charlemagne's policy towards the Church, although his exact contribution has often been disputed. It was probably his work on Latin grammar, leading towards the re-creation of a classically based language, which was his most significant achievement; it has even been claimed that it was his insistence on the pronunciation of every syllable in Latin (very different from the 'lazy' way in which the evolved Latin of France or Italy was spoken at the time) which in effect created a new spoken language for the clergy and clerical bureaucrats of Charlemagne's immense Empire.

The decline of monasticism?

Bede showed us the conversion of the English proceeding side by side with the foundation of monasteries. Gregory the Great had been the first monastic pope, and a great enthusiast for monasticism, particularly of Benedictine monasticism. Augustine himself was a monk, as were his followers, and he founded the monastery of St Peter and St Paul at Canterbury. The foundation of monasteries sometimes preceded, and always soon followed the conversion of kingdoms. Nunneries were founded too, often with royal women (widows or daughters) as abbesses: probably the most famous was Strensall (or Whitby), which was presided over by Abbess Hild, the daughter of Edwin's nephew. Like all rural nunneries of which we know from this period, in England or Gaul, it was what some people call a 'double monastery', in that it housed monks as well as nuns. But 'rural nunnery' is a better term, since only urban nunneries (as in Gaul), could survive without a community of male priests attached: urban nunneries could call on the episcopal clergy for their liturgical and sacramental needs, while rural nunneries needed resident male clergy. A 'double monastery' was always presided over by an abbess, rather than an abbot.

It is with a rural nunnery that we can see, in Bede, the first hint of his worries about English monasticism. Given that a perennial headache for abbesses was keeping men away from their nuns, abbesses of double monasteries were playing with fire. This was literal in the case of Coldingham (Berwickshire): God sent heavenly flames to burn it to the ground, as had been foretold by a vision, according to Bede. God had seen that 'the cells built for praying and for reading have become haunts of feasting, drinking, gossip, and other delights', while the virgins spent their time imperilling their virginity, and making friends with men from outside the monastery.[9] But other such rural nunneries seem to have operated very successfully: Hild's community served virtually as a seminary for the training of bishops and priests for the Northumbrian Church. Monastic communities for men and women were the centres of the Northumbrian Renaissance. Yet, paradoxically, it seems, Bede and Alcuin were living at a time when things were apparently going very wrong with monastic life in England.

At the very end of the *Historia Ecclesiastica* Bede celebrates the way in which monasticism was sweeping across Northumbria at the time of writing (731).

> In these favourable times of peace and prosperity, many of the Northumbrian race, both noble and simple, have laid aside their weapons and taken the tonsure, preferring that they and their children should take monastic vows rather than train themselves in the art of war. What the result will be, a later generation will discover.[10]

This comes in a chapter which mentions two comets (in 729) that portend disaster, and which apparently presaged 'a terrible plague of Saracens' – an attack on southern Gaul by the Muslim Arabs and North Africans who had conquered Spain in 711, that talks about the 'serious commotions and setbacks' of the beginning of the reign of King Ceolwulf of the Northumbrians, but which also refers to the increase in the number of believers, and the peace that reigns with the Picts and the Irish. It is thus not immediately apparent whether 'a later generation' should expect good news or bad. Bede's *Letter to Egbert* from 734, however (introduced p. 170), makes it perfectly clear.

In that letter not only does Bede complain about bishops, but about the state of monasticism: indeed, he puts forward a plan for reform which will deal with both problems. 'There are innumerable places, as we all know, allowed the name of monasteries by a most foolish manner of speaking, but having nothing at all of a monastic way of life'.[11] He suggests that these places become bases for new bishops, and if these monasteries do not have enough land to support a bishop properly, then other similarly useless monasteries should be closed down and have their land added to the estates of episcopal monasteries. It is fascinating to note that Bede, a supposedly unworldly monk, should show his extremely practical political and economic common sense in this letter: he does not only complain that there are too many 'pseudo'-monasteries, but also that these are taking land which would otherwise go to the king's warriors, to reward them for defending the kingdom. The sons of nobles and warriors are forced to go abroad to seek their fortune; or, because they do not have an estate on which to settle and marry after leaving the king's retinue, they give themselves over to loose living and fornication. Some nobles, on the other hand,

> by a still heavier crime, since they are laymen and not experienced in the usages of the life according to the rule or possessed by love of it, give money to kings, and under the pretext of founding monasteries buy lands on which they may more freely devote themselves to lust, and in addition cause them to be ascribed to them in hereditary right by royal edicts, and even get those same documents of their privileges confirmed, as if in truth worthy of God, by the subscription of bishops, abbots and secular persons. And thus, having usurped for themselves estates and villages, and being henceforward free from divine as well as from human service, they gratify their own desires alone, laymen in charge of monks; nay, rather, it is not monks that they collect there, but whomsoever they may perchance find wandering anywhere, expelled from true monasteries for the fault of disobedience, or whom they can allure out of the monasteries, or, indeed, those of their own followers whom they can persuade to promise to them the obedience of a monk and receive the tonsure. With the unseemly companies of these persons they fill the monasteries which they have built and – a very ugly and unheard-of spectacle – the very same men now are occupied with wives and the procreation of children.[12]

The implications of this passage for the significant changes in property law which are occurring in England, and almost certainly other parts of the British Isles, will be discussed later in this chapter. But for the purposes of the history of monasticism, the crucial fact is that large numbers of monasteries were being founded, and that, even if they were presided over by husband and wife, these monasteries did maintain some kind of monastic life. Bede seems to regard them as monasteries in name only, but Bede himself came from a very austere and learned monastic tradition, and we would be rash to assume that all his fellow-clerics in Northumbria or elsewhere shared his rigorist position.

It is thus possible to use Bede's *Letter* to suggest a picture of monasticism in decline in Northumbria and by extension (since we have no reason to think that the situation was different elsewhere) in the rest of England. Indeed, since we know that similar developments were occurring in Ireland, we might think that the problem was a universal one in Britain and Ireland. We are much less well informed on monastic life in the late eighth and early ninth centuries, however, so we might be being misled by silence. For Northumbria, for instance, we have little apart from the letters Alcuin wrote from Aachen, complaining about the sad decline from earlier standards, and the Latin poem *De Abbatibus*, written by Æthelwulf early in the ninth century, which does, however, extol the sanctity and devotion of the monks and abbots of his monastery (sometimes identified as Crayke, to the north of York).

It may be that we are in danger of taking Bede's worries too literally. What his letter suggests is that monasteries were becoming integrated into the life of the Anglo-Saxons to a much greater extent than either he or Alcuin approves. As in Ireland, they are becoming important places: bases of secular aristocratic power and centres of wealth and economic production. They are places where drunkenness was commonplace, and where secular poems about warriors and heroes were sung. Alcuin wrote to an unknown bishop (probably Unuuona of Leicester) complaining about such things:

> Let God's words be read at the episcopal dinner-table. It is right that a reader should be heard, not a harpist; patristic discourse, not pagan song. What has Hinieldus to do with Christ?[13]

Hinieldus is normally taken to be a reference to Ingeld, a hero to whom a passing reference is made in the Old English poem *Beowulf* (which some think may indeed have been composed by monks in such a monastery at this time).

A better example than *Beowulf* of a product of this 'new monasticism' may be the monastery of Flixborough, which was in the kingdom of Lindsey (now just to the north of Scunthorpe, Lincolnshire). It was excavated between 1989 and 1991, and has not yet been fully published. But preliminary reports show that it was a rich site. There were traces of numerous halls, some connected by paths; there were a number of graves; the site was surrounded by a ditch, as is common on monastic sites.[14] Although in the eighth century Lindsey was under Mercian overlordship, most of the sixty-eight coins were Northumbrian, although there were also examples from East Anglia, Wessex and Frisia: they range from coins produced *c.* 700 to coins minted by Alfred of Wessex in 874/5. (Few seventh- or tenth-century coins circulated in Lindsey, so this coin-date range may not be the actual date-range of the monastery.) There was a good deal of local pottery, and Ipswich ware, but also an amount of imported continental pottery, as well as imported glass and quern-stones, suggesting that the site engaged in trade. Iron objects were common (303 knives), and there were signs of iron-working. Hundreds of fragments relating to textile production (loom weights, needles and so on) survive, 'suggesting the production of cloth on an industrial scale'.[15] There is precious little to suggest that it is actually a monastic site. It could be a *wic*, a trading-place (see below, pp. 196–201); it could be an aristocratic centre. But among the finds were clear signs of literacy: twenty-seven writing styli, and an inscribed lead plaque, possibly from a relic chest. Styli have been found on sites that are definitely monastic, but never before in such numbers: there were six from Whitby, and just two from Jarrow, a major site for the production of writing. So there is a strong chance that Flixborough was a monastic site; which does not exclude it from being an aristocratic centre and a trading-place at the same time. One could compare this to the monastic site at Brandon in Suffolk, or to Whithorn in Galloway. The monastery of Whithorn provided significant evidence for craft production and imported luxuries: it has the largest assemblage of imported glass from any site in western Britain.[16] Irish archaeologists, looking at secularised monasteries of this type in the eighth century, have come up with the concept of the 'monastic town': a monastery in legal terms, but economically and socially very little different from the towns of other parts of western Europe.

What archaeology can do is to show us the material basis of life at a particular site; it can say relatively little about spirituality. The historian can marvel at the Lindisfarne Gospels; the archaeologist can find the place, on the north of the island, where calves were slaughtered to provide vellum for the production of manuscripts.[17] Bede and Alcuin may have been right: there may have been a decline of spirituality. But this may have been because of the very success of monasteries as institutions, and in particular their economic success. It was a familiar cycle throughout the Middle Ages: spirituality was prized, and attracted money and land, and rich monasteries found it difficult to sustain their ideals. The answer was reform: as with any utopian endeavour Trotsky's continuous revolution was the only way to maintain the ideals. It does not look as if the reforms suggested by Bede and Alcuin had any time to take effect before the wealth of the monasteries proved their undoing in an even more drastic way. Before the eighth century was out, Lindisfarne was plundered by the Vikings; in the first decades of the ninth century that was the fate of most monasteries in Britain.

The rise of Mercia

With the completion of Bede's *History* in 731 we lose a source of major importance for the history of the whole of Britain, not just for the Anglo-Saxon kingdoms. Indeed, we lose Bede as an informative source long before that: the last section of the *History* reveals very little of what was happening in the first three decades of the eighth century. In the century and a half that ensues, before most of the Anglo-Saxon kingdoms fall to the assault of Scandinavian invaders, we do not have any detailed narrative source, and even the various annals that survive for Britain (which give us vital but often disconnected and unexplained details of events of political significance) are not as extensive as those which exist in Ireland. We do have other sources, however, in particular a growing number of charters, which tell us not only about political relationships, but also about dispute settlement, and ideas about land, property rights and kinship – some of the most fundamental concepts in any society. We also come into a period when burial archaeology does not dominate so much, and where we have more evidence of ecclesiastical establishments, rural settlements and, above all, the new towns of the later seventh and eighth centuries. Coins began to be minted in Britain again, in the second quarter of the seventh century, and they too come to be an important historical source in the pre-Viking period.

It is all too easy for English historians in particular to present the eighth and early ninth centuries with hindsight. Knowing that the Viking invasions were to put an end to all but one of the dynasties of the Anglo-Saxon world, the kingdoms can be seen to have fatal flaws. The words of zealous churchmen can be taken at face value: Bede's *Letter to Egbert* and Alcuin's two letters to Northumbria, written in the wake of the Viking attack on Lindisfarne, can be used to show the general moral decline of the kings themselves, as well as the decline of monasticism. The strongest attack on the policies of the kings, however, was addressed in around 746 to Æthelbald of Mercia (716–57), the strongest king of his day, by Boniface and seven of his fellow bishops (all of them apparently of Anglo-Saxon origin), from the safety of Francia.

> For if the race of the English – as is noised abroad throughout those provinces and is cast up against us in France and in Italy, and is used as a reproach by the pagans themselves – spurning lawful marriage, lives a foul life in adultery and lasciviousness after the pattern of the people of Sodom, it is to be expected that from such intercourse with harlots there will be born a degenerate people, ignoble, raging with lust; and in the end the whole people, sinking to lower and baser things, will finally neither be strong in secular warfare nor stable in faith, neither honoured by men nor loved by God. Just as it has happened to other races of Spain and Provence, and to the Burgundian peoples; who thus, turning from God, committed fornication, until the omnipotent Judge allowed avenging punishments for such crimes to come and destroy them, through ignorance of the law of God, and through the Saracens.[18]

Boniface's complaint was primarily that Æthelbald himself was guilty of fornication, and, worse, that he committed this in nunneries with virgins consecrated to God; and that he had violated the privileges of churches and monasteries and plundered their property – just like his predecessor Ceolred of the Mercians and like King Osred of the Northumbrians (705–16), Boniface adds. It is one of the strongest letters ever sent to an English king, tempered only by a few remarks near the beginning, that 'we have heard' that he gave many alms, that he upheld the law and maintained peace in his kingdom, and that he was a defender of widows and the poor: all the things that characterised a good king in the eyes of the Church.

Æthelbald was murdered in 757, after a reign of over forty years – by his own bodyguard, which does suggest that he had a preternatural facility for alienating people. But he had reigned longer than any previous Anglo-Saxon king of importance, and had maintained dominance over all the other southern kingdoms for longer than any previous *bretwalda*: in a charter of 736 he even styled himself by what may well be the Latin version of the Old English title: *rex Britanniae*, or 'king of Britain'. In the last years of his life Wessex seems to have been in rebellion against him, but since the late 720s he had controlled southern England, and ruled parts of Wessex and Essex – most notably the important town of London – directly. It looks as if Boniface's no doubt very public letter even persuaded Æthelbald of the need to make his peace with the Church: in 749 he freed the churches of his kingdom from all public burdens except the two fundamental ones: repairing bridges and maintaining fortresses.

Æthelbald's murder not surprisingly resulted in a civil war, which resulted in victory for Offa, like Æthelbald a descendant of the brother of the great seventh-century Mercian king Penda. Offa too had an unusually long reign, from 757 to 796. He did not immediately inherit the kind of overlordship which Æthelbald had acquired, but he did win that, and more, by the 790s: he became a king whose power in Britain was even acknowledged on the Continent, by Charlemagne, king of the Franks (who, four years after Offa's death, became 'Emperor of the Romans') and by the pope. His route to power has to be reconstructed from hints, sometimes from charters which show him in the company of subordinate kings. There is one, for instance, which shows him with Ealdfrith, king of Lindsey (north Lincolnshire): the only evidence from the eighth century that the kingdom of Lindsey still existed in any form at all. Offa's rise to power certainly does not seem to have been without occasional setback. Cynewulf of the West Saxons seems to have preserved his independence, until his murder in 786 while visiting his mistress – an incident described at length in the 755 entry of the *Anglo-Saxon Chronicle* (retrospectively placed alongside his accession), which is reckoned to be the first piece of narrative prose in English. Offa won dominance in Wessex by helping one side in the civil war which followed Cynewulf's death. East Anglia seems to have been generally docile, but in 794 Offa had its King Æthelberht beheaded, presumably for disobedience. Kent too did not submit without a struggle, although it is from Kent that comes a document which Sir Frank Stenton called 'the most uncompromising assertion of an overlord's authority that has come down from the whole Anglo-Saxon period':[19] the revocation by Offa of a grant that King Egbert of Kent had made, because 'it was not right for a man to grant away land which his lord had given him, without his lord's assent.' Offa seems to have controlled the crucial centre of London. A charter thought to date from this period describes the granting of land to St Peter and the needy people of God in Thorney 'in the terrible place which is called Westminster' – the earliest reference to a foundation on what was then an island in the Thames, a mile upstream from the site of Saxon London.[20]

Like Æthelbald, Offa decided to advertise his power by new titles. Sometimes he used the rather convoluted 'king of the Mercians and of other neighbouring nations'. But in 774 he took on two new titles: *rex Anglorum* and *rex totius Anglorum patriae*. There is some ambiguity about the first: did he mean 'king of the Angles' (excluding Saxons) or (more likely) 'king of the English'? But the second one is interesting: 'king of the whole fatherland [or country] of the English'. Assuming the *patria* refers to a particular territory, it is a very early example of a territorial rather than a national title: a step along the road to the title of 'king of England'. Stenton suggested that this title was not mere swagger: he did not take it until 774, the year in which he seems to have imposed his own candidate on the kingdom of Northumbria, and was thus able to claim overlordship north as well as south of the Humber.[21] At this point Offa had power over more territory in Britain than any king before him, and more than any subsequent king until the tenth century.

There is some evidence that earlier in the eighth century the Welsh had been raiding with impunity across into Mercia. The pillar of Eliseg (see below, p. 205) records that Eliseg, king of Powys, had recovered land from the English. Offa took the offensive: although the *Welsh Annals* record a battle between the Welsh and the English at Hereford early in Offa's reign, thereafter they record three invasions of Wales by Offa. In the second half of his reign Offa caused the Dyke to be built: the largest public undertaking in Britain since Hadrian's Wall, whether we are talking about linear size or the expenditure of resources (see above p. 145). In practice it was possibly more of a boundary marker than an actual line of defence, making it the last of the various boundary earthworks of the Anglo-Saxon period, of which there are numerous in southern and eastern England. On the other hand, the Dyke did follow the defensive lie of the land, and ignored the realities of settlement in the border region. There are what are probably early English place-names on the Welsh side of the Dyke; more significantly, perhaps, most parishes contiguous to the Dyke are actually bisected by it, and if many of these parishes (as elsewhere in England) preserve the bounds of earlier estates, Offa seems to have ridden roughshod over local feelings in order to separate his kingdom as a whole from the Welsh.

Offa used other titles to express his power which are even more interesting than those noted above: 'King, constituted by the King of Kings' and, in a charter of 764, 'King of the Mercians, from the royal line of the Mercians, and constituted as king by the dispensation of Almighty God'.[22] Such titles had not been known before in England, but they are found among the Franks, and the influence almost certainly comes from there. Constitutional innovations of immense importance happened in Francia in the early 750s, when Pippin III, the most recent member of a dynasty who had served as mayors of the palace to the Merovingian kings of the Franks, and who had been effective rulers for sixty years, put the last Merovingian in a monastery and had himself declared king, as Pippin I of the Franks. He took enormous pains to legitimise this deposition. He not only sought papal permission, but (we may presume) persuaded his closest adviser, the West Saxon missionary Boniface, to devise new ecclesiastical ceremonies. In 751 Pippin was anointed with holy oil by Archbishop Boniface, following the precedents of the Old Testament kings, and he was possibly crowned as well. In 754, according to the *Royal Frankish Annals* he and his two sons were anointed again, this time by Pope Stephen II. His sons Charles and Carloman succeeded him in 768. Charles – later to be known as Carolus Magnus, Charles the Elder, or Charlemagne – had his own young sons Pippin and Louis anointed king by the pope in Rome in 781. Six years later, Offa took the same step: the first English anointing was that of his eldest son Ecgfrith.

Offa had no little difficulty arranging this ceremony, since in the 780s he was in conflict with the man who was the most obvious candidate for carrying it out, Archbishop Jænberht of Canterbury. Kent itself had accepted Offa's overlordship after great resistance, and indeed it is not impossible that after the battle of Otford in 776 they preserved their independence from Mercia for ten years or more. Offa's first priority, if he was to enhance his prestige and that of his son, was to have his own archbishopric. Many historians have connected this ambition with the visit to England by papal legates in 786: the first official mission from Rome since the time of Pope Gregory I. The report of this mission survives among the letters of Alcuin, the Northumbrian scholar who had been at Charlemagne's court since 782 (see above, p. 184), but there is no other reliable record of it, so the precise purpose remains unclear. The two legates, George of Ostia and Theophylact of Todi, visited Canterbury and the court of Offa; then Theophylact went to visit *Brittaniae partes* – the Welsh kingdoms? – and George went to Northumbria. Councils were held in Mercia and in Northumbria, which issued twenty canons designed to reform the Church and regulate the lives of the clergy, and also to regulate the lives of the laity, condemning sexual relations with nuns, commanding the payment of tithes, insisting on the fulfilment of oaths, and forbidding pagan customs. Offa would probably have been most interested in canons eleven to fourteen, which declare the correct relationship between kings and the Church. Like a bishop, the king is 'the Lord's anointed': and to disobey a king (let alone assassinate one) is to disobey God. The rich and powerful have a duty to be just and to protect the powerless; violence and unjust tribute on the Church were condemned, and churchmen and laity should live in harmony among themselves. Crucially, however, bishops are declared to be answerable for the souls of the laity on the Day of Judgement, and therefore must be humbly obeyed by kings and the rest of the laity. Bishops are the angels (messengers) of God: 'therefore, if bishops are called angels, they cannot be judged by laymen'.[23] As Catherine Cubitt has shown, there are many parallels between these legatine decrees and Charlemagne's *Admonitio Generalis* of 789, a crucial early document in the Carolingian programme to create a truly Christian society, an earthly mirror of heaven.[24] There are parallels also with Alcuin's style, and his preoccupations concerning public and private virtue, as revealed in his numerous surviving letters: it seems likely that Alcuin had a hand in the drafting of the *Admonitio Generalis*, but perhaps also of the legatine decrees. Offa was unlikely to have been impressed by these ideas, any more than Æthelred and Eardwulf, kings of Northumbria, probably were when Alcuin admonished them using very similar language. The legatine mission is more likely to be part of the Carolingian king's desire to enhance his *own* prestige by promoting moral reform in Europe.

Whatever the inspiration and motives for the legatine visit were, in the following year Offa achieved his ambition. After a council at Chelsea which the *Anglo-Saxon Chronicle* described as *geflitfullic* – contentious – the province of Canterbury was drastically reduced in size, and a new metropolitan province of Lichfield was created. Hygeberht received his *pallium* from Rome in 788. He was the first archbishop of Lichfield, and the last: in 802 Æthelheard of Canterbury was in Rome, and received from Pope Leo III confirmation that Pope Hadrian I's promotion of Lichfield had been invalid. It was almost certainly Hygeberht, however, who anointed and consecrated Offa's son Ecgfrith king in 787. Offa had achieved some kind of parity with the Carolingians. He failed in a more direct attempt, however. Charlemagne was happy for his son Charles to marry one of Offa's daughters, but refused Offa's condition: that Ecgfrith should marry one of Charlemagne's daughters. Indeed, so offended was Charlemagne that he broke off relations with Offa, and closed Frankish ports to English traders. Alcuin was one of those detailed to help restore relations.

Offa and Charlemagne were contemporaries from Charlemagne's accession in 768 until Offa's death in 796. Charlemagne was interested in maintainng relations with kings other than Offa, however. Alcuin reported to Offa that Charlemagne had been so angry that the Northumbrian king Æthelred I had been murdered in 796 that he actually thought of intervening to punish those who had shed royal blood. Osbald reigned for 27 days before being expelled by Eardwulf; when Eardwulf himself was expelled in 808, he took refuge at Charlemagne's court, and according to the *Royal Frankish Annals*, it was on the intervention of Charlemagne and Pope Leo III that he was reinstalled in Northumbria the following year. Ecgberht, expelled from Wessex by Offa in 789, also stayed at the Frankish court, for at least three years, and when he was installed as king of the West Saxons in 802, it may well have been with Frankish support: he was to succeed to Offa's position as overlord of the southern kingdoms, and conquered Mercia itself in 829, styling himself king of the Mercians. Nor was Charlemagne's influence restricted to the English kingdoms. According to Einhard's *Life of Charlemagne* (probably written in the 820s), 'By his generosity he had so impressed the Irish kings with his good will, that they publically declared that he was certainly their lord and they were his subjects and servants.'[25]

Coinage and commerce

The dispute between Offa and Charlemagne in the late 780s, which had resulted in a cessation of trade between Francia and England, was settled, and in the last year of Offa's life they communicated in what Stenton called 'the first commercial treaty in English history'.[26] Charlemagne's letter to Offa shows that the initiative came from Offa: Charlemagne refers to 'your brotherly messages' containing several suggestions. He agreed that pilgrims ought to be allowed to travel freely; but if merchants should be found masquerading as pilgrims, they should be made to pay the necessary tolls; that merchants abroad should be under the protection of the appropriate king; that he would help Offa find the black stones he needed (almost certainly lavastone querns, for milling grain, from the Rhineland), and that he would try to make sure they were of the right size, if only the English would make sure that the cloaks they sent were of sufficient length too.[27]

This letter is precious information about eighth-century trade, about which relatively little is otherwise known from documentary evidence. There is a brief reference in Bede to a Frisian merchant; a brief reference in an eighth-century saint's life to a colony of Frisians, presumably merchants, in York; and so on. Otherwise our evidence for trade in the pre-Viking period comes either from coins or from archaeology, above all the relatively recently discovered evidence from various trading-centres or *wics*.

Coins in the early Middle Ages do not have the inevitable link with trade and commerce that the modern mind imagines. Coins may be minted for the prestige of the minter; or to provide convenient means of paying tribute or tax, or of giving gifts. But, most importantly, they are useful means of dividing up bullion into pieces of equal value. Throughout Europe, in the post-Roman world, the main coinage was a gold coinage (the gold *solidus* was rarely minted; the third-solidus, the *triens* or *tremissis*, was the norm), whose value was ultimately the market value of the precious metal itself. In the first half of the seventh century the Frankish gold coinage was devalued, in progressive and perhaps organised amounts, until a purely silver coinage emerged in the 660s; it has been suggested that Anglo-Saxon gold jewellery of that period could be dated by looking at the purity of the gold, because Frankish coins constituted the most readily available source of precious metal. The first post-Roman coins in Britain are minted in south-east England in the 630s or 640s: the Sutton Hoo gold hoard from the 620s has only Frankish gold coins, while the Crondall hoard of *c.* 640 had several English types, minted in Kent, London and elsewhere: numismatists call these *thrymsas* (from *tremissis*), but it is likely that they were actually called *scillings*. (Interestingly, and oddly, our earliest English law-code, issued by Æthelberht before 616, gives the value of fines in shillings, a generation before any coins were minted in England. Was that how his subjects referred to the Merovingian gold coins which arrived in Kent? Were those coins actually in circulation, or did *scilling* refer to a weight of gold, whether made up into jewellery or in coin?) As in Francia, the gold quality soon declined, and, as in Francia, a silver coinage took over. The laws of Ine (*c.* 690) refer to coins as 'pennies', and this may well be what they were known as: for want of any better evidence, it is normally agreed that these were named after the great Mercian king Penda. Numismatists refer to them as *sceattas* (the *sce* pronounced as 'sh'), reserving the name 'penny' for the new coins which Offa introduced: ironically, the Old Irish word for such coins was *oiffing*, a word derived from 'Offa'. The style and design of these coins is very similar to the late Merovingian silver *denarii.*

Silver sceattas were minted locally in all the Anglo-Saxon kingdoms, it seems, in the eighth century, although it is often not easy to tell where they come from because they bear no readable inscriptions, and their designs often incorporate fairly standard motifs, such as a drastically simplified bust of a Roman Emperor. There is one from Essex which uses the motif of a sphinx, copied from a coin of Cunobelin, presumably a stray find: 'Looking back to Cunobelin and the first century was perhaps a way of asserting their independence from the growing power of Mercia.'[28] Often their coins have quite local distribution, which suggests that if they were used for trade between kingdoms most of them were melted down and reminted. There are few Northumbrian coins found south of the Humber, for instance. In Northumbria the sceatta type continued to be minted until the Vikings took York in 867, although by then the silver content had totally vanished: numismatists call these coins *stycas.*

In the southern kingdoms in the mid-eighth century, a new silver coin type is adopted, which is broader and thinner than the sceattas (but about the same weight), and which resembles the *denarii* minted by King Pippin of the Franks after his coinage reform of 757. Unlike the sceattas, these coins – referred to as pennies by numismatists – always have the names of the kings responsible for the minting. We can thus tell that the first seems to have been minted around 760 by King Beonna of the East Angles, who is otherwise unknown. Other early pennies were minted at Canterbury, but they are particularly associated with Offa (who took over the Canterbury mint), and their general acceptance across southern England may have been a sign of Mercia's dominance; the continuation of the sceatta in the north might reflect a desire to assert their independence, and perhaps also a lack of interest in trading with Pippin's kingdom. Offa's coinage was a product both of a desire to emulate Pippin and then Charlemagne, and a need to match his coinage with that produced across the Channel, to facilitate trade. As prestige items Offa's coins were superb. The earliest coins were very finely designed, with the royal portrait and moneyer's name on one side, and the name and title of the king on the other. The portrait was dropped in later coins, but the name of the king even more strongly emphasised: in this form they were the model for the English silver coinage right down to the time of Henry III in the thirteenth century. The close link with Charlemagne's coinage was a two-way process: Offa increased the weight of his coins slightly later in his reign, to match the reformed coinage of Charlemagne, but it seems that Charlemagne himself was influenced by the designs of Offa's coins.

There is evidence beyond the coinage for the increased importance of trade in the eighth century, but there is one remarkable coin find which reminds one that England was on the edge of a much wider commercial world than just that of northern Europe. The greatest power in the former Roman Empire in the eighth century was not Charlemagne, or the Byzantine Emperor: it was the Caliph, the 'Successor' to Muhammad. Muhammad had preached Islam, or submission to the will of God, at the time of Rædwald and Sutton Hoo; within a generation of his death in 632 his followers had conquered Egypt, Syria and the Persian Empire, and by the early eighth century Muslims ruled an unbroken territory across the southern Mediterranean and the Middle East from Spain across to the borders of India. A revolution in 750 toppled the Ummayyad caliphs: the new Abbasid dynasty moved their capital from Damascus in Syria to Baghdad in modern Iraq, which became the largest and most magnificent city west of China. A year later, Muslim and Chinese armies clashed; later in the 750s riots involving Muslim and Chinese merchants destroyed much of Canton city.[29] The vast commercial empire of the Muslims had its impact upon the North. Islamic silver coins are found in increasing number in Scandinavia in the eighth century, presumably received in return for such northern luxuries as furs. Many may well have travelled further west, to the trading towns in the kingdoms of Francia and England. If so they were soon melted down, as were any gold coins which arrived in the West. But Offa himself issued a gold coinage, where his Anglo-Saxon moneyer tried to imitate the Arabic script of a dinar of the Caliph Al-Mansur, from 774, adding the words OFFA REX to the Arabic design. This survival may represent an attempt to initiate a direct trade with the Islamic world: a sign of Offa's ambition, but also of the greatly increased horizons of the Anglo-Saxon kingdoms by the end of the eighth century.

The rebirth of towns

The new commercial world under Offa and Charlemagne had been developing for several generations, since the second half of the seventh century at least. It is from that time that we can trace the rise of trading-places right across the northern world. These have variously been called proto-towns, ports-of-trade (a term deriving from ethnographic literature), emporia (deriving from Bede's usage) and *wics* (deriving from the place-names). On the Continent, for instance, we have Quentovic, the *vicus* at the mouth of the Canche in Picardy, Schleswig, on the inlet called the Schlei (at the base of Jutland), and Köpingsvik on the island of Gotland in the Baltic. (The last incorporates a word from late Latin *caupo*, merchant, which is also to be found in the Norwegian trading-place near Oslo, called Kaupang, and the London street-name Cheapside.) In England we have, among others, Ipswich, Eoforwic (the Old English word for York, which became Jorvik under the Vikings), and Hamwic. It looks as if the suffix *wic* could be applied to place-names in order to indicate the town-as-trading-place. Thus, Hamwic is also known as Hamtun (and under the Normans became known as Southampton, to distinguish it from the important Hamton in the North), and London is referred to as Lundenwic, Lundenburh and Lundenceastre (Londonchester) in eighth- and ninth-century sources.

At all these English sites excavations since the 1970s have revealed ample evidence of the trade that was taking place in the pre-Viking period. These trading-places all share one characteristic: that if they are associated with former Roman towns they are not within the walls, but outside. Lundenwic was to the west of Roman London (which was probably referred to as Lundenburh = London-fortification): Lundenwic was probably centred on the Strand, where the place-name of Aldwych preserves the Anglo-Saxon name (= old-*wic*). At Canterbury the *wic* may be at a site along the river Stour to the east of the city, where an area called *wic* is mentioned in Domesday Book and where there is now a Fordwich. At York, redevelopment in the 1980s in a street called Fishergate, a short distance downstream from the Roman and medieval towns, revealed the riverside trading settlement. These changes of site might be due to the availability of property – perhaps Church and/or king had control of property within the Roman walls – or perhaps simply to the fact that it was easy to lay out streets and build houses and latrine pits in an area that was not a mass of Roman rubble (particularly if one wanted to build in wattle and daub rather than in reused Roman masonry).

Hamwic is the best known and most extensively excavated of these sites. The later medieval town was to the west of the peninsula on which modern Southampton originated, on the River Test, and Hamwic was to the east, on the River Itchen. Some fifty large excavations have uncovered perhaps 4 per cent of the settlement.[30] At the Six Dials site a street grid was found, with a main north-south street some 14 metres wide: it seems to have been laid out around 690. Much of the area within the grid-system was crammed with houses, mostly some 4–5 metres wide and 12 metres long: very similar in type to those known from rural sites. There were some specialised workshops, but many of the houses showed signs of being used for industrial activity of some sort, working metal, bone and pottery. Rather than having individual property boundaries, with ditches or fences, areas of the settlement appear to have been divided up by fences along the road: whether these indicate family groups, or areas controlled by individual landlords, is a matter for speculation. There is a good deal of local pottery, but also quantities of pottery from north-eastern France. Little of this pottery is found in England outside Hamwic, and most of it is domestic pottery, so it seems likely that the pottery was not being imported as a commercial enterprise, but actually used by Frankish traders based in Hamwic. There were, however, traces of imported glassware, quernstones and other artefacts.The inhabitants of Hamwic left sceattas around in great numbers in the first half of the eighth century: this period appears to be the high point of the economic life of the settlement. It continued until the Viking attacks of the mid-ninth century, but there seems to be little indication of activity after *c.* 900; at some point in the tenth century settlement shifted across to higher ground on the other side of the peninsula. There is little evidence of continental trade in the tenth century: but, then, there is even less at other sites, and Southampton does at least provide some tenth-century pottery from Normandy.[31]

What was the role of Hamwic in the economic life of the West Saxon kingdom? It seems to be a planned town: Cædwalla or Ine are the obvious candidates. Both were involved in the expansion of the kingdom. Cædwalla had taken the Isle of Wight in 685, and thus won control of the waterways approaching Hamwic. However, his reign was short: he abdicated in somewhat mysterious cirumstances, and went on pilgrimage to Rome. Bede always put the best possible gloss on those kings who became monks or pilgrims, seeing it as part of the spiritual success of the Anglo-Saxons, but it is not impossible that he was deposed. We know little about Ine, except for the survival of his law-code and some hints that during his long reign, from 688 to 726, he was successful in increasing the power of the West Saxons, fighting with the Mercians and the South Saxons, and pushing against the independent British kingdoms in Devon and Cornwall. Richard Hodges has suggested that Hamwic was an integral part of his personal attempt to increase his power: that it was created so that he could monopolise the inflow of prestige goods to his kingdom, for distribution to those powerful people inside and outside his kingdom whose favour he needed to buy. One enigmatic clause in his lawcode is interpreted by Hodges as referring to the rations needed to keep the population of Hamwic supplied, levied from each ten hides of the kingdom and transported to the banks of the Itchen:

> As a food-rent from ten hides: ten vats of honey, 300 loaves, twelve ambers of Welsh ale, thirty of clear ale, two full-grown cows or ten wethers, ten geese, twenty hens, ten cheeses, an amber full of butter, five salmon, twenty pounds of fodder and one hundred eels.[32]

It is much more likely that this ideal food-rent is what Ine intended to consume as he and his court made their constant progress around the kingdom (as all early medieval kings did): the logistical problems of transporting three thousand times that quantity of goods (assuming the Tribal Hidage assessment of Wessex at 30,000 hides) would have been phenomenal. But more crucial is the question of Ine's monopoly control of Hamwic's trade. Even apart from the fact that Hodges seems to have modified his own earlier position by suggesting that the fenced areas were aristocratic properties, it does seem more likely that Ine's control extended over no more than the right to exact dues on merchants and craftspeople – which in itself would have been a considerable source of profit. Perhaps he ensured that all trading in his kingdom took place within the precincts of Hamwic: this might help explain why there are so many sceattas within Hamwic and so few found in the rest of the kingdom. Hamwic may not even have been a permanent settlement, but a seasonal fair, to which merchants and craftspeople came for, say, the summer months (this would explain the small number of graves so far discovered).[33] There is little doubt that Hamwic *was* important in the kingdom, at least for three or four generations. It gave its name to its hinterland, Hampshire, and in size it may have outstripped any other early medieval settlements: the only possible rivals were London, Ipswich and York.

A fairly clear reference to the importance of London as an economic centre occurs earlier than anywhere else. The laws of Hlothhere and Eadric, kings of Kent (Eadric succeeded Hlothere in 685 and may have reigned jointly with him before that) are a very early record of London's significance. Clause 16 begins:

> 16.1 If a man of Kent buys property in London, he is to have then two or three honest *ceorls*, or the king's town-reeve, as witness.
>
> 16.2 If then it is attached in the possessions of the man in Kent, he is to warranty the man who sold it to him, at the king's hall in that town, if he knows him and can produce him at that vouching to warranty.[34]

The legal details do not matter here: the political and economic facts are that the king (presumably of Kent) had a reeve and a hall in the town, and that the purchase of property in the town was important enough to be mentioned. London had a mint by the mid-seventh century, and there is a charter of *c.* 670 that refers to it as a port. There is little doubt that Bede was correct when he referred to it in 731 as 'an *emporium* for many nations who come to it by land and sea'.[35] It is, however, likely to be an emporium with a very different kind of function from that of Hamwic. It had a bishop, who was one of the more important in the kingdom. But, more significantly, it was in disputed territory, being at various times Kentish, East Saxon, Mercian and West Saxon, while the 'sub-kings' of Middlesex and Surrey no doubt also felt they had a claim. When Æthelbald of Mercia controlled London in the 730s and 740s tolls on ships coming to London were granted to an array of people, showing how fragmented the profits from London were (in contrast, arguably, to Hamwic): these included the bishop of London, the abbess of Thanet, the bishop of Rochester and the bishop of Worcester. The distribution of coins and coin hoards of the eighth century in the territory in between London and central Mercia – in a strip of land from the Middle Thames up towards Cambridge – has suggested that intermediaries may have controlled the trade, and prevented Mercia from having direct access to it.[36]

Pre-Viking London, to the west of the Roman town, is now thought to have been over 60 hectares in extent, which would make it the largest settlement in eighth-century England (Hamwic was around 45 hectares) and comparable with the great Carolingian trading-place at the mouths of the Rhine, Dorestad. But there have been few extensive excavations here, and much of the evidence rests on stray discoveries of coins, pottery and other objects; only in the Covent Garden excavations was a fairly large segment of the town discovered, with a road and several buildings. The road was some three metres wide, and the gravel surface had been repaired ten times by the mid-ninth century. The long buildings were laid out with the narrow end on the street front; their hearths were made of reused Roman tile, and one had been used as a smithy. Some fifty thousand animal bones were recovered, and oyster-shells from the Thames estuary, giving some idea of the diet. It looks as if the site had been part of a cemetery until the mid-seventh century, and after that the town grew and built over the burial ground. The earliest traces of settlement in London may be of sixth-century date, however, and are from around Trafalgar Square, at the centre of the later settlement; the last material (apart from a hoard from *c.* 870, recovered from the bed of the Thames) is from the early ninth century. By the time of King Alfred, at the end of the century, the population appears to have shifted once more within the walls of Roman London. The Viking wars presumably made fortified settlements more necessary: it is an interesting fact that none of these trading places of the pre-Viking period that we are discussing, from Hamwic to York, was fortified in any way. There are traces once more of the building of wooden wharves, as in the Roman period; it looks as if traders on the Strand site pulled their boats up on the beaches. Before the end of the ninth century there are documents which mention a 'trading shore' in London, and the right of the bishops of Worcester and Canterbury to moor ships along the length of their properties. Excavations at Bull Wharf, Queenhithe, have found traces of the first of the new wharves, made out of reused timbers from houses and ships.

The third large trading-place in the south-east of Britain is Ipswich, on the banks of the River Orwell. There are traces of early seventh-century settlement here, only a few miles from a main residence of the kings of East Anglia at Rendlesham and their main burial ground at Sutton Hoo: it may be that from the beginning it was an establishment with royal connections, like Hamwic. The production of the pottery called 'Ipswich ware' began here before 650, and continued throughout the pre-Viking period. Extensive excavation did not reveal any pre-Viking houses, because upper layers had been disturbed by later building. There were plenty of rubbish pits from the seventh to ninth centuries, however, to show that there was occupation over an area perhaps as large as 50 hectares. The waste-products of several predictable crafts have been found: spinning and weaving, bone-working, leather-working (specifically shoe-making), iron-working and so on. Ipswich ware predominates in the surviving pottery, as indeed it does in many other sites: examples are known in Kent and Yorkshire. But there is also imported pottery, from the Rhineland and Low Countries and also from northern France. Beonna, king of the East Angles in 760, was the first English king to mint pennies in imitation of Pippin I's *denarii*, as we have seen: an indication of the close commercial ties that must have existed between his port and the Continent.

The northern-most site which can be compared to these south-eastern trading places is York. For a long time all that we had were some references in literary works. Alcuin's long Latin poem on *The Bishops, Kings and Saints of York*, for instance, said York was 'a haven for ocean-going ships from the farthest ports'.[37] But it seemed that the site of the *emporium* mentioned by Bede and Alcuin, or the colony of Frisian merchants mentioned in the *Life of St Liudger*, would never be found. In 1982 Richard Hodges wrote, 'Many excavations have sought seventh- to ninth-century layers and yet none have been found so far. At some stage we have to accept the power of this kind of negative evidence.'[38] But this was before the evidence of stray finds from the Anglo-Saxon period had been put together, which suggested, for instance, that the Roman bridge over the Ouse was still in use, or before the demolition of Redfearn's Glass factory, 46–54 Fishergate, on the banks of the Ouse south of the medieval city walls. That demolition allowed the excavation of a later medieval Gilbertine priory, beneath which were found clear traces of a trading-settlement of the pre-Viking period, which produced similar material to the other towns mentioned above.

All this concentration on the south and east of England will have made the historian more interested in the 'Celts' rather impatient. Were any similar developments taking place in the West? The short answer is 'No'. There is certainly evidence for trade, but it seems to be on a small scale: in particular, it did not call for the establishment of specialist communities such as those we have been looking at. Such evidence as we have relates to the 'Irish Sea province' as a whole: that is, to Ireland as well as to the western seaboard of Britain. Indeed, because of the accident of survival, the literary evidence for Ireland is better than for western Britain. As we have already seen, thanks to fifth-century Irish settlement in western Britain, particularly in western Wales and south-west Scotland, there were close links across the Irish Sea; Irish and Welsh hagiography (admittedly mostly written much later) suggest that in the sixth and seventh centuries there were close ecclesiastical links as well. Indeed, it was partly the Church that brought a need for trade on some scale during the early Middle Ages: the liturgy could not take place without the importation of wine. Bede, on the other hand, stated in the very first chapter of his *History* that vines grew in Ireland, and arguably he is better placed than we are to know this; nor does the liturgy require huge quantities of wine, and the Irish literary evidence suggests that in the pre-Viking period ale was the drink of kings and aristocrats, not wine.

There are odd pieces of evidence, many of them from hagiographical sources, which are difficult to assess. When St Columbanus came to the

Atlantic port of Nantes, he apparently waited until a ship engaged in trade with Ireland arrived, so that he could cadge a lift. The *Life of St Filibert*, written at the island monastery of Noirmoutier (not far from Nantes), described how 'an Irish ship with a diversity of goods on board put into shore and supplied the brethren with an abundance of shoes and clothing'; the ninth-century *Miracula* of the same saint describes how Noirmoutier engaged in the salt trade (the salt pans of the Atlantic coastal areas of Poitou were renowned throughout the Middle Ages).[39]

The changing patterns of the western seaways can best be traced in the find-spots of imported pottery. The late Roman table-wares from the Seine basin are to be found mostly in the Thames estuary, and may also have entered Britain to a lesser extent up the Solent. The late Roman table-wares from western Gaul had, as one might expect, a more westerly distribution, around the Solent and in the lower reaches of the Severn. The pattern changes totally with the fifth and sixth centuries, with the various types of imported Mediterranean pottery found in Britain. There are still some examples north-west of the Solent, in Somerset and in the lower Severn valley; there are numerous examples in Cornwall, and a scattering of finds in Wales, south-west Scotland and Ireland, but nothing at all in eastern England. Some of this pottery is certainly from the eastern Mediterranean, and some from North Africa; the same type of pottery has been found in Portugal and Spain, which supports the idea that it arrived from the Mediterranean via the Straits of Gibraltar, rather than overland. A much quoted literary source – the *only* literary source – which seems to mention this long-distance trade is the Egyptian *Life of St John the Almsgiver*, which tells the story of a ship going from Egypt to Britain with corn, and receiving tin in exchange; on its return the tin has been miraculously transformed into silver. Since Britain seems a semi-legendary place in Byzantine eyes, and since many classical texts would have told them that tin came from Britain, this story may be no more than a literary construct. It may well be a memory of such a lone commercial enterprise, however: what it does not do, as Peter Brown claimed, is show that 'the fleets of the patriarchs of Alexandria sailed to Cornwall in the early seventh century.'[40] The surviving pottery in Britain could have come from sporadic and small-scale visits by merchants over a period of several decades (more likely in the sixth than the seventh century), rather than 'fleets'.

The best concrete example of trade, and of the existence of an 'Irish Sea province', is not the Mediterranean ware, but the so-called E-ware, much of which may indeed be seventh-century in date. There are several different forms – a jar some 15–20 cms high, a beaker, a bowl, a pitcher – and all are in a coarse unglazed wheel-made pottery, usually made from a distinctive clay. It has been found widely on sites in the whole eastern half of Ireland, at a few sites in Cornwall and southern Wales, and in the Isle of Man and in south-west Scotland. The fort of Dunadd (Argyll) has provided the largest number of examples of any British site.[41] The exact source of this production has still not been established, although parallels have been suggested right across Francia, from the Rhineland to the Atlantic coast. The consensus now seems to be that the pottery originates on the Atlantic coast of Gaul, between the Garonne and the Loire. The difficulty has partly been created by the fact that French archaeologists have concentrated their attentions on the rather fine pottery that can be found on their sites, rather than on this coarse domestic ware. One of the main puzzles is why the coarse pottery was exported to the Irish Sea province (sometimes, as in the case of Ireland and western Scotland, to areas where the use of domestic pottery was not known) and not the finer wares. It is possible that they were exported as containers: the dye-stuff madder has been suggested as a possible product. But the types are so varied (and not all of them suitable as containers) that this seems unlikely as a universal answer. What is likely, however, is that the pottery (and some glassware as well) is just the visible surviving evidence of a much larger trade in perishables. The disappearance of the pottery in the eighth century, therefore, may not indicate the loss of the trade at all, but simply a change in its nature, or a change in packaging.

The historical context of this pottery, and its economic significance, is thus difficult to discern. Because we only have fragments of pot and glass we cannot be certain whether this necessarily reflects trade rather than, say, diplomatic contacts or the surviving remnants of a network of gift-exchange. Had people in Ireland or western Britain had the custom of burial with grave-goods, like the Anglo-Saxons of the sixth and seventh centuries, we would probably have a larger range of imported goods, and hence a better basis for hypothesis. Dark, for instance, finds the absence of Byzantine metalwork in western Britain (apart from one bronze censer from Glastonbury) 'surprising',[42] given how this *is* found in eastern Britain, in Anglo-Saxon areas (as at Sutton Hoo): but this may be a result of different burial customs, allowing different types of artefact to survive in different areas. However, it is clear that the imported pottery is a western British phenomenon, and the hypothesis of two different trade routes, one via the Atlantic and one across the Alps from Italy, seems a reasonable one.

One contrast between the patterns of trade in England and those in the Irish Sea area which may be very significant is in the type of site in which the imported goods are concentrated. In England these seem to be specialist trading centres, removed from political centres; in the Irish Sea area, the imported goods are found on the royal sites themselves. There may be exceptions – Dalkey Island, in Dublin Bay, for instance, may be a classic port-of-trade – and sometimes, as with Tintagel, it may be difficult to see if we are looking at a secular or monastic site. But Dunadd is a more typical secular site. It was a major centre for the king of Dál Riata, and may indeed have been the inauguration site of the kings: a series of impressions carved in the living rock on the hill may correspond to the Irish and Scottish inauguration rituals involving the placing of the foot in such a footprint as a symbolic uniting of king with kingdom.[43] Tribute would perhaps be collected at such a site. Alan Lane suggests that these luxury goods may have been used largely at the royal court, but that some goods were distributed as gifts to lesser aristocrats, and are now to be found at, for instance, the forts of Ardifuir and Kildalloig. There is a crannóg (an artificial island) on Loch Glashan, eight kilometres from Dunadd, which may have functioned as an associated royal centre: in Ireland a fort and a crannóg occasionally function as twin royal residences.[44] Adomnán has St Columba declare that at that moment a volcano has erupted in Italy, 'and before the present year is ended Gallic sailors will tell you the same',[45] but there is very little imported material to be found at this main Dalriadan monastic site: imported manuscript colorant, for instance, has been found at Dunadd, but not at Iona. Perhaps Dalriadan kings tried to maintain a monopoly of trade within their kingdom; perhaps the items did not arrive through trade as such, but by gift exchange through diplomatic links at royal level.

Political change in Wales and Scotland

The main reason for our uncertainty about developments west and north of Anglo-Saxon England is the usual one: a lack of evidence. But there is enough evidence to discern that some of the developments noted for pre-Viking England are happening in much of the rest of Britain too. In particular, in Wales and in Scotland we seem to find a gradual movement towards greater political centralisation. Only the peripheries remained outside these developments. Cornwall, for instance, about whose political workings almost nothing is known in the early Middle Ages, continued to remain free of Anglo-Saxon domination until the tenth century, and still had its own kings in the eleventh.

From the sixth century there were a number of Welsh kingdoms, notably Gwynedd in the north-west, Powys in the central-east, Dyfed in the south-west, and Brycheiniog and Glywysing in the south-east. Other areas, like Ceredigion (the central coastal area) had a regional identity, but not necessarily any independence as kingdoms; sometimes a source may mention a kingdom which otherwise is unknown (as when the annal for 816 in the thirteenth-century *Brut y Tywysogyon* mentions that the kingdom of Rhufoniog was overrun by Saxons).[46] Wendy Davies makes the point forcefully that these kingdoms must not necessarily be seen as monolithic territorial kingdoms. At times there is more than one king in a single kingdom; at other times kings can be seen ranging far beyond where they are 'supposed' to be active.

The major political development of the eighth and ninth century seems to be the growth in the power of the kings of Gwynedd. To some extent they may always have had some preeminence among the Welsh kings. Even at the time of Gildas, Maelgwn of Gwynedd was 'first in stature and also power'; for Bede, Cadwallon of Gwynedd was the 'king of the Britons', and the leader of the British in their struggle against the English. 'King of the Britons' is a phrase used of several later kings of Gwynedd: Rhodri (the *Welsh Annals*, 754); his son Cynan (*Annals of Ulster*, 816); Merfyn (d. 844, in a ninth-century Bamberg manuscript).[47] The climax of this development was with Merfyn's son Rhodri, known as Rhodri Mawr, Rhodri 'the Great'. He married the daughter of the king of Powys, and seems to have acquired this kingdom in 855 and absorbed Ceredigion in 872. He defeated the Viking leader Gorm in 856, although he was eventually forced into Irish exile by the Vikings in 877. Rhodri's six sons, led by Anarawd, continued Rhodri's expansionist policy, leading the kings of the south to seek protection from the West Saxon king Alfred. It was Rhodri's grandson, Hywel Dda (Hywel the Good), who by a marriage alliance united the kingships of Gwynedd and Dyfed, creating the most extensive, though brief, power base of any early medieval Welsh king.

The success of Gwynedd in the late eighth and ninth centuries may be partly a result of the damage wrought on other kingdoms by English attacks. The Pillar of Eliseg, a four-metre-high round stone shaft from near Llangollen, was erected in the middle of the ninth century by Cyngen of Powys, recording in a long Latin inscription how his great-grandfather Eliseg had taken Powys back from the English, over nine years of campaigning.[48] This must have happened some time in the middle of the eighth century. The *Welsh Annals* claim that Powys fell into English hands again in 822, when the Saxons took Degannwy, a hill-fort on the Conwy which was a major political centre in the kingdom of Powys. In such circumstances it is not surprising that Rhodri Mawr of Gwynedd should be able to annex Powys, and how the kings of Gwynedd should achieve the status of the main defender of Wales from English attack.

It is traditionally believed that the decisive period in Scottish history was the reign of Cináed mac Alpín (Kenneth mac Alpine), *c.* 840–58. From then on the dynasties of Dál Riata and Pictland were united; his descendants were the later medieval kings of Scotland; he had a palace at Forteviot, but may have chosen Scone as his dynastic centre, and perhaps brought to Scone the 'Stone of Destiny', a 152 kg block of stone (stolen by Edward I in 1296 to be placed under the coronation throne of the English kings at Westminster, briefly recovered by Scottish nationalists in 1950, and quietly returned to Scotland by John Major in 1996). There was a later story that this king of Dál Riata acquired the kingship of Scotland by massacring many Pictish nobles at Scone, but is quite possible that the Vikings had done this task for him. Indeed, there is a list of things that Cináed *may* have done, but which come from similarly unreliable sources: he may have attacked the Northumbrians at the fortress of Dunbar and the monastery of Melrose, for instance; he may have moved the relics of St Columba to the church of Dunkeld.[49] It is unclear precisely how he managed to unite the two main northern kingdoms of the Picts and the Scots; it is even unclear that he did so.

Historians have whittled away at Cináed's reputation from two directions. It is now thought that Domnall mac Constantín (Donald II), at the very end of the ninth century, was a more crucial figure in the creation of a new Scottish kingdom; it is also clear that Cináed's reign was just one stage in a development that can be traced back into the eighth century. The 'victory' of the Irish kings of Dál Riata over the Pictish kings was possibly the culmination of a long period of intermingling and cultural and dynastic cross-fertilisation.

On the face of it the Pictish kings appeared to have attained an unassailable situation by the middle of the eighth century. The centre of their power had shifted southwards by the end of the seventh century to the agriculturally rich area of Fortrenn (or Fortriu), later Fife and Perthshire. The church of St Andrews, probably founded in the 730s, became closely associated with the dynasty, and the Sarcophagus of St Andrews is a testimony to the European aspirations of the Pictish kings. This was not carved from a single block of stone, as Roman or early medieval sarcophagi usually were: it was made up like the corner-post shrines known to the British: four stone slabs slotted into four upright corner-posts. The two front corner-posts, which have broad faces, are decorated with complex interlaced animals; the surviving end panel is decorated by very fine geometric interlace, inset with four panels, two containing serpents, a third with two cats (?) and the fourth with two monkeys (?).[50] There are plenty of parallels for the interlace decoration in the art of the eighth century. The front panel is more exceptional. To the right is a tall standing figure in classical robes, tearing apart the jaws of a lion; to the left are hunting scenes with a mounted hunter killing a lion, a standing figure with his hounds; and various other animals. Parallels to the iconography can be found in Scotland and elsewhere; the large standing figure very probably depicts David killing the lion. If this sarcophagus is from the late eighth century, this is contemporary with Charlemagne (whose court nickname was David). But as a piece of sculpture imitating classical archetypes (above all in the figure of David himself) there is actually nothing comparable surviving from Charlemagne's Francia. Frankish diplomats visiting the Pictish church at St Andrews would have been impressed by this royal monument; high quality sculpture might have been more familiar to representatives of the courts of Northumbrian or Mercian kings, but they too would at least have seen that the Pictish kings belonged to the same cultural world as themselves, and not to a barbarian fringe.

The identification of the personage originally placed in the sarcophagus is impossible, not just because of the difficulties of precise dating by stylistic means, but because of the considerable muddle and confusion of the genealogies in Scotland. It is generally thought that the Pictish kings were being increasingly influenced by Gaelic culture and more and more closely linked with the Dál Riata dynasty. Smyth, for instance, points out how Pictish kings like Ciniod and Óengus were already bearing Gaelic names in the early eighth century.[51] But in the generation or two before Cináed mac

Alpín, we have Constantine, son of Fergus, ruling in Dál Riata, appearing as Castantin son of Uurguit, king of the Picts, in Pictish king-lists; his brother and successor Óengus II (d. 834) is Unuist son of Uurguist of the Picts. Constantine's son Drest and Óengus's son Eóganán (Uuen) are also apparently kings of both Picts and Scots. Smyth mentions the theory that these are signs of a Pictish takeover of the Scots, 'a sequel to the triumph of the Pictish king Óengus I over Dál Riata in 741'[52] but dismisses this on the grounds that 'it is inconceivable if the Picts were the dominant military faction in the century after 740 that the Scots could suddenly emerge under Kenneth mac Alpin precisely at the end of that period in such a strong position as to impose their Gaelic language and institutions on the Picts.'[53] He suggests instead that there was a gradual Gaelic infiltration of the Pictish east, with the help of the Columban clergy, and points out that the *Annals of Ulster* note that Óengus was deprived of his overlordship in 750 with the help of Teudubr, king of Strathclyde, and that the Dál Riata king invaded Fortriu in 768.

More recently, however, Dauvit Broun has looked carefully at the king-lists, and come up with a different theory, which would at least restore the achievement of whichever Pictish king was buried in the St Andrews sarcophagus.[54] The only evidence which is relatively reliable, he argues, is that provided by the *Annals of Ulster*. All those kings who by a conflation of the Dál Riata and Pictish king-lists can be thought of as being kings of both Scots *and* Picts are referred to by the *Annals* as the kings of the Picts only, and there is one king of Dál Riata in the *Annals* who does not appear in the king-lists at all. If one tries to merge the data in the *Annals* with those in the king-lists there are impossible conflicts. But if one assumes the primacy of the *Annals* as a witness, then one can conclude that the Pictish kings who are said to be kings of Dál Riata were actually inserted into the Dalriadan accounts at a later date, after the amalgamation of the dynasties: in reality they were merely kings of the Picts. We thus have a situation where Gaelic culture may be encroaching in Pictish lands in the eighth century, but where the Picts are definitely the dominant political force. The St Andrews sarcophagus may belong to a dominant political figure – the Offa of the north. Onuist (Óengus) son of Uurguist (Fergus), d. 761, is a possible candidate. But his grandson, the first in Scotland to be given the grandiloquent name of Constantine (and who ruled from 789 to 820), may have signalled his right to equality with his contemporary Charlemagne by this impressive imitation of Roman glories: stylistic arguments do not preclude Constantine being the occupant of the sarcophagus.

Land and property

We have three main sources of written evidence for land ownership: law-codes, charters, and wills. Of these, charters are by far the most important.

Through them we can discern something of the changes in the nature of landownership which occurred during the early Middle Ages, and which are crucial to our understanding of early medieval society. Power comes from the possession of land in the early Middle Ages, as indeed right down to the nineteenth or twentieth centuries, but it was more obvious in the early Middle Ages, since with land comes not only the profits of agriculture, but also control of the people who live on that land. This fact is rather hidden in, say, Anglo-Saxon charters, because certain formulae were adopted which do not mention peasants. An Anglo-Saxon charter will say, for instance:

> I Cynewulf, king of the West Saxons, will grant and humbly make over to the Apostle and servant of God, St Andrew, with the consent of my bishops and magnates, for the love of God and for the expiation of my sins, and also, what is sad to relate because of some harrassing of our enemies, the race of the Cornishmen, some portion of land. That is eleven hides near the river which is called Wellow, for the increasing of the monastery which is situated near the great spring which they call Wells.[55]

There is no mention of the people without which the land would be worthless: the free and semi-free peasants, and the slaves. The peasants remained tied to the land rather than to their lord: this is made clear in a law of Ine of Wessex, concerning a noble who moves on (perhaps to newly won estates in the West Country): if he does move on, he may only take with him from the land his reeve, his smith and his children's nurse, and he must ensure that a proportion of his land is sown before leaving (twelve hides of sown land if he has twenty hides altogether).[56]

It seems that the eighth century is the crucial century for changes in ideas about land in both England and Wales; the charters just do not survive for any conclusions to be made about Scotland. For Wales almost the only relevant manuscript is the Book of Llandaff, a twelfth-century manuscript containing 158 charters, apparently ranging from the sixth to the eleventh centuries. Wendy Davies, who has studied this volume, has argued that later editors added phrases and sentences rather than altering earlier texts, and thus it may be possible to reconstruct what the original charter may have said. The charters relate to south-east Wales, and up to the third quarter of the ninth century some relate to what is now south-west Herefordshire, which indicates that this area was until then in Welsh rather than Anglo-Saxon or Viking hands. Unlike the Anglo-Saxon charters, they occasionally recorded the gift of land together with its *heredes*, or tenants. *Hereditarii* are also mentioned, who seem to be more important people who have some kind of hereditary right in the profits of the land, and sometimes seem to be due some annual rent: one charter of 780 mentions six measures of beer and a sester of honey, together with bread and meat in unspecified quantities.[57] About one-third of the charters come from the century from *c.* 680 to *c.* 785, and this is the crucial period of change. At the beginning of this period all grants of land are made by kings, occasionally with close members of his family. From around 710, and especially after the 730s, lay people begin to give grants of land, occasionally with the consent of the king mentioned, but sometimes without any mention of the king at all. This is, as Davies pointed out, 'a fundamental social change'.[58] It is possible, Davies suggests, that up to the early eighth century the king owned all the land, though this does not seem at all likely. Instead 'one might tentatively postulate a process' by which land which had once been inalienable, whether it was in the hands of the king or of other landowning groups, gave way to the idea that tenancies of royal land were alienable, and ultimately by the mid-eighth century it had become possible to alienate land that had been inherited from one's kin. Land ceased to be passed down automatically to one's legal heirs; it became something that could be acquired, and alienated, and perhaps bought on the open market. (It is very difficult to tell whether the legal language of 'donation' sometimes actually hides the economic reality of purchase.)

It is possible that the influence of the Church can be seen in this process. The Church needed land in order to survive economically; this was impossible without the idea that land could be alienated from the kinship group. In Roman law this was relatively easy; landowners had some restrictions on their ability to alienate their land, but these were not significant. Roman landowners could make wills, to give their property to whomsoever they wished; as far as we can see this was impossible in early Welsh, or early Anglo-Saxon, law. The changes of the eighth century that can be discerned in the Book of Llandaff seem to have resulted in a situation that was much closer to Roman law: a move to a society where certain individuals had more freedom of action.

Interestingly, this same process seems to have occurred at almost precisely the same time in the Anglo-Saxon kingdoms, even though the Welsh kingdoms had been Christian for perhaps two centuries longer than their Anglo-Saxon neighbours. The charters are rather different in form and language, however, as has already been mentioned. It is likely that the Welsh charters went back to Romano-British origins; they may indeed be evidence that pre-Roman (or at least non-Roman) ideas of property survived in Britain, on the fringes of the Roman Empire, and continued after that Empire's collapse. Anglo-Saxon charters, on the other hand, seem to have Italian antecedents. It has been thought that the idea of the charter may have been introduced by Wilfrid from Italy, or perhaps (at the same time) by Theodore of Canterbury; but perhaps the idea went back three-quarters of a century earlier, to the time of Augustine of Canterbury.

There are over 1500 surviving Anglo-Saxon charters, although most of them are only preserved in collections of charters (called cartularies) which were compiled in monasteries after the Norman Conquest, and the historian always has to be conscious of the possibility of forgery or of additions and subtractions made by the scribes. But there are around 200 charters which are in contemporary or near-contemporary form, written on single sheets of parchment or, occasionally, written into the fly-leaves of books, or on blank pages of Gospel books. The earliest surviving original is a grant by King Hlothhere of Kent to Abbot Brihtwold and his monastery of the estate of *Westan ae* on the (then) island of Thanet in Kent, 'with everything belonging to it, fields, pastures, marshes, small woods, springs, fisheries . . . As it has been owned hitherto, by the well-known boundaries indicated by me and my reeves.'[59] Like all early Anglo-Saxon charters it is a thoroughly ecclesiastical document. It is written in Latin, in uncial script, like the finest Gospel books. It is sustained not so much by secular legal penalties as by ecclesiastical ones: 'may whoever attempts to contravene this donation be cut off from all Christendom, and debarred from the body and blood of our Lord Jesus Christ.' It is dated by a Roman method of dating, the indiction (based on the fifteen-year tax cycle in the Roman Empire), which was used widely by the Church on the Continent in the seventh century, but would have been meaningless outside ecclesiastical circles. ('The seventh indiction' means the seventh year of that particular cycle, and could be 664 or 679 or 694, or other dates at fifteen-year intervals, but we happen to know that Hlothhere was king in 679.) The document was thus certainly drawn up by ecclesiastics, and very probably by Brihtwold or one of his monks. The list of witnesses – twelve names, headed by Hlothhere, each name preceded by a cross and the words *signum manus*, 'sign of the hand' – were all written by the same scribe, but apparently not the scribe who drew up the rest of the document (one of the signs that it is probably an original).

The status of a document like this is problematic. It is almost certainly not in itself the legal act which transferred the rights over the property, as in a modern contract. That legal act was probably an oral one, perhaps symbolised by the handing over of something physical – a twig, a piece of turf. The charter was a record of what had happened. Nor is the list of 'witnesses' necessarily a list of people who attended the original ceremony. Brihtwold may have sent the document around to the various people who were most concerned, to get them to agree to its terms. The document indeed proclaims that the donation was made 'with the consent of Archbishop Theodore and Eadric, my brother's son, and also of all the leading men'; it adds, in the supposed words of the king, 'may it be contradicted by no-one, neither by me nor by my kindred nor by others', on penalty of rendering 'account to God in his soul on the day of Judgement'. The people most likely to contravene the donation were the legal heirs of the donor, who were being effectively deprived of their inheritance by this charter, or else other lords nearby who thought they had some claim to the land: the 'witness list' may be in part an attempt to forestall such opposition by making any potential complainant agree to the terms of the document.

As in Wales, the earliest Anglo-Saxon charters were donations by kings; some early charters are from self-styled 'sub-kings', which invariably note the consent of 'the' king (Wulfhere, king of the Mercians, for instance, in the case of an early grant by Frithuwald, sub-king of Surrey). But in the course of the eighth century we begin to find grants made by bishops and by lay aristocrats: men like Dunwald, who in 762 granted to the monastery of St Peter and St Paul at Canterbury land which had been granted to him by King Æthelberht II of Kent, or Oslac, ealdorman of the South Saxons, who granted land to the Church in 780, and had King Offa of the Mercians confirm the donation.

What rights were actually being confirmed by charters? As with so many other problems in the history of barbarian kingdoms in the West, we are very much constrained by our ignorance of what the situation was *before* the introduction of writing. A traditional methodology has been to take evidence from wherever one can within the various Germanic kingdoms in Europe: by piecing it all together one might understand the situation better. However, this is making the dangerous assumption that all Germanic societies were organised in the same way, and that the earliest evidence from written documents is somehow free of influence from the peoples among whom they lived. The earliest Frankish law-code, for instance, the *Pactus Legis Salicae*, drawn up a century before Æthelberht I of Kent's lawcode, was written in Latin and, some have argued, by people familiar with Roman provincial law. The fact that Roman provincial law may have influenced early Germanic lawcodes is difficult to prove, because local Roman law does not survive intact in written form itself, and was presumably different in each province. Did it lie behind practice in both Wales and England in the seventh and eighth centuries? What were the differences between the changes in ideas about property in Wales and in England? What difference did charters actually make?

One commonly held theory (explained clearly by Wormald, for instance)[60] is that the early Anglo-Saxons made a clear distinction between land inherited from the kin and land which was acquired by other means, whether by conquest or by gift. The former could not be alienated; the latter could. However, not all kings would have agreed that land given by a king in reward for service could be alienated: such gifts could be revoked, and did not necessarily pass to the heirs. There was no doubt much confusion and occasion for legal dispute over which land was alienable and which was not. This was a confusion which the Church could not tolerate. A charter could make sure that any land acquired from the king could not be claimed back by the king or by anyone else. Such land, which initially was all in the hands of the Church, was known in Old English as *bookland*: land for which there was a 'book': a 'book' meant any written record, not just something bound between boards – the word is cognate with both *birch* and *bark*, suggesting that the earliest Anglo-Saxon documents were in fact on wood (like the letters at Vindolanda: see above p. 47) rather than parchment. Land that has been booked to the Church was, by the church's own law, inalienable; but this did not stop the Church offering to laymen tenancies in its land.

The opportunities which this offered to aristocrats ought to be obvious: indeed, in a sense it *created* an aristocracy. Before the charter, a powerful man might control inherited land and acquired land; on his death, the inherited land might be divided up among his various heirs and the acquired land might be recovered by the king. Under such circumstances, it is difficult to conceive of an hereditary aristocracy. On the other hand, if an aristocrat donated much of his land to a monastery while alive, he and his immediate heirs could probably continue to control and use that land, either through controlling the monastery directly or through acquiring tenancies of land from the monastery. At first, perhaps, the land that was booked was land that had been acquired rather than inherited; but probably the two categories were soon confused and merged. We can now see, perhaps, why Bede was so worried by the number of 'pseudo-monasteries' which had sprung up, he said, in the thirty years previous to his letter of 734. Some at least of these may well have been the eighth-century equivalents of tax havens: ways of exploiting the system for the benefit of individuals by using the letter rather than the spirit of the law. Through lavish donation to the church, an individual could acquire credit in heaven, but could also assemble a power base that was largely unassailable by kings or rival aristocratic families. Any talk of 'Church reform', of course, might be seen as a real threat: Bede, after all, talked about the desirability of dispossessing monasteries. But the concept of bookland ultimately spread beyond the Church, and lay property rights strengthened.

It would be wrong to think that a charter gave people *ownership* of land: a charter gave its possessor certain rights over land and people, above all the right to collect the food-rent. But other people had rights in the land too. Unless the charter specified otherwise (as some do from the mid-eighth century onwards) the king was still able to demand certain services from those on the land, even on lands which had been granted to the Church. Estates might be granted with an immunity from the obligation to work on palace-buildings, or to feed and house the king and his court on their itineraries, but three obligations that went with the holding of land were almost never remitted: service in the army, the building of fortresses and the construction of bridges.[61] Even the general grant of privileges issued by Æthelbald of Mercia to the Church, at Gumley in 749 (in the wake of St Boniface's criticisms: see above, p. 189), did not let the Church off the last two obligations. Offa may well have invoked the obligation to build fortresses to gather together the labour for the biggest fortification of all: his Dyke. Although much of the land was slipping outside direct royal control in the eighth century, rulers were determined to lay down what landholders owed the king for their privileged position. It was an important element in the move to a more institutionalised and less personal kind of rule.

Can we see any of these fundamental changes in the ownership and control of land 'on the ground', so to speak, through archaeology? These changes do coincide chronologically with what Anglo-Saxon archaeologists have come to call the 'Middle Saxon Shift'. (Archaeologists, but not historians, use 'Middle Saxon' to mean not the inhabitants of Middlesex, but the central period of Anglo-Saxon history, basically the seventh to the ninth centuries.) This 'Middle Saxon Shift', the desertion of early settlement sites and the shift of population to new sites, seems to happen in quite widely separated areas: Bishopstone (Sussex), Cassington (Oxon), Chalton (Hants) and Thirlings (Northumberland) were all deserted in the late seventh or early eighth centuries. None of them were on the best agricultural land. Their relocation would seem to have been rather different from the characteristically moving settlements of northern Francia in the post-Roman period, where periodically the centre of a settlement would be relocated a kilometre or two away, to a new site within the same general area. It has been suggested that it was part of a general reorganisation of the land.[62] Earlier Anglo-Saxon settlements, with the earliest cemeteries, were frequently on poor land; the new settlements tended not to be associated with cemeteries, and to be on richer valley soils. Perhaps the requirements of tribute to kings or lords forced communities to reorganise, in order to maximise their resources?

More recently this model has come under serious criticism. There are real problems of dating, partly caused by the gradual disappearance of grave-goods, but also the virtual disappearance of pottery over large parts of southern England,[63] and real problems of the identification of settlement sites, given the difficulty of carrying out the large-scale fieldwork which is necessary to put together a complete picture of a particular early medieval landscape. We still need a lot more detailed excavations of the type carried out at West Heslerton (North Yorks); but also the type of broad regional surveys like the East Anglian survey conducted in recent years alongside the Sutton Hoo research project. What is the relationship between these apparent settlement changes and the broader social and political changes which have been discussed in this chapter? Can this be linked to changes in burial practice and cemetery location, in the emergence of what archaeologists have called Final Phase cemeteries, which must be related in some way to the establishment of Christianity in the countryside?[64] There is a lot going on in eighth-century Britain, very little of which can be said to have attracted definitive explanation.

9

Viking attack and settlement

The earliest raids

One of the earliest known Viking raids in Britain is famously recorded in the *Anglo-Saxon Chronicle* under 793:

> In this year dire portents appeared over Northumbria and sorely frightened the people. They consisted of immense whirlwinds and flashes of lightening, and fiery dragons were seen flying in the air. A great famine immediately followed those signs, and shortly after that in the same year, on 8 June, the ravages of the heathen men miserably destroyed God's church on Lindisfarne, with plunder and slaughter.[1]

The first appearance of the Vikings was thus associated with other natural expressions of God's wrath, including fiery dragons (which have been interpreted as a poetic reference to the aurora borealis). Two letters written by Alcuin from Charlemagne's court at Aachen give a contemporary view. They too blame this attack of the heathen on God's will. Alcuin reassured the bishop of Lindisfarne that perhaps God was punishing them harshly because He loved them more, but went on to suggest that the best way of avoiding such attacks was to make sure that he and the monks avoided drunkenness and fine clothes. (It is clear that he assumed that life in the monastery continued despite the attack.) In his accompanying letter to King Æthelred of Northumbria he noted that the sin which called down this attack was not that of the monks alone: he castigated the king for allowing fornication, adultery and incest in his kingdom, even involving nuns, and again mentions dress, though here in an interesting context:

> Consider the dress, the way of wearing the hair, the luxurious habits of the princes and people. Look at your trimming of beard and hair, in which you have wished to resemble the pagans. Are you not menaced by terror of them whose fashion you wished to follow?[2]

This strongly suggests that 'the pagans', who can here only be the Scandinavians, already had close contacts with the Northumbrians before this first attack. It is a hint that cannot be followed up in any other source, but two facts are worth recalling: the evidence from female dress noted by John Hines, which suggested the presence of Norwegians in northern and eastern England in the sixth century, and the existence of a colony of Frisian traders in York in the eighth century. Frisia would have been a port of call for any Danish traders en route for England, and 'Frisian' might be used as shorthand for any traders from across the sea. Does this thought conflict with something that Alcuin says earlier in the same letter?

> Lo, it is nearly 350 years that we and our fathers have inhabited this most lovely land, and never before has such terror appeared in Britain as we have now suffered from a pagan race, nor was it thought possible that such an inroad from the sea could be made.[3]

This has been taken as surprise at the ability of the Vikings to cross the North Sea, presumably from Norway, in one voyage, to strike unerringly at what must have been the wealthiest coastal settlement on the whole north-eastern coastline of England. Was it that previously Scandinavians had arrived by the safer route from the south, hugging the coasts of Francia and England? But, of course, Alcuin could not have known from which direction the raiders had come: it is more likely that he was commenting on the novelty of this type of sea-borne attack, or, as has been suggested recently, that we should retranslate that last phrase: 'nor was it thought possible that such a destruction should be made', meaning that the destruction of Lindisfarne has shown that God's favour had been unexpectedly withdrawn from this monastery.

A map of the recorded Viking raids of the period *c.* 789 to 833 shows us two raids in Northumbria, one in Dorset, one in south Wales, a few on Francia, and around thirty in Ireland and south-west Scotland.[4] Why so many raids in Ireland, and so few over most of Scotland and England? The answer, of course, is that such maps represent the location of written records rather than of actual raids, and may paradoxically reflect a mirror-image of reality. Put simplistically, there were many raids recorded in Ireland: there were many monasteries whose monks could record those raids, and those monasteries survived the raids and thus preserved their records for us. There are very few known raids in Northumbria, and, apart from the raid on Lindisfarne, those raids were recorded in the West Saxon *Anglo-Saxon Chronicle* at the very end of the ninth century, by compilers who were really not very interested in the northern kingdoms. That is because almost no Northumbrian monastery survived through the Viking period to make a local record of the raids. There are no raids recorded in Scotland at all: there are very few sources surviving from the period, again quite possibly because of the severity of the Viking attacks (although Kathleen Hughes suggested that early Picts and Scots had actually not been very interested in creating historical records).[5] If one looks at a map of the North Sea, one can see very easily that if Norwegians were involved in raiding Britain, their ships would first reach the Shetlands, and then the Orkneys, and so on down the eastern coast of Scotland to Northumbria, or down the west coast past the Western Isles to Ireland. Northern and eastern Scotland was likely to have been the first part of the mainland of Britain to experience Viking attacks, but no record survives of them at all in documentary records. However, there are some thirty Viking-period hoards from Scotland, many of which may be the result of the burial of treasure in order to hide it from the Vikings. (The fact that the known hoards were not recovered, of course, may indicate fatalities inflicted by the raiders.) One of the best known is the St Ninian's Isle treasure, hidden beneath the floor of a chapel and excavated in 1958. The largest is that of Skaill in Orkney (from *c.* 960), which contained over a hundred pieces of silver: ingots, brooches, armrings, and 'hack-silver' (silver cut up into fragments convenient for exchange). The only Scottish hoard which contained gold as well as silver was that found on the site of the monastery at Iona. This included over 360 coins, almost all of which were Anglo-Saxon: the date of the last suggests that the hoard was buried just before the Viking attack on Iona at Christmas 986.[6] This raid on Iona was around two hundred years after the first. A raid on a monastery was not something final: a monastery was a valuable producer of wealth, not to be destroyed, but to milk, again and again.

Lindisfarne may have been the first Viking raid known to Alcuin, but it was certainly not the first raid on Britain, or even on one of the English kingdoms. In 789 a group of ships arrived in Dorset: they were, interestingly, mistaken for traders – perhaps Anglo-Saxons were used to Scandinavian traders – and the reeve of Portland came out to greet them. He was killed, and the town attacked. In 792, Offa of Mercia was organising coastal defences, presumably to protect the eastern shores of his kingdom from Scandinavian attacks. Not long afterwards Charlemagne was forced to undertake similar measures, as the first attacks were made on the Low Countries and northern France. But defence against swift raiding expeditions was extremely difficult. The whole of Western Europe, not just the coasts but anywhere within reach of navigable rivers, was vulnerable to these raids in the first half of the ninth century. Not only did Vikings raid far up rivers like the Seine, Loire and Garonne, but in 844 they even reached and sacked Lisbon and Seville. By the early 840s they were establishing bases in the territories they were raiding, at Noirmoutier, at the mouth of the Loire, and at various places in Ireland, most notably near the mouth of the Liffey, securing their ships near Baile Átha Cliath, in the Black Pool (= Dub Linn), and thus establishing the foundations of what was to be the first town in Ireland. It seems likely that the Viking kingdom of Dublin was established by those Scandinavians who had already established their domination over much of Scotland and the Isles.

The Viking raids were to have a profound effect on the development of

Western European societies, and indeed had an even more profound effect on the Scandinavian world itself. The raids by (mostly) Danes and Norwegians on Western Europe, and the raids by (mostly) Swedes in the Baltic, and up the Russian rivers as far as the Black Sea and the Caspian, brought back massive amounts of wealth to Scandinavia. That wealth probably destabilised Scandinavian society, and encouraged the growth of more powerful chieftains and, eventually, the growth of national kingdoms. In Western Europe the raids led eventually to permanent Scandinavian settlements. The place-names of north-east Caithness, Orkney and Shetland are today almost totally Norse in origin, suggesting a massive displacement of the earlier Pictish population. The Isle of Man, an ideal base from which to reach either Ireland or Western Britain, also became heavily settled, as shown by both archaeology and the place-names. Indeed, Man still retains its Tynwald, or *thing-völlr*, 'assembly-field', comparable to the Thingvellir the Scandinavian settlers established in western Iceland, and to the site of place-names such as Dingwall (Sutherland). In Yorkshire and Lincolnshire the large number of placenames ending in *-by* and *-thorpe* are witness to an apparently extensive Danish settlement; across the Channel the map displays a similar pattern in the only region in Western Europe which still displays the name of the invading Northmen: Normandy. These 'French Northmen', of course, invaded England in 1066; but so did 'real' Northmen, under Harald Hardrada of Norway, and the last Danish invasion of England was threatened as late as 1085. The Western Isles of Scotland remained in the hands of the kings of Norway until the treaty of Perth in 1266; the Northern Isles were not transferred from the kingdom of Norway to that of Scotland until 1472. Scandinavians had a profound impact on Western Europe, and a prolonged impact on parts of it: the main theme of this chapter is to try to be more specific about the true nature and extent of this impact.

The Vikings

One of the many unsolved problems of the Viking period in European history is precisely what caused it. It used to be thought – in the Middle Ages itself – that overpopulation was the problem: that the polygamous Scandinavians produced so many children that they needed to grab land outside Scandinavia. Nowadays the explanations are more subtle, but none, individually, particularly persuasive. Were there some other social or political changes taking place which persuaded Scandinavians to go on raids and, ultimately, to emigrate? Icelandic sagas in the thirteenth or fourteenth century would say that Norwegians were fleeing the tyranny of Harald Finehair, who was trying to impose his will on much of the country, but this may well in part reflect contemporary concerns (Iceland had to submit to Norwegian rule in 1264) rather than ninth-century reality. Were the

Scandinavians responding to the massive political changes taking place in the Continent, as the Frankish rulers from Charles Martel onwards extended their power outwards from their homeland in north-east Gaul? The first known act of a Danish king – the building of a large earthwork, the Danevirke, right across the southern part of the Jutland peninsula – took place in 737 (this is dated by the tree-rings in the timbers felled for the purpose), and this was presumably in response to Frankish aggression. As the Franks moved against the Saxons, towards the end of the eighth century, in a savage series of campaigns, the Danes must have become even more worried. It has been suggested (rather fancifully?) that the early Viking raids targeted churches and monasteries in part as a result of the participation in them by Saxon exiles, still fiercely resenting the brutal way in which Charlemagne had imposed Christianity on Saxony at swordpoint.

The intensification of the Viking raids in the 830s and 840s may have been a result of profound commercial change. Some years ago Richard Hodges and David Whitehouse boldly sketched out a global economic model.[7] They argued that Charlemagne's growing ambitions, and his expanding territories – by 800 the most extensive seen in Europe between the Roman Empire and Napoleon – were increasingly dependent on a monetary economy based on silver. Much of the silver he needed came from silver dirhems minted in the Abbasid Caliphate, which were being minted in larger quantities in the late eighth and early ninth centuries. This silver, they argue, reached the West not via the Mediterranean, but via the trade-routes of Russia and the Baltic: in other words, Scandinavians were middlemen for this lucrative exchange. Pirates preyed on this commerce in the early years of the ninth century. But economic problems in the Caliphate, caused by the megalomaniac schemes of Harun al-Rashid and his successors and by civil disturbances, drastically reduced the flow of silver after the 820s. Both the Carolingian Empire and the *nouveaux riches* of the Scandinavian world suffered; the response in the Carolingian Empire was political unrest (Charlemagne's son Louis the Pious was deposed at one point) and in the Scandinavian world it was the intensification and expansion of raiding. It is a fascinating hypothesis, but one that can be proved only by much further research. But it does suggest the ways in which we have to think in global terms; and shows how Britain was, to some extent, merely on the sidelines.

The connections between raiding and commerce are much closer than usually given credit for. After all, the word 'Viking' itself – usually taken as equivalent to 'brutal sea-raider' – may well mean 'someone who frequents *viks*' or *wics*: the trading places in northern Europe which have often preserved the *wic* element in their place-names. If the Carolingian expansion had disrupted traditional trading networks, which Scandinavians may have been using for centuries, the transition from peaceful trading to armed raiding might have been a very easy one to make. The reeve of Portland might have been one of the first who realised, belatedly, that this transition had taken place. And once it had been established how vulnerable parts of

Western Europe actually were, the incentive to mount raids must have been irresistible. Commerce in the Scandinavian world flourished: much of the raided booty may well have ended up at trading-places, to be exchanged for what individual Scandinavians wanted and needed.

Were the Vikings simply engaging in commerce by other means? 'Should we view the Vikings as little more than groups of long-haired tourists who occasionally roughed up the natives?'[8] The tendency of research over the last thirty years has been to downplay the traditional image of the bloodthirsty Viking, to remove the horns from his helmet in the name of archaeological accuracy, and to argue that, despite his paganism, he was little different from the Anglo-Saxons or Irish who served as his victims. Raiding, after all, was a traditional activity for those peoples as well. All European aristocracies at the time essentially defined themselves by their status as warriors; and any idea that warfare was always an honourable affair can be dispelled by looking, for instance, at Charlemagne's wars against the Saxons. In Ireland, the traditional idea that, if nothing else, the pagan Vikings taught the Christian Irish the despicable habit of attacking churches and monasteries was countered by evidence that the Irish were already doing that in the eighth century, and didn't need lessons from anyone.[9]

It is possible to argue in the other direction, however. The Icelandic sagas of the thirteenth and fourteenth centuries, which preserve, however inaccurately, memories of the pagan Viking past, often display a sardonic delight in mayhem that is unlike anything else in medieval Europe, with an apparent admiration for the berserker, whose frenzy for blood led him into battle without fear of the consequences. Several sagas carry the tradition of the blood-eagle, which might indeed have been a genuine method by which the Vikings sacrificed their enemies to Odin. It is described in the *Orkneyinga Saga*, in the story of how Einarr searched for and killed the son of the king of Norway, who had attempted to gain power in Orkney at the end of the ninth century.

> Einarr carved the bloody eagle on his back by laying his sword in the hollow at the backbone and hacking all the ribs from the backbone down to the loins, and drawing out the lungs; and he gave him to Odin as an offering for his victory.[10]

Odin was the All-Father, but he was also the god of war: a sinister figure, whose cult may have been favoured in particular by warriors. For Christian writers, it was the paganism of the raiders which was their most obvious distinguishing characteristic: they were sometimes called *piratae*, but most often *pagani* or *hæthene men*. The earliest Vikings who settled in Britain seem to have converted to Christianity relatively quickly and quietly: but this was two or three generations after the initial Viking raids, and new Vikings could be found who adhered to the old beliefs and, for instance, ostentatiously placed the hammer of the god Thor on the coins they minted in York in the early tenth century. Were the early Vikings from a pagan culture which did foster an attitude to bloodshed which was different to that found in Christian Europe, and motivated by a hostility to the Christian Church? The fact is that our sources simply do not allow us to know the answer. Written sources from the Viking world do not begin until the eleventh century, and although the Icelandic traditions, written down from the twelfth century, may preserve genuine fragments of much earlier written records, their interpretation is not easy. For the ninth and tenth century our only contemporary written sources are written by the victims of the Vikings, or their descendants: by churchmen, who see the Vikings as pagans who specifically target churches and monasteries for their attacks.

The Great Army in England

There were numerous recorded raids in Ireland and in the Low Countries in the 820s and 830s, but relatively little activity, apparently, in England. The rate of attacks changed dramatically in the 840s. The east coast was widely ravaged in 841; a Northumbrian king was killed in battle against a Viking force in 844; in 850 and 854 it was recorded that a Danish army wintered in a base in eastern England. But the Vikings did not have it all their own way: a Kentish force defeated the Danes off Sandwich in 851, in the first recorded naval battle in English history, while in the same year King Æthelwulf of the West Saxons (Alfred's father) defeated a large Danish army which had attacked Canterbury and London and defeated the Mercian king.

In 859 a Viking force which had been raiding up the Somme crossed the Channel and attacked Winchester; when it was repelled it returned to its attacks in Francia. The ability of Viking armies to move from one side of the Channel to the other, to take advantage of whatever situation appeared to be the most advantageous, was a feature of the last decades of the ninth century, as was the emergence of ever larger Viking armies. The 'Great Army' – the *Anglo-Saxon Chronicle* calls it the *micel here*, but sometimes simply the *here*, the Army – was assembled, and arrived in England late in 865.

> [They] took up winter quarters in East Anglia; and there they were supplied with horses, and the East Angles made peace with them.[11]

The horses were needed for their first campaign of the following year: an expedition up to Northumbria, which resulted in the capture of the main Northumbrian centre at York. A later tradition has it that this happened on the Feast of All Saints, November 1. The Vikings seem to have held it until the spring of 867, when an attempt by two rival Northumbrian kings, Osbert and Ælla, to remove them ended in a massive defeat of the Northumbrians, the death of both kings, and the establishment of Viking control over this Anglo-Saxon kingdom, or at least its southern part. (The history of northern Northumbria is very murky, but it seems that an independent Anglo-Saxon kingdom survived here throughout the Viking period, just as one survived in Wessex.)

The account of these events in the *Anglo-Saxon Chronicle* is brief and confused, and the various elaborations added by later English and Anglo-Norman historians may not be reliable. Even more controversial is the question of the reliability of later Icelandic traditions about these events. Alfred P. Smyth has tried to use these sources to give an idea of the complexity of the political interactions not just within England, but right across Britain and Ireland. He has reconstructed – often from much later, and, for most scholars, very largely fictitious accounts – the career of Ragnarr loðbrók (Ragnar Hairy-breeks) and his son Ívarr inn beinlausi (Ivar the Boneless) who, in these later Scandinavian traditions, dominate the history of the Vikings in the West in these years. The most famous Icelandic tradition about Ragnarr was that he led an expedition against Ælla of Northumbria, and was captured by him and put to death by being placed in a pit of poisonous snakes: this story has parallels with other folk tales in Scandinavia, and may have been developed in order to explain why Ragnarr's son Ívarr later invaded Northumbria and put Ælla to death. The twelfth-century Danish historian Saxo wrote about Ragnarr as someone who led expeditions against Scotland and in Ireland; he may even be the *Reginherus* who, according to a Frankish source, attacked Paris in 845. Smyth suggests that he was a Danish leader of a large Viking fleet, which was involved in large-scale raiding in the West, and tried to oust the Norwegians from their stronghold in Dublin and eastern Ireland: it was there, perhaps, that Ragnarr died, in the mid-850s.

Ragnarr's son Ívarr first appears, in the Irish sources, in the early 850s, and in six out of the nine references to him in the contemporary annals he is acting together with Óláfr, whom later tradition took to be his brother: in fact he was a Norwegian, who had won himself the kingship of Dublin. The two take part in expeditions in Ireland and in Scotland in the 850s and early 860s. In 871, according to the *Annals of Ulster*, they take and destroy Dumbarton, the main fortress of the kings of Strathclyde, after a prolonged siege. After this expedition

> Amlaíb [Óláfr] and Ímar [Ívarr] returned to Áth Cliath [Dublin] from Alba [northern Britain], with two hundred ships, bringing away with them in captivity to Ireland a great prey of Angles and Britons and Picts.[12]

The Irish sources are much more explicit than the English about the involvement of the Vikings in an international slave trade. Wealthy prisoners were ransomed; but others might well be sold abroad. Later tradition associates 'the sons of Ragnarr' with the expedition that undoubtedly took place around 860 on the coasts of Arab Spain and beyond. One set of Irish annals (although not contemporary ones) mention the slaves that were brought back:

> And they carried off a great host of them as captives to Ireland, and these are the Black Men of Ireland, for *Mauri* is the same as *black men*, and *Mauretania* is the same as *blackness*.[13]

According to the *Annals of Ulster*, Ívarr died in Ireland two years later, in 873, and it makes a remarkable claim: 'Ímar, the king of the Northmen of the whole of Ireland and Britain, ended his life.' It is partly this claim, from a source not given to exaggeration, that persuaded Smyth that the Ímar or Imhar of the Irish sources (*mh* is pronounced *v* in Old Irish) is the same as the Iuuar or Ingwar of the English sources and the Ívarr of the Old Norse sources. Ímar is absent from Ireland, or from the Irish sources, between the time he plundered the great Neolithic tombs of the Boyne valley in 863 and when he returned to Dublin from Northern Britain in 871 with his captives. Was he a leader of the Great Army in England during this absence?

The *Anglo-Saxon Chronicle* does not mention anyone who could be Ívarr in the activities of the Great Army in England, although under 878 it mentions that the (unnamed) brother of 'Inwær' or 'Iwer' and 'Healfdene' was killed in Devon, with 840 of his men. Other sources, later Scandinavian and English ones, suggest that Ívarr was actually the most important leader. Æthelweard, writing his *Chronicle* at the end of the tenth century, for instance, ascribed the Danish invasion of East Anglia to 'Iguuar'. All Scandinavian sources have Ívarr as the main instigator of the attack on Northumbria, and as the king who had Ælla murdered. 'And Ívarr, who dwelt at York, carved the eagle on Ælla's back,' as a poem by Sighvat the Skald put it in the eleventh century.[14] According to the twelfth-century historian Henry of Huntingdon, it was he ('Hinguarus') who led the Danish forces into Mercia in 868, taking Nottingham but declining to meet the combined Mercian and West Saxon forces in battle. The Danes retreated to York, and stayed there for a year; in 869 the *Chronicle* says that the army crossed Mercia into East Anglia, fought and killed King Edmund and took the kingdom. Abbo of Fleury (at the end of the tenth century) thinks that it was a sea-borne invasion. He has the Danish messenger to the East Anglian king make the following announcement:

> My August lord and unconquerable sovereign Inguar, a terror by land and sea, having by force of arms brought several countries into his subjection, has landed with a great fleet on the desirable shores of this territory, with the intention of fixing his winter quarters here, and in pursuance thereof commands you to share with him your ancient treasures, and your hereditary wealth, and to reign in future under him.[15]

Abbo says that Edmund refused to submit to this because a Christian could not submit to a pagan: indeed, that he offered to submit if Ívarr converted. Edmund was beaten, tied to a tree, shot full of arrows and beheaded. When he was taken from the tree, they found 'his ribs laid bare by numberless gashes, as if he had been put to the torture of the rack, or had been torn by savage claws' – which Smyth takes to be the sacrifice of the blood-eagle. Abbo says that he got the story of Edmund's death from Archbishop Dunstan, who heard Edmund's armour-bearer tell the story to King Æthelstan (924–39). His body was, of course, ultimately buried at Bury St Edmunds, where his cult as a saint continued throughout the Middle Ages.

Ívarr disappears from the English scene at this point. He does not seem to be in the army which set up a base at Reading, to attack Wessex; a much later source says that he went back to Northumbria to join his brother Ubba, sacking Ely on his way north,[16] and from there he must have planned his joint expedition with Óláfr of Dublin against the Britons of Dumbarton, eventually returning to Dublin in triumph, as 'king of the Northmen of the whole of Ireland and Britain'.

With his brother Ubba (who is mentioned in several of the sources) in Northumbria and his brother Hálfdan still with the Great Army in East Anglia, Ívarr might have preserved his role in English affairs had he not died. But Hálfdan, at least, played a part in what follows. After the 871 entry in the *Anglo-Saxon Chronicle* we are much better informed: Alfred, for whom the *Chronicle* was originally compiled, starts to play a major role in events, and also, presumably could have been more useful as an informant. But it is also from 871 that Wessex becomes a major target for the Great Army. They establish a base at Reading, and launch attacks into the heartland of the West Saxon kingdom. Events do not go all their own way. King Æthelred and his brother Alfred do have a major victory at Ashdown (the Berkshire Downs), and are then defeated at Basing. Twice that year, according to the *Chronicle*, a West Saxon army under the king defeated the Danes, at *Meretun* and at Wilton, and on both occasions the *Chronicle* says that the West Saxons won, and yet 'let the Danes have possession of the battlefield', which certainly lets us wonder what kind of victory it was. In the middle of this campaigning Æthelred died, and Alfred became sole king of the West Saxons. At the end of the 871 entry, the longest entry in the *Chronicle* so far (apart from the anecdote under 755), it records that nine Danish earls and one king had been killed. The Danes withdrew to winter quarters in London, but it was not a retreat, and it is quite likely that Alfred had to pay for the peace that he had won. At London the Vikings mint coins, in the name of Hálfdan. But Hálfdan was not the only Viking leader, because the Great Army was no longer the only army. The Great Army had been joined in Reading that year by what the *Chronicle* calls the Summer Army.

In 873 both armies, apparently, went to Northumbria, to put down a revolt against their power: they reinstated the archbishop of York and established a new puppet king. Then they launched an assault on Mercia, wintering in Repton (Derbyshire) in 873/4 and taking Mercia in 874. King Burghred followed a long line of early Anglo-Saxon kings across the Alps to Rome, where he died, as a pilgrim, and a puppet king ruled in his place. Thanks to the excavations conducted by the Biddles at Repton between

1974 and 1988, we now know rather more about this particular episode: it is one of the few historical *events* in the Viking period (as opposed to historical processes) that archaeology has illuminated. It is unlikely that Repton was a random choice of wintering-place for the Viking army. Repton was a monastery, ruled by an abbess. St Guthlac had come to live there in the eighth century, and it was the burial place of the murdered King Æthelbald of Mercia (d. 757), of King Wiglaf (d. 840) and of prince Wigstan. The latter was murdered too, and regarded as a martyr: there was a cult of St Wystan later in the Middle Ages, and the church at Repton is dedicated to him. The astonishing crypt which is still visible, with its carved monolithic columns with spiral decoration, was a mausoleum and cult-site for the Mercian dynasty. Securing this site was a preliminary to the elimination of the Mercian dynasty the following year. When the Danes came to Repton they built earthworks which linked the church into a D-shaped enclosure, whose straight edge was formed by the River Trent. It enclosed an area of less than an acre: evidence for those who believe that Viking armies were small (that is, to be counted in three figures rather than four or five). Tiny pieces of metal book-fittings were found trampled into the floor of one building, suggesting that the Vikings had systematically stripped the monastery of all its wealth. Outside the encampment was a mass grave, containing the remains of around 250 people. There is some controversy over what this means. It has been suggested that they may be the graves of Vikings, who had died of disease during the winter; it seems unlikely that they were slaughtered monks, as there is no sign of violence on the skeletons themselves. It has also been argued that the women in the grave, around 20 per cent of the whole, were of a different physical type: perhaps local women enslaved by the marauders; Graham-Campbell coyly suggests that they were 'native English camp followers who had taken partners among the Viking army'.[17] One of those buried must have been one of the Vikings. He had been killed by a great blow to his left hip. He was buried much more carefully than the others, under a mound of stones, and with his weapons: a Thor's hammer hung from his neck, unequivocally indicating his paganism.

After the conquest of Mercia, the two armies separated: Hálfdan went back to Northumbria, and the Summer Army, under Guthrum, Oscetel and Anwend, went to Cambridge. Hálfdan now concentrated his attentions on the north. In 876 he 'shared out the land of the Northumbrians, and they proceeded to plough and to support themselves':[18] the only reference to Viking colonisation of the land in the whole of the *Chronicle*. It is not impossible that in 874 he had heard of the death of his brother Ívarr, and planned to try and inherit some of his power in the north and west. Even the *Anglo-Saxon Chronicle*, which was rarely interested in the events of the north, noted his activity under 875: '[He] took up winter quarters by the River Tyne. And the army conquered the land and often ravaged among the Picts and the Strathclyde Britons'.[19] The *Annals of Ulster* record his attack on the Picts in 875, and note that he killed Eystein, son of Óláfr, king of

Dublin. He returned to Northumbria to settle his men on the land, and then returned to Ireland to try again to establish his power there. It looks as if he could persuade few to follow him, and the *Annals of Ulster* record that he was killed in the course of a *belliolum*, a small battle.[20]

The Summer Army was meanwhile having considerable success in the South. It moved from Cambridge into the heart of Alfred's kingdom in 876, as far as Wareham (Dorset), where the Vikings used a nunnery as the basis for their encampment, much as they had used a monastery at Repton. However, Alfred did persuade them to swear an oath to leave immediately, on a holy ring – 'a thing which they would not do before for any nation', adds the *Chronicle*. (Such oaths are mentioned in the Icelandic sagas.) But they forswore their oath, apparently, and slipped off to Exeter. Alfred managed to dislodge them in 877, when they went to Mercia and shared out some of the land to settle on. But in the middle of winter, after Twelfth Night in 878, they slipped into Wessex again, and forced most of the population to submit to them. It may be that the *Anglo-Saxon Chronicle* exaggerates the scale of the Viking victory in order to enhance the scale of Alfred's subsequent triumph: we have no real way of telling. The *Chronicle* relates how Alfred alone, with a few men, held out against the Vikings, hiding in the woods and fens, and eventually emerging from his stronghold in the marshes at Athelney (Somerset) to rally the forces of Somerset, Wiltshire and parts of Hampshire. He met the Danes at Edington (Wiltshire), and defeated them soundly. As part of the peace-treaty Guthrum agreed to convert to Christianity. Moreover, this time he kept the agreement: he and thirty of his more important followers were baptised at Aller near Athelney.

It was not quite the end of Alfred's immediate problems. Guthrum's Summer Army stayed within Wessex in 879, at Cirencester; and a third Viking army came up the Thames, to establish a base at Fulham – ideally placed for raiding up river into Wessex. But the threat passed. Guthrum's army returned to East Anglia, and 'shared out the land', while the Fulham army went overseas to Francia. For the next four years, the *Chronicle* restricts itself – with a mixture of triumph and relief, perhaps – to noting the movements of this army on the Continent, from Ghent, along the Meuse, up the Scheldt, and then up the Somme, and up the Seine to Paris, where they established their winter quarters in 886, and then up the Marne, where they wintered two years. For all this time, the *Chronicle* gives very little information on England, and the only time between 880 and 892 that the army made an assault on Wessex it was clearly very little threat: part of the army attacked Rochester, but Alfred put them to flight and took their horses.

Those twelve years of peace must have been extremely important for Alfred, enabling him to consolidate his own position and to prepare his army for future onslaughts. The remains of the Great Army, in the north, and the Summer Army in the east, seem to have been occupied with their own affairs, while the Fulham Army found far more useful opportunities in Francia. Although the renewed assaults between 892 and 896 were sustained and serious, it is clear that Alfred had learned how to cope with the threat, even when, for a while, the army from Francia was joined by the armies from Northumbria and East Anglia. The *Chronicle* summed it up in 896 as follows:

> By the grace of God, the army had not on the whole afflicted the English people very greatly; but they were much more seriously afflicted in those three years by the mortality of cattle and men, and most of all in that many of the best king's thegns who were in the land died in those three years.[21]

Thereafter, after Alfred's death in 899, the West Saxons would be on the offensive, and would gradually annex to themselves what the Vikings had conquered from other Anglo-Saxon peoples.

Alfred and the defence against the Vikings

The West Saxons managed to preserve their independence, when every other Anglo-Saxon people lost theirs. How did this happen? Undoubtedly Alfred himself had something to do with it, even if we do not necessarily have to believe everything announced by the West Saxon propaganda machine (whether that of the late ninth or of the nineteenth and twentieth centuries). On the other hand, Alfred was certainly aided by a number of factors over which he had no control. The West Saxons were the last target of the Vikings, partly for geographical reasons: many of the invaders must have been too preoccupied with controlling newly won territories further north or east to devote all their attention to the West Saxons. Alfred's great victory at Edington almost exactly coincided with news that the great Charles the Bald (840–77) had died in Francia, and that his West Frankish kingdom had fallen into the hands of incompetents: this was a very useful and unexpected distraction.

Alfred may have learnt lessons from Charles the Bald. Charles had been relatively successful in building defences (notably fortified bridges, denying access by water up some of France's main rivers), and in encouraging local defence on the peripheries of the kingdom. Alfred had ideas of his own, however. The *Anglo-Saxon Chronicle* makes much of Alfred's attempts to meet the Vikings in their own element: attempts that have earned him the title of 'Father of the English Navy'. They were not particularly remarkable, save perhaps as an expression of determination. In 875 the navy captured one Viking ship and put six others to flight; in 882 he captured two ships and forced the surrender of two others; and in 885, his navy seized sixteen ships on the River Stour in east Anglia, but was defeated by a Danish force on the way home. The last mention of Alfred's navy in the *Chronicle* is the most farcical. In 896 the Vikings of Northumbria and East Anglia were attacking the south coast of Wessex in 'warships which they had built many years before'. Alfred put to sea in ships twice as long as those old Viking ships, some with more than sixty oars: 'they were built neither on the Frisian nor the Danish pattern, but as it seemed to him that they could be most useful.'[22] Some of these ships tried to attack marauding Vikings in an estuary. They were so unmanoeuvrable that they ran aground, and the Danes were able to attack them. Although only one Viking ship returned home (the crew of one ran ashore and were handed in at Winchester), Alfred's own forces were badly mauled. It is interesting that among those killed by the Vikings were a king's reeve and a king's companion (or *geneat*), together with three named (and thus important) Frisians: Wulfheard, Æbbe and Æthelhere. It looks very much as if Alfred had to import sea-faring talent from the Frisians of the Low Countries.

Alfred's programme of fortification was probably more important. An intriguing document known as the Burghal Hidage gives us an idea of how Alfred organised his fortresses; and that, in fact, tells us a good deal about Alfred's power. The document as we have it seems to be a copy of a document drawn up under Alfred's son, but it is generally thought that it incorporates procedures laid down under Alfred. It is a list of burhs or fortresses established in Wessex, together with the number of hides needed to man their defences. A formula is given by which one can calculate the hidage:

> For the maintenance and defence of an acre's breadth of wall 16 hides are required. If every hide is represented by 1 man, then every pole of wall can be manned by 4 men. Then for the maintenance of 20 poles of wall 80 hides are required, and for a furlong 160 hides are required by the same reckoning, as I have stated above.[23]

The formula continues, listing the number of hides needed to defend a wall up to a length of twelve furlongs (a mile and a half). Every pole of wall – some 5 metres – needed four men to defend it, and thus needed four hides in the surrounding territory to supply the men. (For those interested in such things, there are forty poles to a furlong, and eight furlongs to the mile.) As a consequence of the formula, the hide was by no means of equal value in each county. In Hampshire, most notably, is the burh of Winchester; but since Alfred's burh of Winchester reused the extensive Roman walls, it needed 2400 men to defend it. *Hamtun* (Southampton) is also in the shire, and valued at 150 hides. Hampshire thus had to supply 2550 men, far more than any other shire in the Burghal Hidage – and, long after the Viking threat has disappeared, after the Norman Conquest, Hampshire is still assessed for tax purposes at 2550 hides. It is a wonderful example, at the same time, of Alfred's organisational skill, and of the inertia of the English administrative system.

The Burghal Hidage thus shows a number of things. It shows how Alfred covered the kingdom with a system of garrisoned forts, spaced so that no settlement would be further than 30 miles from one: the garrisons could defend the localities, but could also harass any invading Danish force, and impede its movement. It shows how Alfred was powerful enough to organise his kingdom into a cohesive defensive force like no other in Europe, and to set up a system of royal exploitation of manpower. And it shows that, whether or not the Viking armies were large or small, Alfred was able (in theory at least) to put one of the largest attested early medieval armies into garrison and field. 27,070 men were needed just to garrison the forts of Wessex; and it seems that Alfred intended to put a similar sized force into his field armies as well. It is almost inconceivable that invading Viking forces could have mustered similar numbers. The *Chronicle* says that Alfred 'had divided his army into two, so that always half its men were at home, half on service, apart from the men who guarded the boroughs [burhs]'.[24] There are, however, hints in the *Chronicle* that the army had its organisational problems; in 893, the English army stopped the Danes from retreating to their ships in Essex with their booty, and they besieged the Danes on a small island on the Thames:

> Then the English forces besieged them for as long as their provisions lasted; but they had completed their term of service and used up their provisions, and the king was on the way there with the division which was serving with him.[25]

Short-term problems there may have been; but it does seem that Alfred had managed to put together a military force and a system of defences without parallel in Europe.

For Alfred, however, the true defence of Wessex possibly lay not in ships, walls or warriors, but in God's grace. The *Anglo-Saxon Chronicle* says little about Alfred apart from his military activities, but we can learn more about the person from a much-disputed source, Asser's *Life of Alfred*. The majority of scholars agree that this is, as it purports to be, a near-contemporary life of the king, by someone who knew him well, in latter years. The text itself says that Asser was summoned to the king's presence in around 885, 'from the remote, westernmost parts of Wales'.[26] The *Life* says that it was written in 893, after eight years in which Asser had divided his time between the royal court and various ecclesiastical duties in Wales and in south-west England. At some time in the 890s he became bishop of Sherborne (Dorset), and he died in around 908. It is perhaps odd that the first ever secular life of a living English king should be written by a Welshman. It was, as Asser explained, at a time when Alfred had been extending his control over southern Wales. He says that the kings of Dyfed and Brycheiniog had submitted themselves to Alfred's overlordship in order to win protection from the sons of Rhodri Mawr of Gwynedd, and that the kings of Glywysing and Gwent had been driven to seek protection from Alfred 'by the might and tyrannical behaviour of Ealdorman Æthelred – that is, of the ruler of the Mercians.[27] Eventually even the sons of Rhodri Mawr, having got no benefit from their alliance with 'the Northumbrians' (that is, presumably, with the Vikings of York), threw in their lot with

Alfred. Asser puts his summons to the royal court, however, not so much in the context of Anglo-Welsh relations, as with Alfred's desire to renew Christian learning in his kingdom.

The Alfred of the *Life* is quite a different figure from the Alfred of the *Chronicle*. He is an active warrior, but he is much more than that: a person in agony from an unspecified illness and persistent piles, a man tormented by his lusts, and also anguished by his lack of divine and secular learning. Like Charlemagne (whose *Life* by Einhard was an inspiration to Asser), he called to his court men of learning and wisdom: four Mercians, including Werferth, bishop of Worcester and Plegmund, archbishop of Canterbury; Grimbald, a monk of St-Bertin in Flanders, and John, from Saxony in Germany; and Asser himself. ('Asser' is a Hebrew word meaning 'blessed': the Welsh equivalent might have been 'Gwyn'.) Alfred founded monasteries, and brought people from Gaul to fill them; he encouraged learning, in Latin but also in English: we have the translations of Latin texts which he commissioned, with the prefaces which are written in the first person, as by the king. He was, for Asser, in many ways the ideal king, like 'the holy, highly esteemed and exceedingly wealthy Solomon, king of the Hebrews'.[28]

> What shall I say of his frequent expeditions and battles against the Vikings and of the unceasing responsibilities of government? What of his daily involvement with the nations which lie from the Mediterranean to the farthest limit of Ireland? – for I have seen and read letters sent to him with gifts from Jerusalem by the patriarch Elias. And what of the cities and towns to be rebuilt and others to be constructed where previously there were none? And what of the treasures incomparably fashioned in gold and silver at his instigation? And what of the royal halls and chambers marvellously constructed of stone and wood at his command? And what of the royal residences of masonry, moved from their old position and splendidly reconstructed at more appropriate places by his royal commands? And what of the mighty disorder and confusion of his people – to say nothing of his malady – who would undertake of their own accord little or no work for the common needs of his kingdom?[29]

For Asser, what Alfred achieved was wholly due to his own superhuman efforts; he did it despite, rather than with, his subjects.

The *Life* finishes six years before Alfred's death, although Asser outlived his subject by nearly a decade: another oddity. It is this accumulation of oddities which has led a number of scholars to believe that Asser's *Life* was actually a forgery, dating from the late tenth or even eleventh century. V.H. Galbraith was the most distinguished of these sceptics, and Alfred P. Smyth the most recent.[30] The intemperate nature of the academic reaction which followed Smyth's own intemperate book was more akin to the vitriolic debates familiar to early medievalists in Smyth's native Dublin than to the relatively measured tone of most Anglo-Saxonists (in which some might discern complacency).[31] So far the consensus has not shifted: all those who have joined the debate, apart from Smyth, believe that Asser is a genuine contemporary of Alfred's. But Smyth has made people think clearly about the reliability of Asser, and what this means for our picture of Alfred himself. Was he really this neurotic king, virtually crippled by disease, who was not able to learn to read Latin until he was nearly forty?

> The man who pondered on the mysteries of human consciousness in an afterlife also had the ability to lead in war. For no man, born in Alfred's world, who shrank from treading on the entrails of the dying, could ever hope to gain the respect of his warband in that life and death struggle with the Norse enemy.[32]

Smyth's argument is that, without Asser's text, Alfred emerges as a much more assured and gifted figure, a learned man with an appreciation of the power of the vernacular, and a decisive leader.

The Vikings in the north and west

At Alfred's birth, a well-established pattern of British political geography existed. There were a number of English kingdoms, from Edinburgh south to the Channel; a number of British kingdoms to the West, from Strathclyde south to Cornwall; there were the kingdoms of the Picts and the Scots in the north and north-west. By the time of Alfred's death in 899, the independent English were restricted to Wessex, western Mercia and the northern part of Northumbria – Bernicia/Lothian; the rest of England and much of the former territory of the Picts was controlled by the Vikings. There was no longer a kingdom of the Picts at all. Strathclyde had suffered a severe blow by the capture of Dumbarton in 871, by Ívarr and Óláfr. A year later, Artgal of Strathclyde, the last name in the genealogy of the Strathclyde dynasty, was killed by Constantine II; his son married Constantine's daughter, and thereafter the rulers of the sub-kingdom of Strathclyde were members of the Scottish dynasty.[33] In both England and Scotland, therefore, the Vikings may have been indirectly responsible for the emergence of a single national kingdom. As we have seen, two of the major problems in early medieval British history are linguistic ones: why did Romano-Britons come to speak English rather than Welsh, and why did the Pictish language disappear so completely? The explanation to the second question may involve the Vikings. Without the Vikings, it is rather puzzling. We have seen (above, pp. 207) how the Pictish dynasty seems to be largely dominant in the eighth century; yet in the middle of the ninth century the kingdom of Scotland is unified, under Cináed mac Alpín (840/2–858), a Gaelic rather than a Pictish king. If the question of the emergence of the *Regnum Scottorum* – the problem which Wormald has called 'an object lesson in the frustrations of life as an early medieval historian'[34] – is to be solved at all, then it has to explain how a Gaelic king could come to unite Scotland, and apparently wipe out the Pictish culture and language. One explanation, as mentioned earlier, is what we might call 'creeping Gaelicisation', but it is not easy to see how this could have happened. The Pictish language appears to have been *p*-Celtic, like Welsh, and thus would not have been comprehensible to speakers of *q*-Celtic, like the Dalriadans. We have to imagine a situation where the Dalriadans were put into an unassailable social and political superiority; as Wormald has said, 'twenty-five years' study of the Barbarian West's warrior aristocracies has yet to acquaint me with one that rolled over and died of osmosis'.[35] There was a later story that much of the Pictish aristocracy were wiped out by Cináed and his men, while the latter were guests at a banquet in Scone; but the eclipse of that aristocracy might also have been the result of the depredations of the Vikings.

This is admittedly almost entirely hypothetical. There is only one battle with the Vikings in Scotland mentioned in the annals: one in 839, in which Éoganán mac Óengusa was killed. Other evidence suggests that it was the Dalriadans who were most hard hit by the Vikings: after all, it was their monastery of Iona which was attacked twice, in 802 and 825. After the first attack, the monks were given Kells, near Dublin, as a safer base; after the second the story of Blathmac, who was martyred by the Vikings after having hidden the relics of Columba from them, reached as far as the Carolingian court, and was celebrated in a poem by the Frankish scholar Walafrid Strabo.[36] But the absence of evidence need not be too much of a hindrance; there is always a lack of evidence about the internal history of the Pictish kingdom. Later traditions, for what they are worth, certainly believed that the Vikings devastated Pictland in the mid-ninth century.[37] It is quite possible that Viking attacks dealt severe blows against Pictish armies, and thus against its warrior aristocracy, which would have seriously affected the political and social cohesion of the kingdom, and that the Dalriadans took advantage of this. Wormald again: 'The Scots may have been among the beneficiaries of a markedly destabilized ninth century scene – whether or not they were among the few who rode the Viking tiger without ending up inside it.'[38] The Pictish kingdom probably did not simply fall into Cináed's hands, however; later Scottish traditions assert that he campaigned in Pictland (and indeed that he attacked Northumbria as well, sacking Dunbar and Melrose).[39] Tradition had it that he died at Forteviot: he had taken over the main Pictish palace complex in Fortriu. Under him and his son Constantine II (Causentín mac Cináeda, 862–76) a process of 'Gaelicisation' may have begun: the twisting of the genealogies to imply long-standing links between the Pictish and Scottish dynasties, the use of ecclesiastical propaganda to stress the significance of Iona as the source of Pictish Christianity, and so on. It is possible that the evangelising missionaries of the Céli Dé ('Servants of God') reform movement were at the forefront of the forging of this new Scottish identity: the old Pictish Church could be portrayed as decadent and betraying the ideals of its founder,

Columba. Columba, as Scottish apostle to the Picts, could symbolise the new national unity. Columba's relics, or some of them, were moved to Dunkeld, to create a new national shrine, and several of the later Scottish kings bore names which showed devotion to this saint – Máel Coluim, 'Servant of Columba', or Malcolm) – and Iona became a resting place for the bodies of the Scottish kings.

From the point of view of documentary history, the part of the northern Viking world that we know best is that group of islands between the Shetlands and the northern coasts of Scotland: the Orkneys. And we know about them thanks to an Icelandic story-teller. Between the twelfth and the fourteenth century Icelanders wrote huge amounts of poetry and prose, particularly the latter. Their prose sagas told stories of everyday life on Iceland – farming and feuding – but also about the settlement of this new land, which was theirs for the taking (and empty apart from a few easily disposable Irish monks). Sometimes these sagas tell of the connections Icelanders retained with the rest of the Viking world: they visit Norway, above all, but also Britain and Ireland. Egil, in *Egils Saga*, visits Eiríkr Bloodaxe in York, and characters in *Njáls Saga* take part in the battle of Clontarf, just to the north of Norse Dublin, in 1014: Earl Sigurd of the Orkneys met his end there. Icelanders also wrote histories of their home countries: *Knutlinga Saga* is a history of Denmark, and *Heimskringla* is a history of Norway. But only one part of Viking Britain was treated this way, in a surviving work: the Orkneys. *Orkneyinga Saga* was written in Iceland, around 1200. It has a fanciful legendary introduction, but may well become more historical from the late ninth century, the time of Harald Finehair of Norway. Harald himself, according to the saga, came to the Orkneys in order to put a stop to certain Vikings who were using the Orkneys and Shetlands as a base from which to raid Norway. He himself plundered in the Hebrides, and as far south as Man, before returning home, investing one of his men, Sigurd, with the title of earl of Orkney. From Orkney Sigurd proceeded to conquer much of the northern part of Scotland; he defeated Earl Máel Brigte of the Scots, but while riding home one of the teeth of Máel Brigte's severed head, which was hanging from his saddle, scratched Sigurd's thigh, and he died of the infected wound. Much of the late ninth- and tenth-century material in the saga is like that: good stories which may have some basis in historical reality, but mostly beyond verification. The picture it presents is one of serious political instability: Orkney was very well situated between Norway and the new British and Icelandic homes of the Vikings, and the possession of Orkney was thus a prize worth fighting for. It was a matter of note for the saga-writer that Earl Thorfinn (in the later tenth century) actually died in his bed.[40] The saga is almost entirely about the earls and their military activities, and says little about the population of the Orkneys. There are a few references to the farmers, however: farmers who complained about the ability of the earl to defend them against attacks from Vikings, or farmers who were unable to pay tax complained about excessive dues.[41] It is possible that these were Viking settlers, as were those 'men of Orkney' who decided to support one candidate for the earldom rather than another.[42] As we shall see in the next section, it looks as if the Vikings totally displaced – or annihilated – the indigenous population of these islands, as well as that of the Shetlands.

The history of Viking activity in western Britain is rather different from that in England. Over most of England there is a general cessation of Viking aggression from the beginning of the tenth century (partly because of the onset of English aggression), until the end of the tenth century and the renewed attacks which eventually led to the conquest of England by Denmark. But there is almost continuous activity in the Irish Sea region, because of the proximity to the British mainland of Viking kingdoms in Ireland and on the Isle of Man. The Vikings established various bases on the east coast of Ireland from the middle of the ninth century, which kept their independence from the native Irish until well into the eleventh century.

The ogam inscriptions on the Isle of Man, along with various church dedications, show that in the pre-Viking period Man had close connections with Ireland. The Manx language, which is *q*-Celtic like Irish (and unlike the Celtic languages of mainland Britain), may date from this period. Three major graves from this period were excavated between 1943 and 1946 by the archaeologist Gerhard Bersu (during his internment as an enemy alien): the mound at Ballateare contained the body of a warrior, with his armour and his weapons (apparently ritually broken), and the remains of sacrifices of a woman and various animals, while in the mound at Balladoole was a ship about ten metres in length, with a warrior with weapons and horse equipment, and again the traces of animal sacrifices. From the ninth century Man was ruled by various kings from different parts of the Norse world: Dublin, even the Orkneys. It was not until the eleventh century, when Godred (a survivor of the battle of Stamford Bridge in 1066) arrived in Man, that the Norse kingdom of Man begins to have a relatively well-documented and continuous history. Man itself was transferred along with the Hebrides to the king of Scotland in 1266, on the death of Magnus, the last Norse king of Man; finally, as a result of the Anglo-Scottish wars of England's three Edwards, it came to England. The bishop of the *ecclesia Sodorensis*, the bishop of the *Suðreyjar* (Old Norse for 'Southern Isles', which included Man and the Hebrides), continued to be under the control of the archbishop of Trondheim in Norway, however. The current title of the bishop of Sodor and Man preserves the memory of this Norwegian diocese, which was only transferred into the province of York in the fifteenth century.

The raids on Wales were probably launched from both Ireland and Man. The earliest recorded was in 852. In 876 Rhodri Mawr of Gwynedd was forced to go into exile in Ireland. In 877 there was the first of many attacks on Anglesey, and a Viking army wintered in Dyfed. Not all these attacks were by sea, however: in the 890s there were two attacks by the Vikings from the direction of Mercia. Attacks continued in the mid- and late tenth century, and the Welsh began to pay tribute to the Vikings. Wendy Davies concludes that between around 960 and 1025 Scandinavians were actually controlling Gwynedd, either from Man or Dublin or indeed from bases within Wales itself. The various members of the Gwynedd dynasty were referred to as 'holding' Gwynedd: they were not called 'kings', and they were paying tribute to the Vikings.[43] The *Annals of Ulster* even begin calling the king of Strathclyde *rí Bretan*, 'king of the Britons', a grandiose title which earlier, and later, was normally given to the kings of Gwynedd.

Scandinavian settlement in Britain

At several points in the *Chronicle* mention is made of 'sharing out the land': this occurred in Northumbria, Mercia and East Anglia. In 877, for instance, *gefor se here on Miercne lond ond hit gedeldon sum*: 'the Army went into the land of the Mercians and shared it out'. Presumably it denotes the point at which the conquerors moved from being landless warriors to landed gentry. We know almost nothing about how this happened, or on what scale. Documentary sources tell us very little about Viking settlement: for that we have to turn to place-names and to archaeology. From these kinds of evidence we can, firstly, get some sort of idea of *where* Viking settlement took place. In England those place-names are to be found throughout East Anglia, the East Midlands and the North, but they are most dense in Yorkshire, Lincolnshire and the East Midlands. They are also to be found on the west coast: in Pembrokeshire and along the south coast of Wales; in Lancashire and around the Solway Firth; on the Isle of Man, and Scottish Isles such as Islay, Skye and Lewis. In north-east Caithness, and across the water in Orkney, and beyond in Shetland, the Viking place-names have almost totally replaced any earlier names. It is possible, of course, that modern maps do not give a reasonable impression of earlier Viking settlement: it has been argued that in the Western Isles most of the Gaelic place-names are not pre-Viking, but post-Viking, and that therefore in the Viking period the Scandinavian element in the place-names might have been as overwhelming in the Western as in the Northern Isles.[44]

Maps of place-name elements shows the geographical distribution of the names, but they again tells us little about numbers, nor how the Vikings actually settled the land. If we have a settlement called Grimsby ('Grim's place'), are we dealing with one Dane called Grim, who founded a farmstead or perhaps took over an existing one, or a whole group of Danes, who recognised Grim as their leader? In other words, was Viking settlement in Britain an aristocratic affair – a military elite moving in to exploit an Anglo-Saxon, Welsh or Pictish peasantry – or was it the product of large-scale settlement from Denmark and Norway? On the whole the debate has been conducted with historians on the one side, often arguing for a small-scale

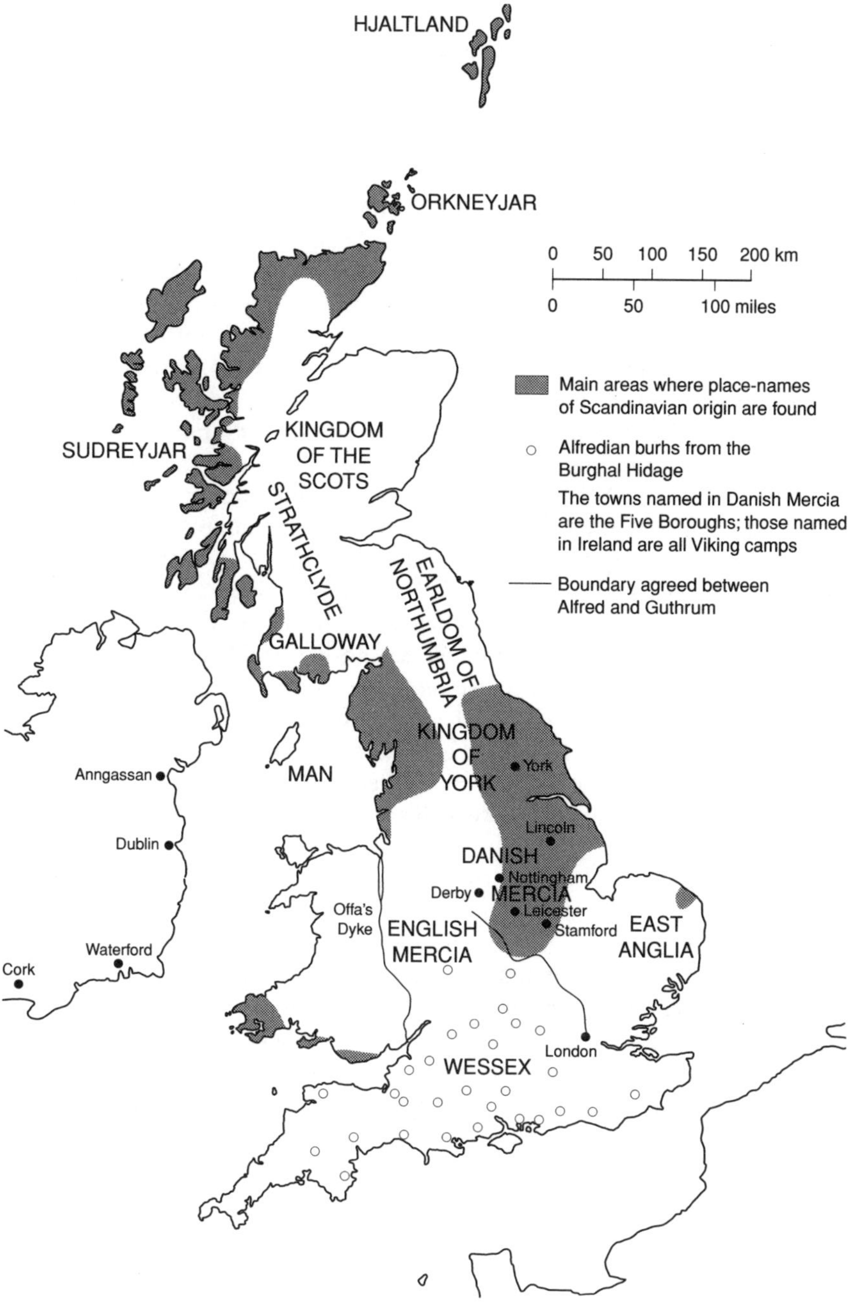

Map 6 Britain in *c.* 900

aristocratic settlement, and the philologists and place-name specialists on the other, usually arguing for popular migration.

A common argument from place-name scholars is that people like Grim do not name their settlements: settlements are named by consensus among the surrounding population. After all, it is Grim's neighbours who need to specify that they are going to meet at 'Grim's place' to get drunk that evening. Thus, the existence of Grimsby, and many other place-names like it, which are wholly Scandinavian in origin, suggest a relatively large or predominant local population of Scandinavians. They can be opposed to what have come to be called 'Grimston hybrids', such as are rather more common in East Anglia, for instance, than the 'Grimsby' types. Grimston, and words like it, are formed from a Scandinavian personal name followed by the Old English equivalent of *-by*, such as *-ton* or *-ham*. In cases like those, the theory runs, the local population is English, and if they talk about 'Grim's place', they say it in English and not Danish. There are no doubt problems in individual cases. A Scandinavian personal name does not have to belong to a Scandinavian, for instance; likewise, it is not impossible that Anglo-Saxons started using the Danish suffixes *-by* and *-thorp* to form their own place-names. For English to take on Scandinavian linguistic habits in itself denotes substantial influence. But the real problem is to date the place-name formations and this linguistic influence. Another problem is that we cannot be sure that a Scandinavian place-name necessarily indicates a new settlement, rather than a renaming of an existing Anglo-Saxon place. In our sources the best known renaming is that of the Anglo-Saxon *Northworthy*, which the Danes renamed Derby, but others are known.[45] Is the changing of names common, until growing centralisation and bureaucratisation, as with Domesday Book in 1087, impose some kind of stability?

Cameron has noted that in the East Midlands (Derby, Notts, Leics and Lincs) there are 303 names ending in *-by* recorded in Domesday Book (1087), as well as several dozen others recorded in later sources. Of the 303, 207 seem to be compounded with a personal name, of which almost all were Danish in type. Others are descriptive names, like Ferriby (Lincs), 'the village near the ferry', most of which are wholly Scandinavian in style, and some have ethnic prefixes, like Frisby (Leics), 'the village of the Frisians', Normanby (Lincs), 'the village of the Norwegians', or Ingleby (Derby, Lincs), 'the village of the English'. Many of the words, Cameron argues, are purely Danish from the point of view of the grammar; sometimes even when English personal names are used, they seem to be Danicised forms of English names.[46] Altogether, about 87 per cent of these *-by* names are purely Scandinavian compounds, and the percentage is as high as 91 per cent in Lincolnshire. More significantly, Cameron suggests that if one looks at the distribution of Scandinavian place-names in the landscape at a local level – at how they relate to the contours, the geology (including the soils) and the neighbouring settlements – one could conclude that the Vikings come as colonists, and not conquerors. The newcomers seem to have followed the river valleys to select the sites of their settlements, avoiding the higher ground, but also avoiding the main rivers, whose banks were already well settled by the English. Likewise, the English had settled on the best stretches of glacial sand and gravel, leaving the less attractive sites for the Danes. The Danes do not seem to have settled near the Five Boroughs – Derby, Nottingham, Leicester, Lincoln and Stamford – which formed their main administrative centres in the East Midlands, but at some distance away; the English had already settled densely around these towns. Of course, this does not take into account the possibility that Danish warriors took over the lordships of existing villages, without changing their names; but it does look as if the densest settlement, as indicated by the wholly Scandinavian place-names, was to a large extent respecting the existing structure of settlement and landholding.

In Scotland there is a quite different range of Scandinavian names, in part relating to the importance of Norwegians rather than Danes, and in part the result of the different linguistic substratum (Celtic rather than Germanic), but also a product of the much longer settlement. Some of the place-names show the particular interest of the Vikings in the islands and coastline. In the west most Scottish islands have endings in *-ay* or *-a* (Old Norse *-ey*), most headlands end in ON *-nes* (Gaelicised as *-nish*), and hill-names often end in ON *-fjell* (Gaelicised to *-val*).[47] In Lewis, ninety-nine of the 126 village-names are purely Scandinavian, while nine of the others have Scandinavian elements, but the natural features are much more likely to be Celtic in origin.[48] It has thus been suggested that 'the moors and hills were chiefly the domain of a subjugated Celtic-speaking class whose tasks were, among other things, to attend to the shielings, the sheep and the peat-bogs, activities in which it was necessary to know the names of topographical features.'[49] Elsewhere it may be possible to detect the way in which settlements were made in the landscape. Nicolaisen has suggested that in Orkney the farm-names formed from ON *boer/-bðr* might have been the earliest, core, settlements; those formed from *-land*, *-bólstaýr*, *-garth*, and *-skaill* were somewhat more recent; those formed from *-staðr* (modern *-sta*, *-stay* or *-ston)* were secondary settlements; while those ending in ON *-qvi* (modern *-quoy*) were peripheral establishments, perhaps pastoral dependencies of a main farm. But looking at these and other name-types (such as those formed from *-setr* or *-bólstaðr*) has suggested to others that drawing up settlement histories at a parish level from such evidence is far from straightforward.[50] Comparison with similar name-forms in Iceland (which was settled and named from the late ninth century, perhaps predominantly from Scotland) hardly helps, although it does suggest that the earliest settlements may not be any of these names formed with some kind of farm suffix: the earliest Icelandic farms tended to be named after features like hills or promontories. Of the fifteen Orkney farm-names preserved in the *Orkneyinga Saga*, twelve have topographical names, seven of which end in *-ness*.[51]

A final area worth looking at is north-west England: Lancashire and

Cumbria. There is a strong influence of *q*-Celtic (as in Irish and Scottish Gaelic) in the Viking place-names of this part of the world, which has led many scholars to think that there was a movement from the Viking colonies on the east coast of Ireland. In place-names like Ireby and Ireleth, it is fairly clear there are settlements of Irish.[52] But in other cases the 'Irish' element may in fact come not across the Irish Sea, but just across the Solway Firth from Galloway, an area which was Gaelicised before the arrival of the Vikings. In addition to this influx of 'Scottish Vikings', there was probably also settlement of Danes from across the Pennines: place-names ending in *-by*, ubiquitous in Yorkshire but quite absent in Scotland and Ireland, are found in Cumbria – but they are found also on the Isle of Man.[53]

The extent of Viking settlement and linguistic influence is not just to be measured in terms of place-names. Indeed, far more important (though much less geographically precise) is the influence of the Scandinavian languages themselves. In the Northern Isles and Caithness, for instance, the native language was totally replaced by Norwegian. The Norse dialects, known as 'Norn', were eventually replaced by Scots in the post-medieval period, but in the islands Norn was still spoken until the eighteenth century. In the Western Isles, where a variety of Norse may have been widely spoken, it was replaced by Gaelic rather than the Germanic Scots, and at a much earlier date, probably soon after Norwegian rule ended in the thirteenth century.

Perhaps the most interesting aspect of the linguistic inheritance of the Vikings is the impact which they had on the English language itself. That is strongest in local dialect, in those areas more heavily settled by the Vikings, such as Scotland and Yorkshire. Scandinavian words such as *laik* (to play) or *lait* (to search) survive in abundance. But the Scandinavian impact upon standard English was also considerable. Sometimes Old Norse simply supplied a second word, which happened to survive when the Old English one did not: thus, Chaucer still uses *ey* to mean 'egg', from OE *æg*, but our word comes from ON *egg*. Shakespeare's Corporal Nym comes from the OE word *nim*, 'to take' or 'to steal', but nowadays we use just the ON *taka*, 'to take'. Sometimes both words survive, sometimes with different meanings. Old Norse *angr* and Old English *wræþþ* give us 'anger' and 'wrath', while *illr* and *yfel*, which mean the same thing in ON and OE respectively, give us 'ill' and 'evil'. The word for a short garment in the two languages has come to us as *shirt* (from OE) and *skirt* (from ON). As can be seen, Old Norse has given us some of the most everyday words in the English language: others are bag, cake, dirt, fellow, knife, sister, skin, sky, or call, get, give, smile, and want. Even 'they', 'them' and 'their' are Scandinavian.[54] One of the explanations for this is that standard English derived in particular from London English, as one might expect, but that London English was heavily influenced in the later Middle Ages by the large number of immigrants from the East Midlands: that is, from the former Danelaw. Had standard English evolved from, say, the dialect of Dorset, the results might have been very different.

The distribution maps of archaeological material to a large extent confirms the same geographical patterns of settlement as the place-names, but such material is much less plentiful and just as difficult to interpret. If we take just those clearly Viking graves, for instance, where burials were made with grave-goods of typically Scandinavian type (and in a context where the native inhabitants of Britain had long since abandoned the idea of burial with grave-goods) we are left with a few dozen in Orkney and Shetland, some of the Hebrides (especially Oronsay, Colinsay and Islay) and above all on Man; but on the mainland of Britain, apart from northern Caithness, there are very few indeed. The total in northern England was in 1981 assessed at between five and eighteen, depending on how one regards the evidence (many of these graves were discovered in the nineteenth century and not published properly); the total in southern England is far less. (This is excluding the large numbers of burials dating from the Vikings' stay in Repton: see above p. 224.) Judging on Viking graves alone, one would hardly believe that there was any Scandinavian settlement in England. The usual argument used to explain this in fact suggests a situation opposite to that believed by many place-name experts: Scandinavians who settled were immediately influenced by the burial customs of those native to Britain. If place-names like Grimsby suggest that whole Scandinavian communities were founded in Britain, then the burials suggest that only in certain places, like the Isle of Man, did that happen. Indeed, some of the graves may well not represent settlement at all: the single warrior's grave at Sonning, just down the Thames from Reading, could have been dug by the garrison encamped temporarily at Reading in 870. The remarkable lack of burials with grave-goods, which are often (rashly) called 'pagan burials', may possibly indicate that conversion to Christianity was fairly rapid. But we cannot assume that all furnished burials were those of pagans; nor, indeed, that all pagan Vikings were buried with grave-goods. A recently excavated grave at Buckquoy (Orkney) has grave-goods, and is dated by a coin to the mid-tenth century or later; but that cannot be taken as evidence that it is pagan.[55]

Unfortunately, other forms of archaeological evidence are not easy to use as proof of Scandinavian settlement; we have already seen in this book (in relation to the Anglo-Saxon settlements) how difficult it is to detect ethnic identity from archaeological evidence. As we shall see in the next chapter, there has been a great deal of activity in York over the last thirty years to investigate 'Jorvik', or Viking York. The excavations are of considerable importance, and millions of tourists have seen the results at the Jorvik Viking Centre. There, one can take a 'time-car' and travel through a reconstruction of the 'Viking' houses. The people in the streets are talking Old Norse. But nothing discovered in the excavations tells us whether the people who lived in those houses, under the rule of Viking kings, were actually Scandinavian or English. The decision to represent the inhabitants as 'Viking' is based on an assumption about the density of Viking settlement, and perhaps about the propensity for Scandinavians to settle in towns, that really has no historical or archaeological evidence behind it.

Rather better evidence for the presence of Vikings in the kingdom of York comes from the Yorkshire countryside, in the surviving sculpture. Scandinavians did not have a tradition of sculpting monuments back in Scandinavia. There are plenty of stones with incised decoration, and runic inscriptions, particularly in Sweden; quite a few of the inscriptions in fact record the death of someone in Britain. Stone-carving was a well-developed form in England, however, and continued under the Vikings. What the surviving sculptures of northern England show is that sculptures were produced in the tenth and eleventh centuries following the taste of the Vikings: using the Viking art styles that were developed in Scandinavia, and placing pagan iconography on stones shaped in the form of Christian crosses, and taking sculpture out of its earlier monastic context, making it, perhaps, a way for the new elite to express its status. The most impressive example is probably the cross from Gosforth in Cumbria, a tall stone shaft with a cross on top, like the pre-Viking Ruthwell Cross, and (like Ruthwell) with the scene of the crucifixion, but in addition with several panels illustrating the Viking legend of Ragnarok, the violent death of the gods. The Sigurd legend can be found illustrated on crosses in both Yorkshire and the Isle of Man. There is nothing to prove that this sculpture was all produced for Scandinavian patrons: the prestige of the Vikings may have influenced Anglo-Saxon taste. And one can only speculate on what religious meaning such crosses had for those who created them, and for those who viewed them. Was Ragnarok equated with the Christian Apocalypse? Was Sigurd, the dragon-slayer, seen as a version of Christ, the victor over evil? Or was there a real resurgence of paganism in a land in which, around the year 900, the structures and authority of the Church must have been under serious threat?

10

From Vikings to Danes and Normans

The conquests of the West Saxon kings

At the time of the death of King Alfred, the kingdom of the West Saxons was bounded to the south by the Channel, and to the north by the Thames and the (Bristol) Avon. North of the Thames was Mercia, under the control of the man whom West Saxon sources consistently call 'ealdorman' Æthelred, but who was clearly regarded as king by the Mercians. The West Saxon title was presumably a reminder that he had accepted the overlordship of Alfred, his father-in-law, and his charters are all confirmed by Alfred. After Alfred's death, however, he and his wife issued charters without reference to Alfred's heir Edward. Other English 'ealdormen' survived too, independent of the Danes and of the West Saxons: Eadwulf of Bamburgh, whose territory ran all the way from the Tees to the Firth of Forth, and various others between the Pennines and the Irish Sea. The rest of England, the Danelaw, lived in only slightly less obscurity under various Scandinavian leaders.

King Edward, known as Edward the Elder (899–924), would eventually add the whole of England south of the Humber to his territory. His first war, however, was against his cousin Æthelwold, who at one time persuaded the Danish army of East Anglia to attack Mercia and Wessex on his behalf, and it was some time before he led his army against the Danes themselves. That is not to say that he was taking no action at all: Stenton pointed to two fascinating charters from 926, where Æthelstan (Edward's son) confirmed the possession by English landowners of property 'bought from the heathen at the command of King Edward and ealdorman Æthelred', in one case in Bedfordshire and the other in Derbyshire.[1] It was as if there was a surreptitious attempt to bring control on the ground back to the English. But it also suggests that relations with the Danes south of the Humber were not uncordial. That it was the power of the Northumbrian Danes that worried Edward is suggested by his first campaign, which was aimed against them, and which culminated in a major victory at Tettenhall in Staffordshire, in 910. The Northumbrian kings were killed there, and Northumbria was not able to intervene to help the Southern Danes in subsequent years; indeed, the weakened kingdom of Northumbria fell to a force of Vikings from Ireland in 919.

By 918, however, in just eight years of campaigning and fortress-building, Edward had conquered the south. One Viking stronghold after another was reduced, and the allegiance of Viking and Englishman assured. Nottingham and Lincoln were the last to submit. This major success was not a result of the efforts of Edward alone, however. In 911 his ally Æthelred of Mercia had died, and his widow Æthelflæd, with the highly unusual title of 'Lady of the Mercians'– *Æþelflæd Myrcna hlæfdige* – ruled the Mercians. She was Edward's sister, and seems to have been keen to support his endeavours, as she seems to have done even when her husband was alive, although it could well be that this policy suited Mercian aims too. We must certainly not assume that her power was due to her sisterly position. Throughout the ninth century queens in Mercia seem to have been quite prominent and powerful, while queens among the West Saxons seem deliberately to have been kept in obscurity.[2] She was one of a whole series of powerful queens, often widows acting as regents, in the late ninth and tenth centuries. She built ten fortresses in the few years after 911, and was strengthened enough by that to send expeditions against the Danes of the East Midlands, and into Brycheiniog in Wales. There she attacked Brecenanmere (the lake known as Llyn Syfadden in modern Welsh) in Wales, and captured the king's wife, who may well have been staying on the artificial island of Llangorse crannog, which excavation has revealed to be a high-status residence.[3]

Æthelflæd died in 918, at Tamworth. Edward immediately seized this royal site, and the Mercian aristocracy accepted Edward as their lord; the following year Edward ended the chances of Æthelflæd's daughter Ælfwynn becoming a rallying point for Mercians by taking her off forcibly to a nunnery in Wessex. Thereafter Mercia was fully a part of the West Saxon kingdom: as important a gain as the conquests over the Danes in the east. It was probably, however, the culmination of a long process, for even under Alfred the old rivalries may have come to be replaced, for some, by a sense of solidarity. As Simon Keynes has pointed out recently, Alfred's court had been 'crawling' with Mercians, notably the 'groupies and friends' of Alfred's wife Ealhswith; he suggests that the *Anglo-Saxon Chronicle* was not written from a narrowly West Saxon viewpoint in Alfred's reign, but in the knowledge that Mercia, Kent and Sussex were already within the West Saxon orbit.[4]

It is likely that Edward continued the garrisons that had been established in various fortified places under Æthelred and Æthelflæd: coins were struck at several of these places, such as Chester, Hereford, Oxford, Shrewsbury, Stafford, and Tamworth, which suggests that they may have been not only military centres, but places to which new settlers were being encouraged to move. It may have been Edward who at least began the major administrative organisation of Mercia which survives to this day in the shire structure. Shires had been in existence in Wessex before the Viking invasions: they were either remnants of earlier small kingdoms, or else territories dependent on an administrative centre (Dorset: Dorchester; Somerset: Somerton; Wiltshire: Wilton; Hampshire: (South)hamton). In western Mercia the shire division seems to cut across earlier divisions: this may have been deliberate policy, in a West Saxon bid to replace any earlier Mercian institutions around which Mercian opposition to West Saxon rule might coalesce. The shire divisions of what had been eastern Mercia, but which had been the Danelaw from the late ninth century, may well retain the military territories of the Danes: the county towns of Bedford, Cambridge, Huntingdon, Leicester and Northampton were all centres of operation for Viking armies.

Edward's rapidly won dominance in southern England soon extended itself westwards. Even under his father Alfred some Welsh princes had looked to the West Saxon king to protect them from their traditional Mercian enemies. Now three major Welsh kings, including those of Gwynedd and Dyfed, became Edward's men, and the *Chronicle* implies that other lesser Welsh kings followed them.

A new political situation had emerged in the north by the end of the 910s. A Viking leader called Ragnald attacked the Northumbrian coast in 915, and at Corbridge defeated forces led by Constantine, king of the Scots, and Ealdred, the Anglo-Saxon 'ealdorman' of Bernicia. In 918 Ragnald joined a large Viking fleet from Ireland and attacked again. The Scots and the English failed to dislodge him, and in 919 he took York, and declared himself king. His cousin Sihtric, with an army from Dublin, attacked north-west Mercia. Edward countered that menace, and then moved northwards; the result was recorded in what Stenton called 'one of the most famous passages in the whole *Anglo-Saxon Chronicle*':[5]

> Then he went from there [Nottingham] into the Peak District to Bakewell, and ordered a fortification to be built in the neighbourhood, and manned. And then the king of the Scots and all the people of the Scots, and Ragnald, and the sons of Eadwulf [including Ealdred] and all who live in Northumbria, both English and Danish, Norsemen and others, and also the king of the Strathclyde Welsh and all the Strathclyde Welsh, chose him as father and lord.[6]

As Stenton pointed out, each of these rulers was in an insecure position; some pledge of protection from the man who was clearly the most formidable warrior-king in Britain was welcome. We have no idea of what promises were given, nor do we know whether any of the northern rulers would actually have agreed with the description of the occasion in the *Chronicle*. For Edward it hardly mattered that there was no reality in this position of preeminence within Britain; but as a propaganda coup it was unprecedented. No previous English king had been accorded such a dominant position.

Edward died near the River Dee in 924, in the course of a campaign against the men of Chester, who had rebelled against him together with their Welsh allies: at least a part of Mercia was not prepared to accept his rule. But things seemed to change after his death. His eldest son, Æthelstan, had been brought up in Mercia, at the court of Æthelred and Æthelflæd, and he may even have been recognised as king there before his father died. His Mercian experience may be significant; it may have given him a stronger base than Edward had for a move on the North. He does seem to have been interested in fostering unity among those whom the West Saxons had conquered in the south. A charter of 931, for instance, has among the witnesses, present along with the king in Devon, seven men with Scandinavian names: 'there is little doubt,' wrote Stenton optimistically, 'that they were the successors of the earls who had led the Danish armies of eastern England in the time of Edward the Elder.'[7] Æthelstan moved quickly in the north. Ragnald had died in 921, being replaced by his cousin Sihtric. Sihtric proposed an alliance with Æthelstan, and married his sister at Tamworth in 926. But Sihtric died the following year, and Guthfrith, the Viking king of Dublin, came over to support Sihtric's young son Olaf. Æthelstan attacked, and drove first Olaf and then Guthfrith back to Ireland. The West Saxon forces took York, and destroyed the fortifications that the Vikings had built there. But before this there was another historic meeting, by which he confirmed the dominant position that Edward had established. The meeting was at Eamont, near Penrith (Cumbria), in territory that might have been thought to belong to the king of Strathclyde. The *Chronicle* again:

> In this year appeared fiery lights in the northern quarter of the sky, and Sihtric died, and King Æthelstan succeeded to the kingdom of the Northumbrians; and he brought under his rule all the kings who were in this island: first, Hywel, king of the West Welsh, and Constantine, king of the Scots, and Owain, king of the people of Gwent, and Ealdred, son of Eadwulf from Bamburgh. And they established peace with pledge and oaths in the place which is called Eamont, on 12 July [927], and renounced all idolatry, and afterwards departed in peace.[8]

There are all sorts of problems raised in this text (as in most texts relating to the poorly documented reigns of Edward and Æthelstan). Was Hywel really king of the 'West Welsh', by which name the English referred to the Cornish, or was he Hywel of Dyfed? Why is the king of Strathclyde not mentioned, or is Owain of Gwent in fact Owain of Strathclyde? What is this 'idolatry'? Is it the remnants of Viking paganism, or is it a vague word, by which the Chronicler can make a generalised point about the religious superiority of the West Saxons?

There is certainly evidence that close relations with Wales continued under Æthelstan. The Welsh kings met him at Hereford, and agreed on a yearly tribute of hounds, hawks, oxen, gold and silver, and settled the southern boundary at the River Wye. Welsh princes stayed with the king, and witnessed his charters. The most powerful of the Welsh kings – Hywel of Dyfed (Hywel Dda, the Good) – was, to the dismay of modern nationalists, positively Anglophilic. He apparently had an English penny minted in his name: the sole surviving example came from the English mint at Chester (coins not being minted in Wales itself until after the Norman Conquest of England); he gave one of his sons an English name Edwin.[9] And it was possibly following the English model that he caused a law-book to be issued which bears his name: even though the manuscripts that survive have all been added to at later stages, there may be elements from Hywel's day. He had a law-book with his name on it, as Alfred did; but the differences actually suggest a good deal about the differences between Welsh law and Anglo-Saxon law. Anglo-Saxon kings issued laws, with the consent of their council. Hywel's law, like the law-books that survive from Ireland, is not royal law; it is actually put together by lawmen.

Æthelstan's reign was crucial for another area of Britain too. The south-west – the modern counties of Devon and Cornwall – is an area whose history is very hazy in the early Middle Ages. There is a good deal of hagiography, and later tradition about the kings, but none of that is reliable as history; mostly we have to write the history of the south-west in terms of what its English conquerors were doing. The place-names show clearly the distinctions in the peninsula: the names of central and western Cornwall are very largely Celtic in character, while those of Devon are almost entirely English. Most of Devon seems securely in West Saxon hands by the end of the seventh century, and King Ine's wars against the Cornish king Gereint enable the West Saxon king to grant some land west of the River Tamar (and thus in Cornwall) to the monastery of Glastonbury. No further West Saxon king is known to have disposed of Cornish land until Ecgberht (802–39).[10] We know of three battles against the Cornish in his reign, each of which resulted in a Cornish defeat. The Cornish preserved their independent dynasty, however. The *Welsh Annals* refer to a King Dungarth of the Cerniu (a later manuscript adds 'that is, Cornwall'), who was drowned in 875; he may be the Doniert who set up a monument near Liskeard in Cornwall. No later Cornish kings are known for certain, although a tenth-century cross, now in Penzance, seems to refer to a King Riocatus.[11] It is possible that the 'Hywel of the West Welsh' referred to as offering submission to Æthelstan in the last quotation from the *Anglo-Saxon Chronicle* was not actually a king of the West Welsh (Cornish) at all. But it may be that the tradition related by William of Malmesbury (*c.* 1125) was based on fact: that it was Æthelstan who was responsible for eliminating Cornish independence. William also said that the king 'cleansed that city [Exeter] by purging it of that vile people';[12] although Exeter had been West Saxon since the seventh century it is possible that there had been a Cornish community in the town. In 936 Æthelstan appointed Bishop Conan of Crediton (himself possibly a Cornishman, judging by his name) to be 'Abbot of St German', with episcopal responsibility for Cornwall; St Germans was raised to the status of a bishopric by Æthelred II in 994.

Possibly the most significant event of Æthelstan's fifteen-year reign (924–39) was the battle of *Brunanburh*. Although the site of this battle is unknown, it is usually assumed to have taken place in northern England, because of the later tradition that it occurred as a result of a northern invasion. Olaf, the son of Guthfrith, whom Æthelstan had expelled from York in 927, assembled a massive fleet in Ireland, joined with the kings of Strathclyde and Scotland, and invaded Northumbria. The only real source for the battle is an Old English poem, incorporated into the *Anglo-Saxon Chronicle*'s record for 937. It tells how Edward's sons, Æthelstan and his brother Edmund ætheling,

> clove the shield-wall, hewed the linden-wood shields with hammered swords, for it was natural to men of their lineage to defend their land, their treasure, and their homes, in frequent battle against every foe.[13]

The battle ended, we are told, with five kings and seven of Olaf's earls dead on the battlefield. The aged Constantine of the Scots lost his young son.

> Never yet in this island before this, by what books tell us and our ancient sages, was a greater slaughter of a host made by the edge of the sword, since the Angles and Saxons came hither from the east, invading Britain over the broad seas, and the proud assailants, warriors eager for glory, overcame the Britons and won a country.[14]

It set the seal on what Æthelstan had been claiming for some time, that he was 'King of the English, raised to the throne of the kingdom of Britain by the right hand of the Almighty'. On one of his coins he is 'king of Britain'. In the charters issued by the king, there is a good deal of repetition of formulae, and many of them are composed in the same very elaborate and high-flown Latin, using grandiloquent words for the king's own position, including *basileus* and *imperator* (words used in Greek and Latin of an Emperor). Æthelstan undoubtedly had a clerical staff who travelled with him, who produced these documents: the business of issuing charters was now the business of the donor rather than (as in the earliest days of the charter in England) that of the recipient. But a private document from Winchester calls him *Angelsaxonum Denorumque gloriosissimus rex*, 'most glorious king of the Anglo-Saxons and Danes': interesting for its recognition of Danish separateness, but also for one of the earliest appearances of the word 'Anglo-Saxon' in Britain.[15] That his titles were no mere propaganda is suggested by the high-flown phrases used of him abroad: to a Frank he 'excelled in fame and praise all earthly kings of modern times',[16] and to an Irish monk he was 'the pillar of the dignity of the western world'.[17]

Æthelstan also showed his status in his dealings with Continental kings. His predecessors had already established significant marriage arrangements:

Alfred's daughter Ælfthryth married the count of Flanders, and Edward the Elder married his daughter Eadgifu to Charles III ('the Simple'), the Carolingian king of West Francia. When Charles was captured and imprisoned by his enemies, Æthelstan welcomed his son Louis to England: eventually Louis did return to France in 936, as Louis IV, and thus gained his nickname of 'd'Outremer': Louis 'from beyond the sea'. It was presumably in an attempt to forestall any such return that Charles's captor, Hugh, Duke of the Franks (ancestor of the Capetian dynasty which was to replace the Carolingians in 987), sent a mission to Æthelstan in 926 (led by the son of Baldwin of Flanders and Ælfthryth of Wessex). The presents he sent were magnificent, including (it is said by the historian William of Malmesbury or his source), the sword of Constantine the Great (which had a nail from Christ's cross in the hilt), the lance of Charlemagne (which had once been the lance which had pierced Christ's side), and various other relics, including pieces of the Holy Cross and the crown of thorns.[18] The mission returned with agreement for a marriage alliance between Hugh and Æthelstan's sister Eadhild. Soon after the other great monarch of Europe, Henry the Fowler of Germany, made similar overtures: his son Otto – one day Emperor Otto the Great – married Æthelstan's sister Edith.

Such alliances could set up links which would last a long time. The Latin version of the *Anglo-Saxon Chronicle*, written in the eleventh century by a noble layman, Æthelweard, was written for the abbess of Essen, the granddaughter of Otto and Edith. Ecclesiastical links might be an outcome of such marriages, too: Ælfthryth, Alfred's daughter, gave her estate at Lewisham to an abbey in Ghent. And these alliances even resulted in military involvement. The first time an English monarch lent military aid to a continental ally was in 939, when Otto invaded Lotharingia, and Æthelstan sent a fleet which was intended to help Louis IV (but which totally failed to do so). Æthelstan also established links with Brittany, by helping Alan the Great win back his counties from the ever-encroaching power of the Vikings in northern France. He even established the first diplomatic relations with Norway, then ruled by Harald Finehair, and when in York he was presented with a Norwegian warship. Later Norse tradition called Harald's son Håkon *Athalsteins fóstri*, Æthelstan's foster-son: there is really no reason to doubt that Harald wanted to give his son an education at the court of one of the few European kings to rival himself in ambition.

Æthelstan died in 939 and was succeeded by his eighteen-year-old brother Edmund. The battle of Brunanburh was revealed not to have been such a watershed as the *Anglo-Saxon Chronicle* had implied. Olaf Guthfrithsson came again from Dublin, retook York in 939, and, after attacking Northampton and Tamworth in 940, won by treaty the four northernmost shires of the former Danelaw: Leicester, Derby, Nottingham and Lincoln. Olaf died the following year, after sending an army into Anglian Northumbria as far north as Dunbar, and was succeeded by his cousin Olaf Sihtricson. This Olaf soon lost the four shires – a contemporary

English poem preserved in the *Chronicle* puts it in terms of the Danes being liberated from the oppression of the Norwegians of York – and he and his rival Ragnald Guthfrithson were both baptised at Edmund's court, and soon afterwards both expelled from the north. Edmund acted swiftly to restore his lost reputation. He allied with the new king of the Scots, Malcolm, and attacked what the *Chronicle* calls *Cumbraland*: the land of the Cymry, or Britons: possibly not just what is now Cumbria, but also further north, into the kingdom of Strathclyde. Edmund gave this land to the king of the Scots, in return for his alliance. Even though the king of Strathclyde soon returned to his kingdom, it is an interesting recognition of the boundaries of English ambition, and that the king of the Scots was more useful as an ally than as a target for conquest.

The last chapter in the history of Viking England was played out in the reign of the last of Edward's sons, Eadred, who succeeded after Edmund's murder (he was apparently stabbed by the accused party during a legal case) in 946. Harald Finehair's son Eiríkr had been driven from his Norwegian throne by his brother Håkon, Æthelstan's foster-son. Eiríkr, whose image still does valiant publicity work for the York Archaeological Trust as 'Eric Blood-Axe', landed in Northumbria, and was acclaimed by the Norse there as king. Eadred had some problems dislodging him; the situation in the North was confused by the continuing attempts of Olaf Sihtricson to reestablish himself in York. It is possible that it was this rivalry which ended Eiríkr's power in the North; whatever the details, Eadred emerged as king in York again by 954. With hindsight we know Eiríkr to be the last Viking to have a kingdom in England in the tenth century, but Eadred himself was by no means sure. In his surviving Old English will, his largest bequest was 1600 pounds 'for the redemption of his soul and the benefit of his people that they may redeem themselves from famine and from a heathen army if they need'.[19]

The conquests of the Scottish kings

It was not just the West Saxon dynasty that was able ultimately to benefit from the turmoil introduced into political relationships in Britain by the arrival of the Vikings. We have already seen how the unification of Picts and Scots, in the name of the Scottish dynasty of Dál Riata, may have been a consequence of Viking raiding. The Scottish kings extended their power further in the course of the ninth and tenth centuries, following in the wake of the Vikings.

Their first advance was a crucial one, even if it is difficult to discern. As we have seen (above, p. 221), in 870–1 the Viking leaders Ívarr and Oláfr had besieged the fortification of Dumbarton, the ancient seat of the British kings of Strathclyde, and led back large numbers of captives to Dublin. The king survived, though some time later he was killed on the insistence of King

Constantine of the Scots (son of Cináed mac Alpín). Alfred Smyth argues that Eochaid, king of the Britons of Strathclyde, who was expelled in 889, was the last king of his dynasty, and the last Briton to rule Strathclyde.[20] A much later Welsh source places, sometime in the late ninth century, the story that those Strathclyde Britons who refused to submit came south and sought exile in Gwynedd. The kingdom of Strathclyde continued into the tenth century, but as a Scottish sub-kingdom, always subordinate to the kings of the Scots. It may be that on more than one occasion it was the heir of the Scottish kingdom who held the Strathclyde kingdom (rather as heirs to the throne of the United Kingdom today are Princes of Wales), but some of the dynastic struggles of the later tenth and early eleventh centuries were perhaps caused by those who did not accept this system – who wanted to succeed to the larger kingship earlier, or who wanted to set up a rival dynasty.

Strathclyde had long been a rival of the Scottish kings; but so had the English in the south of Scotland. The collapse of the Northumbrian kingdom in the face of Viking attack, and the problems of the Viking kings of York, led to the gradual extension of Scottish suzerainty in the south. It seems that Strathclyde was able to extend its control into Galloway and Cumbria, and that in the east the Scottish kings whittled away at the power of the Angles, who for a while were represented by the independent kings or ealdormen of Bamburgh. On more than one occasion the ealdorman of Bamburgh relied on Scottish help in defending Bernicia against the Danes; it may be that he became subordinate to the Scots early in the tenth century. Scottish kings are also taking direct action in 'England'. Malcolm I was raiding in England as far south as the Tees in 949, and around the time that Eric Bloodaxe was expelled from York. In 954, the Scottish king took Edinburgh from the Angles. According to a later Durham tradition, King Edgar of the English ceded Lothian to Cináed II (presumably in 973). The process culminated in the battle of Carham in 1018, near the Tweed, when Malcolm II of Scotland defeated the Northumbrians under their earl Uhtred. Two centuries earlier, it was the land on either side of the Firth of Forth which was in dispute between the English and the kings in the north; after the battle of Carham the territory in dispute had shifted much further south, to between the Tyne and the Tweed, or even the Tees and the Tweed. One consequence of the victory of the West Saxon dynasty was thus a displacement of royal centres of power from the north, leaving a vacuum into which energetic and ambitious Scottish kings could easily insert themselves.

The English kings of the later tenth century

One must not exaggerate the degree of unity which England had achieved by the eleventh century. On Eadred's death in 955, the West Saxons, Mercians and Northumbrians separately chose the young Eadwig as king.

In 957 the Mercians and Northumbrians changed their minds, in favour of Eadwig's younger brother Edgar (then only fourteen years old). When Eadwig died in 959, the kingdom reunited again – but it would be wrong to think that such a reunification was inevitable. Both English and French history have usually been written in hindsight, from the standpoint that a unified kingdom was ordained, inevitable and (for some reason) desirable. But it was not impossible that, had Eadwig survived, the kingdom of England would have fallen apart into its constituent regions, as, by that time, the French kingdom of the Carolingians had done. The division between north and south was revived again in 1016 and perhaps envisaged again in 1035; the loyalty of those north of the Humber to the government of Winchester and, later, Westminster, remained suspect long beyond William the Conqueror's brutal suppression of the 1069 revolt – and northern resentment at a southern-based government has remained a factor in English political and social history down to at least 2000.

What was astonishing about the generation after 955 was that between that time and 980, when Viking forces sacked Southampton and ravaged both Thanet and Cheshire, there was no mention of the major theme of the *Chronicle*: war. On the face of it England was content under West Saxon rule, and England's neighbours remained at peace. Those who wrote about Edgar after his death, and after the renewed attacks of the Vikings, saw Edgar's reign as idyllic compared to that of his son Æthelred 'the Unready'. The one secular event for which Edgar is remembered is his so-called 'delayed' coronation of 973. He was crowned at the great Roman site of Bath, and anointed by St Dunstan, the archbishop of Canterbury, in a carefully scripted religious ceremony: it was possibly no accident that the ceremony took place when he became thirty, the age at which Christ began his mission, and at which a man could proceed to the priesthood. It is rather unlikely, however, that he had been reigning for so long without the benefit of coronation: the occasion of 973 was probably just one of his regular crown-wearings.[21] Ælfric, abbot of Eynsham, records that all eight kings in Britain came to acknowledge his supremacy, and three manuscripts of the *Chronicle* record that he sailed to Chester, where six kings pledged to support him 'by sea and land' (the same phrase used of the agreement between Edmund and Malcolm of the Scots, thirty years earlier). The chronicler known usually as Florence of Worcester (early twelfth century) says that these kings rowed Edgar on the River Dee, and named them as Kenneth, king of the Scots, Malcolm, king of the Cumbrians (Strathclyde), Maccus, 'king of many islands', Dufnal, Sifeth, Huwel, Jacob and Juchil. As Stenton noted, this is too accurate for Florence not to have got the information from a reasonably reliable source, because all those kings were contemporaries of each other in 973.[22] Kenneth had become king of the Scots in 971; Dufnal was Dunmail, king of Strathclyde, who was succeeded by his son Malcolm when he was on pilgrimage to Rome in 975; Maccus was a king in the Scottish Isles; Jacob was Iago, king of Gwynedd (950–79); and Hywel was Iago's relative and rival.

Edgar's relations with his neighbours seem to have been good; those with his foreign subjects were also conducted with tact. A lawcode survives which he issued at a certain *Wihtbordesstan*, in 962/3, where he set down his philosophy of law.

> It is my will that secular rights be in force in every province, as good as they can best be devised, to the satisfaction of God, and for my full royal dignity and for the benefit and security of poor and rich; and that I have in every borough and in every shire the rights belonging to my royal dignity, as my father had; and my thegns are to have their dignity in my time as they had in my father's. And it is my will that secular rights be in force among the Danes according to as good laws as they can best decide on. Among the English, however, that is to be in force which I and my councillors have added to the decrees of my ancestors, for the benefit of all the nation.[23]

He goes on to say that a system of sureties and witnesses, to avoid the sale of stolen goods, should be set up in 'all the nation, whether Englishmen, Danes, or Britons', which is an interesting recognition of the multi-ethnic basis of the 'nation'. But the reference to the Danes in the paragraph above is even more interesting: it recognises that the Danes in what was now being called the Danelaw should decide on what law they should live by just as they had, presumably, before the West Saxon conquest. This promise of autonomy probably did more than anything else to ensure peace within the kingdom.

Three manuscripts of the *Anglo-Saxon Chronicle*, at 959, in a passage which is obviously not contemporary, sum up Edgar's reign.

> He improved the peace of the peoples more than the kings who were before him in the memory of man. And God also supported him so that kings and earls willingly submitted to him and were subjected to whatever he wished. And without battle he brought under his sway all that he wished. ... [He] continually and frequently directed all his people wisely in matters of church and state. Yet he did one ill deed too many: he loved evil foreign customs and brought too firmly heathen manners within this land, and attracted hither foreigners and enticed harmful people to this country.[24]

It is possible that this refers to his relations with Scandinavians, and was written after the renewed attacks of the 980s; perhaps it is intended to suggest that the downfall of the dynasty of Alfred began with Edgar.

Edgar died in 975. By an early marriage he had had a young son called Edward; by a later marriage, with Ælfthryth (who had been associated with him as queen in the 973 ceremonies), he had a son called Æthelred, probably no more than ten in 975. Edward became king. What little is known about him comes from a later age which regarded him as a martyr and a saint; but even in that tradition it is said that he was subject to violent rages.

No doubt he had his political troubles, for a faction would inevitably have grown up around his step-mother Ælfthryth. Just like any fairy-tale step-mother, she invited him to stay with her and the young Æthelred, at Corfe in Dorset, and there, in 978, he was murdered. The earliest accounts of the murder, some thirty years after the event, accuse the retainers of his half-brother Æthelred, who met him, seized him, and stabbed him; a century later come the first accusations aimed at Queen Ælfthryth. Whoever was responsible, no-one was ever punished. Edward the Martyr's body ended up in the nunnery at Shaftesbury, and miracles began to take place. It was not an auspicious beginning for the reign of his young half-brother Æthelred. It shows the strength of the traditional West Saxon dynasty that an under-age boy should be accepted as king (a very rare occurrence in Anglo-Saxon politics), but one might wonder whether it was really such a good idea.

The tenth-century Reformation

The history of the Church is the history of one reform movement after another, each in vain trying to recreate the presumed ideals of an earlier era. What has come to be known as the 'tenth-century Reformation' had little or nothing in common with Luther's, except in its determination to return to that mythical past. The Church had suffered even more than other institutions from the Viking attacks of the ninth century, and the growing stability of the tenth century was an occasion for a re-establishment, but also of renewal. The Church that was recreated, above all under King Edgar, was obviously not the same as the pre-Viking Church: it could not be. It was a new kind of Church, with a new kind of monasticism, which very much followed the lead of the Frankish Church.

We have also already seen how in the eighth century Anglo-Saxon churchmen like Boniface and Alcuin were at the forefront of ecclesiastical reform in the Frankish Church. Those reforms were aimed partly at bringing the Church back to the norms of canon law and removing the influence of the lay aristocracy, and partly at restoring the spiritual life of the Church, through a renewed emphasis on monastic ideals, on education and on scholarship. There was also a greater centralisation, centred on the figure of the Carolingian ruler, particularly after the restoration of the title of Emperor in 800, and on the Pope. Liturgical forms were introduced from Rome, and imposed on the whole Empire; a monastic uniformity was also imposed, based on the monastic Rule whose cause had been taken up by Pope Gregory the Great in the sixth century – that of St Benedict of Nursia. Charlemagne's son Louis the Pious had been king of Aquitaine before becoming Emperor in 814; he and his advisor St Benedict of Aniane had made the *Rule of St Benedict of Nursia* the sole rule to be used in Aquitanian monasteries, and in a series of reforming councils after 814 the Carolingian Church accepted that Benedictine monasticism should become standard in all the Empire's monasteries. It was not necessarily the *Rule* that Benedict himself would have recognised: the liturgy was more important in the life of the monk than in Benedict's *Rule*, for instance, and manual work less. But the reform was important in terms of centralisation, and also control: no longer did individual abbots have the freedom to devise their own ways of life for their monks.

The second phase of reform on the Continent came after the collapse of the Carolingian Empire into various kingdoms and numerous independent duchies and counties. Reforming ideals were kept alive, but they needed a new focus, which was not dependent on a weakened monarchy, and which, indeed, did not necessarily place monasteries under the control of any lay powers. Various reformed monasteries were founded, notably in two areas of considerable political fragmentation, Burgundy and Lotharingia. The most important of these was undoubtedly Cluny, founded in Burgundy by Duke William of Aquitaine, and placed by him under papal protection. Berno was the first abbot, but it was the second abbot, Odo (927–42), who established Cluny as a major centre of reform, thanks largely to his own international stature. Other important monasteries were Brogne (near Namur), founded by St Gerard, from which St Peter's in Ghent was reformed, and Gorze, a decayed monastery near Metz, put on its feet again by John. These monasteries were not under the control of any individual aristocratic family, and that was no doubt a reason for their success: numerous different aristocratic families were happy to donate land and wealth, reasonably secure in the knowledge that it would not be used for secular aristocratic purposes.

To some extent England had experienced the initial phase of reform. Bede's *Letter to Egbert*, and various letters written from the Continent by men like Boniface and Alcuin, show the desire in clerical circles for a reform of ecclesiastical, and specifically monastic, life in England. There were a number of reforming councils, such as Clovesho in 747, and the councils connected with the visit of the papal legates in 786. Some progress may well have been made, but the disruption brought by the Vikings, both of the church itself and of the survival of the Church's records, make it difficult to be certain. In his Preface to the Old English translation of Gregory the Great's *Pastoral Care*, King Alfred lamented the state of Church life in his day, above all its learning, in comparison to the great days of the past. Interestingly, he does not at first blame the Vikings, but just 'decay': indeed, the Viking invasions were 'punishments' sent by God *because* the English had allowed learning to decay.

> So completely had learning decayed in England that there were very few men on this side of the Humber who could [. . .] translate a letter from Latin into English, and I think there were not many beyond the Humber. There were so few of them that I cannot even recollect a single one south of the Thames when I succeeded to the kingdom. [. . .]

> Remember what temporal punishments came upon us, when we neither loved wisdom ourselves nor allowed it to other men; we possessed only the name of Christians, and very few possessed the virtues. When I remembered all this, I remembered also how, before everything was ravaged and burnt, the churches throughout all England stood filled with treasures and books, and likewise there was a great multitude of the servants of God. And they had very little benefit from those books, for they could not understand anything in them, because they were not written in their own language.[25]

Bishop Asser, whose help Alfred acknowledges in that Preface, himself comments interestingly on the state of monastic life.

> For many years past the desire for the monastic life had been totally lacking in that entire race (and in a good many other peoples as well!), even though quite a number of monasteries which had been built in that area still remain but do not maintain the rule of monastic life in any consistent way. I am not sure why: either it is because of the depredations of foreign enemies whose attacks by land and sea are very frequent and savage, or else because of the people's enormous abundance of riches of every kind, as a result of which (I suspect) this kind of monastic life came all the more into disrespect.[26]

There are many such complaints about the state of the Church, not just from the ninth century, but from the tenth and eleventh centuries as well. After 1066, English writers blame the Conquest on God's wrath for the state of the Church, just as Alfred was blaming the Vikings on exactly the same thing. In many cases it is just a question of changing ideals: the expectations of the lifestyle of the clergy were changing throughout the tenth and eleventh centuries. Thus we read Bishop Æthelwold, in the later tenth century, talking about Edgar.

> He cleansed holy places from all men's foulnesses, not only in the kingdom of the West Saxons, but in the land of the Mercians also. Assuredly he drove out canons who abounded beyond measure in the aforesaid sins, and he established monks in the foremost places of all his dominion for the glorious service of the Saviour Christ (. . .) he was himself ever enquiring about the welfare of the monks, and he kindly exhorted her [Queen Ælfthryth] to take thought for the nuns in the same way.[27]

Much suffering can be visited on harmless victims by reforming zealots whose values are not those of a former age. 'Men's foulnesses' presumably refers to the married life of clergy; henceforth celibacy was to be demanded from all clerics.

Alfred's complaints about the Church were no doubt justified to some extent, however. Undoubtedly the Vikings had wrought considerable destruction (or, if one prefers, had completed the process of decay that had been there when they arrived). All the great monasteries in Northumbria come to an end, save only St Aidan's monastery at Lindisfarne; and the history of that monastic community shows the problems faced by the Church under the Vikings. The monks had eventually decided to abandon Lindisfarne, its island site being indefensible from Viking attack, and they and the bishop of Lindisfarne traipsed around the north for years, carrying the sacred relics of St Cuthbert, before settling at Chester-le-Street, on the River Wear, in 883, and eventually moving upstream to the site of Durham in 995. As far as we know, no other monastic communities survived at all in the areas taken over by the Vikings.

More significant from the point of view of the health of the Church, many bishoprics did not survive either. Without bishoprics, it was difficult for the life of the Church to carry on at all. In the north, the archbishopric of York seems to have a continued existence, though perhaps not an unbroken one; the bishopric of Hexham disappears; so, south of the Humber, do the bishoprics of Dunwich, Elmham, Leicester, Lincoln, and possibly Lichfield. Under Edward and Æthelstan the two dioceses of Wessex were expanded into six. In 'English' Mercia, the dioceses of Worcester, Hereford, and possibly Lichfield, continued, but there were no new dioceses. In the Danelaw, for a long time the existing bishops of Dorchester and London coped with the whole area: Dorchester-on-Thames had once been within the diocese of Leicester, but the Danish takeover of that area caused the bishop of Leicester to flee south, and for a long time the bishopric of Dorchester extended effectively over the whole of the East Midlands from the Thames to the Humber. As Pauline Stafford had said, the history of the restoration of bishoprics in the first half of the tenth century is like the history of West Saxon royal control itself: 'closest and fullest south of the Thames, especially in Wessex, more careful and cautious in Mercia, a question more of aspiration than fact in eastern and northern England.'[28] When the Normans arrived in England in 1066, the distribution of bishoprics across the country still remained very uneven.

Even when bishops had survived, their incomes may have been seriously diminished. It seems that the archbishops of York were particularly severely hit, and to recompense them the archbishops had Nottinghamshire added to their diocese, and were given several large estates south of the Humber. But when St Oswald, bishop of Worcester, was translated to the archbishopric of York in 872, a new solution was found: he kept his see of Worcester together with York, and down to 1016 the two were always kept together, the rich Mercian see subsidising the income of the poor northern archbishopric.

The process known to historians now as the 'tenth-century Reformation', however, has much more to do with changes in monastic life than in episcopal organisation. There had been some attempt at a restoration of monastic life as early as the reign of Alfred. He founded a monastery at Athelney, though it is interesting to note that to fill it he had to import monks from abroad. Recruitment abroad continued as a practice in the tenth century: Æthelstan appointed the German Theodred as bishop of East Anglia, and in the documents he appears surrounded by clerics with German names.[29] There was considerable continental influence on the next generation of reformers too, though its extent and nature is in some dispute.

There is no doubt, however, about the most influential of the reformers. St Dunstan came from Somerset; his father had lands adjoining those of Glastonbury, which was a pilgrimage centre maintained by secular clergy rather than monks. Dunstan spent some time studying there, but went to court, like many young noblemen. Unlike most noblemen, he became a monk there, under the influence of Bishop Ælfheah of Winchester. According to his first biographer, he miraculously saved King Edmund's life, when staying at Cheddar Palace, and was thus appointed abbot of Glastonbury. He was at Glastonbury from around 940 to 956, and in this period reformed it as a Benedictine community. He was on very good terms with Edmund and Eadred, but was exiled briefly by Eadwig; according to the same text it was because he had remonstrated with the king for leaving his coronation banquet for a spot of lechery. Dunstan spent his exile at the monastery of St Peter's in Ghent, which had been reformed from Brogne. It is impossible to say how far he was influenced by the monastic practices he found there, but it is known that at some point in his life he took one small but crucial decision to change to a continental practice: he abandoned writing in the style in which he had been trained (known to palaeographers as insular minuscule) and took up the standard continental handwriting, known as Caroline minuscule after its origins at the time of Carolus Magnus (Charlemagne). Samples of his handwriting show that he did not write it very fluently, and he mixed in insular habits: 'in short, his is exactly the sort of script that a middle-aged English abbot might adopt as a result of a year's enforced furlough in Flanders.'[30] Careful study of his handwriting has also led to a suggestion by Mildred Budny about his role in the frontispiece for the Bodleian manuscript known as 'St Dunstan's Classbook'. This frontispiece has the tall figure of Christ, walking on clouds, and at his feet, a tiny figure of a monk abasing himself before the divine presence: an inscription reads 'I ask you, merciful Christ, to watch over me, Dunstan. May you not permit the Taenarian storms to swallow me.' The first line quotes from a poem by the ninth-century Frankish churchman Hrabanus Maurus; the second recalls a line from the classical poet Statius. The lines are written in Dunstan's hand, and he may have added some of the red lead decoration to the page; but Christ and the figure of the monk are by a different hand, and the inscription on the Christ figure can be identified as by the scribe who drew up one of Dunstan's charters.[31] The manuscript contains various Latin, Greek, Old Breton, Old Welsh and Old English texts, including book I of Ovid's *Ars Amatoria*, the only copy to survive from pre-Conquest Britain, and an Old English homily on 'The Finding of the True Cross'.

Together with the humble monk of the frontispiece, the whole gives the impression of a learned and pious monk: a figure on the face of it rather far removed from the powerful figure of the early *Lives* of St Dunstan, where we find 'a concept of episcopal sanctity which, while elevating asceticism as a virtue, stressed authority and proximity to the king.'[32]

When Dunstan was recalled by King Edgar he was given in rapid succession the sees of Worcester, then London, and then Canterbury. Even if he did not hold any two of these sees at once, for any length of time, Dunstan was still in breach of canon law, which forbade the translation of a bishop from one see to another. But for him and for Edgar, we may presume, it was monastic reform which had priority, not the niceties of Church law. Dunstan was archbishop of Canterbury from 960 to 988, and presided over some of the most sweeping changes to affect the English church between the conversion and the Protestant Reformation. But he was not alone in his reforming campaign. Within three years Edgar had handed over the most important sees of southern England to reformers: to Dunstan, Oswald and Æthelwold.

Oswald was the nephew of Oda, archbishop of Canterbury (941–58), who himself was the son of a Dane who had come over with Ívarr the Boneless (according to the *Life of St Oswald*). Oswald had trained at the monastery of Fleury, on the Loire, which was a magnet for all reformers not so much for its religious practices but for the fact that it housed the body of St Benedict of Nursia, whose Rule was at the heart of the reformers' programme.[33] (The monks of Fleury – now St-Benoit-sur-Loire – had stolen the body from Monte Cassino in the late seventh century, though the monks of Monte Cassino themselves denied that the theft had ever taken place.) Oswald was made bishop of Worcester in 961, and, as we have seen, became archbishop of York in 971, without giving up the see of Worcester: he died in 992.

Æthelwold was a young man at the court of Æthelstan, and then joined the household of Bishop Ælfheah of Winchester; he was ordained priest on the same day as Ælfheah's nephew Dunstan. He became a monk at Dunstan's abbey of Glastonbury, and wanted to leave in order to learn about reformed monasticism abroad, but was refused permission by the king. Instead he was given the abbacy of the run-down monastery of Abingdon, which he reformed with the help of monks from Glastonbury and Winchester – one of whom he sent to Fleury, to gain the knowledge that he had been denied. He was given the see of Winchester by Edgar in 963, and presided there for twenty-one years. After only one year, with the approval of Edgar and of the Pope, he expelled the cathedral clergy from Winchester, and replaced them with monks. Subsequently he reformed several monasteries, above all Peterborough, Ely and Thorney. He wrote flowery and obscure Latin, and clear Old English, and among his pupils was Ælfric, whose homilies and didactic works in Old English were one of the means by which the spiritual ideals of the Reformation could spread to the laity and to priests with no Latin. But for art historians his name lives on above all in the *Benedictional of St Æthelwold*, one of the finest and most elaborately decorated of all tenth-century illuminated manuscripts. It is a salutary reminder that a monastic revival was not, in the tenth century, an austere affair. One of the things that *twelfth*-century reformers most objected to in the reformed Benedictinism of the tenth and eleventh centuries was its delight in celebrating God with grandeur and lavishness, whether in architecture, sculpture, furnishings, liturgy or music.

Æthelwold himself was responsible for major building in Winchester: the reorganisation of the south-eastern corner of the area within the Roman walls as an ecclesiastical town. Walls were built to separate the three main monasteries: the Old Minster, the New Minster, and Nunnaminster. The Old Minster had been built in the seventh century, becoming the cathedral in the 660s, and was the burial-place of most of the West Saxon kings, up to Alfred. The New Minster and Nunnaminster ('the nuns' monastery') were founded by Edward the Elder, although they may have been planned by Alfred, and Nunnaminster seems to have been built on an estate belonging to Alfred's queen Ealhswith. The church of the New Minster was built just four metres north of that of the Old Minster: it was twice the size, and was the new resting place of the kings, or at least of Alfred and Edward. All three of these monasteries were reformed between 964 and 966, and building-works started not long afterwards. The Old Minster church was extended westwards, over the tomb of St Swithun, and a large west-work built up. This was a massive building several stories high where, perhaps (as in some German west-works) there was a throne from which the king could survey the entire church. The west-work was immediately opposite the royal palace, and could thus have served as the symbolic meeting-place between bishop and king, or 'church' and 'state'. Not to be outdone, in the following decade the New Minster also acquired a west tower: a description suggests that there were six storeys, each adorned with sculpture corresponding to the saint to which the internal chapel was dedicated. In the 990s, the Old Minster church was given an eastern extension as well.[34] To the east of these three monasteries, in the south-east corner of the Roman town, was the bishop's palace, which may have been begun by Æthelwold, and immediately to the west was the royal palace: altogether an impressive complex of buildings for what was the chief residence of one of the most powerful kings in Europe. But this is only one of the many projects of church building and restoration that was going on throughout southern England. None of the major buildings is now standing above ground: all England's cathedrals were replaced by the Normans in the first generations after the conquest of 1066. But some idea of the scale of late Anglo-Saxon buildings can be gained from surviving rural churches, such as St Mary's, Deerhurst (Gloucs), which still stands to a height of several storeys.[35]

The culmination of the reform process was the council held in Æthelwold's cathedral city in 973 which produced the document known as the *Regularis Concordia Anglicae nationis monachorum sanctimonialiumque*, 'an agreement on the way of life for the monks and nuns of the English nation'. It provided details about the liturgy for the monastic day and year and the duties of monastic officials, and ends with elaborate details for the ceremonies to be performed on the death of a monk. Many similarities can be traced with continental documents of this type from the ninth and tenth centuries, although, as Dom David Knowles noted, there are some purely English elements: a comment about heating during the winter, a concession to the national fondness for the pealing of church-bells, the idea that monastic processions will take place in the streets around the monastery and not just within the monastic enclosure, and the assumption that a lay congregation would take part at Mass on Sundays and at feasts.[36] More significantly, though, the *Regularis Concordia* emphasised the importance of the king and queen as patrons of English monasticism – prayers for the king and queen are specified throughout the liturgy – and laid down that in cathedrals served by a monastic clergy, the monks shall elect the bishop, and the bishop should live as a monk. The *Regularis Concordia* owed something to the reformed monasticism of the Continent in the tenth century, but perhaps even more to the early reform movement of Louis the Pious and Benedict of Aniane. One late tenth-century manuscript actually binds up the *Regularis Concordia* together with the Carolingian monastic legislation of 816–19.[37]

By the time of the Council of Winchester (near the end of Edgar's reign), the process of the 'monasticisation' of the English Church was already well under way. But it is not at all easy to know how far it had proceeded, or how lasting the effects of this 'reformation' were. At Winchester Æthelwold may have expelled the old clerks and replaced them with monks in direct and brutal fashion, but other cathedral communities, like Christ Church Canterbury, changed almost imperceptibly. Numerous monasteries were founded, but it is clear that despite the *Regularis Concordia*, many of them still continued to be regarded as 'family monasteries', and nephews succeed uncles as abbots or even as bishops. Peterborough was prospering, for instance, at the end of the Anglo-Saxon period: but its abbot was Leofric, the son of Leofric, earl of Mercia, who had donated much land to it, and the younger Leofric was also abbot of Burton, Crowland, Thorney and the elder Leofric's foundation of Coventry. It was the type of pluralism that would be much condemned by the Normans when they took over the Church in England. However, it has been estimated by Knowles that three-quarters of the bishops of the period 960 to 1066 were monks, and if one excludes the reign of Edward the Confessor (1042–65) the proportion would be nearer nine-tenths.[38] The flourishing of art and of Old English literature – almost all known literature in the vernacular probably comes from this last century of the Anglo-Saxon kingdom – can be seen as another sign of the success of the reformation, since most of it proceeded from the monasteries. The church building and the art was important not only in a cultural sense, of course; it was the direct result of the transfer of large amounts of landed wealth from lay into ecclesiastical hands. The propaganda of the Norman writers of the period after 1066, determined to judge the late Anglo-Saxon Church unfavourably, by using the even higher standards of the late eleventh and twelfth-century papal reformers, should not allow us to lose sight of the achievement of Dunstan and his colleagues.

The Danes in England

One of the most celebrated monuments of Denmark is a large triangular stone, a great beast on one side, with a figure of Christ bound to the cross on another, both in the Viking art-style known as Mammen. On the third side begins an inscription: 'King Harald ordered these monuments to be made after his father Gorm and his mother Thyra. It was this Harald who won for himself all Denmark and Norway and made the Danes Christian.'[39] The words 'and Norway' are inscribed separately, under the great beast, and the claim about conversion is placed under the figure of Christ. The stone is in central Jutland, at Jelling, and stands between two huge mounds, and next to another stone whose inscription reads 'King Gorm made these monuments in memory of his wife Thyra, Denmark's adornment.' One mound has been excavated: although the burial chamber was empty, it can be dated by dendrochronology to the year 958. It is possible that Harald, known as Harald Bluetooth, moved his father's body into the small church which he had built in between the Jelling stone and the burial mound. Denmark was much more politically centralised than either Norway or Sweden from as far back as the eighth century, and from the time of Harald the kings began to have ambitions that took them beyond Denmark itself. Harald's conversion to Christianity was possibly part of this attempt to emulate other powerful kings of Europe.

Denmark was made up of four main territories: the peninsula of Jutland (separated from Germany since the mid-eighth century by the great earthworks known as the Danevirke), the islands of Fyn and Sjælland, and Skåne, the latter of which became only after 1648 the southern province of the kingdom of Sweden. Harald has left impressive traces of his attempt to weld these provinces into a united kingdom in the shape of five fortresses, all built on the same careful geometric plan: two on Jutland, one on Fyn, and one each – both called Trelleborg – on Sjælland and in Skåne. It used to be thought that these had been built as part of the preparations for the invasion of England by Harald's son Swein Forkbeard, but we know from dendrochronological analysis that the timbers for Trelleborg in Sjælland were cut between September 980 and May 981, some years before Harald's death in 987. What the fortresses do show, however, is that Denmark has for the first time emerged as a political entity which could challenge neighbouring kingdoms. Harald became king of Norway in the late tenth century, and twice attacked Germany, under its powerful Ottonian rulers; Swein (or, variously, Sven, Svein, Sweyn, Swegn, Swegen) and Cnut (Knútr, Knut, Canute) became kings of England in the early eleventh century.

Viking raids on England began again in 980, five years after the death of Edgar, and during the long reign of Æthelred II, more generally known as Æthelred the Unready. His reputation has no doubt suffered because of the tenor of the account in the *Anglo-Saxon Chronicle*, which was probably often drafted with the help of hindsight.[40] It is all very well to point out that Unræd means 'poorly advised' rather than 'unready', but the poor advice was in part a result of some disastrous appointments by Æthelred of advisers and generals. In other respects, however, he did his best. His policy of appeasement by paying large sums of money to marauding Danes was perhaps not advisable (although it was possibly cheaper than putting together a large enough army to fight them).[41] But this was not his only policy. He used diplomacy and bribery to divide his enemies and recruit allies, persuading the young Olaf Tryggvason of Norway to join with him in 994, and in 1012 recruiting Thorkell the Tall, with forty-five ships, to his side. Archaeology suggests that from the 990s he was refurbishing defences, and building new fortifications, and in 1008 he parcelled up his kingdom into naval districts, called 'ship-sokes', in an effort to provide a proper financial support for the English navy.[42] It is possible that weak government may have attracted the Danes to England; so may the increasing costs of royal government in Scandinavia, no longer supported by the influx of silver from Russia and the Abbasid caliphate. But these were no longer the relatively small-scale tentative attacks which began the 'first Viking period'. These were large expeditions, with royal leaders, and the leaders soon learnt that extorting money was easier and more profitable than seeking booty in piecemeal fashion. The amounts paid in what became known as 'Danegeld' soon rose, from 4,500 kg of silver in 991, to 11,000 kg in 1002 and 22,000 kg in 1012. These are huge amounts of bullion: to relate it to the actual coinage, the 50,000 Anglo-Saxon pennies of this period which have been found on the Baltic island of Gotland would weigh some seventy kg, while the 22,000 kg paid over in 1012 could have been minted into over fifteen million silver pennies. The taxation system needed to cope with raising these sums was advanced compared to anywhere else in Europe at the time: it could be argued that the power and wealth of the English kings in the late eleventh century was largely a result of the taxation system that Danegeld had forced on the kingdom. But the kingdom was also wealthy enough to sustain such a taxation system.

> It was the wealth of England, not the inadequacy of the English defences, that tempted so many continental adventurers to come here in search of loot and tribute. England was rich and the English people were ready to pay large sums of tribute for the sake of peace.[43]

Sawyer argued that it was England's wool production that brought England its wealth, and notes that the proliferation of towns and mints show the exceptional nature of England's economic strength: he suggests that ten per cent of England's population lived in towns in 1066, a high proportion, perhaps even exceeding that of the late fourteenth century.

The most active and experienced of the leaders of Scandinavian expeditions to England during Æthelred's reign was Harald's son Swein Forkbeard. After various highly profitable expeditions, Swein decided to conquer England: he did so in a rapid campaign in 1013, forcing Æthelred into exile with his in-laws in Normandy. Swein died the following year. His son Cnut was chosen as king of England by the Danish fleet, but it took him two years to establish himself against Æthelred (who died in April 1016) and against Æthelred's son Edmund II Ironside (who died in November of the same year). In 1015 the West Saxons submitted temporarily to Cnut; in 1016 the Northumbrians submitted to him and in October 1016 Cnut defeated Edmund at *Assandun* and a treaty was agreed which gave England north of the Thames to him, reserving the south for Edmund. After Edmund's death, a matter of days later, Cnut was the unopposed king of the English: it was in Denmark and Norway that he had to face opposition. At the height of his power Cnut had established a wide-ranging territory for which there was no precedent in northern Europe. In 1027 the claim was made that he was *rex totius Angliae et Denemarchiae et Norreganorum et partis Suanorum*, 'king of the whole of England and Denmark and Norway and of parts of Sweden'. Cnut may have been the last great Viking, but he was also to initiate a political pattern which was to become familiar to the English in the course of later centuries: a king who maintained a close interest in his territories abroad. He wintered in Denmark in 1019/20, in 1022/23 (probably), in 1025–26 and in 1026/27; he fought the kings of Norway and Sweden in 1026; he visited Rome in 1027, and campaigned in Scotland; and he campaigned in Norway in 1028/29. When he was away one of his earls acted as regent, as happened when he was absent from Denmark. But he was certainly not absent from England as frequently as, say, Henry II or Richard I in the twelfth century, and he seems to have provided a degree of stability and good government that had been rare under Æthelred.

Like William the Conqueror after him, Cnut as king of England did a great deal to emphasise continuity with previous Anglo-Saxon kings. He issued a lawcode that was little more than a confirmation of earlier law – indeed, it may have been compiled by the same man who had been responsible for the later laws of Æthelred II: Wulfstan, Archbishop of York. Cnut even married Emma, the widow of Æthelred II: she, as the daughter of Richard I, count of Normandy, and thus as a descendant of Vikings, perhaps identifying herself more easily with a Dane than with an Anglo-Saxon. Even Richard II's court in Normandy had not entirely separated itself from its Viking heritage; in around 1025 a poet from the court of Oláfr of Norway was welcomed at Rouen.[44] Cnut's court was even more Danish in tone. Several Old Norse poems that were composed in Cnut's honour, and which may have been recited before him in Winchester, have been preserved in later Icelandic texts. Ottar the Black's 'Knútsdrápa', recorded in *Knýtlingasaga*, is one of the best known. Its verses commemorate Cnut's victories in Scandinavia and in England in the time-honoured terms used of Viking heroes:

> 5. You made war in green Lindsey, Prince. The Vikings wrought there what violence they would. In your rage, withstander of the Swedes, you brought sorrow on the English, in *Helmingborg* to the west of the Ouse.
>
> 8. Mighty Scylding, you fought a battle beneath the shield at *Assandun*. The blood-crane got morsels brown with blood. Prince, you won renown enough with your great sword, north of *Danaskógar* [Forest of Dean?], but to your men it seemed slaughter indeed.[45]

Ottar was apparently employed by Cnut at the English court; but it is very tempting to associate another poet with Cnut's court: the *Beowulf*-poet.

There has always been a tendency to date *Beowulf*, the greatest of all early English poems, as early as possible. Once it was firmly believed that portions of it went almost as far back as the events it describes: the visit of Beowulf and his Geats to Heorot, the court of Hrothgar, king of the Danes, the killing of the monster Grendel and his mother, and the subsequent fight between Beowulf, now king of the Geats (in Sweden), and a dragon. A coincidence of names between one of the Danes and a Danish king mentioned by Gregory of Tours in his sixth-century *History*, allows scholars to suggest a mid-sixth century date for the historical Hrothgar and Beowulf (if they are historical). More recent scholarship has shown that the Christian elements were not interpolated into an early version of the poem, but were so deeply embedded that the poem as we have it could hardly be earlier than the eighth century. Historians have seen it fitting in well into an eighth-century context, and perhaps a specifically monastic one:[46] indeed, when Alcuin of York complained about secular poetry being enjoyed by monks he mentions a character, Ingeld, who does actually appear in *Beowulf* (see above, p. 187). After all, could a poem celebrating the deeds of Danes really have been written after the Viking attacks? Well, some have answered, 'yes', pointing out that by the middle of the tenth century many English were living perfectly happily alongside Vikings; but then adding that it would be difficult to conceive of the poem after the renewal of Viking raids in 980.

The fact remains that the sole manuscript of *Beowulf*, rescued but with rather charred edges from the fire that nearly destroyed the Cotton collection of medieval manuscripts in 1731, is generally agreed to be from the period 975–1025. The shorthand for this is usually '*c*. 1000', which actually conceals the fact that the manuscript could be from the last decade of this period of fifty years, that is, from Cnut's reign. Kiernan, who has done the most rigorous analysis of the manuscript in recent times, has argued that the manuscript may actually be a first draft: the stories may have existed beforehand, but the poem was itself composed at the time.[47] If not Cnut's court, then perhaps Æthelred's: he had Danes at his court, and even an Icelandic skaldic poet, called Gunnlaug Serpent's Tongue. But if one is looking for a context in which an Anglo-Saxon poet might have celebrated the great deeds of ancient Danes, then the court of Cnut is probably the best place of all. As we have seen in the verses by Ottar the Black, above, Cnut is described as a 'mighty Scylding'. Is it really coincidence that *Beowulf* begins with praise of Scyld and his descendants?

> Indeed, we have heard of the glory of the Spear-Danes, kings of the nation in days gone by – how those princes performed deeds of courage. Often Scyld Scefing dragged away the mead benches from bands of foes, from any tribes – struck terror into the Heruli. From the time when first he was found destitute (he received consolation for that) he flourished beneath the skies, prospered in honours until every one of those who dwelt round about him across the whale's road had to obey him, pay him tribute. That was a great king![48]

Cnut himself was (or claimed to be) a Scylding, a descendant (like the poem's Hrothgar) of the great king Scyld. Cnut too had grown in power until all those round across the whale's road – the sea – had to obey him and pay him tribute. *Beowulf* was a skilful historical reconstruction of the past age of heroes, containing within it, in the character and speech of Hrothgar, a 'mirror for princes'. 'Scylding' appears some fifty times in *Beowulf*, but nowhere else before 1100, except in the Old Norse skaldic verse of the earlier eleventh century, where it is used of just three kings, one of whom is Cnut.[49]

The court of Cnut was one of the most cosmopolitan and linguistically varied of any early medieval courts. There were plenty of Englishmen who, discontented with Æthelred or simply wanting to profit from a career in Cnut's large Empire, threw in their lot with the Danish king. One of the most significant was Godwin, who had received an earldom by 1018; he publicised his new loyalty by giving his first four sons Danish names: Swegn, Harold, Tostig and Gyrth (this Harold was the last Anglo-Saxon king, killed at Hastings in 1066). Charters issued by Cnut show both Danes and English in the lists of witnesses. A grant to Orc, in 1024, has thirteen Danish *ministri* as witnesses, and seven English, but most have a rather higher proportion of English. The evidence of charters and of Domesday Book (1087) suggest that there were numerous Danes given estates in this period; but it was nothing like the scale of William the Conqueror's grants to Normans after 1066. The difference was that Cnut could rely on support from many Englishmen – and he could not trust all Scandinavians.[50]

Sir Frank Stenton censoriously noted that 'in the ordering of his own life Cnut ostentatiously disregarded conventions which were beginning to govern the behaviour of civilized kings':[51] he regarded his first wife Ælfgifu of Northampton as his queen even after he had married Æthelred's widow

Emma (whom Anglo-Saxon sources refer to unhelpfully as Ælfgifu), and even appointed her as his regent in Norway in 1030. But Stenton also disapproved of 'the barbarian strain in Cnut's mentality', by which he means the ruthlessness by which any conqueror is likely to have to enforce his power. Cnut killed Eadwig, Æthelred's son (though failed to kill Edmund Ironside's two sons, in exile in Hungary); he killed a number of prominent Englishmen without trial early in his reign, including Eadric Streona, whom he himself had appointed to control Mercia in 1017. Given that Eadric had a history of defection, it is hardly surprising that he was beheaded, as the *Encomium Emmae* put it, 'so that soldiers may learn from this example to be faithful, not faithless, to their kings'.[52] On the whole, Cnut relied upon Scandinavians as his earls earlier in his reign. The 'earl' (ON *jarl*) was the equivalent of the former 'ealdorman', and indeed, had been a term that appears earlier than Cnut, in the former Danelaw. Although Stenton had argued that there was a difference: the ealdormanry had 'to some degree expressed local self-consciousness',[53] while the earl was a royal appointment within a territory defined by the king, more recent historians have seen little difference between the two. The Scandinavian earls were mostly men who had taken part in the wars of conquest: men like Thorkell the Tall, from Sjælland, earl of East Anglia; Eiríkr, son of the earl of Lade in Norway, earl of Northumbria, and his son Hákon, earl of Worcestershire; Úlfr, a Dane who married Cnut's sister and whose sister Gytha married Earl Godwin; and Úlfr's brother Eilífr. But there were also English earls, particularly later in Cnut's reign, most significantly Godwin, a 'new man'; but also some continuations from the previous regime, such as Leofwine, an 'ealdorman of the provinces of the Hwicce' in 997 but still apparently holding some authority under Cnut. Leofwine's son Leofric begins attesting charters as earl in Mercia in 1032, and seems then to be second in the hierarchy after Godwin; like Godwin he played an important role under King Edward the Confessor too, until his death in 1057, even if perhaps he is now better known for his wife Godgifu, Latinised in later tradition as Lady Godiva. He apparently had a brother, somewhat incongruously called Norman.

A major element in Cnut's control of England were his troops: his housecarl and his lithsmen. The housecarl (ON *húskarl*), literally 'housemen', were companions of lords and soldiers, although in the sources they often appear as landowners: the rewards for their service. The *liðsmann* is a 'fleetman', although in Scandinavian terminology 'fleet' often stands for 'army'; we do not see them as landowners in the sources. Housecarls, Nicholas Hooper argues, were no different from the military retinues that kings and aristocrats maintained throughout the early Middle Ages, and later.[54] The housecarl served in armies, perhaps served in garrison duty, and may have been used in tax collection and in domestic duties within the household. The lithsmen, however, functioned much more like the standing armies of later times. They operated for pay, at a very high level, and when disbanded would take their ships with them. A special tax, the *heregeld*, was instituted to pay for them; when 32 ships' companies were paid in 1041, the tax provoked a revolt in Worcester. It was probably the deep unpopularity of the *heregeld* that inspired Edward the Confessor to pay off all the lithsmen in 1050, and to abolish the *heregeld* in the following year.

One can chart to some extent the role and influence of Danes in England during Cnut's reign; but one must not forget that England had perhaps a rather greater impact upon Denmark during the almost thirty-year period of joint rule, under Cnut (1014–35) and his sons Harold I Harefoot (1035–40) and Harthacnut (1040–42). It is clear, for instance, that Cnut remodelled the Danish coinage on the English system, with regular issues of coins centrally controlled. Cnut also continued Swein's policy with regard to the Danish Church. The conversion of Denmark had largely proceeded under the auspices of the archbishops of Hamburg-Bremen, and Denmark was regarded as part of the German archbishop's province. Swein Forkbeard drove out the German bishops; the twelfth-century historian Adam of Bremen, whose sympathies can be guessed from his name, regarded this as a return to paganism, but it was of course merely a part of Swein's foreign policy, which Cnut continued. Adam of Bremen notes that Cnut appointed Englishmen to the sees of Lund (Skåne), Roskilde (Sjælland) and Odense (Fyn), while the Dane whom he appointed to the see of Ribe (Jutland) had been educated in England. Cnut's visit to Rome in 1027 was partly for pilgrimage, but was also in part designed to restore reasonable relations with the German Emperor. The occasion was the imperial coronation of Conrad II, with whom Cnut arranged a marriage alliance for their children; he also negotiated a reduction in customs for pilgrims and traders coming to Rome from England and Scandinavia.[55]

The end of the Viking Age?

Some of the Vikings who had been active as raiders in northern France were given a province by Charles the Simple in 911. This was not conceding to a victorious group: the Norwegian leader Rollo (Hrólfr) had been defeated by the Franks, and the intention was that the defeated Vikings should defend the area, at the mouth of the Seine, from other Scandinavians. Rollo's successors took advantage of the weakness of Frankish royal authority to spread their power westwards, and to become the most powerful non-royal power-base in northern France. The province of the Northmen was called *Nor(d)mannia*: Normandy. We call its inhabitants Normans, although in the eleventh century sources they were commonly called *Franci*. There are Viking place-names in Normandy, and a number of Old Norse words entered the French language, above all those to do with sea-faring. But by the eleventh century these descendants of the Vikings had little to distinguish them from the bulk of the population of Normandy, who were French-speaking, apart, perhaps, from their own traditions of their past. In the mid-tenth century the young duke Richard I had to be sent to Bayeux to pick up some Old Norse, because there were no native-speakers to be found in Rouen – a story which points out both the strengths and the weaknesses of Scandinavian traditions in Normandy.

One of the first Normans to arrive in England was Emma, the daughter of Richard I of Normandy and his Danish wife Gunnor. She came in 1002 to marry Æthelred II, and among her children was Edward the Confessor (king 1042–65); she was also the great-aunt of Duke William of Normandy, later the Conqueror of England (king 1066–87). It was the beginning of a series of contacts between Normandy and England which continued right up to the Conquest of 1066. When Swein of Denmark conquered England, Emma and her family spent their exile at her brother Duke Richard II's court. After Æthelred's death, Emma married Cnut himself, and bore him a son, Harthacnut. In the *Encomium Emmae Reginae*, which she commissioned, all memory of her first husband, the failed Æthelred, is suppressed. Emma's son Edward married Edith, the daughter of Earl Godwin and Gytha, the sister of two Danish jarls. Both Emma and her daughter-in-law Edith spent time at Edward's court, and both were for a time disgraced. Edward was childless: Edith's brother Harold II succeeded Edward, but was deprived of the throne by Emma's great-nephew William. The complex inter-relationships of these two women, Emma and Edith, and their families have recently been explored in a fascinating book by Pauline Stafford.[56]

Because of Edward's parentage, he favoured Normans, as is well known. Indeed, the idea that he intended William of Normandy, his closest male relative, as his heir, rather than Harold, the son of his overpowerful earl Godwin, is not implausible: even though this is one of the propaganda messages hammered home after the Conquest, in multimedia formats, both parchment and embroidery (for of course the Bayeux Tapestry is an embroidery not a tapestry), it does not mean that it was not true. Edward did favour Normans. He appointed several Normans to important positions in the church: Ulf became bishop of Dorchester in 1049, Robert, from the Norman monastery of Jumièges, became bishop of London in 1044 and archbishop of Canterbury in 1051, while William, another Norman, was bishop of London from 1051 to 1075. Both Ulf and Robert lost their positions as a result of the conflict between Edward and Earl Godwin: even in 1052 Godwin and his sons, including the future Harold II, were defining themselves by opposition to the Normans. There were lay appointments too: Ralf of Mantes, from the frontier lands between Norman dukes and French kings (but also the son of Edward's sister Godgifu), was given Herefordshire to defend against the Welsh, and there he built castles and introduced other Norman military customs. There were possibly castles elsewhere, and there were Norman churches and monasteries which held estates in England.

However, these familiar facts should not be treated as if it was Edward preparing England for the Conquest. They may just be part of the evidence that Edward's England was very open to exchange across the Channel. Edward did also appoint Lotharingians to three bishoprics, for instance. English Church calendars show the number of cross-Channel saints that were venerated in England, but two new Church festivals were probably introduced through contact with Greeks in southern Italy, or in Rome.[57] Edward had contacts all over Europe, including Flanders, Germany and Italy, while it was in Hungary that he had sought refuge when Cnut was on the English throne.

We have strayed far too far from the end of the first millennium for the purposes of this book; a more detailed discussion of the impact of the Normans upon England and Britain will be found in the second volume of this series. William's reign does mark the end of an era for England, however: it saw the last of the invasions of England. On September 18 1066 Harald Hardrada of Norway landed in Yorkshire, following up a claim to England he had inherited from King Harthacnut's ally Magnus, and he was defeated and killed at the battle of Stamford Bridge, east of York, two days later. A week later, in the night of 27/28 September, William of Normandy crossed the English Channel. Three years later, Cnut's nephew Swein Estridsson invaded with a large Danish fleet, invited by northerners dissatisfied with William's conquest. The combined forces seized York. William put down the English rebellion, but was unable to dislodge the Danes except by paying them tribute. In 1075, it was Norman earls who rebelled and called on Danish help, but their revolt had been crushed before the fleet arrived (although the Danes plundered York). Ten years later, William heard strong rumours of a further invasion by Danes, this time led by Swein's son Cnut, and William energetically prepared to defend England. The fleet was assembled, but it never set sail; Cnut was himself the victim of a rebellion in 1086. Nils Lund claimed that the failure of this expedition 'marked the end of the Viking Age. No more Scandinavian plunderings or invasions of Britain, France or Germany occurred'.[58]

Those living in the north or west of Britain might have been surprised to hear this. No more plunderings or invasions from Scandinavia, perhaps, but Scandinavians continued to dominate in northern and western Scotland, and continued to control the Irish Sea from their bases on the east coast of Ireland and the Isle of Man. At the time of Earl Rognvald Kali of Orkney, in the mid-twelfth century, the *Orkneyinga Saga* tells us of three men who go off on a Viking expedition to the Hebrides, and then to the Scillies 'where they won a great victory and a massive share of plunder on St Columba's Day'.[59] After that, Svein Asleifarson went out with five longships on a raiding expedition, returning, as he always did, in the autumn; later still, he went with seven ships to the Hebrides, where there was nothing left worth plundering, and to Ireland, 'where they looted everywhere they could', and on to Dublin, where he eventually lost his life.[60] The saga was written some half a century after these events: even allowing for literary exaggeration, the author must have been convinced that the Viking Age was by no means over in some parts of Britain.

Although much of this chapter has concerned the largest and wealthiest of the kingdoms of Britain, we ought to end by considering the other kingdoms in Britain, and how they emerged from the Viking era – remembering, as always, the meagre amounts of comprehensible data.

As we have seen, Normans were already present on the borders of Wales even before the Conquest, because of Edward's appointment of Ralf of Mantes in Herefordshire, and a band of Normans was employed as mercenaries in Scotland as early as 1054, at the battle of Dunsinane. These facts in a sense represent the fate of Wales and Scotland in the course of the twelfth and thirteenth century: Normans were to whittle away at Welsh power until they finally overwhelmed it, under Edward I; in Scotland Normans and others from northern France were welcomed in, to create a 'modernised' kingdom which was in the end able to resist Anglo-Norman aggression.

Let us start, however, with Dunsinane, and with the one early Scottish king that almost everyone knows: Macbeth (Mac Bethad). Almost nothing of what everyone knows about Macbeth is true, however. Macbeth did not stab Duncan in his bedchamber; he defeated him in open battle in 1040. He was not a hated ruler, it seems: a contemporary spoke of him as 'the generous king', 'the ruddy complexioned, yellow-haired tall one whom I celebrate'.[61] He went on pilgrimage in 1050, to Rome, like his English and Danish contemporary King Cnut. He was not killed at Dunsinane; he lived to fight for his kingdom for another three years after his defeat in that battle. And the invasion of Scotland which led to Dunsinane was hardly a liberation from tyranny, as Shakespeare portrays it: it was inspired by Edward the Confessor's desire to have a compliant king on the throne of Scotland. Malcolm III had been in exile in England for some years, and was reimposed on his throne by an army largely made up of Anglo-Scandinavians from the north of England. On the other hand, Macbeth was no doubt hated by some: he came from a family powerful in the north of Scotland, and tried to oust the royal family which, for a long time, had been based in the centre and east of Scotland, between Edinburgh and Perth.

Malcolm III's English connections, which put him on the throne in 1058, were rather more dangerous after 1066. Scotland had welcomed Anglo-Saxon exiles after Hastings, and in particular harboured Edgar Ætheling, the grandson of King Edmund Ironside, and his sister Margaret, who had been in exile in Hungary under Cnut. The English Margaret of Hungary, as she was known, or St Margaret as she is now known (because of her piety), married Malcolm III of Scotland: one of those crucial marriages which had significant repercussions, like that of Emma, wife in turn of Æthelred and Cnut. Initially the marriage caused serious disagreements between William I and the Scots; in the end, however, it brought about close connections between the Anglo-Norman and Scottish dynasties. Margaret's daughter

Edith married Henry I, and was the grandmother of Henry II; and Margaret's daughter Mary was the mother of King Stephen.

Under the two Williams there was considerable military activity against the Scots, accentuated by the fact that the border was by no means settled, and Scottish kings at times successfully maintained their claims to Cumbria and Northumberland. In 1072 William forced Malcolm III to become his vassal, at Abernethy, an event which became crucial in later Norman propaganda. Malcolm's son Duncan became a hostage, and was brought up, trained and knighted at the Norman court. Although Duncan himself only reigned for a year, it is perhaps from that time that one can trace the start of the Norman influence in Scotland. In the early twelfth century Alexander I started building castles, as at Stirling, and giving land to his vassals in return for military service. But it was the reign of his successor David I that was even more important. He too had been brought up and knighted in England, at Henry I's court. One of his first acts when he became king in 1124 was to give a large estate to a leading Norman follower, Robert de Brus. Brus was a little village near Cherbourg in Normandy; Robert de Brus was the ancestor of King Robert the Bruce of Scotland. But David also held the Honour of Huntingdon in southern England, and through that connection (which involved him in the civil wars of Stephen's reign, for instance), Scotland obtained ready access to the new ideas of the twelfth century, and Scotland's old institutions began to be replaced by ones that were much more recognisably part of the European mainstream.

The Welsh story was very different. Through much of the tenth century the various Welsh rulers seem to have accepted English overlordship, although that did not necessarily prevent the continuation of sporadic raiding across the frontiers, in both directions. In the early eleventh century this raiding was often carried out not by English kings, but by the semi-independent earls of Cnut or Edward. In the middle of the eleventh century, however, arrived one of the most successful and aggressive Welsh rulers for a long time: Gruffudd ap Llywelyn. He seems first of all to have become ruler of Powys, and then, after Iago of Gwynedd's murder in 1039, of Gwynedd as well. For years he struggled to get control of south-east Wales, and had done so by 1055. Twice Gruffudd was able to inflict considerable defeats on English forces. Eventually Harold Godwinsson took over the earldom of Hereford, and launched a combined sea and land expedition against Gruffudd. The Welsh ruler was defeated: Harold took his head back to Edward the Confessor and married his widow. The defeat came just at the wrong time for the Welsh: weakening them politically on the eve of the Norman Conquest. By the end of the century Norman barons had definitively won much of the south coast of Wales, and were pushing westwards from Chester. What Anglo-Saxons had never achieved (and perhaps never wanted) – the elimination of Welsh political independence – had begun.

Epilogue

William of Normandy's conquest of England in 1066 was, it turned out, a watershed in the history not just of England but of all the kingdoms in Britain. It established that close link with France which was to be of crucial political and cultural importance for the rest of the Middle Ages (for Scotland as well as England), and allowed easy access to Britain for the many new cultural and intellectual developments that were sweeping Europe in the eleventh and twelfth centuries. An alternative history scenario in which Harold II did not die on the battlefield of Hastings on October 14 1066, but succeeded in repelling the Norman invader as he had repelled the Norwegian invader three weeks earlier would no doubt have to imagine a very different England emerging in the course of the eleventh and twelfth centuries. But one would surely have to envisage very different histories for the Welsh and the Scottish as well: proximity to the Norman world changed those two polities just as profoundly and rapidly.

As is the way of history, the Norman Conquest was not just the beginning of a new world, but the end of an old one. It was the last successful invasion of Britain, after a millennium indelibly marked by invasion. This was the last time that a military elite from outside Britain was able to impose itself on the island. That is, of course, a somewhat strange fact to celebrate, and no consolation at all to the Welsh and the Scottish, who had to cope with the impositions, or attempted impositions, of the English military elite throughout the Middle Ages and beyond, let alone to the Irish, whose fortunes were irrevocably tied to the island of Britain after the English (or, more properly perhaps, Cambro-Norman) invasion of 1169. Immigrants with less political clout would continue to arrive in Britain from various parts of the world for the rest of the second millennium, of course, and will do so, one hopes – for immigrants have done so much to enrich British economy and society – well into the third millennium.

This book, and the series to which it belongs, has been a long time in the making, and in a sense is even more relevant now than when it was planned.

Irish and Scottish devolution were barely under discussion at that point, and the debate about whether to go into the single European currency had not started. The murders of Englishmen by other Englishmen because of the colour of their skin, and the hate campaigns conducted by some newspapers against other nations, have reminded us that racism and xenophobia are still powerful forces in our society; the bogeys of 'illegal immigrants' and 'bogus asylum seekers' have brought ugly passions to the surface. We have seen the interesting spectacle of tough immigration controls urged on us by the sons of immigrants, such as the former Conservative ministers Michael Howard and Michael Portillo. All these developments of the last years of the second millennium (remembering, as historians must, that the last year of the second millennium is 2000) serve to remind the British that nationalism and national identity are still very live issues, as are Britain's relations with its neighbours, across the English Channel and across the Irish Sea.

No-one could pretend that the history of the first millennium AD is going to be seen by most people as relevant to these issues. But the main theme of this book has really been the complex history of the emergence of the three main political units of modern Britain, and the emergence of political and/or national identities. For those who think historically this has interesting lessons. Each of those three units has a very different history. Wales is unique in the history of Western Europe: the one area of the former Roman Empire which was not taken over by a barbarian military elite, and which developed its own political institutions and preserved its own independence in the post-Roman period. England's story is not unique: there were other barbarian peoples who moved into parts of the former Roman Empire and totally transformed its culture and identity. But the English did this on a larger scale than other barbarian peoples, and more thoroughly. The Britons who formed the bulk of the population of what became England effectively disappear from sight, ultimately subsumed into a new nation. Scotland's history is unusual too: becoming the home of four early medieval nationalities – Pictish, Irish, British and English – it nevertheless developed its own national and political identity despite its divisions and its different languages and traditions.

The long perspective of 'our island story' provided by this book does illustrate a number of things that might be useful for the British to remember today. That the growth of national states inevitably means the extinction of cultures judged to be 'less important'. (The last native speaker of Cornish died around 1800; the last Norse speakers in the Orkneys died in the eighteenth century; the last native speakers of Pictish and Welsh in Scotland died out many centuries earlier than that.) That there is no neat connection between culture and identity on the one hand, and biological groups on the other. (The 'Celtic peoples' of the north and west of Britain are probably largely descended from the people who were in Britain before the Celtic language was introduced; the English are probably largely descended from Celtic-speaking peoples.) That there was no inevitability about the emergence of these nationalities in Britain. (That the Scots emerged as the leading dynasty in what came to be called Scotland might never have happened without the Vikings, and without the Vikings England would never have emerged as a politically united people as early as it did.) That the development of Britain – above all in this period, perhaps – was the result of innumerable interactions between Britain and other parts of Europe. And finally, and most important, that there is no one history of Britain in this period: there can only be the history imagined by one person, with that person's assumptions, prejudices and areas of ignorance, based on his or her own knowledge and interpretation of a contentious body of difficult sources, which, thanks to archaeologists, grows in size and complexity with every year that passes.

Notes

Chapter 1

1. Somewhere between the 2,262,000 listed in the 1901 census as 'persons engaged in agriculture' and the 609,105 listed as 'agricultural labourers and shepherds': see *Encyclopedia Britannica*, 11th edition (1910), vol. 1, p. 413.
2. K. Dark and P. Dark, *The Landscape of Roman Britain* (Stroud, 1997), pp. 31–2.
3. See the maps in chapter 1 of B. Jones and D. Mattingley, *Atlas of Roman Britain* (Oxford, 1990).
4. W.C. Sellar and R.J. Yeatman, *1066 And All That* (first published 1930; Harmondsworth, 1960), *Important Note* to p. 13.
5. See the discussion in F. Wallis, ed., *Bede: The Reckoning of Time* (Liverpool, 1999), pp. 307–12.
6. Bede, *Historia Ecclesiastica* (*HE*), I.1; in *Bede's Ecclesiastical History of the English People*, ed. B. Colgrave and R.A.B. Mynors (Oxford, 1969), pp. 14–21 (though the older edition, by Charles Plummer (Oxford, 1898) shows the borrowings more clearly).
7. A.P. Smyth, *Warlords and Holy Men: Scotland AD 80–1000* (London, 1984), pp. 59–60.
8. S. Ireland, *Roman Britain: A Sourcebook*, 2nd edn (London, 1996): Herodian, document no. 17 (p. 24) and Claudian, no. 276 (p. 159).
9. On all this see under the relevant headings in A.L.F. Rivet and C. Smith, *The Place-Names of Roman Britain* (London, 1979).
10. W.S. Hanson, *Agricola and the Conquest of the North* (London, 1987), pp. 22–3.
11. D.N. Dumville, quoted by P. Sims-Williams, *Cambridge Medieval Celtic Studies*, 26 (1993), p. 27
12. B. Yorke, 'The Jutes of Hampshire and Wight and the origins of Wessex', in S. Bassett, ed., *The Origins of Anglo-Saxon Kingdoms* (Leicester, 1989), pp. 84–96.
13. Bede, *HE*, I.15; transl. Colgrave and Mynors, pp. 50–1.
14. B. Yorke, 'Fact or fiction? The written evidence from the fifth and sixth centuries AD', *Anglo-Saxon Studies in Archaeology and History* 6 (1993), p. 49.
15. A.J. Mainmain, *Anglo-Scandinavian Pottery from Coppergate* (The Archaeology of York, 16/5) (York, 1990), p. 386; T.P. O'Connor, *Bones from Anglo-Scandinavian Levels at 16–22 Coppergate* (The Archaeology of York, 15/3) (York, 1989), p. 137.

Chapter 2

1. '*The Ruin*': see S.A.J. Bradley, ed., *Anglo-Saxon Poetry* (London, 1982), p. 402.
2. T. Pratchett, *The Last Continent* (London, 1998), p. 138.

3. Strabo IV.5.2; S. Ireland, *Roman Britain: A Sourcebook*, 2nd edn (London, 1996), no. 14 (p. 20).
4. Caesar, *Gallic Wars* V.12 and 14, translated as *The Conquest of Gaul* by S.A. Handford (revised by J. F. Gardner) (Harmondsworth, 1982), pp. 110–11.
5. Tacitus, *Agricola*, 11; transl. H. Mattingley (revised S.A. Handford), *The Agricola and the Germania* (Harmondsworth, 1970), pp. 61–2.
6. *Gallic Wars* V.12; transl. Handford, p. 110.
7. P. Salway, *Roman Britain* (Oxford, 1981), pp. 43, 47
8. P. Salway, *The Oxford Illustrated History of Roman Britain* (Oxford, 1993), p. 12.
9. G. Webster, *The Cornovii* (London, 1975), p. 18.
10. *Gallic Wars* II.4; transl. Handford, p. 59.
11. M. Millett, *The Romanization of Britain: An Essay in Archaeological Interpretation* (Cambridge, 1990), p. 10.
12. K. Dark and P. Dark, *The Landscape of Roman Britain* (Stroud, 1997), p. 42.
13. N. Higham, *Rome, Britain and the Anglo-Saxons* (London, 1992), p. 20.
14. *Gallic Wars* IV.26; transl. Handford, p. 100.
15. Ireland, *Roman Britain*, no. 30 (p. 34).
16. On which see D. Braund, *Ruling Roman Britain: Kings, Queens, Governors and Emperors, from Julius Caesar to Agricola* (London, 1996), pp. 10–23; Plutarch, *Life of Caesar*, 23, 2–4.
17. J. Foster, *The Lexden Tumulus: A Re-appraisal of an Iron Age Burial from Colchester, Essex* (Oxford, 1986).
18. A.L.F. Rivet and C. Smith, *The Place-Names of Roman Britain* (London, 1979), pp. 298–300.
19. *Gallic Wars* V.13; transl. Handford, p. 110.
20. As Salway, *Roman Britain*, p. 46.
21. Salway, *Roman Britain*, p. 14.
22. B. Jones and D. Mattingley, *Atlas of Roman Britain* (Oxford, 1990), p. 51.
23. D. Miles and S. Palmer, 'White Horse Hill', *Current Archaeology* 142 (1995), pp. 372–8.
24. See Dark and Dark, *Landscape*, p.16, citing L. Sellwood, 'Tribal boundaries viewed from the perspective of numismatic evidence', in B. Cunliffe and D. Miles, ed., *Aspects of the Iron Age in Central Southern Britain* (Oxford, 1984), pp. 191–204.
25. Strabo, *Geography* IV.v.3; Ireland, *Roman Britain*, no. 14 (p. 20).
26. Jones and Mattingley, *Atlas*, p. 57.
27. *Gallic Wars*, III.8; transl. Handford, p. 76.
28. Strabo, *Geography* IV.5.3; Ireland, *Roman Britain*, no. 37 (p.37).
29. Ireland, *Roman Britain*, no.56 (p. 44).
30. *Agricola* 14; transl. Mattingley, p. 64.
31. Richard Reece, *My Roman Britain* (Cirencester, 1988), p. 9 (but note that different reprintings of this have different paginations, and different reprintings are not signaled, and therefore pagination is unreliable) Braund, *Ruling Roman Britain*, p. 111.
32. Rosalind Niblett, 'A royal burial at St Albans', *Current Archaeology* 132 (Jan. 1993), 484–8, at p. 484.
33. Tacitus, *Annals*, XIV.32; transl. M. Grant, *The Annals of Imperial Rome* (Harmondsworth, 1971), p. 329.
34. *Agricola* 21; transl. Mattingley, pp. 72–3.
35. *Agricola* 24; transl. Mattingley, p. 74.
36. *Agricola* 27; transl. Mattingley, p. 77.
37. *Histories*, I.2; Ireland, *Roman Britain*, no. 110 (p. 84).
38. G.S. Maxwell, *The Romans in Scotland* (Edinburgh, 1989), pp. 101–10.
39. D.J. Breeze, *Roman Scotland: Frontier Country* (London, 1996), p. 111.
40. Breeze, *Roman Scotland*, p. 69.
41. D. J. Breeze and B. Dobson, *Hadrian's Wall*, 3rd edn (Harmondsworth, 1987), p. 213.
42. Breeze, *Roman Scotland*, p. 112.
43. Higham, *Rome*, p. 36.
44. A. Robertson, 'Roman finds from non-Roman sites in Scotland: more Roman "drift" in Caledonia', *Britannia* 1 (1970), pp. 198–213; L. Macinnes, 'Baubles, bangles and beads: trade and exchange in Roman Scotland', in J.C. Barrett, A.P. Fitzpatrick and L. Macinnes, eds, *Barbarians and Romans in North-West Europe* (British Archaeological Reports, IS 471) (Oxford, 1989), pp. 108–16.

Chapter 3

1. H.L. Mencken, *The American Language: An Inquiry into the Development of English in the United States*, 4th edn (New York, 1936), pp. 223–4.
2. S. Ireland, *Roman Britain: A Sourcebook*, 2nd edn (London, 1996), no. 67 (p. 52).
3. A. Birley, *The People of Roman Britain* (London, 1979), p. 91.
4. *Agricola* 21, transl. Mattingly, p. 73.
5. Birley, *People*, pp. 15–6.
6. Ireland, *Roman Britain*, no. 502 (pp. 229–30).
7. G. Webster, *The Cornovii* (London, 1975), p. 58.
8. Birley, *People*, p.104.
9. Ireland, *Roman Britain*, no. 224 (pp.129–32).
10. Ireland, *Roman Britain*, no. 225 (pp. 132–3).
11. T. Williams, 'Allectus' Palace?', *Current Archaeology* 158 (July, 1998), p. 72.
12. Birley, *People*, p. 37.
13. Birley, *People*, p. 39
14. M. Millett, *The Romanization of Britain* (Cambridge, 1990), p. 58.
15. Cited in B. Jones and D. Mattingley, *Atlas of Roman Britain* (Oxford, 1990), p. 158.
16. A.K. Bowman, *Life and Letters on the Roman Frontier: Vindolanda and its People* (London, 1994), p. 36.
17. *Tab. Vindol.* II 164; Bowman, *Life and Letters,* p. 106.
18. Bowman, *Life and Letters*, pp. 69–70.
19. *Tab. Vindol.* II 233; Bowman, *Life and Letters*, p. 123.
20. Bowman, *Life and Letters*, p. 88.
21. *Tab. Vindol.* II 292; Bowman, *Life and Letters*, p. 128.
22. P. Salway, *Roman Britain* (Oxford, 1981), p. 410.
23. On the Franks in the Roman Empire, see E. James, *The Franks* (Oxford, 1988), pp. 38–44.
24. As estimated by James in T.F.C. Blagg and A.C. King, eds, *Military and Civilian in Roman Britain: Cultural Relationships in a Frontier Province* (British Archaeological Reports, BS 136) (Oxford, 1984). p. 163.
25. E. Cleary in M. Todd, ed., *Research on Roman Britain: 1960–89* (London, 1989), p. 237.
26. N. J. Higham, *An English Empire: Bede and the Early Anglo-Saxon Kings* (Manchester, 1995), pp. 114–15.
27. J. Wacher, *The Towns of Roman Britain* (London, 1974), p. 59.
28. G.A. Webster, 'Fort and town in early Roman Britain', in J.S. Wacher, ed., *The Civitas Capitals of Roman Britain* (Leicester, 1966), pp. 31–45.
29. R.F.J. Jones, in R.F.J. Jones, ed., *Britain in the Roman Period: Recent Trends* (Sheffield, 1991), p. 54.
30. See B.C. Burnham and J.S. Wacher, *The Small Towns of Roman Britain* (London, 1990).
31. M. Todd, in S. J. Greep, ed., *Roman Towns: the Wheeler Inheritance: A Review of Fifty Years' Research* (Council for British Archaeology Research Report, 93) (London, 1993), p. 7.
32. Feris and Jones, in Jones, ed., *Britain in the Roman Period*, pp. 103–9.
33. R. Reece, *My Roman Britain* (Cirencester, 1988), p. 70.
34. M. Todd, in Greep, ed., *Roman Towns*, p. 6.
35. S. Frere, *Britannia: A History of Roman Britain*, 3rd edn (London, 1987), p. 253.
36. See F.A. Pritchard, 'Ornamental stonework in Roman Britain', *Britannia* 17 (1986), pp. 169–89.
37. S. Roskams, in Jones, ed., *Britain in the Roman Period,* p. 68.
38. R. Reece, 'Town and country: the end of Roman Britain', *World Archaeology* 12 (1980), p. 78.
39. M. Todd, in Greep, ed., *Roman Towns*, p. 8.
40. And here I summarise K. Dark and P. Dark, *The Landscape of Roman Britain* (London, 1997), p. 120.
41. D. Miles, in Todd, ed., *Research on Roman Britain*, p.115.
42. Reece, *My Roman Britain*, p. 157.
43. D. Miles, in Todd, ed., *Research in Roman Britain*, p. 117.
44. Dark and Dark, *Landscape*, p. 11.

45. Dark and Dark, *Landscape*, p. 87.
46. D.J. Breeze, *Roman Scotland: Frontier Country* (London, 1996), p. 90.
47. K. Branigan, 'Villa settlement in the West Country', in K. Branigan and P. Fowler, eds, *The Roman West Country: Classical Culture and Celtic Society* (Newton Abbot, 1976), pp. 120–41.
48. B.R. Hartley and R. Leon Fitts, *The Brigantes* (Gloucester, 1989), p. 74.
49. Millett, *Romanization*, pp. 118–19.
50. J.R.L. Allen and M.G. Fulford, 'The Wentlooge Level: a Romano-British saltmarsh reclamation in south-east Wales', *Britannia* 17 (1986), pp. 91–117.
51. See Potter, in Todd, ed., *Research on Roman Britain*, pp. 158–60.
52. Dark and Dark, *Landscape*, p. 104.
53. Miles in Todd, ed., *Research on Roman Britain*, p. 126.
54. Ireland, *Roman Britain*, no. 210 (pp. 124–5).
55. Millett, *Romanization*, p. 30.
56. See Dark and Dark, *Landscape*, p. 111; D. Williams, 'A consideration of the sub-fossil remains of *Vitis vinifera* L., as evidence for viticulture in Roman Britain', *Britannia* 8 (1977), 327–34.
57. Dark and Dark, *Landscape*, p. 128.
58. Dark and Dark, *Landscape*, pp. 129–30.
59. See Millett, *Romanization*, pp. 168–9.
60. See map 5:10 in Jones and Mattingley, *Atlas*.
61. P. Salway, *Roman Britain*, p. 507.
62. K. Jackson, *Language and History in Early Britain* (Edinburgh, 1953).
63. P. Russell, 'Recent work in British Latin', *Cambridge Medieval Celtic Studies* 9 (Summer, 1985), pp. 19–29.
64. E.P. Hamp, 'Social gradience in British spoken Latin', *Britannia* 6 (1975), pp. 150–62; C. Thomas, *Christianity in Roman Britain to AD 500* (London, 1981), pp. 69–73.
65. See E. James, 'Gregory of Tours and the Franks', in A.C. Murray, ed., *After Rome's Fall: Narrators and Sources of Early Medieval History* (Toronto, 1998), pp.51–66.

Chapter 4

1. M. Hunter, 'Germanic and Roman antiquity and the sense of the past in Anglo-Saxon England', *Anglo-Saxon England* 3 (1974), p. 10.
2. *Gallic Wars* VI.13, transl. Handford, p. 140.
3. *Natural History* XVI. 251; transl. H. Rackham, *Pliny: Natural History* IV (Cambridge, Mass., 1915), p. 551.
4. *Gallic Wars* VI. 14, transl. Handford, p. 141.
5. *Gallic Wars*, VI. 16; transl. Handford, pp. 141–2.
6. Claudius 25; transl. R. Graves, revised M. Grant, *Suetonius: The Twelve Caesars* (Harmondsworth, 1979), p. 202.
7. *Nat. Hist.* 30, 12; translated in J.C. Mann and R.G. Penman, eds, *Literary Sources for Roman Britain* (London Association of Classical Teachers – Original Records 11) (London, n.d.), p. 64.
8. M. Henig, *Religion in Roman Britain* (London, 1984), p. 25.
9. *Gallic War* VI.17; transl. Handford, p. 142.
10. Henig, *Religion*, p. 43.
11. Henig, *Religion*, p. 55.
12. See map 8:16 in B. Jones and D. Mattingley, *An Atlas of Roman Britain* (Oxford, 1990).
13. S. Ireland, *Roman Britain: A Source Book*, 2nd edn (London, 1996), nos. 402–4 (p. 200).
14. Henig, *Religion*, pl. 44.
15. Justin, *Apologia I pro Christianis 66: Patrologia Graeca*, 5, col. 429.
16. P. Veyne, *Did the Greeks Believe in Their Myths? An Essay on the Constitutive Imagination* (Chicago, 1988), pp. 61–2.
17. Tacitus, *Annals* XIV.31; transl. Grant, p. 318.
18. Henig, *Religion*, p. 79.

19. Henig, *Religion*, p. 131.
20. L. Allason-Jones, *Women in Roman Britain* (London, 1989), p. 153.
21. Henig, *Religion*, p. 145.
22. Ireland, *Roman Britain*, no. 370 (p. 194).
23. Henig, *Religion*, p. 145; for full text see *Britannia* 13 (1982), pp. 408–9.
24. Henig, *Religion*, pp. 151–2.
25. *Adversus Judaeos* 7.4: Salway, *Roman Britain*, p. 718.
26. *In Ezekiel*, 1: *Patrologia Latina*, 35, col. 723.
27. P. Salway, *Roman Britain* (Oxford, 1981), p. 719.
28. J. Morris, *British History and the Welsh Annals* (London and Chichester, 1980), p. 85.
29. Suggested by Chandler: see C. Thomas, *Christianity in Roman Britain to AD 500* (London, 1981), p. 106.
30. Orosius, quoted by Thomas, *Christianity*, p. 54.
31. Lupus, *Life of St Germanus*, 14: transl. in F.D. Hoare, *The Western Fathers* (London, 1954), p. 297–8.
32. Passages from Prosper translated in Thomas, *Christianity*, p. 301.
33. D.N. Dumville, 'Late seventh- or eighth-century evidence for the British transmission of Pelagius', *Cambridge Medieval Celtic Studies* 10 (Winter, 1985), pp. 39–52.
34. F. O'Brien, *The Dalkey Archive* (London, 1973), p. 38
35. *Confessio* 61, in A.B.E. Hood, *St Patrick: His Writings and Muirchu's Life* (London and Chichester, 1978), pp. 53–4.
36. *Letter*, c.1: transl. Hood, p. 55.
37. *Letter*, c. 14; transl. Hood, p. 57.
38. W. Davies, *Wales in the Early Middle Ages* (Leicester, 1982), pp. 162–3.
39. Davies, *Wales*, pp. 148, 151–3.
40. R. McCluskey, ed. *The See of Ninian: A History of the Medieval Diocese of Whithorn and the Diocese of Galloway in Modern Times* (Ayr, 1997), p. 3.
41. Bede, *HE*, III.4: transl. Colgrave and Mynors, pp. 221–3.
42. See L. Alcock, *Arthur's Britain: History and Archaeology, AD 367–634* (London, 1971), pl. 25a, opposite p. 368.

Chapter 5

1. The author's student notes from a lecture series by Brown, c. 1969.
2. Bede, *HE*, I.21; transl. Colgrave and Mynors, p. 67.
3. See O. Maenchen-Helfen, *The World of the Huns* (Berkeley, 1973), p. 125.
4. Ammianus, 20.1.1; transl. W. Hamilton, *Ammianus Marcellinus: The Later Roman Empire (AD 354–378)* (Harmondsworth, 1986), p. 185.
5. Ammianus 26.4.5 and 27.8.4; transl. Hamilton, pp. 318 and 342. For St Jerome's recollection of seeing these cannibals in Gaul (perhaps exhibited as captives, in the late 360s), see J.N.D. Kelly, *Jerome: His Life, Writings and Controversies* (London, 1975), pp. 26–7.
6. Ammianus 27.8.1; transl. Hamilton p. 342.
7. Ammianus 28.3.9; transl. Hamilton p. 358.
8. S. Ireland, *Roman Britain: A Source Book*, 2nd edn (London, 1996), no. 258 (pp. 151–2).
9. As argued for northern Britain in B.R. Hartley and R. Leon Fitts, *The Brigantes* (Gloucester, 1988), p. 109.
10. Zosimus, VI. 5. 2–3; transl. Ronald T. Ridley, *Zosimus: New History* (Sydney, 1982), pp. 128–9. See Ireland, *Roman Britain*, no. 286.
11. Zosimus, VI. 10. 2; transl. Ridley, p. 130; Ireland, *Roman Britain*, no. 287.
12. E.A. Thompson, 'Peasant revolts in late Roman Gaul and Spain', *Past and Present* 2 (1952), pp. 11–23; R. Van Dam, *Leadership and Community in Late Antique Gaul* (Berkeley, 1985), pp. 25–56; G. Halsall, 'The origins of the *Reihengräberzivilisation*: forty years on', in J. Drinkwater and H. Elton, eds, *Fifth-Century Gaul: A Crisis of Identity?* (Cambridge, 1992), pp. 196–207.
13. D. Dumville in M. Lapidge and D. Dumville, *Gildas: New Approaches* (Woodbridge, 1984), pp. 51–9.
14. Gildas c. 66; translated in M. Winterbottom, ed., *Gildas: The Ruin of Britain and Other Documents* (London and Chichester, 1978), p. 52.

15. Gildas c. 26; transl. Winterbottom, p. 28.
16. P. Sims-Williams thinks that the double occurrence of the 44 years is purely coincidental: 'Gildas and the Anglo-Saxons', *Cambridge Medieval Celtic Studies* 6 (Winter, 1983), p. 20.
17. I. Wood in Lapidge and Dumville, *Gildas*, p. 23.
18. Gildas, c. 4; transl. Winterbottom, p. 17.
19. Gildas, c.18; transl. Winterbottom, p. 22.
20. Gildas, c.19; transl. Winterbottom, p. 23.
21. Gildas, c.23; transl. Winterbottom, p. 26.
22. Gildas, c.26; transl. Winterbottom, p. 28.
23. Bede, *HE*, V.24; transl. Colgrave and Mynors, p. 563.
24. M. Miller, 'Bede's use of Gildas', *English Historical Review* 90 (1975), pp. 241–61.
25. *Welsh Annals*; transl. J. Morris, *Nennius: British History and the Welsh Annals* (London and Chichester, 1980), p. 45.
26. *Historia Brittonum*, c. 56; transl. Morris, *Nennius*, p. 35.
27. K. Jackson, 'The Arthur of history', in R.S. Loomis, ed., *Arthurian Literature in the Middle Ages* (Oxford,1959), p. 3.
28. R. Barber, *The Figure of Arthur* (London, 1972), pp. 21–33.
29. O. Padel, 'The nature of Arthur', *Cambrian Medieval Celtic Studies* 27 (Summer, 1994), p. 31.
30. M. Dillon, 'The Irish settlements in Wales', *Celtica* 12 (1977), pp. 1–12.
31. See C. Thomas, *And Shall These Mute Stones Speak? Post-Roman Inscriptions in Western Britain* (Cardiff, 1994), pp. 183–96.
32. *Historia Brittonum*,14; transl. Morris, *Nennius*, p. 20.
33. Thomas, *And Shall These Mute Stones Speak?*, pp. 53–6.
34. Thomas, *And Shall These Mute Stones Speak?*, p.70.
35. Letter 3.9; transl. O.M. Dalton, *The Letters of Sidonius* (Oxford, 1915), vol 1, p. 76.
36. See A. Chédeville and H. Guillotel, *La Bretagne des saints et des rois, Ve-Xe siècle* (Rennes, 1984), p. 29; G. Ashe, '"A certain very ancient book": traces of an Arthurian source in Geoffrey of Monmouth's *History*', *Speculum* 56 (1981), pp. 301–23.
37. E.A. Thompson, 'Britonia', in M.W. Barley and R.P.C. Hanson, eds, *Christianity in Britain 300–700* (Leicester, 1968), p. 206.
38. Bede, *HE* I.15; transl. Colgrave and Mynors, p. 51.
39. Rolf H. Bremmer, Jr, 'The Nature of the Evidence for a Frisian Participation in the *Adventus Saxonum*', in A. Bammesberger and A. Wollmann, eds, *Britain 400-600: Language and History* (Heidelberg, 1990), pp. 353–71.
40. The sequence of maps in J. Hines, 'Philology, archaeology and the *adventus Saxonum vel Anglorum*', in A. Bammesberger and A. Wollmann, eds, *Britain 400-600: Language and History* (Heidelberg, 1990), pp. 34–6 (and see H.-W.Böhme, 'Das Ende der Römerherrschaft in Britannien und die angelsächsische Besiedlung Englands im 5. Jahrhundert', *Jahrbuch des Römisch-Germanischen Zentralmuseums* 33 (1986), pp. 469–574) have been amended in K.R. Dark, *Civitas to Kingdom: British Political Continuity 300–800* (London, 1994), p. 219.
41. John Hines, 'The becoming of the English: identity, material culture and language in early Anglo-Saxon England', *Anglo-Saxon Studies in Archaeology and History* 7 (1994), 49–59.
42. See, most recently, C. Hills, 'Spong Hill and the Adventus Saxonum', in C.E. Karkov, K.M. Wickham-Crowley and B.K. Young, eds, *Spaces of the Living and the Dead: An Archaeological Dialogue* (American Early Medieval Studies 3) (Oxford, 1999), pp. 15–26.
43. Guy Halsall, *Settlement and Social Organization: The Merovingian Region of Metz* (Cambridge, 1995), p. 248.
44. P. Jackson, 'Footloose in archaeology', *Current Archaeology* 144 (Dec. 1995), pp. 466–70.
45. H. Härke, '"Warrior Graves"? The background of the Anglo-Saxon weapon burial rite', *Past and Present* 126 (1990), pp. 22–43.
46. M.E. Jones, *The End of Roman Britain* (Ithaca, NY, 1996), p. 26.
47. Hines, 'Becoming of the English', p. 58, summarising the implied arguments of Martin Welch and others.
48. M. Welch, 'Late Romans and Saxons in Sussex', *Britannia* 2 (1971), pp. 232–7, and in M.

Welch, *Early Anglo-Saxon Sussex* (British Archaeological Reports, BS 112) (Oxford, 1983).
49. Jones, *End,* pp. 24–5.

Chapter 6

1. Discussed in R. Folz, *The Coronation of Charlemagne* (London, 1974), pp. 120–1.
2. N.J. Higham, *An English Empire: Bede and the Early Anglo-Saxon Kings* (Manchester, 1995, pp. 74–111.
3. D. Whitelock, ed., *English Historical Documents, I, c. 500–1042*, 2nd edn (London, 1979), no. 54 (pp. 479–80).
4. Bede, *HE* III.24.
5. F. Kelly, *A Guide to Early Irish Law* (Dublin, 1988), p. 18.
6. Bede, *HE* II.5.
7. See Wendy Davies, *Patterns of Power in Early Wales* (Oxford, 1990), pp. 9–15.
8. E. James, *The Origins of France* (London, 1982), pp. 24 and 31.
9. Bede, *HE* I.15; transl. Colgrave and Mynors, p. 53.
10. *Felix's Life of Saint Guthlac*, ed. B. Colgrave (Cambridge, 1956), c. 34 (pp. 108–11), cited in P.H. Sawyer, *From Roman Britain to Norman England* (London,1978), p. 51.
11. M. Gelling, 'Why aren't we speaking Welsh?', *Anglo-Saxon Studies in Archaeology and History* 6 (1993), p. 51.
12. P. Wormald, 'Celtic and Anglo-Saxon kingship: some further thoughts', in B. E. Szarmach and V. D. Oggins, eds., *Sources of Anglo-Saxon Culture* (Kalamazoo, MI, 1986) pp. 51–83 at p. 153.
13. P. Wormald, 'Celtic and Anglo-Saxon Kingship: some further thoughts', in P. E. Szarmach and V. D. Oggins, eds., *Sources of Anglo-Saxon Culture* (Kalamazoo, MI, 1986), pp. 151–83, at p. 153.
14. K. McCone, *Pagan Past and Christian Present in Early Irish Literature* (Maynooth, 1990), p. 108.
15. W.A. Chaney, *The Cult of Kingship in Anglo-Saxon England* (Manchester, 1970), pp. 64–5.
16. J. McClure, 'Bede's Old Testament Kings', in P. Wormald *et al.*, eds, *Ideal and Reality in Frankish and Anglo-Saxon Society* (Oxford, 1983), p. 91.
17. K. Jackson, *The Oldest Irish Tradition: A Window on the Iron Age* (Edinburgh, 1964).
18. Sawyer, *From Roman Britain to Norman England*, pp. 51–6.
19. R. North, *Heathen Gods in Old English Literature* (Cambridge, 1997), p. 115.
20. T.M. Charles-Edwards, 'Kinship, status and the origins of the hide', *Past and Present*, 56 (1972), p. 7. For fuller and more recent discussion, see T.M. Charles-Edwards, *Early Irish and Welsh Kinship* (Oxford, 1993).
21. Charles- Edwards, 'Kinship', p. 18.
22. Whitelock, *EHD 1*, no. 32 (p. 400).
23. *Life of Guthlac*, 17–18; transl. Colgrave, p. 81.
24. Bede, *HE* IV.21, transl. Colgrave and Mynors, p. 401.
25. T.M. Charles-Edwards, 'The authenticity of the *Gododdin*: an historian's view', in R. Bromwich and R. Brinley Jones, eds, *Astudiaethau ar Yr Hengerod* (Cardiff, 1978), p. 46.
26. Bede, *HE* III.14; transl. Colgrave and Mynors, pp. 257–9.
27. R. Frank, 'The ideal of men dying with their lord in *The Battle of Maldon*: anachronism or *nouvelle vague*?' in I. Wood and N. Lund, ed., *People and Places in Northern Europe, 500–1600: Essays in Honour of Peter Hayes Sawyer* (Woodbridge, 1991), p. 106.
28. The football analogy – the history of England as a knockout competition between various minor local clubs, until at last Mercia and Wessex meet for the Cup Final (with serious crowd troubles in eastern England putting the Mercians off their game at the final moment) – is developed by Steven Bassett in Bassett, ed., *The Origins of Anglo-Saxon Kingdoms* (London, 1989), pp. 26–7.
29. J.M. Spearman and J. Higgitt, eds, *The Age of Migrating Ideas: Early Medieval Art in Northern Britain and Ireland* (Edinburgh and Stroud, 1993).
30. Bede, *HE* I. 34; transl. (adapted) Colgrave and Mynors, p. 117.

31. H. Moisl, 'The Bernician royal dynasty and the Irish in the seventh century', *Peritia* 2 (1983), pp. 115–16.
32. D.P. Kirby, *The Earliest English Kings* (London, 1991), p. 84.
33. Bede, *HE* III.14; transl. Colgrave and Mynors, p. 257.
34. Bede, *HE* II.9; transl. Colgrave and Mynors, p. 167.
35. Bede, *HE* II.5; transl. Colgrave and Mynors, p. 151.
36. Bede, *HE* 2.16; transl. Colgrave and Mynors, p. 193.
37. *Life of Wilfrid* c. 17; Whitelock, *EHD 1,* no. 154 (p. 754).
38. A.P. Smyth, *Warlords and Holy Men: Scotland AD 80–1000* (London, 1984), p. 25.
39. F.J. Byrne, *Irish Kings and High-Kings* (London, 1973), p. 112.
40. Bede, *HE* IV.26; transl. (adapted) Colgrave and Mynors, p. 427.
41. Eddius, *Life of Wilfrid*, 60: ed. and transl. B. Colgrave, p. 130–31. I am following here T.M. Charles-Edwards, 'Early medieval kingships in the British Isles', in S. Bassett, ed., *The Origins of Anglo-Saxon Kingdoms* (London, 1989), 31–2.
42. Bede, *HE* III.24 and II.5; transl. (adapted) Colgrave and Mynors, pp. 295 and 15.
43. Bede, *HE*, IV.3 and V.19; transl. Colgrave and Mynors, pp. 337 and 525.
44. Bede, *HE* IV.26; transl. (adapted) Colgrave and Mynors, p. 429.
45. Bede, *HE* III. 4. See Cyril Hart, 'The Tribal Hidage', *Transactions of the Royal Historical Society* 21 (1971), pp. 336–7.
46. Adomnán of Iona, *Life of Columba*, I.1; transl. R. Sharpe (Harmondsworth, 1995), p. 111.
47. See Kathleen Hughes, 'Where are the writings of early Scotland?', in K. Hughes (ed. D. Dumville), *Celtic Britain in the Early Middle Ages* (Woodbridge, 1980), pp. 1–21.
48. S. Foster, *Picts, Gaels and Scots: Early Historic Scotland* (London, 1996).
49. Adomnán, *Life of St Columba*, III.5; transl. R. Sharpe, p. 209.
50. Following Foster, *Picts, Gaels and Scots*, pp. 37–8.
51. See the distribution maps in Foster, *Picts, Gaels and Scots*, p. 31 (*pit*- names) and p. 73 (symbol-stones), and the discussion of the latter, pp. 71–9.
52. Foster, *Picts, Gaels and Scots*, p. 78.
53. Here I follow Smyth, *Warlords and Holy Men*, pp. 59ff.
54. As noted by Smyth, *Warlords and Holy Men*, p. 69.
55. K. Jackson, 'Angles and Britons in Northumbria and Cumbria', in *Angles and Britons: O'Donnell Lectures* [no editor] (Cardiff, 1963), pp. 71–2.
56. Jackson, 'Angles', p. 71.
57. Bede, *HE* IV.12; my translation.
58. See K.R. Dark, *Civitas to Kingdom: British Political Continuity 300–800* (London, 1994), p. 88.
59. V.E. Nash-Williams, *The Early Christian Monuments of Wales* (Cardiff, 1950), no. 138.
60. Nash-Williams, no. 103.
61. For a critique of Wendy Davies's position see K.R. Dark, *Civitas to Kingdom*, pp. 140–8.
62. Kate Pretty, 'Defining the Magonsæte' and Margaret Gelling, 'The early history of Western Mercia', in Bassett, *Origins*, pp. 176 and 191.
63. Wormald, in J. Campbell, ed. *The Anglo-Saxons* (London, 1982), p. 121.

Chapter 7

1. T.M. Charles-Edwards, 'The social background to Irish *peregrinatio*', *Celtica* 11 (1976), pp.43–59.
2. *Anglo-Saxon Chronicle*, 891: Whitelock, *EHD I*, no. 1, pp. 200–01.
3. Bede, *HE* III. 4; transl. Colgrave and Mynors, p. 223.
4. D.N. Dumville, *Saint Patrick, AD 493–1993* (Woodbridge, 1993), pp. 140–5.
5. Genereus and Pilu: see A.O. and M.O. Anderson, ed., *Adomnán's Life of Columba* (Oxford, 1991), pp. 196–7 and 214–15.
6. R. North, *Heathen Gods in Old English Literature* (Cambridge, 1997), p. 50.
7. Letter 6.10 in the edition by D. Norberg, *Registrum Epistolarum* (Corpus Christianorum 140) (Turnhout, 1982).
8. Letter 6.51 in the Norberg edition.

9. See I.N. Wood, 'Frankish hegemony in England', in M.O.H. Carver, ed., *The Age of Sutton Hoo: The Seventh Century in North-Western Europe* (Woodbridge, 1992), pp. 235–41.
10. Letter 11.56 in the Norberg edition; copied in Bede *HE*, I.30; transl. Colgrave and Mynors, pp. 107–9.
11. M. Lapidge and M. Herren, ed., *Aldhelm: The Prose Works* (Cambridge, 1979), pp. 160–1. John Blair has discussed the evidence for temples in *Anglo-Saxon Studies in Archaeology and History* 8 1995.
12. Bede, *HE*, I.27; transl. Colgrave and Mynors, p. 87.
13. Letter 11.39 in the Norberg edition, reproduced by Bede in *HE* 1.29.
14. Bede, *HE* II.2; transl. Colgrave and Mynors, p. 141.
15. As noted in P.H. Sawyer, *From Roman Britain to Norman England* (London, 1978), p. 50.
16. *Historia Brittonum* 63; transl. J. Morris, ed., *Nennius: British History and the Welsh Annals* (London and Chichester, 1980), p. 38.
17. Bede, *HE* II.14; transl. Colgrave and Mynors, p. 189.
18. Bede, *HE* II.16; transl. Colgrave and Mynors, p. 193.
19. North, *Heathen Gods*, pp. 333–4.
20. *HE* III.1; transl. Colgrave and Mynors, p. 215.
21. Ine, law 76: Whitelock, *EHD I*, no. 32, p. 407.
22. Bede, *HE* III.7; transl. Colgrave and Mynors p. 235.
23. Bede, *HE* III.18; transl. Colgrave and Mynors. p. 269.
24. Bede, *HE* III.8; transl. Colgrave and Mynors, p. 239.
25. Bede, *HE* III.19; transl. Colgrave and Mynors, p. 269.
26. Bede, *HE* III.21; transl. Colgrave and Mynors p. 281.
27. Bede, *HE* III.4; transl. Colgrave and Mynors, pp. 223–5.
28. D. Ó Cróinín, *Early Medieval Ireland, 400–1200* (London, 1995), pp. 149–68.
29. As noted by Ó Cróinín, *Early Medieval Ireland*, pp. 166–7.
30. Ibid., p. 167.
31. The letter quoted in note 11 above; on this see M.W. Herren, 'Scholarly contacts between the Irish and the southern English in the seventh century', *Peritia* 12 (1998), pp. 24–53.
32. Bede, *HE* III.5; transl. Colgrave and Mynors, p. 227.
33. Translated in Whitelock, *EHD I*, no. 170 (pp. 799–810).
34. Whitelock, *EHD I*, no. 170 (p. 802).
35. Whitelock, *EHD I*, no. 31 (pp. 396–8).
36. Whitelock, *EHD I*, no. 32 (p. 399).
37. K.L. Jolly, *Popular Religion in Late Anglo-Saxon England: Elf Charms in Context* (Chapel Hill, NC, 1996), p. 125.
38. For the Minster hypothesis, see J. Blair and R. Sharpe, eds, *Pastoral Care before the Parish* (Leicester, 1992), and the debate in the journal *Early Medieval Europe* beginning with E. Cambridge and D. Rollason, 'The pastoral organization of the Anglo-Saxon Church: a review of the "Minster Hypothesis"', *Early Medieval Europe* 4 (1995), pp. 87–104.
39. Bede, *HE*. III.27; transl. Colgrave and Mynors p. 313.
40. Bede, *HE* V.9, transl. Colgrave and Mynors, p. 477.
41. A letter of 746, transl. E. Emerton, *The Letters of Saint Boniface* (New York, 1940), pp. 122–3.
42. Translated by Colgrave and Mynors, p. 575.
43. Ibid., p. 575.
44. S. Allott, *Alcuin of York* (York, 1974), letter 56, p. 73.
45. Transl. C.H. Talbot, *The Anglo-Saxon Missionaries in Germany* (London, 1954), pp. 231–2; quoted by R. Fletcher, *The Conversion of Europe: From Paganism to Christianity, 371–1386 AD* (London, 1997), p. 214.

Chapter 8

1. R.L.S. Bruce-Mitford, *The Art of the Codex Amiatinus* (Jarrow Lecture 1967), p. 2.
2. N. Netzer, 'The *Book of Durrow*: the Northumbrian connection', in J. Hawkes and S. Mills, eds, *Northumbria's Golden Age* (Stroud, 1999), p. 325.

3. Cited in Netzer, '*Book of Durrow*', pp. 320–1, from E.A. Lowe, *Codices Latini Antiquiores* II, pp. xiv–xv.
4. C.L. Neuman de Vegvar, *The Northumbrian Renaissance. A Study in the Transmission of Style* (London and Toronto, 1987), p. 270.
5. C.L. Neuman de Vegvar, 'The Travelling Twins: Romulus and Remus in Anglo-Saxon England', in Hawkes and Mills, *Northumbria's Golden Age*, pp. 257–9.
6. L. Webster, 'The iconographic programme of the Franks casket', in Hawkes and Mills, *Northumbria's Golden Age*, p. 244.
7. P. Meyvaert, in B. Cassidy, ed., *The Ruthwell Cross* (Princeton, NJ, 1992).
8. See E. James, 'Alcuin and York in the eighth century', in P.L. Butzer and D. Lohrmann, eds, *Science in Western and Eastern Civilization in Carolingian Times* (Basel, 1993), pp. 34–7.
9. Bede, *HE* IV.25; transl. Colgrave and Mynors, p. 425.
10. Bede, *HE* V.23; transl. Colgrave and Mynors, p. 561.
11. Whitelock, *EHD I*, no. 170, p. 804.
12. Whitelock, *EHD I*, no. 170, pp. 805–6.
13. Translated in D. Bullough, 'What has Ingeld to do with Lindisfarne?, *Anglo-Saxon England*, 22 (1993), p. 124.
14. K. Leahy, 'The Middle Saxon site at Flixborough, North Lincolnshire', in Hawkes and Mills, *Northumbria's Golden Age*, pp. 87–94 and B. Whitwell in *Current Archaeology* 126 (Sept/Oct 1991), pp. 244–7.
15. Leahy, 'Flixborough', p. 91.
16. E. Campbell, in P. Hill, ed., *Whithorn and St Ninian. The Excavation of a Monastic Town, 1984–91* (Stroud, 1997), p. 297.
17. A suggestion made by D. O'Sullivan at a conference on early monasticism, Kellogg College, Oxford, November 1998.
18. Whitelock, *EHD I*, no. 177, pp. 819–20.
19. F.M. Stenton, *Anglo-Saxon England*, 2nd edn. (Oxford, 1947), p. 206.
20. *Current Archaeology* 162, p. 220.
21. Stenton, *Anglo-Saxon England*, pp. 210–1.
22. J.M. Wallace-Hadrill, *Early Germanic Kingship in England and on the Continent* (Oxford, 1971), pp. 111–12.
23. C. Cubitt, *Anglo-Saxon Church Councils, c. 650–c. 850* (London, 1995), p. 166.
24. Cubitt, *Councils*, pp. 161ff.
25. P.E. Dutton, ed., *Charlemagne's Courtier: The Complete Einhard* (Peterborough, Ontario, 1998), p. 25.
26. Stenton, *Anglo-Saxon England*, p. 219.
27. Whitelock, *EHD I*, no. 197; S. Allott, *Alcuin of York* (York, 1974), no. 40.
28. D.M. Metcalf in J. Campbell ed., *The Anglo-Saxons* (London, 1982), pp. 62–3.
29. H. Kennedy, *The Prophet and the Age of the Caliphates* (London, 1986), pp. 121–2.
30. R. Hodges, *The Anglo-Saxon Achievement* (London, 1989), p. 80.
31. M. Brisbane, 'Hamwic (Saxon Southampton): an 8th century port and production centre', in R. Hodges and B. Hobley, eds, *The Rebirth of Towns in the West, AD 700–1050* (CBA Research Report 68) (London, 1988), pp. 103–4.
32. Ine 70.1: Whitelock, *EHD I*, no. 32 (p. 406).
33. Suggested by Hodges, *Achievement,* p. 89.
34. Whitelock, *EHD I*, no. 30 (p. 395).
35. Bede, *HE* II.3; transl. Colgrave and Mynors, p. 143.
36. Hodges, *Achievement,* p. 96; see map 29.
37. P. Godman, ed., *Alcuin: The Bishops, Kings and Saints of York* (Oxford, 1982), p. 5.
38. R. Hodges, *Dark Age Economics: The Origins of Towns and Trade, AD 600–1000* (London, 1982), pp. 73–4.
39. On this evidence see now J. Wooding, *Communication and Commerce along the Western Sealanes, AD 400–800* (British Archaeological Reports, Brit. Series 654) (Oxford, 1996), pp. 67 and 72.
40. P. Brown, *The World of Late Antiquity* (London, 1971), p. 156.
41. See map, Wooding, *Communication*, p. 99.
42. K.R. Dark, *Civitas to Kingdom: British Political Continuity, 300–800* (London, 1994), p. 211.
43. M.R. Nieke and H.R. Duncan, 'Dalriada: the establishment and maintenance of an Early

Historic kingdom in northern Britain', in S.T. Driscoll and M.R. Nieke, eds, *Power and Politics in Early Medieval Britain and Ireland* (Edinburgh, 1988), p. 16.

44. A. Lane, 'Trade, gifts and cultural exchange in Dark-Age Western Scotland', in B.E. Crawford, ed., *Scotland in Dark Age Europe* (St Andrews, 1994), p. 111.
45. *Life of Columba*, I.28; A.O. and M.O. Anderson, ed., *Adomnán's Life of Columba* (Oxford, 1991), p. 55.
46. W. Davies, *Wales in the Early Middle Ages* (London, 1982), p. 98.
47. On all this see Davies, *Wales*, pp. 104–6.
48. V. E. Nash-Williams, *The Early Christian Monuments of Wales* Univ. of Wales Press: Cardiff, 1950, pp. 123–5.
49. On all this, see B. T. Hudson, *Kings of Celtic Scotland* (Westport, CT, 1994), pp. 37–47.
50. See I. Henderson, 'Descriptive Catalogue', in S.M. Foster, ed., *The St Andrews Sarcophagus: A Pictish Masterpiece and its International Connections* (Dublin, 1998), pp. 19–35.
51. A.P. Smyth, *Warlords and Holy Men: Scotland AD 80–1000* (London, 1984), p. 177.
52. Ibid., p. 178.
53. Ibid., p. 178.
54. D. Broun, 'Pictish kings 761–839: integration with Dál Riata or separate development?', in Foster, *St Andrews Sarcophagus*, pp. 71–83.
55. Probably in 766: Whitelock, *EHD I*, no. 70, p. 497.
56. Ine 63, 64: Whitelock, *EHD I*, no. 32, p. 406.
57. W. Davies, *An Early Welsh Microcosm* (London, 1978), p. 47. It should be noted that Davies's work on Llandaff has been seriously criticised; see J.R. Davies, 'Church, property, and conflict in Wales, AD 600–1100', *Welsh History Review* 18 (1997), pp. 387–91 for a brief résumé.
58. Ibid., p. 63.
59. See Whitelock, *EHD I*, no. 56, pp. 482–3; photograph in Campbell, ed., *Anglo-Saxons*, p. 98.
60. Wormald in Campbell, ed., *Anglo-Saxons*, pp. 97–8.
61. See N. Brooks, 'The development of military obligations in eighth- and ninth-century England', in P. Clemoes and K. Hughes, eds, *England Before the Conquest* (Cambridge, 1971), pp. 69–84.
62. Initially by C.J. Arnold and P. Wardle, 'Early medieval settlement patterns in England', *Medieval Archaeology* 25 (1981), pp. 145–9.
63. H.F. Hamerow, 'Settlement mobility and the 'Middle Saxon Shift': rural settlements and settlement patterns in Anglo-Saxon England', *Anglo-Saxon England* 20 (1991), p. 13.
64. A. Boddington, 'Modes of burial, settlement and worship: the Final Phase reviewed', in E. Southworth, ed., *Anglo-Saxon Cemeteries: A Reappraisal* (Stroud, 1990), pp. 177–99.

Chapter 9

1. Whitelock, *EHD I*, no. 1 (p. 181).
2. Whitelock, *EHD I*, no. 193 (p. 843).
3. Whitelock, *EHD I*, no. 193, p. 842.
4. Map 49 in D. Hill, *An Atlas of Anglo-Saxon England* (Oxford, 1981).
5. K. Hughes, 'Where are the writings of early Scotland?', in Hughes, *Celtic Britain in the Early Middle Ages: Studies in Scottish and Welsh Sources* (Woodbridge, 1980), pp. 20–1.
6. J. Graham-Campbell and C.E. Batey, *Vikings in Scotland: An Archaeological Survey* (Edinburgh, 1998), p. 233.
7. R. Hodges and D. Whitehouse, *Mohammed, Charlemagne and the Origins of Europe: Archaeology and the Pirenne Thesis*, 2nd edn. (London, 1989).
8. J.M. Wallace-Hadrill, 'The Vikings in Francia' (Stenton Lecture, University of Reading 1974), reprinted in Wallace-Hadrill, *Early Medieval History* (Oxford, 1975), p. 220.
9. A.T. Lucas, 'The plundering and burning of churches in Ireland, 7th to 16th century', in E. Rynne, ed., *North Munster Studies* (Limerick, 1967), pp. 172–229.
10. Quoted by A.P. Smyth in his discussion of the blood-eagle: *Scandinavian Kings in the British Isles, 850–880* (Oxford, 1977), p. 191, using the translation of A.B. Taylor, *The Orkneyinga Saga* (Edinburgh, 1938), p. 142.

11. *Anglo-Saxon Chronicle* under 866: at this time the Anglo-Saxons began the new year on September 24, so Autumn 866 is what we call 865.
12. S. Mac Airt and G. Mac Niocaill, eds., *The Annals of Ulster (to AD 1131)* (Dublin, 1983), p. 327.
13. *Three Fragments*: quoted in Smyth, *Scandinavian Kings*, pp. 161–2.
14. Whitelock, *EHD I*, no. 16 (p. 337).
15. Smyth, *Scandinavian Kings*, pp. 206 and 239, quoting Abbo of Fleury's *Passio Sancti Eadmundi*. On Smyth's use of evidence, see D. Ó Corráin, 'High-kings, Vikings and other kings', *Irish Historical Studies* 21 (1978–9), pp. 283–323.
16. Smyth, *Scandinavian Kings*, p. 228.
17. J. Graham-Campbell, ed., *Cultural Atlas of the Viking World* (Oxford, 1994), p. 129.
18. Whitelock, *EHD I*, no. 1 (p. 195).
19. Whitelock, *EHD I*, no. 1 (p. 194).
20. On this see Smith, *Scandinavian Kings*, pp. 255–66.
21. Whitelock, *EHD I*, no. 1 (p. 205).
22. Whitelock, *EHD I*, no. 1 (p. 206).
23. D. Hill, 'The Burghal Hidage: the establishment of a text', *Medieval Archaeology* 13 (1969), pp. 90–1.
24. Whitelock, *EHD I*, no 1 (p. 202).
25. Whitelock, *EHD I*, no. 1 (p. 202).
26. Asser, c. 79; transl. S. Keynes and M. Lapidge, eds, *Alfred the Great: Asser's 'Life of King Alfred' and Other Contemporary Sources* (Harmondsworth, 1983), p. 93.
27. Asser 80; transl. Keynes and Lapidge, p. 96.
28. Asser 77; transl. Keynes and Lapidge, p. 92.
29. Asser 91; transl. Keynes and Lapidge, p. 101.
30. V.H. Galbraith, 'Who wrote Asser's Life of Alfred?', in Galbraith, *An Introduction to the Study of History* (London, 1964), pp. 88–128, and A.P. Smyth, *King Alfred the Great* (Oxford, 1995), esp. pp. 149–324.
31. For a more sympathetic, though nevertheless critical, view, see J.L. Nelson, 'Waiting for Alfred', *Early Medieval Europe* 7 (1998), 115–24.
32. Smyth, *Alfred*, p. 600.
33. Following Smyth, *Warlords*, pp. 219–29 and D. Ó Corráin, 'The Vikings in Scotland and Ireland in the ninth century', *Peritia* 12 (1998), 296–339.
34. P. Wormald, 'The emergence of a *Regnum Scottorum*: a Carolingian hegemony?', in B.E. Crawford, ed., *Scotland in Dark Age Britain* (St Andrews, 1996), p. 131.
35. Wormald, 'Emergence', p. 134.
36. B.T. Hudson, *Kings of Celtic Scotland* (Westport, CT, 1994), p. 34.
37. See D. Broun, 'The origins of Scottish identity in a European context', in B.E. Crawford, ed., *Scotland in Dark Age Europe* (St Andrews, 1994), pp. 26–8.
38. Wormald, 'Emergence', p. 140.
39. Hudson, *Kings*, p. 43.
40. Transl. M. Pálsson and P. Edwards, *Orkneyinga Saga: The History of the Earls of Orkney* (Harmondsworth, 1978), p. 33.
41. Ibid., pp. 28, 32, 39.
42. Ibid., p. 35.
43. W. Davies, *Patterns of Power in Early Wales* (Oxford, 1990), p. 59.
44. G. Fellows-Jensen, 'Viking settlement in the Northern and Western Isles', in A. Fenton and H. Pálsson, eds, *The Northern and Western Isles in the Viking World: Survival, Continuity and Change* (Edinburgh, 1984), pp. 148–68.
45. K. Cameron, *Place-Name Evidence for the Anglo-Saxon Invasion and Scandinavian Settlements* (Nottingham, 1977), p. 117.
46. Ibid., p. 120.
47. B.E. Crawford, *Scandinavian Scotland* (Leicester, 1987), p. 104.
48. Ibid., p. 96.
49. M. Oftedal, 'Names of lakes on the Isle of Lewis in the Outer Hebrides', in H. Bekker-Nielsen, P. Foote and O. Olsen, eds, *Proceedings of the Eighth Viking Congress, Århus 1977* (Odense, 1981), pp. 183–8.
50. Crawford, *Scandinavian Scotland*, pp. 104–14.
51. Ibid., p. 111.
52. D. Kenyon, *The Origins of Lancashire* (Manchester, 1991), p. 132.

53. G. Fellows-Jensen, 'Scandinavian settlement in Cumbria and Dumfriesshire: the place-name evidence', in J.R. Baldwin and I.D. Whyte, eds, *The Scandinavians in Cumbria* (Edinburgh, 1985), p. 67.
54. All these examples are taken from C. Barber, *The English Language: A Historical Introduction* (Cambridge, 1993), pp. 130–4.
55. Despite Crawford, *Scandinavian Scotland*, p. 121.

Chapter 10

1. F.M. Stenton, *Anglo-Saxon England*, 2nd edn (Oxford, 1947), pp. 318–19.
2. A point made by P. Stafford in *Queens, Concubines and Dowagers: The King's Wife in the Early Middle Ages* (London, 1983), p. 140.
3. E. Campbell and A. Lane, 'Llangorse: a tenth century royal crannog in Wales', *Antiquity* 63 (1989), pp. 675–81; M. Redknap, *The Christian Celts: Treasures of Late Celtic Wales* (Cardiff, 1991), pp. 16–25.
4. S. Keynes, 'King Alfred and the Mercians', in M.A.S. Blackburn and D.N. Dumville, eds, *Kings, Currency and Alliances: History and Coinage of Southern England in the Ninth Century* (Woodbridge, 1998), pp. 39–41.
5. Stenton, *Anglo-Saxon England*, p. 330.
6. Whitelock, *EHD I*, no. 1 (p. 217).
7. Stenton, *Anglo-Saxon England*, p. 347.
8. Whitelock, *EHD I*, no. 1 (p. 218).
9. According to Stenton, *Anglo-Saxon England*, p. 337.
10. On this see S.M. Pearce, *The Kingdom of Dumnonia* (1978), pp. 113–14.
11. Pearce, *Dumnonia*, p. 168.
12. William of Malmesbury, *De Gestis Regum Anglorum*, 134; Whitelock, no. 8, p. 307.
13. Whitelock, *EHD I*, no. 1 (p. 219).
14. Whitelock, *EHD I*, no. 1 (p. 220).
15. Thus Stenton, *Anglo-Saxon England*, pp. 348–9.
16. Cited by William of Malmesbury. See M. Wood, 'The making of King Aethelstan's empire: an English Charlemagne?', in P. Wormald *et al.*, eds, *Ideal and Reality in Frankish and Anglo-Saxon Society* (Oxford, 1983), p. 251.
17. On the occasion of his 'untroubled death', 939: in *The Annals of Ulster*, transl. S. Mac Airt and G. Mac Niocaill (Dublin, 1983), p. 387.
18. William of Malmesbury, 135; Whitelock, *EHD I*, no. 8 (pp. 308–9).
19. Whitelock, *EHD I*, no. 107 (p. 555).
20. Smyth, *Warlords*, pp. 215ff.
21. As Julie Ann Smith plans to argue, forthcoming.
22. Stenton, *Anglo-Saxon England*, p. 364.
23. Whitelock, *EHD I*, no. 41 (p. 435).
24. Whitelock, *EHD I*, no. 1 (p. 225).
25. Whitelock, *EHD I*, no. 226A (pp. 888–9).
26. Asser, *Life of Alfred*, 93; transl. Lapidge and Keynes, p. 103.
27. Whitelock, *EHD I*, no. 238 (p. 922).
28. P. Stafford, *Unification and Conquest: A Political and Social History of England in the Tenth and Eleventh Centuries* (London, 1989), p. 183.
29. Wood, 'The making of King Aethelstan's empire', p. 261.
30. N.P. Brooks., 'The career of St Dunstan', in N. Ramsay, M. Sparks and T. Tatton-Brown, eds, *St Dunstan: His Life, Times and Cult* (Woodbridge, 1992), p. 17.
31. See M. Budny, '"St Dunstan's Classbook" and its frontispiece: Dunstan's portrait and autograph' in Ramsay *et al.*, eds, *St Dunstan*, p. 142.
32. D. Rollason, 'The concept of sanctity in the early *Lives* of St Dunstan', in Ramsay *et al.*, eds., *St Dunstan*, p. 272.
33. See J. Nightingale, 'Oswald, Fleury and continental reform', in N. Brooks and C. Cubitt, eds, *St Oswald of Worcester: Life and Influence* (London, 1996), pp. 23–45.
34. For all this see Biddle, '*Felix Urbs Winthonia*: Winchester in the age of monastic reform', in D. Parsons, ed., *Tenth-Century Studies: Essays in Commemoration of the Council of Winchester and Regularis Concordia* (London, 1975), pp. 123–40 and 233–7.

35. See H.M. Taylor, 'Tenth-century church building in England and on the Continent', in Parsons, ed., *Tenth-Century Studies*, pp. 141–68 and 237–41.
36. D. Knowles, *The Monastic Order in England*, 2nd edition (Cambridge, 1963), p. 44.
37. As noted by P. Wormald, 'Æthelwold and his Continental counterparts', in B. Yorke, ed., *Bishop Æthelwold: His Career and Influence* (Woodbridge, 1988), p. 31.
38. Knowles, *Monastic Order*, pp. 700-01.
39. For this stone and its setting see, e.g., J. Graham-Campbell, ed., *Cultural Atlas of the Viking World* (Oxford, 1994), pp. 118–9.
40. S. Keynes, 'The declining reputation of King Æthelred the Unready', in D. Hill, ed., *Ethelred the Unready* (British Archaeological Reports, British Series 59) (Oxford, 1978), p. 230.
41. M.K. Lawson, *Cnut. The Danes in England in the Early Eleventh Century* (London, 1993), p. 37.
42. All this argued by R. Abels, 'English tactics, strategy and military organisation in the late tenth century', in D. Scragg, ed., *The Battle of Maldon, AD 991* (Oxford, 1991), pp. 144–5.
43. P.H. Sawyer, 'The wealth of England in the eleventh century', *Transactions of the Royal Historical Society*, 5th series 15 (1965), p. 145.
44. D. Bates, *Normandy Before 1066* (London, 1982), p. 21.
45. Whitelock, *EHD I*, no. 15 (pp. 335–6).
46. See e.g. P. Wormald, 'Bede, *Beowulf*, and the conversion of the Anglo-Saxon aristocracy', in R.T. Farrell, ed., *Bede and Anglo-Saxon England* (British Archaeological Reports, British Series, 46) (Oxford, 1978), pp. 32–95.
47. See K.S. Kiernan, *Beowulf and the Beowulf Manuscript* (Brunswick, NJ, 1981); a late date is separately argued by both K.S. Kiernan and R. Frank in C. Chase, ed., *The Dating of Beowulf* (Toronto, 1981), pp. 9–21 and 123–39.
48. *Beowulf*, lines 1–11; transl. M. Swanton, *Beowulf* (Manchester, 1978), p. 35.
49. R. Frank, 'Skaldic verse and the date of *Beowulf*', in Chase, *Dating of Beowulf*, pp. 126–7.
50. As noted by Lawson, *Cnut*, p. 174.
51. Stenton, *Anglo-Saxon England*, p. 391.
52. *Encomium Emmae* II.15, quoted in S. Keynes, 'Cnut's earls', in A.R. Rumble, ed., *The Reign of Cnut: King of England, Denmark and Norway* (London, 1994), p. 67.
53. Stenton, *Anglo-Saxon England*, pp. 392–3.
54. N. Hooper, 'Military developments in the reign of Cnut', in Rumble, *Reign of Cnut*, pp. 89–100.
55. On all this see N. Lund, 'Cnut's Danish kingdom', in Rumble, *Reign of Cnut*, esp. pp. 39–41.
56. *Queen Emma and Queen Edith: Queenship and Women's Power in Eleventh-Century England* (Oxford, 1997).
57. F. Barlow, *The English Church, 1000–1066*, 2nd edn (London, 1979), p. 21.
58. N. Lund, 'The Danish Empire and the end of the Viking Age', in P. Sawyer, ed., *The Oxford Illustrated History of the Vikings* (Oxford, 1997), p. 181.
59. *Orkneyinga Saga* 100; transl. H. Pálsson and P. Edwards (Harmondsworth, 1978), p. 207.
60. Ibid., 101, 107; transl. Pálsson and Edwards, pp. 209, 217.
61. Quoted in G.W.S. Barrow, *Kingship and Unity: Scotland 1000–1306* (Edinburgh, 1981), p. 26.

Bibliography

Primary sources in translation

Adomnán of Iona, Life of St Columba, transl. R. Sharpe (Harmondsworth, 1995) or A.O. and M.O. Anderson, eds, *Adomnán's Life of Columba* (Oxford, 1991)

Æthelwulf: De Abbatibus, ed. A. Campbell (Oxford, 1967)

Alcuin of York [Letters], transl. S. Allott (York, 1974)

Alcuin: The Bishops, Kings and Saints of York, ed. P. Godman (Oxford, 1982)

Alcuin, *Life of St Willibrord*, transl. C.H. Talbot, *The Anglo-Saxon Missionaries in Germany* (London, 1954), pp. 3–22

Aldhelm: The Poetic Works, ed. M. Lapidge and J. Rosier (Cambridge, 1985)

Aldhelm: The Prose Works, ed. M. Lapidge and M. Herren (Cambridge, 1979)

Ammianus Marcellinus, The Later Roman Empire (AD 354–378), transl. W. Hamilton with A. Wallace-Hadrill (Harmondsworth, 1986)

The Anglo-Saxon Chronicle, ed. G.N. Garmonsway (London, 1972) and in Whitelock, *English Historical Documents I*, no. 1

The Annals of Ulster (to AD 1131), ed. S. Mac Airt and G. Mac Niocaill (Dublin, 1983)

Anonymous Monk of Lindisfarne, *Life of Cuthbert*, in B. Colgrave, ed., *Two Lives of Saint Cuthbert* (Cambridge, 1940)

Anonymous Monk of Whitby, *The Earliest Life of Gregory the Great*, ed. B. Colgrave (Lawrence, Kansas, 1968)

Asser: *Alfred the Great: Asser's 'Life of King Alfred' and Other Contemporary Sources,* transl. S. Keynes and M. Lapidge (Harmondsworth, 1983)

Attenborough, F.L., *The Laws of the Earliest English Kings* (Cambridge, 1922)

Bede: A Biblical Miscellany, ed. W.T. Foley and A.G. Holder (Liverpool, 1999)

Bede, Ecclesiastical History of the English People, ed. and transl. B. Colgrave and R.A.B. Mynors (Oxford, 1969)

Bede, *The Life of St Cuthbert*, in B. Colgrave, ed., *Two Lives of Saint Cuthbert* (Cambridge, 1940)

Bede: On the Tabernacle, ed. A.G. Holder (Liverpool, 1994)

Bede: On the Temple, ed. S. Connolly (Liverpool, 1995)

Bede: On Tobit and On the Canticle of Habakkuk, ed. S. Connolly (Dublin, 1997)

Bede: The Reckoning of Time , ed. F. Wallis (Liverpool, 1999)

Beowulf, transl. M. Swanton (Manchester, 1978)

Boniface: *The Letters of Saint Boniface*, transl. E. Emerton (New York, 1940), and in C.H. Talbot, *The Anglo-Saxon Missionaries in Germany* (London, 1954), pp. 65–149

Bradley, S.A.J., ed., *Anglo-Saxon Poetry* (London, 1982)

Caesar, *The Conquest of Gaul*, transl. S.A. Handford, revised J.F. Gardner (Harmondsworth, 1982)

Constantius, *Life of St Germanus*, transl. F.R. Hoare, *The Western Fathers* (London, 1954), pp. 284–320

Douglas, D.C. and Greenaway, G.W., eds, *English Historical Documents II, 1042–89*, 2nd edn. (London, 1981)
Eddius Stephanus, The Life of Wilfrid by, ed. B. Colgrave (Cambridge, 1927)
Einhard: *Charlemagne's Courtier: The Complete Einhard*, ed. P.E. Dutton (Peterborough, Ontario, 1998)
Felix's Life of Saint Guthlac, ed. B. Colgrave (Cambridge, 1956)
Gildas, The Ruin of Britain and Other Documents, ed. and transl. M. Winterbottom (London and Chichester, 1978)
The Gododdin of Aneirin, ed. J.T. Koch (Cardiff, 1997)
Historia Brittonum: see Nennius
Ireland, S., *Roman Britain: A Sourcebook* (2nd edn, London, 1996)
Koch. J.T. and Carey J., *The Celtic Heroic Age: Literary Sources for Ancient Celtic Europe and Early Ireland and Wales*, 2nd edn, (Andover, Mass., 1997)
Mann, J.C. and Penman, R.G., eds, *Literary Sources for Roman Britain* (London Association of Classical Teachers – Original Records 11) (London, 1977)
Nennius, *British History and The Welsh Annals*, ed. and transl. John Morris (London and Chichester, 1980)
Orkneyinga Saga: The History of the Earls of Orkney, transl. M. Pálsson and P. Edwards (Harmondsworth, 1978)
Patrick, *St Patrick: His Writings and Muirchu's Life*, ed. and transl. A.B.E. Hood (London and Chichester, 1978)
Pliny, Natural History, transl. H. Rackham (Cambridge, Mass., 1915)
Robertson, A.J., *The Laws of the Kings of England from Edmund to Henry I* (Cambridge, 1925)
Sidonius Apollinaris: transl. O.M. Dalton, *The Letters of Sidonius* (Oxford, 1915)
Suetonius, The Twelve Caesars, transl. R. Graves, revised M. Grant (Harmondsworth, 1979)
Tacitus, The Agricola and the Germania, transl. H.A. Mattingley, revised S.A. Handford (Harmondsworth, 1970)
Tacitus, The Annals of Imperial Rome, transl. Michael Grant, revised edn (Harmondsworth, 1971)
Welsh Annals: see Nennius
Whitelock, D., ed., *English Historical Documents, I, c. 500–1042*, 2nd edn (London, 1979)
Willibald, *The Life of St Boniface*, transl. C.H. Talbot, *The Anglo-Saxon Missionaries in Germany* (London, 1954), pp. 25–62
Zosimus, New History, transl. Ronald T. Ridley (Sydney, 1982)

General: Britain to *c.* 500

Collingwood, R.G. and Myres, J.N.L., *Roman Britain and the English Settlements* (2nd edn, Oxford 1937)
Dark, K. and Dark, P., *The Landscape of Roman Britain* (Stroud, 1997)
Frere, S., *Britannia: A History of Roman Britain*, 3rd edn (London, 1987)
Hartley, B.R. and Fitts, R.L., *The Brigantes* (Gloucester, 1988)
Jones, B. and Mattingley, D., *An Atlas of Roman Britain* (Oxford, 1990)
Jones, R.F.J., ed., *Roman Britain: Recent Trends* (Sheffield, 1991)
Millett, M., *The Romanization of Roman Britain: An Essay in Archaeological Interpretation* (Cambridge, 1990)
Reece, R., *My Roman Britain* (Cirencester, 1988)
Salway, P., *Roman Britain* (Oxford, 1981)
Salway, P., *The Oxford Illustrated History of Roman Britain* (Oxford, 1993)
Smyth, A.P., *Warlords and Holy Men: Scotland AD 80–1000* (London, 1984)
Todd, M., *The Coritani* (London, 1973)
Todd, M., ed., *Research on Roman Britain, 1960–89* (Britannia Monograph Series no. 11) (London, 1989)
Webster, G., *The Cornovii* (London, 1975)

General: Britain *c.* 500–*c.* 1087

Campbell, J., ed. *The Anglo-Saxons* (London, 1982)
Davies, W., *Wales in the Early Middle Ages* (Leicester, 1982)
Foster, S., *Picts, Gaels and Scots: Early Historic Scotland* (London, 1996)
Gelling, M., *The West Midlands in the Early Middle Ages* (Leicester, 1992)
Higham, N.J., *The Kingdom of Northumbria, AD 350–1100* (Stroud, 1993)
Hill, D., *An Atlas of Anglo-Saxon England* (Oxford, 1981)
John, E., *Reassessing Anglo-Saxon England* (Manchester, 1996)
Loyn, H., *Anglo-Saxon England and the Norman Conquest*, 2nd edn (London, 1991)
Sawyer, P.H., *From Roman Britain to Norman England* (London, 1978)
Smyth, A.P., *Warlords and Holy Men: Scotland AD 80–1000* (London, 1984)
Stafford, P., *The East Midlands in the Early Middle Ages* (Leicester, 1985)
Stenton, F.M., *Anglo-Saxon England*, 2nd edn (Oxford, 1947)
Yorke, B., *Wessex in the Early Middle Ages* (London, 1995)

Chapter 1

Gelling, M., *Signposts to the Past. Place-names and the History of England* (London, 1978)
Hanson, W.S., *Agricola and the Conquest of the North* (London, 1987)
Mainmain, A.J., *Anglo-Scandinavian Pottery from Coppergate* (The Archaeology of York, 16/5) (York, 1990)
O'Connor, T.P., *Bones from Anglo-Scandinavian Levels at 16–22 Coppergate* (The Archaeology of York, 15/3) (York, 1989)
Rivet, A.L.F. and Smith, C., *The Place-Names of Roman Britain* (London, 1979)
Sellar, W.C. and Yeatman, R.J., *1066 And All That* (first published 1930; Harmondsworth, 1960)
Yorke, B., 'The Jutes of Hampshire and Wight and the origins of Wessex', in S. Bassett, ed., *The Origins of Anglo-Saxon Kingdoms* (London, 1989), pp. 84–96
Yorke, B., 'Fact or fiction? The written evidence from the fifth and sixth centuries AD', *Anglo-Saxon Studies in Archaeology and History* 6 (1993), pp. 45–50
Wainwright, F.T., *Archaeology and Place-Names and History* (London, 1962)

Chapter 2

Birley, A., *The People of Roman Britain* (London, 1979)
Braund, D., *Ruling Roman Britain: Kings, Queens, Governors and Emperors, from Julius Caesar to Agricola* (London, 1996)
Breeze, D.J., *Roman Scotland: Frontier Country* (London, 1996)
Breeze, D.J. and Dobson, B., *Hadrian's Wall* 3rd edn (Harmondsworth, 1978)
Dannell, G.B., 'Eating and drinking in pre-conquest Britain: the evidence of amphora and Samian trading, and effect of the invasion of Claudius', in B.C. Burnham and H.B. Johnson, eds, *Invasion and Response: the Case of Roman Britain* (British Archaeological Reports, British Series 73) (Oxford, 1979), pp. 177–84
Foster, J., *The Lexden Tumulus: A Re-appraisal of an Iron Age Burial from Colchester, Essex* (Oxford, 1986)
Hanson, W.S., *Agricola and the Conquest of the North* (London, 1987)
Higham, N., *Rome, Britain and the Anglo-Saxons* (London, 1992)
James, S., *The Atlantic Celts: Ancient People or Modern Invention?* (London, 1999)
Macinnes, L., 'Baubles, bangles and beads: trade and exchange in Roman Scotland', in J.C. Barrett, A.P. Fitzpatrick and L. Macinnes, eds, *Barbarians and Romans in North-West Europe* (British Archaeological Reports, IS 471) (Oxford, 1989), pp. 108–16
Maxwell, G.S., *The Romans in Scotland* (Edinburgh, 1989)
Miles, D. and Palmer, S., 'White Horse Hill', *Current Archaeology* 142 (1995), pp. 372–8
Niblett, R., 'A royal burial at St Albans', *Current Archaeology* 132 (1993), pp. 484–8
Robertson, A., 'Roman finds from non-Roman sites in Scotland: more Roman "drift" in Caledonia', *Britannia* 1 (1970), pp. 198–213

Sellwood, L., 'Tribal boundaries viewed from the perspective of numismatic evidence', in B. Cunliffe and D. Miles, eds, *Aspects of the Iron Age in Central Southern Britain* (Oxford, 1984), pp. 191–204

Chapter 3

Allen, J.R.L. and Fulford, M.G., 'The Wentlooge Level: a Romano-British saltmarsh reclamation in south-east Wales', *Britannia* 17 (1986), 91–117
Birley, A., *The People of Roman Britain* (London, 1979)
Blagg, T.F.C. and King, A.C., eds, *Military and Civilian in Roman Britain : Cultural Relationships in a Frontier Province* (British Archaeological Reports, British Series 136) (Oxford, 1984)
Bowman, A.K., *Life and Letters on the Roman Frontier: Vindolanda and its People* (London, 1994)
Branigan, K., 'Villa settlement in the West Country', in K. Branigan and P. Fowler, eds, *The Roman West Country: Classical Culture and Celtic Society* (Newton Abbot, 1976), pp. 120–41
Burnham, B.C. and Wacher, J.S. *The Small Towns of Roman Britain* (London, 1990)
Fulford, M., 'Demonstrating Britannia's economic dependence in the first and second centuries', in T.F.C. Blagg and A.C. King, eds, *Military and Civilian in Roman Britain* (British Archaeological Reports, British Series 136) (Oxford, 1984), pp. 129–44.
Greep, S.J., ed., *Roman Towns: The Wheeler Inheritance. A Review of 50 Years' Research* (CBA Research Report 93) (London, 1993)
Hamp, E.P., 'Social gradience in British spoken Latin', *Britannia* 6 (1975), pp. 150–62
Higham, N.J. 'Roman and native in England north of the Tees: Acculturation and its limitations', Barrett, J.C. ed., *Barbarians and Romans in North-West Europe* (British Archaeological Reports, Intern. Series 471) (Oxford, 1989), pp. 153–74
Higham, N.J., *An English Empire: Bede and the Early Anglo-Saxon Kings* (Manchester, 1995)
Jackson, K., *Language and History in Early Britain* (Edinburgh, 1953)
James, E., *The Franks* (Oxford, 1988)
James, E., 'Gregory of Tours and the Franks', in A.C. Murray, ed., *After Rome's Fall: Narrators and Sources of Early Medieval History* (Toronto, 1998), pp. 51–66
James, S., 'Britain and the late Roman army', in T.F.C. Blagg and A.C. King, eds, *Military and Civilian in Roman Britain* (British Archaeological Reports, British Series 136) (Oxford, 1984), pp. 161–86
Jones, R.F.J., 'A false start? The Roman urbanization of western Europe', *World Archaeology* 19 (1987), pp. 47–57
Pritchard, F.A. 'Ornamental stonework in Roman Britain', *Britannia* 17 (1986), pp. 169–89
Reece, R. 'Town and country: the end of Roman Britain', *World Archaeology* 12 (1980), pp. 77–92
Russell, P., 'Recent work in British Latin', *Cambridge Medieval Celtic Studies* 9 (Summer, 1985), pp. 19–29
Thomas, C., *Christianity in Roman Britain to AD 500* (London, 1981)
Wacher, J., ed. *The Civitas Capitals of Roman Britain* (Leicester, 1966)
Wacher, J., *The Towns of Roman Britain* (London, 1975)
Webster, G.A., 'Fort and town in early Roman Britain', in J.S. Wacher, ed., *The Civitas Capitals of Roman Britain* (Leicester, 1966), pp. 31–45
Williams, D., 'A consideration of the sub-fossil remains of *Vitis vinifera* L., as evidence for viticulture in Roman Britain', *Britannia* 8 (1977), pp. 327–34
Williams, T., 'Allectus' Palace?', *Current Archaeology* 158 (July, 1998), p. 72

Chapter 4

Alcock, L., *Arthur's Britain: History and Archaeology, AD 367–634* (London, 1971)
Allason-Jones, L., *Women in Roman Britain* (London, 1989)
Barley, M.W. and Hanson, R.W.C., eds, *Christianity in Britain, 300–700* (Leicester, 1968)

Dumville, D.N., 'Late seventh- or eighth-century evidence for the British transmission of Pelagius', *Cambridge Medieval Celtic Studies* 10 (Winter, 1985), pp. 39–52
Henig, M., *Religion in Roman Britain* (London, 1984)
Hunter, M., 'Germanic and Roman antiquity and the sense of the past in Anglo-Saxon England', *Anglo-Saxon England* 3 (1974), pp. 29–50
McCluskey, R., ed., *The See of Ninian: A History of the Medieval Diocese of Whithorn and the Diocese of Galloway in Modern Times* (Ayr, 1997)
Thomas, C., *Christianity in Roman Britain to AD 500* (London, 1981)
Veyne, P., *Did the Greeks Believe in Their Myths? An Essay on the Constitutive Imagination* (Chicago, 1988)

Chapter 5

Alcock, L., *Arthur's Britain: History and Archaeology, AD 367–634* (London, 1971)
Anderson, M.O., *Kings and Kingship in Early Scotland* (Edinburgh, 1973)
Anderson, M.O., 'Dalriada and the creation of the kingdom of the Scots', in D. Whitelock, R. McKitterick and D. Dumville, eds, *Ireland in Early Medieval Europe* (Cambridge, 1982), pp. 106–132
Ashe, G., '"A certain very ancient book": traces of an Arthurian source in Geoffrey of Monmouth's *History*', *Speculum* 56 (1981), pp. 301–23
Bannerman, J., *Studies in the History of Dalriada* (Edinburgh, 1974)
Barber, R., *The Figure of Arthur* (London, 1972)
Böhme, H.-W., 'Das Ende der Römerherrschaft in Britannien und die angelsächsische Besiedlung Englands im 5. Jahrhundert', *Jahrbuch des Römisch-Germanischen Zentralmuseums* 33 (1986), pp. 469–574
Bremmer, R.H., Jr, 'The nature of the evidence for a Frisian participation in the *Adventus Saxonum*', in A. Bammesberger and A. Wollmann, eds, *Britain 400–600: Language and History* (Heidelberg, 1990), pp. 353–71.
Charles-Edwards, T.M., 'The Arthur of History', in Rachel Bromwich *et al.*, eds, *The Arthur of the Welsh: The Arthurian Legend in Medieval Welsh Literature* (Cardiff, 1991), pp. 15–33
Chédeville, A. and Guillotel, H., *La Bretagne des saints et des rois, Ve-Xe siècle* (Rennes, 1984)
Cleary, A.S.E., *The Ending of Roman Britain* (London, 1989)
Dark, K.R., *Civitas to Kingdom: British Political Continuity 300–800* (London, 1994)
Dark, S.P., 'Palaeoecological evidence for landscape continuity and change in Britain, ca AD 400–800', in K.R. Dark, ed., *External Contacts and the Economy of Late Roman and Post-Roman Britain* (Woodbridge, 1996) pp. 23–51
Dillon, M., 'The Irish Settlements in Wales'. *Celtica* 12 (1977), pp. 1–12
Dumville, D.N., 'Sub-Roman Britain: History and legend', *History* 62 (1977), 173–92
Halsall, G., 'The origins of the *Reihengräberzivilisation*: forty years on', in J. Drinkwater and H. Elton, eds, *Fifth-Century Gaul: A Crisis of Identity?* (Cambridge, 1992), pp. 196–207
Halsall, G., *Settlement and Social Organization: The Merovingian Region of Metz* (Cambridge, 1995)
Härke, H., '"Warrior Graves"? The background of the Anglo-Saxon weapon burial rite', *Past and Present*, 126 (1990), pp. 22–43
Higham, N.J., *The English Conquest: Gildas and Britain in the Fifth Century* (Manchester, 1994)
Hills, C., 'The archaeology of Anglo-Saxon England in the pagan period: a review', *Anglo-Saxon England* 8 (1979), pp. 297–329
Hills, C., 'Spong Hill and the Adventus Saxonum', in C.E. Karkov, K.M. Wickham-Crowley and B.K. Young, eds, *Spaces of the Living and the Dead: An Archaeological Dialogue* (American Early Medieval Studies 3) (Oxford, 1999), pp. 15–26
Hines, J., *The Scandinavian Character of Anglian England in the pre-Viking Period* (British Archaeological Reports, British Series 124) (Oxford, 1984)
Hines, J., 'Philology, Archaeology and the *adventus Saxonum vel Anglorum*', in A. Bammesberger and A. Wollmann, eds, *Britain 400–600: Language and History* (Heidelberg, 1990), pp. 17–36

Hines, J., 'The Becoming of the English: Identity, Material Culture and Language in Early Anglo-Saxon England', *Anglo-Saxon Studies in Archaeology and History* 7 (1994), pp. 49–59
Jackson, K., 'The Arthur of History', in R.S. Loomis, ed., *Arthurian Literature in the Middle Ages* (Oxford, 1959), pp. 1–11
Jackson, P., 'Footloose in Archaeology', *Current Archaeology* 144 (Dec. 1995), pp. 466–70
Jones, M.E., *The End of Roman Britain* (Ithaca, NY, 1996)
Kelly, J.N.D., *Jerome: His Life, Writings and Controversies* (London, 1975)
Maenchen-Helfen, O., *The World of the Huns* (Berkeley, 1973)
Musset, L., *The Germanic Invasions*, transl. E. and C. James (London, 1975)
Lapidge, M. and Dumville, D., eds. *Gildas: New Approaches* (Woodbridge, 1984)
Miller, M., 'Bede's use of Gildas', *English Historical Review* 90 (1975), pp. 241–61
Miller, M., 'Matriliny by treaty: The Pictish foundation legend', in D. Whitelock, R. McKitterick and D. Dumville, eds, *Ireland in Early Medieval Europe* (Cambridge, 1982), pp. 133–161
Morris, J., *The Age of Arthur: A History of the British Isles from 350 to 650* (London, 1973)
Padel, Oliver., 'The nature of Arthur', *Cambrian Medieval Celtic Studies* 27 (Summer, 1994), pp. 1–31
Scull, C., 'Archaeology, early Anglo-Saxon society and the origins of Anglo-Saxon kingdoms', *Anglo-Saxon Studies in Archaeology and History* 6 (1993), pp. 65–82
Sims-Williams, P., 'The settlement of England in Bede and the *Chronicle*', *Anglo-Saxon England* 12 (1983), pp. 1–41
Sims-Williams, P., 'Gildas and the Anglo-Saxons', *Cambridge Medieval Celtic Studies* 6 (Winter, 1983), pp. 1–30
Thomas, C., *And Shall These Mute Stones Speak? Post-Roman Inscriptions in Western Britain* (Cardiff, 1994)
Thompson, E.A., 'Peasant revolts in late Roman Gaul and Spain', *Past and Present* 2 (1952), pp. 11–23
Thompson, E.A., 'Britonia', in M.W. Barley and R.P.C. Hanson, eds, *Christianity in Britain 300–700* (Leicester, 1968), pp. 201–05
Van Dam, R., *Leadership and Community in Late Antique Gaul* (Berkeley, 1985)
Welch, M., 'Late Romans and Saxons in Sussex', *Britannia* 2 (1971), pp. 232–7
Welch, M., *Early Anglo-Saxon Sussex* (British Archaeological Reports, British Series 112) (Oxford, 1983)

Chapter 6

Bassett, S., ed., *The Origins of Anglo-Saxon Kingdoms* (London, 1989)
Byrne, F.J., *Irish Kings and High-Kings* (London, 1973)
Carver, M., *Sutton Hoo: Burial Ground of Kings?* (London, 1998)
Chaney, W.A., *The Cult of Kingship in Anglo-Saxon England* (Manchester, 1970)
Charles-Edwards, T.M., 'Kinship, status and the origins of the hide', *Past and Present*, 56 (1972), pp. 3–33
Charles-Edwards, T.M., 'The authenticity of the *Gododdin*: an historian's view', in R. Bromwich and R. Brinley Jones, eds., *Astudiaethau ar Yr Hengerod* (Cardiff, 1978), pp. 43–71
Charles-Edwards, T.M., 'Early medieval kingships in the British Isles', in S. Bassett, ed., *The Origins of Anglo-Saxon Kingdoms* (London, 1989), pp. 28–39
Charles-Edwards, T.M., *Early Irish and Welsh Kinship* (Oxford, 1993)
Davies, W., *Patterns of Power in Early Wales* (Oxford, 1990)
Dornier, A., ed., *Mercian Studies* (Leicester, 1977)
Dumville, D.N., 'The ætheling: a study in Anglo-Saxon constitutional history', *Anglo-Saxon England* 8 (1979), pp. 1–33
Folz, R., *The Coronation of Charlemagne* (London, 1974)
Frank, R., 'The ideal of men dying with their lord in *The Battle of Maldon*: anachronism or *nouvelle vague?*' in I. Wood and N. Lund, eds, *People and Places in Northern Europe, 500–1600: Essays in Honour of Peter Hayes Sawyer* (Woodbridge, 1991), pp. 95–106

Gelling, M., 'Why aren't we speaking Welsh?', *Anglo-Saxon Studies in Archaeology and History* 6 (1993), pp. 51–6
Hart, C., 'The Tribal Hidage', *Transactions of the Royal Historical Society* 21 (1971), pp. 133–57
Higham, N.J., *An English Empire: Bede and the Early Anglo-Saxon Kings* (Manchester, 1995)
Hughes, K., 'Where are the Writings of Early Scotland?', in K. Hughes (ed. D. Dumville), *Celtic Britain in the Early Middle Ages* (Woodbridge, 1980), pp. 1–21
Jackson, K., 'Angles and Britons in Northumbria and Cumbria', in *Angles and Britons* (O'Donnell Lectures), (University of Wales Press: Cardiff, 1963)
Jackson, K., *The Oldest Irish Tradition: A Window on the Iron Age* (Edinburgh, 1964)
James, E. *The Origins of France, from Clovis to the Capetians, AD 500–1000* (London, 1982)
Kelly, F., *A Guide to Early Irish Law* (Dublin, 1988)
Kirby, D.P., *The Earliest English Kings* (London, 1991)
McClure, J., 'Bede's Old Testament Kings', in P. Wormald *et al.*, eds, *Ideal and Reality in Frankish and Anglo-Saxon Society* (Oxford, 1983), pp. 76–98
McCone, K., *Pagan Past and Christian Present in Early Irish Literature* (Maynooth, 1990)
Moisl, H., 'Anglo-Saxon royal genealogies and Germanic oral tradition', *Journal of Medieval History* 7 (1981), pp. 215–48
Moisl, H., 'The Bernician Royal Dynasty and the Irish in the Seventh Century', *Peritia* 2 (1983), pp. 103–26
North, R., *Heathen Gods in Old English Literature* (Cambridge, 1997)
Richter, M. *Ireland and her Neighbours in the Seventh Century* (Dublin, 1999)
Spearman, J.M. and Higgitt, J., eds, *The Age of Migrating Ideas: Early Medieval Art in Northern Britain and Ireland* (Edinburgh and Stroud, 1993)
Wallace-Hadrill, J.M., *Early Germanic Kingship in England and on the Continent* (Oxford, 1971)
Wormald, P., 'Bede, the *Bretwaldas* and the origins of the *Gens Anglorum*, in P. Wormald *et al.*, eds, *Ideal and Reality in Frankish and Anglo-Saxon England* (Oxford, 1983), pp. 99–129
Wormald, P., 'Celtic and Anglo-Saxon Kingship: some further thoughts', in P.E. Szarmach and V.D. Oggins, eds., *Sources of Anglo-Saxon Culture* (Kalamazoo, MI, 1986), pp. 151–83

Chapter 7

Blair, J., 'Anglo-Saxon pagan shrines and their prototypes', *Anglo-Saxon Studies in Archaeology and History* 8 (1995), pp. 1–28
Blair, J. and Sharpe, R., eds, *Pastoral Care Before the Parish* (Leicester, 1992)
Bullough, Donald A., 'What has Ingeld to do with Lindisfarne?', *Anglo-Saxon England* 22 (1993), pp. 93–125
Cambridge, E. and Rollason, D., 'The pastoral organization of the Anglo-Saxon Church: a review of the "Minster Hypothesis"', *Early Medieval Europe* 4 (1995), pp. 87–104
Chadwick, N.K., 'The conversion of Northumbria: a comparison of sources', in N.K. Chadwick, ed. *Celt and Saxon: Studies in the Early British Border* (Cambridge, 1963), pp. 138–66
Charles-Edwards, T.M., 'The social background to Irish *peregrinatio*', *Celtica* 11 (1976), pp. 43–59
Dumville, D.N., *et al., Saint Patrick, AD 493–1993* (Woodbridge, 1993)
Edwards, N. and Lane, A., eds, *The Early Church in Wales and the West* (Oxbow Monograph 16) (Oxford, 1992)
Fletcher, R., *The Conversion of Europe: From Paganism to Christianity, 371–1386 AD* (London, 1997)
Gameson. R., ed., *St Augustine and the Conversion of England* (Stroud, 1999)
Herren, M.W., 'Scholarly contacts between the Irish and the southern English in the seventh century', *Peritia* 12 (1998), pp. 24–53
Higham, N.J., *The Convert Kings: Power and Religious Affiliation in Early Anglo-Saxon England* (Manchester, 1997)
Jolly, K.L., *Popular Religion in Late Anglo-Saxon England: Elf Charms in Context* (Chapel Hill, NC, 1996)

Lapidge, M., ed., *Archbishop Theodore* (Cambridge, 1995)
Mayr-Harting, H., *The Coming of Christianity ot Anglo-Saxon England*, 3rd edn (London, 1991)
North, R., *Heathen Gods in Old English Literature* (Cambridge, 1997)
Rollason, D., *Saints and Relics in Anglo-Saxon England* (Blackwell, 1989)
Wood, I. 'The Franks and Sutton Hoo', in I. Wood and N. Lund, eds, *People and Places in Northern Europe, 500–1600: Essays in Honour of Peter Hayes Sawyer* (Woodbridge, 1991), pp. 1–14
Wood, I.N., 'Frankish hegemony in England', in M.O.H. Carver, ed., *The Age of Sutton Hoo: The Seventh Century in North-West Europe* (Woodbridge, 1992), pp. 235–42

Chapter 8

Abels, R.P., *Lordship and Military Obligation in Anglo-Saxon England* (Berkeley, 1988)
Arnold, C.J. and Wardle, P., 'Early medieval settlement patterns in England', *Medieval Archaeology* 25 (1981), pp. 145–9
Boddington, A., 'Modes of burial, settlement and worship: the Final Phase reviewed', in E. Southworth, ed., *Anglo-Saxon Cemeteries: A Reappraisal* (Stroud, 1990), pp. 177–99
Brisbane, M., 'Hamwic (Saxon Southampton): an 8th century port and production centre', in R. Hodges and B. Hobley, eds, *The Rebirth of Towns in the West, AD 700–1050* (CBA Research Report 68) (London, 1988), pp. 101–8
Brooks, N., 'The development of military obligations in eighth- and ninth-century England', in P. Clemoes and K. Hughes, eds, *England Before the Conquest* (Cambridge, 1971), pp. 69–84
Broun, D., 'Pictish kings 761–839: integration with Dál Riata or separate development?', in S.M. Foster, ed., *St Andrews Sarcophagus: A Pictish Masterpiece and its International Connections* (Dublin, 1998), pp. 71–83
Brown, P., *The World of Late Antiquity* (London, 1971)
Bruce-Mitford, R.L.S., *The Art of the Codex Amiatinus* (Jarrow Lecture 1967)
Campbell, E., 'Trade in the Dark Age West: a peripheral activity?', in B.E. Crawford, ed., *Scotland in Dark Age Britain* (St Andrews, 1996), pp. 79–91
Cassidy, B., ed., *The Ruthwell Cross* (Princeton, NJ, 1992)
Cubitt, C., *Anglo-Saxon Church Councils, c. 650–c. 850* (London, 1995)
Dark, K.R., *Civitas to Kingdom: British Political Continuity, 300–800* (London, 1994)
Davies, J.R., 'Church, property, and conflict in Wales, AD 600–1100', *Welsh History Review* 18 (1997), pp. 387–406
Davies, W., *An Early Welsh Microcosm* (London, 1978)
Foster, S.M., ed., *The St Andrews Sarcophagus: A Pictish Masterpiece and its International Connections* (Dublin, 1998)
Hamerow, H.F., 'Settlement mobility and the 'Middle Saxon Shift': rural settlements and settlement patterns in Anglo-Saxon England', *Anglo-Saxon England* 20 (1991), pp. 1–17
Hawkes, J. and Mills, S., eds, *Northumbria's Golden Age* (Stroud, 1999)
Hill, P., ed. *Whithorn and St Ninian. The Excavation of a Monastic Town, 1984–91* (Stroud, 1996)
Hodges, R., *Dark Age Economics: The Origins of Towns and Trade, AD 600–1000* (London, 1982)
Hodges, R., *The Anglo-Saxon Achievement* (London, 1989)
Hudson, B.T., *Kings of Celtic Scotland* (Westport, CT, 1994)
James, E., 'Alcuin and York in the eighth century', in P.L. Butzer and D. Lohrmann, eds., *Science in Western and Eastern Civilization in Carolingian Times* (Basel, 1993), pp. 34–7
Kennedy, H., *The Prophet and the Age of the Caliphates* (London, 1986)
Lane, A., 'Trade, gifts and cultural exchange in Dark-Age Western Scotland', in B.E. Crawford, ed. *Scotland in Dark Age Europe* (St Andrews, 1994), pp. 103–15
Leahy, K., 'The Middle Saxon site at Flixborough, North Lincolnshire', in J. Hawkes and S. Mills, eds, *Northumbria's Golden Age* (Stroud, 1999), pp. 87–94
Levison, W., *England and the Continent in the Eighth Century* (Oxford, 1946)
Netzer, N., 'The *Book of Durrow*: the Northumbrian Connection', in J. Hawkes and S. Mills, eds, *Northumbria's Golden Age* (Stroud, 1999), pp. 315–26

Neuman de Vegvar, C.L., *The Northumbrian Renaissance. A Study in the Transmission of Style* (London and Toronto, 1987)
Neuman de Vegvar, C.L., 'The Travelling Twins: Romulus and Remus in Anglo-Saxon England', in J. Hawkes and S. Mills, *Northumbria's Golden Age* (Stroud, 1999), pp. 257–9
Nieke, M.R. and Duncan, H.R., 'Dalriada: the establishment and maintenance of an Early Historic kingdom in northern Britain', in S.T. Driscoll and M.R. Nieke, eds, *Power and Politics in Early Medieval Britain and Ireland* (Edinburgh, 1988), pp. 6–21
Thomas, C., 'Westminster', *Current Archaeology* 162 (April/May 1999), pp. 218–22
Wallace-Hadrill, J.M., *Early Germanic Kingship in England and on the Continent* (Oxford, 1971)
Webster, L., 'The Iconographic Programme of the Franks Casket', in J. Hawkes and S. Mills, *Northumbria's Golden Age* (Stroud, 1999), pp. 227–46
Whitwell, B., *Current Archaeology* 126 (Sept/Oct 1991), pp. 244–7
Wooding, J., *Communication and Commerce along the Western Sealanes, AD 400–800* (British Archaeological Reports, British Series 654) (Oxford, 1996)

Chapter 9

Abels, R.P., *Alfred the Great: War, Kingship and Culture in Anglo-Saxon England* (New York, 1998)
Anderson, P.S., 'Norse settlement in the Hebrides: What happened to the natives and what happened to the Norse immigrants?', in I. Wood and N. Lund, eds, *People and Places in Northern Europe, 500–1600: Essays in Honour of Peter Hayes Sawyer* (Woodbridge, 1991), pp. 131–47
Barber, C., *The English Language: A Historical Introduction* (Cambridge, 1993)
Bailey, R.N., *Viking-Age Sculpture in Northern England* (London, 1980)
Batey, C.E., Jesch, J. and Morris, C.D., eds, *The Viking Age in Caithness, Orkney and the North Atlantic* (Edinburgh, 1993)
Broun, D., 'The origins of Scottish identity in a European context', in B.E. Crawford, ed., *Scotland in Dark Age Europe* (St Andrews, 1994), pp. 21–31
Cameron, K., *Place-Name Evidence for the Anglo-Saxon Invasion and Scandinavian Settlements* (Nottingham, 1977)
Clancy, T., 'Iona, Scotland and the Céli Dé', in B.E. Crawford, ed., *Scotland in Dark Age Britain* (St Andrews 1996), pp. 111–30
Crawford, B.E., *Scandinavian Scotland* (Leicester, 1987)
Crawford, B.E., ed., *Scandinavian Settlement in Northern Britain* (London, 1995)
Davies, W., *Patterns of Power in Early Wales* (Oxford, 1990)
Fellows-Jensen, G., 'Viking settlement in the Northern and Western Isles', in A. Fenton and H. Pálsson, eds, *The Northern and Western Isles in the Viking World: Survival, Continuity and Change* (Edinburgh, 1984), pp. 148–68
Fellows-Jensen, G., 'Scandinavian settlement in Cumbria and Dumfriesshire: the place-name evidence', in J.R. Baldwin and I.D. Whyte, eds, *The Scandinavians in Cumbria* (Edinburgh, 1985), pp. 65–82
Fenton, A. and Pálsson, H., eds, *The Northern and Western Isles in the Viking World: Survival, Continuity and Change* (Edinburgh, 1984)
Galbraith, V.H., 'Who wrote Asser's Life of Alfred?', in V.H. Galbraith, *An Introduction to the Study of History* (London, 1964), pp. 88–128
Graham-Campbell, J., ed., *Cultural Atlas of the Viking World* (Oxford, 1994)
Graham-Campbell, J. and Batey, C.E., *Vikings in Scotland: An Archaeological Survey* (Edinburgh, 1998)
Hall, R., *Viking-Age York* (London, 1994)
Hill, D., 'The Burghal Hidage: the establishment of a text', *Medieval Archaeology* 13 (1969), pp. 84–92
Hill, D. and Rumble, A.R., eds, *The Defence of Wessex: The Burghal Hidage and Anglo-Saxon Fortifications* (Manchester, 1996)
Hodges, R. and Whitehouse, D., *Mohammed, Charlemagne and the Origins of Europe: Archaeology and the Pirenne Thesis*, 2nd edn (London, 1989)

Hughes, K., 'Where are the writings of early Scotland?', in K. Hughes (ed. D.N. Dumville), *Celtic Britain in the Early Middle Ages* (Woodbridge, 1980), pp. 1–21
Kenyon, D., *The Origins of Lancashire* (Manchester, 1991)
Lucas, A.T., 'The plundering and burning of churches in Ireland, 7th to 16th century', in E. Rynne, ed., *North Munster Studies* (Limerick, 1967), pp. 172–229.
Morris, C.D., 'Raiders, traders and settlers: the early Viking age in Scotland', in H.B. Clarke, M. Ní Mhaonaigh and R. Ó Floinn, eds, *Ireland and Scandinavia in the Early Viking Age* (Dublin, 1998), pp. 73–103
Nelson, Janet L., '"A king across the sea": Alfred in Continental perspective', *Transactions of the Royal Historical Society*, 5th series, 36 (1986), pp. 45–68
Nelson, Janet L., 'Reconstructing a royal family: reflections on Alfred, from Asser, Chapter 2', in I. Wood and N. Lund, eds, *People and Places in Northern Europe, 500–1600* (Woodbridge, 1991), pp. 47–66
Nelson, Janet L., 'Waiting for Alfred', *Early Medieval Europe* 7 (1998), pp. 115–24
Ó Corráin, D., 'High-kings, Vikings and other kings', *Irish Historical Studies* 21 (1978–9), pp. 283–323
Ó Corráin, D., 'The Vikings in Scotland and Ireland in the ninth century', *Peritia* 12 (1998), pp. 296–339
Oftedal, M., 'Names of lakes on the Isle of Lewis in the Outer Hebrides', in H. Bekker-Nielsen, P. Foote and O. Olsen, eds, *Proceedings of the Eighth Viking Congress, Århus 1977* (Odense, 1981), pp. 183–8
Richards, J.D., *English Heritage Book of Viking Age England* (London, 1991)
Ritchie, A., *Viking Scotland* (London, 1993)
Sawyer, P.H., 'The two Viking ages of Britain: a discussion', *Medieval Scandinavia* 2 (1969), pp. 163–207
Sawyer, P.H., *The Age of the Vikings*, 2nd edn (London, 1971)
Sawyer, P.H., ed. *The Oxford Illustrated History of the Vikings* (Oxford, 1997)
Smyth, A.P., *Scandinavian York and Dublin: The History and Archaeology of Two Related Viking Kingdoms*, 2 volumes (Dublin, 1975 and 1979)
Smyth, A.P., *Scandinavian Kings in the British Isles, 850–880* (Oxford, 1977)
Smyth, A.P. *King Alfred the Great* (Oxford, 1995)
Wallace-Hadrill, J.M., *The Vikings in Francia* (Stenton Lecture, University of Reading 1974), reprinted in J.M. Wallace-Hadrill, *Early Medieval History* (Oxford, 1975), pp. 217–36
Wormald, P., 'The emergence of a *Regnum Scottorum*: a Carolingian hegemony?', in B.E, Crawford, ed., *Scotland in Dark Age Britain* (St Andrews, 1996), pp. 131–60

Chapter 10

Abels, R., 'English tactics, strategy and military organisation in the late tenth century', in D. Scragg, ed., *The Battle of Maldon, AD 991* (Oxford, 1991), pp. 143–55
Barlow, F., *Edward the Confessor*, 2nd edn (London, 1979)
Barlow, F., *The English Church, 1000–1066*, 2nd edn (London, 1979)
Barrow, G.W.S., *Kingship and Unity: Scotland 1000–1306* (Edinburgh, 1981)
Bates, D., *Normandy before 1066* (London, 1982)
Biddle, M., '*Felix Urbs Winthonia*: Winchester in the Age of Monastic Reform', in D. Parsons, ed., *Tenth-Century Studies* (London, 1975), pp. 123–40 and 233–7
Brooks, N.P., 'The career of St Dunstan', in Ramsay *et al.*, eds, *St Dunstan: His Life, Times and Cult* (Woodbridge, 1992), pp. 1–23
Budny, M., '"St Dunstan's Classbook" and its frontispiece: Dunstan's portrait and autograph' in Ramsay *et al.*, eds, *St Dunstan: His Life, Times and Cult* (Woodbridge, 1992), pp. 103–42
Campbell, E. and Lane, A., 'Llangorse: a tenth century royal crannog in Wales', *Antiquity* 63 (1989), pp. 675–81
Chase, C., ed., *The Dating of Beowulf* (Toronto, 1981)
Chibnall, M., *Anglo-Norman England, 1066–1166* (Oxford, 1986)
Foot, S., 'The making of *Angelcynn*: English identity before the Norman Conquest', *Transactions of the Royal Historical Society* 6th series, 6 (1996), pp. 25–49

Frank, R., 'Skaldic verse and the date of *Beowulf*', in C. Chase, ed., *The Dating of Beowulf*, pp. 123–39

Hooper, N., 'Military developments in the reign of Cnut', in A.R. Rumble, *Reign of Cnut: King of England, Denmark and Norway* (London, 1994), pp. 89–100

Keynes, S., 'The declining reputation of King Æthelred the Unready', in D. Hill, ed., *Ethelred the Unready* (British Archaeological Reports, British Series 59) (Oxford, 1978), pp. 227–53

Keynes, S., 'A tale of two kings: Alfred the Great and Æthelred the Unready', *Transactions of the Royal Historical Society*, 5th series, 36 (1986), pp. 195–217

Keynes, S., 'Cnut's earls', in A.R. Rumble, ed., *The Reign of Cnut: King of England, Denmark and Norway* (London, 1994), pp. 43–86

Keynes, S., 'King Alfred and the Mercians', in M.A.S. Blackburn and D.N. Dumville, eds, *Kings, Currency and Alliances: History and Coinage of Southern England in the Ninth Century* (Woodbridge, 1998), pp. 1–45

Kiernan, K.S., *Beowulf and the Beowulf Manuscript* (Brunswick, NJ, 1981)

Knowles, D., *The Monastic Order in England*, 2nd edn (Cambridge, 1963)

Lawson, M.K., *Cnut. The Danes in England in the Early Eleventh Century* (London, 1993)

Lund, N., 'Cnut's Danish kingdom', in A.R. Rumble, *Reign of Cnut: King of England, Denmark and Norway* (London, 1994), pp. 27–42

Lund, N., 'The Danish Empire and the end of the Viking Age', in P. Sawyer, ed., *The Oxford Illustrated History of the Vikings* (Oxford, 1997), pp. 156–81

Nightingale, J., 'Oswald, Fleury and continental reform', in N. Brooks and C. Cubitt, eds, *St Oswald of Worcester: Life and Influence* (London, 1996), pp. 23–45

Ortenberg, V., *The English Church and the Continent in the Tenth and Eleventh Centuries: Cultural, Spiritual and Artistic Exchange* (Oxford, 1992)

Parsons, D., ed., *Tenth-Century Studies: Essays in Commemoration of the Council of Winchester and Regularis Concordia* (London, 1975)

Pearce, S.M., *The Kingdom of Dumnonia: Studies in History and Tradition in South-West Britain* (Padstow, 1978)

Ramsay, N., Sparks, M. and Tatton-Brown, T., eds, *St Dunstan: His Life, Times and Cult* (Woodbridge, 1992)

Redknap, M., *The Christian Celts: Treasures of Late Celtic Wales* (Cardiff, 1991)

Rollason, D., 'The concept of sanctity in the early *Lives* of St Dunstan', in Ramsay *et al.*, eds, *St Dunstan: His Life, Times and Cult*, pp. 261–72

Rumble, A.R., ed., *The Reign of Cnut: King of England, Denmark and Norway* (London, 1994)

Sawyer, P.H., 'The wealth of England in the eleventh century', *Transactions of the Royal Historical Society*, 5th series, 15 (1965), pp. 145–64

Stafford, P., *Queens, Concubines and Dowagers: The King's Wife in the Early Middle Ages* (London, 1983)

Stafford, P., *Unification and Conquest: A Political and Social History of England in the Tenth and Eleventh Centuries* (London, 1989)

Stafford, P., *Queen Emma and Queen Edith: Queenship and Women's Power in Eleventh-Century England* (Oxford, 1997)

Stafford, P., 'Queens, nunneries and reforming churchmen: gender, religious status and reform in tenth- and eleventh-century England', *Past and Present* 163 (1999), pp. 3–35

Taylor, H.M., 'Tenth-century church building in England and on the Continent', in D. Parsons, ed., *Tenth-Century Studies* (London, 1975), pp. 141–168 and 237–41

Wood, M., 'The making of King Aethelstan's Empire: an English Charlemagne?', in P. Wormald, *et al.*, eds, *Ideal and Reality in Frankish and Anglo-Saxon Society* (Oxford, 1983), pp. 250–72

Wormald, P., 'Bede, *Beowulf*, and the conversion of the Anglo-Saxon aristocracy', in R.T. Farrell, ed., *Bede and Anglo-Saxon England* (British Archaeological Reports, British Series, 46) (Oxford, 1978), pp. 32–95

Wormald, P., 'Æthelwold and his Continental counterparts: context, comparison, contrast', in B. Yorke, ed., *Bishop Æthelwold: His Career and Influence* (Woodbridge, 1988), pp. 13–42

Index

Abbreviations: a = abbot; abp = archbishop; b = bishop; k = king; mon = monastery; w = wife